Open to The World

Interdisciplinary Perspectives on Themes in Christian Theology

Aaron Yom

Seymour Press *SP*
Capitol Heights, MD

Seymour Press

Capitol Heights, MD

Table of Content

Preface

I have written this book as a supplement to a course in interdisciplinary studies, especially dealing with the theology and science interface. Collecting lecture notes and essays I had written over the years, I organized them under the rubric of four Christian theological themes that are not entirely disconnected to one another. In a nutshell, this is an honest attempt to go against naturalistic tendencies of today's interdisciplinary efforts, all the while raising the bar for the theology and science dialogue, for better or worse.

My emphasis on the open nature of reality is the common thread that weaves the various pieces of ideas and information concerning the cross-fertilization of theology and science that I have presented in this book. Essentially, this is what I did when I prepared my lectures at Regent University. In my lectures, I have been emphasizing, again and again, the openness of God, humanity, and nature. Students who I have been teaching all have heard it many times, and they openly joke about it, saying that I have played the broken record in the class and firmly planted this idea in their heads that they probably will never forget it.

I emphasize the open structure of theology and science because I am convinced that this is the most effective weapon against naturalistic reductionism or theological antagonism. I consider studying theology to be a gift of God, the most fascinating intellectual adventure, but due to myopic visions and closed minds of our time, theology is in danger of losing its ground and identity. Let me mention three problems, which I shall attend to and diffuse thoroughly in this book.

First, theology and science suffer from antagonists such as religious fundamentalists and atheist scholars. Concerning religious fundamentalists (e.g., fideists), they deny the findings from the collaborative efforts of theologians and scientists, since they only want to adhere to their own faith traditions. Therefore, in spite of the success of the interdisciplinary studies in the Christian camp, some scholars still see the relationship between religion and science as foes rather than friends. Concerning atheists, like those who belong to New Atheism, they have been defending their thesis that God does not exist and argue that there is plenty of scientific evidence to prove it. For atheists, the theology and science interface or any form of interdisciplinary effort that involves God is just a meaningless effort, and for this reason, they try to prevent fellow scientists to stay within the bounds of a naturalistic worldview that has nothing to do with God.

Second, there is a danger of theologians remaining in the scientific camp, overwhelming the contribution of theology. Both the first generation of theo-scientific scholars and their followers put much effort in patching the gaps between theology and science caused by modernist reductionism and metaphysical dualism, but from what I can see, in today's context, the bridging work has been overdetermined from the side of science. One such case is an incessant effort to merge theology and science within the context of the single matrix of naturalism. Although the conceptual framework of naturalism has been well modified to accommodate the Christian core paradigms such as the theology of nature, nonetheless, it promotes a robust naturalistic theology that tends to marginalize the traditional understanding of God.

Third, although the theology and science dialogue is investing much effort to clear away impediments for the sake of mutuality, the critical component of Christian theology may have been marginalized. For instance, for the sake of continuing the conversation between theology and science, the issue of miracles has been set aside. Even in the divine action project, the issue of miracles is mentioned rarely. Of course, most of us who are engaged with theology and science want to follow the way of non-interventionism. We should not read God's action in terms of God contradicting or overriding the laws of nature. However, this does not mean that God is limited in his work with nature, being unable to produce extraordinary events that are beyond and above nature. In my judgment, one of the main pillars of the bridging work is our affirmation and description of the possibility of miracles. Without it, the bridge between theology and science cannot be sustained, because, from the side of the theological span, the bridge would collapse. We cannot do theology with the missing pillar of God's miracles. After all, the weight of Christian theology rests on miracle claims.

I present this book to diffuse these tendencies, and at the same time, encourage the Christian community to explore the other side of faith, that is, the world of natural and human sciences. I hope that this book opens our eyes to see something more, greater, deeper, and wider than what we are used to.

Abbreviations

CR	Critical Realism
DAP	Divine Action Project
IJST	International Journal of Systematic Theology
NIV	New International Version
SJT	Scottish Journal of Theology
SPS	Society of Pentecostal Studies

Introduction

Niels Gregersen and J. Wentzel van Huyssteen outrightly declare, "Gone are the days in which any attempt to relate theology and science to one another could still possibly—and mistakenly—be seen as a rather esoteric, intellectualist exercise limited to a privileged few." [1] This statement is fitting in the current ethos of the theology and science interface. Living in a scientific society that is fully equipped with state-of-the-art technology, theologians are boldly engaging the world of science, searching for the possible areas of consonance between theology and science. Indeed, such an effort is not esoteric or unconventional anymore. Theological engagements with science are widely acknowledged, and as a result, the cross-fertilization between theology and science has become the most popular theological pursuit in the 21st-century.

Due to the ongoing dialogue between theology and science, Christian theology has become extremely pluralistic and diverse. Scholars nowadays enjoy a cafeteria of theological options that include the theological mingling with evolutionism, emergentism, chaos theory, relativity theory, quantum theory, or process metaphysics. The theological choice has multiplied exponentially for we have a superabundance of theo-scientific possibilities. I do not consider theological pluralism in its association with natural and human sciences as a necessary evil for the Christian community. Assuredly, pluralism in all shapes and forms is the primary impetus behind the growth of Christianity. Even the Bible expresses a good deal of diverse views that may not easily be reconciled. Indeed, from the ancient days to the contemporary era, Christian doctrines flourished because of competing ideas and concepts that gave rise to new theological theories. For this reason, I join the academic guild that pursues an interdisciplinary effort

---

[1] Niels Henrik Gregersen and J. Wentzel van Huyssteen, "Introduction," in *Rethinking Theology and Science: Six Models for the Current Dialogue*, ed. Niels Henrik Gregersen and J. Wentzel van Huyssteen (Grand Rapids: Eerdmans, 1998), 1.

1

to connect the two streams of the contemporary culture, that is, science and religion.

However, although this interdisciplinary effort endorses freedom of human creativity and growth, it nonetheless carries the danger of putting theology in the hands of science-oriented scholars who are inclined to change the substance and grammar of Christian core beliefs to fit the scientific structure of our day. I am concerned with the way in which science is taking control of theology and forces a theological shift that redefines our understanding of who God is, God's action in this world, the validity of Christian realism, and the nature of faith. Science as the dominant form of human rationality leaves no choice for the contemporary theologians to accommodate the traditional theological theories to natural sciences, and as a result, Christian theology is losing its unique features and core doctrinal stances that form the basis for the transforming power of our society and the community of believers.

So, there is a problem. We need to find a way to sustain the theology and science dialogue without marginalizing the core beliefs of Christian theology. More clearly, as Clark Pinnock has pointed out, we must find a way to be conservative "in wanting to maintain the treasures of the past and 'liberal' in its unending search for new ways to express the ever-fresh announcement of God's grace."[2] The question remains. How do we conserve and stay faithful to the Christian message, and at the same time, interpret this truth for the emerging scientific generations in a new, fresh way? From my own analysis, there are four ways we can go about it, namely, naturally, realistically, faithfully, and openly. This analysis aligns well with the current ethos of the contemporary theology and science interface, for theologians and scientists are engaging with the four foundational interdisciplinary categories: nature, critical realism, faith rationality, and the divine action project. As the main topics that structure the following chapters, I present a brief critical examination of each of these developments, respectively.

---

[2] Clark H. Pinnock, *Tracking the Maze: Finding Our Way through Modern Theology from an Evangelical Perspective* (San Francisco: Harper and Row, 1990), 7.

Nature

The contemporary scholars are giving undue attention to nature. This is evident in all fields of study. Philosophically, natural science has become the driving force for the development of metaphysical naturalism, [3] physicalism, [4] and evolutionism. [5] The key tenet of philosophical naturalism is that there is nothing but natural laws, forces, and entities operate in this world. Therefore, it has turned into a counterforce to supernaturalism. Scientifically, nature has become the key to unlocking the secret of our universe. Consequently, scientific empiricism, scientific research programs, and scientific realism, all depend on the careful observation of the modal properties of nature. Even in some academic circles, nature is seen as a religious category. Religious naturalism is a chief output of this movement. [6] Religious naturalists hold to the belief that nature is inherently awe-inspiring due to its sacred qualities. Furthermore, in hopes of promoting the interconnectedness of human community with natural things, socio-

---

[3] Gary L. Drescher, *Good and Real: Demystifying Paradoxes from Physics to Ethics* (Cambridge: The MIT Press, 2006); Richard Carrier, *Sense and Goodness without God: A Defense of Metaphysical Naturalism* (Bloomington: Authorhouse, 2005); D. M. Armstrong, *A World of States of Affairs* (Cambridge: Cambridge University Press, 1997).

[4] Jaegwon Kim, *Physicalism, or Something Near Enough* (Princeton: Princeton University Press, 2005); Andrew Melnyk, *A Physicalist Manifesto: Thoroughly Modern Materialism* (Cambridge University Press, 2003); Jeffrey Poland, *Physicalism: The Philosophical Foundations* (Oxford University Press, 1994); John R. Searle, *The Rediscovery of the Mind* (Cambridge: The MIT Press, 1992).

[5] Francis Crick, *Of Molecules and Men* (New York: Prometheus, 2004); Christof Koch, *The Quest for Consciousness: A Neurobiological Approach* (Englewood: Roberts and Company, 2004); Daniel Dennett, *Freedom Evolves* (New York: Penguin, 2003); Richard Dawkins, *The Selfish Gene* (Oxford; Oxford University Press, 1989).

[6] Stuart Kaufman, *Reinventing the Sacred: The New Science, Reason, and Religion* (New York: Basic Books, 2008); Jerome A. Stone, *Religious Naturalism Today: The Rebirth of a Forgotten Alternative* (Albany: State University of New York Press, 2008); Ursula Goodenough, *The Sacred Depths of Nature* (New York: Oxford University Press, 1998); Willem Drees, *Religion, Science and Naturalism* (New York: Cambridge University Press, 1996); Bernard E. Meland, *The Secularization of Modern Cultures* (New York: Oxford University Press, 1966); Roy W. Sellars, *Religion Coming of Age* (New York: McMillan, 1928).

naturalists work to highlight the importance of living together with each other and with nature.[7]

Following this renewed zeal over nature, those who are involved with the theology and science interface have adopted the naturally-based worldview and began to revise and modify the traditional theological motifs based on the study of nature. There are several major outputs of this nature-based interdisciplinary approach—e.g., panentheism, [8] panpsychism, [9] process metaphysics, [10] religious naturalism, [11] emergentism, [12] theistic evolutionism, [13] substance

[7] Owen Flanagan, *The Geography of Morals: Varieties of Moral Possibility* (Oxford: Oxford University Press, 2017); Joshua Greene, *Moral Tribes: Emotion, Reason, and the Gap between Us and Them* (New York: Penguin, 2014); Jane Bennett, *Vibrant Matter: A Political Ecology of Things* (Durham: Duke University Press, 2010); Thomas W. Clark, *Encountering Naturalism: A Worldview and Its Uses* (Somerville: Center for Naturalism, 2007).

[8] Philip Clayton and Loriliai Biernacki, eds, *Panentheism across the World's Traditions* (Oxford: Oxford University Press, 2014); Arthur Peacocke, *Creation and the World of Science: The Re-shaping of Belief* (Oxford: Oxford University Press, 2004); David R. Griffin, *Panentheism and Scientific Naturalism: Rethinking Evil, Morality, Religious Experience, Religious Pluralism, and the Academic Study of Religion* (Claremont: Process Century Press, 2014); Denis Edwards, *Breath of Life: A Theology of the Creator Spirit* (Maryknoll: Orbis, 2004).

[9] Stuart Kauffman, "Cosmic Mind?" *Theology and Science* 14/1 (2016): 36-47; Steven Shaviro, *The Universe of Things: On Speculative Realism* (Minneapolis: University of Minnesota Press, 2014); Galen Strawson, "Realistic Monism: Why Physicalism Entails Panpsychism," in *Consciousness and Its Place in Nature: Does Physicalism Entail Panpsychism?* (Exeter, Imprint Academic, 2006); David S. Clarke, *Panpsychism and the Religious Attitude* (New York: State University of New York, 2003); Pierre Teilhard de Chardin, *The Divine Milieu* (New York: Harper Collins, 1960).

[10] Catherine Keller, *On the Mystery: Discerning Divinity in Process* (Minneapolis: Fortress, 2008); Joseph A. Bracken, *Christianity and Process Thought: Spirituality for a Changing World* (West Conshohocken: Templeton Foundation Press, 2006); Robert C. Mesle, *Process Theology: A Basic Introduction* (St. Louis: Chalice, 1993); John B. Cobb, Jr., and David R. Griffin, *Process Theology: An Introductory Exposition* (Westminster John Knox Press, 1976).

[11] See above footnote 5.

[12] Niels Henrik Gregersen, "Emergence and Complexity," in *The Oxford Handbook of Religion and Science,* ed. Philip Clayton (Oxford: Oxford University Press, 2008), 767-783; Philip Clayton, *Mind and Emergence: From Quantum to Consciousness* (Oxford: Oxford University Press, 2006); Nancey Murphy, *Bodies and Souls, or Spirited Bodies?* (Cambridge: Cambridge University Press, 2006).

[13] William A. Dembski, *The Design of Life: Discovering Signs of Intelligence in Biological Systems* (Dallas: The Foundation for Thought and Ethics, 2008); Jeffrey P. Schloss, "Evolutionary Theory and Religious Belief" in *The Oxford Handbook of Religion*

dualism,[14] and eco-theology.[15] Scientific theologians who have adhered to these newly found interdisciplinary motifs search for the natural explanation for religious experiences and beliefs, which are to be discerned only by studying what goes on in nature. Consequently, theistic naturalists start with working assumptions that belong to the sphere of the natural sciences, rather than biblical convictions concerning the nature and activity of God. I see both the positive and negative aspects of this approach.

Positively, from the vantage point of Christian studies, there are two areas of theology that have been benefited from the renewed interest in nature: natural theology and theology of nature. These two areas of theology should not be mistaken as the same type of study. They are different. Christopher Southgate and Michael Poole describe the difference this way: "Natural theology is traditionally understood as the consideration of what can be known about God without the aid of revelation," and "theology of nature starts from a religious tradition based on religious experience and historical revelation. But it holds that some traditional doctrines need to be reformulated in the light of current science."[16] Or, more recently, in the current theological ethos, natural theology has to do with giving proofs of God's existence rationally without relying on biblical testimonies or traditional Christian doctrines. By contrast, theology of nature refers to all knowledge of God related to God's creative work in and through the natural and human spheres.

Traditionally, natural theology has been set aside as the deficient form of theology since it went after knowledge of God without the aid

---

and Science, ed. Philip Clayton (Oxford: Oxford University Press, 2008), 187-206; John F. Haught, *Christianity and Science: Toward a Theology of Nature* (Maryknoll: Orbis, 2007).

[14] For more details, see J. P. Moreland, *Consciousness and the Existence of God: A Theistic Argument* (New York: Routledge, 2008), and Alvin Plantinga, *Where the Conflict Really Lies: Science, Religion, and Naturalism* (Oxford: Oxford University Press, 2011).

[15] Peter Scott, *A Political Theology of Nature* (Cambridge: Cambridge University Press, 2003); Michael Welker, *Creation and Reality* (Minneapolis: Fortress, 1999); Jurgen Moltmann, *God in Creation: A New Theology of Creation and the Spirit of God* (Minneapolis: Fortress, 1993); Sallie McFague, *The Body of God: An Ecological Theology* (Minneapolis: Augsburg Fortress, 1993).

[16] Christopher Southgate and Michael Poole, "Introduction," in *God, Humanity, and Cosmos*, ed. Christopher Southgate (New York: T&T Clark, 2011), 7-8.

of revelation. This is the basic tenet of the conservative camp. Those who work within the boundary of theological conservatism do not allow natural knowledge to be the chief source of understanding God's being and act.[17] They were reminded that the Kierkegaardian principle holds true, that there is an infinite qualitative gap between God and finite beings, and that there is no way for us to come to the knowledge of God without God's help. Martin Luther's cry for *sola scriptura* and *sola fide* makes sense for the traditionalists. The abstract, speculative argument for God coming from rationalists was never a good option for the orthodox Christians.

However, natural theology today has found a new power source, the advancement of science. By incorporating scientific innovations, Christian philosophers now have new reasons to ride on the bandwagon of natural theology. New scientific discoveries have become the game-changer for Christian apologists. The cosmological argument, the ontological argument, the teleological argument, the argument from consciousness, the argument from reason, the moral argument, and the argument from religious experience, are but a few examples that show the contemporary Christian defense for God is backed up by new scientific findings.[18] Although their opponents, mainly atheists, have come up against their viewpoints, denying that rational theistic arguments do not really prove God's existence, these reformulated approaches to natural theology have bolstered the old tradition arguments for the existence of God that were thoroughly discounted by modernists such as Immanuel Kant and David Hume.

Concerning theology of nature, unlike natural theology, due to its high regard for God's revelation, it is well received by Christian scholars, even in the evangelical circles. Although some historians note that

---

[17] Karl Barth is a representative figure. Cf. Karl Barth, *The Epistle to the Romans*, trans. Edwyn C. Hoskyns (Oxford: Oxford University Press, 1968). The most recent evaluation of Barth's natural theology from the vantage point of the theology-science dialogue, see Rodney Holder, *The Heavens Declare: Natural Theology and the Legacy of Karl Barth* (West Conshohocken: Templeton Foundation Press, 2012).

[18] A brief introduction to these arguments, and more, is included in *The Blackwell Companion to Natural Theology*. William Lane Craig and J. P. Moreland, eds., *The Blackwell Companion to Natural Theology* (Malden: Wiley-Blackwell, 2012).

theology of nature has been with Christians from the beginning,[19] as it is well attested in the Bible, "The heavens declare the glory of God" (Ps. 19:1), theology of nature in today's setting is much different in scope than the premodern period. Theology of nature today mingles with various scientific findings such as the theory of evolution, Einstein's theory of relativity, and quantum mechanics. We shall see more of these approaches in our discussion of the divine action project, but we need to acknowledge here that contemporary theology of nature takes seriously the scientific description of the natural phenomena for the sake of reformulating distinctively religious concepts such as God's triune life.[20]

On the negative side, there is one noticeable setback. As I have mentioned already, it drives a style of theology prepared to introduce far-reaching changes in the traditional understanding of Christian theology and faith, revising even what was earlier held to be constitutive beliefs fundamental to orthodoxy. For instance, in Pierre Teilhard de Chardin's interdisciplinary matrix, the God of the Bible has transformed into the God of evolution, and this God carried a new name, the "Omega Point," that is, the source of all our evolutionary energy.[21] The idea of God has been thoroughly revised that, in his theo-scientific program, it is very difficult to find the trace of the biblical picture of God. For theologians who are enchanted by naturalism, there seems to be no limit beyond which the revision cannot go. Earlier norms are simply allowed to be swallowed up in the sea of scientific theories. Consequently, as John Polkinghorne laments, theology has lost its transcendental

---

[19] David Lindberg traces the historical root of theology of nature back to the early years of Christianity. According to Lindberg, ancient Christian scholars, such as Augustine and Tertullian had taken advantage of natural philosophy and utilized its study to explain the things of God. See David L. Lindberg, "Early Christian Attitude toward Nature," in *Science and Religion: A Historical Introduction*, ed. Gary B. Ferngren (Baltimore: John Hopkins University Press, 2002). 47-56.

[20] For instance, Wolfhart Pannenberg has taken the scientific theory of "field" and incorporated into the doctrine of the Trinity, denoting the triune God as the unique form of fields of relationship. Wolfhart Pannenberg, "God as Spirit—and Natural Science," *Zygon* 36/4 (2001): 783-825.

[21] Pierre Teilhard de Chardin, *The Phenomenon of Man*, trans. Bernard Wall (New York: Harper and Brothers, 1959), 262-263.

dimensions, for theology underwritten by naturalistic worldview always starts from below, from the experience of nature.[22]

What we need then is to find a way to avoid the two extremes. On the one extreme, we have theological conservativism that has the tendency to stress the ontological difference between God and nature with little regard for their mutually enriching interactions, and on the other hand, we have theological naturalism that has the tendency to relate God to nature indiscriminately, often conflating the two without making a clear distinction. The trick here is to allow the theology's engagement with science to reformulate the traditional understanding of God to some extent and, at the same time, avoid naturalistic metaphysics to determine or underwrite the doctrine of God. We will work on this issue in Chapter One.

Critical Realism

Critical realism has been another dominant philosophical matrix that sustains a healthy conversation between theology and science. This is clearly the case for the vast array of scholars of the past and the present all pitching the tent in the critical realist camp. The first-generation scientific theologians such as Thomas Torrance, Arthur Peacocke, and Ian Barbour, have defended critical realism as the appropriate starting point for the dialogue between theology and science as well as their successors such as Alister McGrath, John Polkinghorne, and Janet Soskice.[23] For these scholars, the key to sustaining a theology and science rapprochement is to bring these two main forces of our culture

---

[22] John Polkinghorne, *The Faith of a Physicist* (Princeton: Princeton University Press, 1994), 64, 80.

[23] Alister E. McGrath, *The Science of God* (Grand Rapids: Eerdmans, 2004); John Polkinghorne, *Reason and Reality: The Relationship between Science and Theology* (London: Trinity Press International, 1991); Ian G. Barbour, *Religion in an Age of Science: Gifford Lectures Series* (New York: Harper Collins, 1990); Janet Soskice, *Metaphor and Religious Language* (Oxford: Clarendon, 1987); Arthur Peacocke, *Intimations of Reality: Critical Realism in Science and Religion* (Notre Dame: University of Notre Dame Press, 1984); Thomas F. Torrance, *Theological Science* (Oxford: Oxford University Press, 1969).

under the single rubric of a realist worldview. But what is critical realism?

As Paul Allen notes, critical realism in today's philosophical milieu is a loaded term, for those who are involved with the theology and science dialogue have taken the liberty of adjusting it to fit their own metaphysical agenda. However, despite its inherent ambiguity, the philosophical model of critical realism retains several distinct features that help us define it. Philosopher Kees von Kooten Niekerk provides a good description:

> *Critical realism* is a philosophical view of the nature of knowledge. On the one hand, it holds that it is possible to acquire knowledge about the external or physical world as it really is, independent of the human mind or subjectivity. This is why it is called *realism*. On the other hand, it rejects the claim of so-called naïve realism that the external world is as we experience it. Valid knowledge of the real world can only be acquired through critical reflection upon experience. That is why it is called *critical*.[24]

What this means is that critical realism affirms the necessity of recognizing the thing-in-itself while understanding the human intellectual involvement in the process of interpreting the object in question. For this reason, under the rubric of critical realism, the order of knowing and the order of being are neither separated nor collapsed into a single category of objectivity or subjectivity. The balance between concreteness and generality, or object and subject, are held in check by the interplay of the concept and the thing-in-itself. Furthermore, as an added benefit, such a realistic movement prevents the errors of naïve realism or instrumentalism.

If we were to follow the ways of naïve realism, we would assume that a concept or a model like a scientific theory such as "force" or

---

[24] Kees van Kooten Niekerk, "A Critical Realist Perspective on the Dialogue between Theology and Science" in *Rethinking Theology and Science: Six Models for the Current Dialogue*, eds. Niels Henrik Gregersen and J. Wentzel van Huyssteen (Grand Rapids: Eerdmans, 1998), 51.

"gravity" describes exactly and literally the actual entity to which it refers. Although the belief in the one-to-one correspondence between our concepts and the thing-in-itself held its ground for a while at the onset of the Enlightenment by scholars like Thomas Reid, [25] it was quickly overturned and replaced by instrumentalism. Instrumentalism stands at the opposite pole to that of naïve realism. It presupposes that our concepts do not really say anything about the real entity out there; rather, they are only instrumental and useful in making predictions or formulating a sophisticated version of scientific theories. John Dewey is a representative figure belonging to this philosophical movement. He writes, "Instrumentalism is an attempt to establish a precise logical theory of concepts, of judgments and inferences in their various forms, by considering primarily how thought functions in the experimental determinations of future consequences." [26] Put differently, from an instrumentalist perspective, scientific models and theories neither refer to actual reality nor reveal the nature of reality. They are just a conceptual tool with which we interpret the world.

Steering away from these two extremes of reductionistic philosophical viewpoints, critical realists attempt to hold a delicate balance between the known and the knower. Thus, the most urgent task for critical realists is the immediate formulation of a particular type of scientific methodology—that is, a scientific approach that correlates the concept with reality without creating an epistemological confusion between what is objectively known and what is subjectively construed. One such approach is the analogical method promoted by Ian Barbour, a well-known pioneer of the theology and science interface.

---

[25] In today's context, naïve realism has metamorphosed into direct realism. For direct realists, experience or our senses provide us with direct awareness of the external world. For more details, see John R. Searle, *Seeing Things as They Are; A Theory of Perception* (Oxford: Oxford University Press, 2015); Galen Strawson, *Selves: An Essay in Revisionary Metaphysics* (Oxford: Oxford University Press, 2009); and John McDowell, *Mind and World* (Cambridge: Harvard University Press, 1994).

[26] John Dewey, "The Development of American Pragmatism," in *John Dewey: The Later Works, 1925-1953*, vol. 2, ed. Jo Ann Boydston (Carbondale: Southern Illinois University Press, 1984), 14.

As a critical realist, Barbour recognized that all sciences, including theology, use models and analogies to make the connection between theory and data. This is largely due to the fact that "in science there is no direct route by logical reasoning from data to theory."[27] A theoretical model, according to Barbour, functions as a bridge that connects data and theory without having to fall back on literalism or instrumentalism, because the logic of analogy is grounded on the principle of similarity-and-difference. The principle of similarity-and-difference is the dialectic of commonality emerging from the comparison of analogues that discloses certain similar cognizable patterns and relations, and differentiation arising from the particular feature of analogues that conveys multiple meanings as a result of not only contrasting features in analogues but also our approach to each analogue with various motivations and from different perspectives. Thus, the logic of analogy is driven by, on the one hand, the elaborate synthesizing power of scientific rationality that helps us bring together in conceptual unities different analogues, or what Barbour calls, the positive analogy, and on the other hand, the negation of the univocal and exhaustive claims of analogues, or what Barbour calls, the negative analogy.

Granted that critical realism is an alternative to naïve realism and instrumentalism for it uses the analogical method, why is critical realism so popular in the theology-science interface? Thomas Torrance gives a good hint. According to Torrance, there is a "real" parallel between theology and science. On the one hand, within the theological reference, (1) God is the object, who exists ontologically independent of human perception; (2) God can be known because he reveals himself to us and we can experience God's being and act objectively; (3) and God can be expressed and articulated via theological concepts and doctrinal models though inadequately.[28] Similarly, within the scientific reference, (1) reality is the object that exists ontologically independent of human awareness; (2) reality can be known through observable events and empirical data; and (3) reality can be modeled based on the interplay of

---

[27] Ian Barbour, *Religion and Science: Historical and Contemporary Issues* (New York: Harper One, 1990), 115.

[28] Torrance, *Theological Science*, 295-99.

theory and data.[29] In short, both theological and scientific activities operate on the common ground, that is, they are driven by and to reality.

However, despite its success, recently, critical realists are faltering. The balance between the realist objective pole and the constructive involvement of the human agency seems too difficult to maintain, and as a result, critical realists are shifting their view to one pole over the other, creating an unwarranted schism within the group. On the one hand, scholars such as Thomas Torrance and Alister McGrath unequivocally tilt their balance to the objective side. For them, scientific inquiries must be genuine questions which are aimed at reality, and appropriate to the nature of the object they aim to investigate. These scholars are more comfortable with the description of science that highlights the correspondence of the human mind to the object in question, not vice versa. On the other hand, scholars such as Bas van Fraassen tilt the balance to the constructive pole. According to Fraassen, science aims to give an adequate empirical picture of reality, never the full picture of reality itself.[30] What is empirically adequate? What is observable and testable is empirically adequate. Hence, as a constructive empiricist, Fraassen denies any ontological status of scientific theories except for those that are based on what is observable. For this reason, Fraassen is called an anti-realist because of his denial of the actuality of the unobservable entities such as "electrons." He thinks that they are mere human constructions.

The more pressing issue is the division of scientific realism and theological realism. Scholars such as Ernan McMullin and his successor, Paul Allen, identify apparent discrepancies in the way scientific theologians try to put together theology and science into a unified whole using critical realism.[31] McMullin gives at least three reasons why we should not cross-link the two worlds by way of critical realism. First, the

---

[29] Ibid., 286–94.

[30] Bas C. van Fraassen, *The Scientific Image* (Oxford: Clarendon, 1980), 12.

[31] Ernan McMullin, "Realism in Theology and Science: A Response to Peacocke," *Religion and Intellectual Life* 2 (1985): 39-47; and Paul L. Allen, *Ernan McMullin and Critical Realism in the Science-Theology Dialogue* (London: Routledge, 2006).

two disciplines do not deal with the same reality.[32] What McMullin wants to emphasize here is the importance of understanding that there are mutually exclusive ontological categories between theology and science (e.g., the reality of God versus the reality of nature). However, for the sake of keeping the dialogue going, scientific theologians have been unapologetically merging the reality of nature and the reality of God as a non-divisible whole, as in the case of panentheism and process theology, creating confusion and misunderstanding. Second, although critical realism draws our attention to how a theory is justified by evidence, theology and science have a different ground of justification. McMullin notes in this regard:

> Though scientists do not always agree on the weight to be given the different criteria, there is still an impressive consensus as to what should count in favor of a theory: predictive accuracy, internal consistency, coherence with other accepted theories, absence of unexplained "coincidence," successful novel predictions, long-term fertility in suggesting more detailed specifications of the associated model, unification of previously disparate domains, and so on.[33]

He adds, "What enables the realism to be a critical one is, then, the quality of the evidence available and the broadly agreed-upon character of the criteria of theory-assessment."[34] By contrast, according to McMullin, for the theology's ground of justification, none of these criteria of scientific realism applies. And third, scientific realism is thoroughly intersubjective. In science, it is never the case that a given theory is only accessible to a limited group of people who have membership like a religious circle. Rather, "it is in principle available to anyone who knows how to use the experimental equipment."[35]

I will critically evaluate McMullin's argument in detail in Chapter Two, so it suffices to say here that McMullin has shown that we have to

---

[32] McMullin, "Realism in Theology and Science," 39.

[33] Ibid., 41.

[34] Ibid.

[35] Ibid.

rethink about the relationship between theological realism and scientific realism and reassess the viability of using critical realism as the chief matrix for sustaining a healthy and fruitful interdisciplinary dialogue. What is needed is a better understanding of theological realism in light of the recent development of scientific realist criteria such as intersubjectivity, underdetermination, and epistemological fallibilism. We will discuss these matters more in detail in Chapter Two.

Faith Rationality

In addition to the discussion of critical realism, the faith-reason dichotomy has become a hotly debated topic in the theology and science dialogue.[36] Although we have come a long way since the heyday of Kant's philosophy that caused a clean break between the matters of faith and the matters of science, those of us who are involved with the interdisciplinary work is still challenged by the ambiguous role of faith

---

[36] The list here represents just a few examples. As the list shows, the literary output regarding the question of the relationship between faith and scientific rationality is extensive and broad. However, in my judgment, despite the vast output of literature, there are more questions raised than questions addressed. This is partly due to the nature of the topic, that is, the elusiveness of "faith." Tom McLeish, *Faith and Wisdom in Science* (Oxford: Oxford University Press, 2014); John F. Haught, *Science and Faith: A New Introduction* (New York: Paulist, 2012); Surrey Farnham, *Science and Faith within Reason: Reality, Creation, Life and Design* (Burlington: Ashgate, 2011); Karl Giberson, *The Language of Science and Faith: Straight Answers to Genuine Questions* (Downers Grove: Intervarsity Press, 2011); Oliver D. Crisp et al., *Theology and Philosophy: Faith and Reason* (New York: T&T Clark, 2011); Andrew J. Kirk, *The Future of Reason, Science and Faith Following Modernity and Post-modernity* (Burlington: Ashgate, 2007); John Milbank, "Faith, Reason, and Imagination: The Study of Theology and Philosophy in the 21st Century," *Transversalités* 101/1 (2007): 69-86; William H. Chalker, *Science and Faith: Understanding Meaning, Method, and Truth* (Louisville: Westminister John Knox Press, 2006); Kenneth Boa and Robert M. Bowman, *Faith Has Its Reasons: Integrative Approaches to Defending the Christian Faith* (Downers Grove: Intervarsity Press, 2005); Mark Richardson and Gordy Slack, eds., *Faith in Science: Scientists Search for Truth* (London: Routledge, 2001); Timothy L. Smith, ed., *Faith and Reason* (South Bend: St. Augustines Press, 2001); L. L. Hench, *Science, Faith, and Ethics* (London: Imperial College Press, 2001); Paul Helm, *Faith with Reason* (Oxford: Oxford University Press, 2000); Stephan Evans, *Faith beyond Reason: A Kierkegaardian Account* (Grand Rapids: Eerdmans, 1998); Jitse M. van der Meer, ed., *Facets of Faith and Science: Historiography and Modes of Interaction*, vol. 1 (Landham: University Press of America, 1996); Alvin Plantinga, *Faith and Rationality: Reason and Belief in God* (Notre Dame: Notre Dame University Press, 1991); Michael Polanyi, Science, *Faith and Society* (Chicago: University Of Chicago Press, 1964).

in the shaping of our knowledge. After the demise of logical positivism, even in the post-critical context that recognizes extra-rational factors in the way we do science, faith seems to be the source of many divisions. The problem of faith can be seen from three distinct and yet related perspectives.

First, our understanding of faith is still hampered by the old philosophical logic of foundationalism. The Barth-Scholz debate sheds some light on this issue. Karl Barth in dialogue with his fellow German philosopher Heinrich Scholz argued that theology is science for two reasons. First, theology is a special kind of science because it is dogmatic—that is, theology produces propositional statements about God rather than about humanity or nature.[37] Second, theology is science because it is based on God's self-revelation, and God's own self-disclosure provides "real" data for all theological reflections. [38] Consequently, according to Barth, although theology is a rational exercise of the mind, it deals with primarily the matters of faith. However, from an empiricist's point of view, Barth's way of doing theology could not be considered a science. This is the basic contention made by Scholz. Since Scholz was not convinced that Barth's description of "science" is adequate, he basically asked for three things from Barth in order to justify and substantiate theology as a science: verifiability of statements, agreement with other sciences, and independence from prior judgment.[39] Simply put, Scholz does not think that Barth's way of doing theology is really evidenced-based. It is rather more like a confessional declaration that depends on the personal decision of faith. For Scholz, the things of God, as contended by Barth, could not be put under the scrutiny of natural-scientific investigations.

What we can take away from Scholz's argument is that Barth's way of doing theology has the potential to exempt theological statements from critical examinations by all scientists. If faith statements are not

---

[37] Karl Barth, *Church Dogmatics* (New York: T & T Clark, 1932, c2009), 1:269.

[38] Ibid., 276.

[39] For more details on Barth-Scholz debate, see Pannenberg, *Historicity*, 11–22. Pannenberg notes that contemporary theologians are still not responding to or fulfilling Scholz's demands.

criticizable and left to the private sector of the church, theology cannot escape the fallout from epistemological foundationalism. What is foundationalism? Stanley Stratton defines foundationalism in the following way. "The idea is that there is a foundation for knowledge which consists of beliefs that are justified but not by relying on any other beliefs."[40] Thus, a faith statement becomes irrefutable, infallible, and self-justifying. However, the consensus today is that foundationalism is impractical and unrealistic. Merold Westphal writes, "That it [foundationalism] is philosophically indefensible is so widely agreed that its demise is the closest thing to a philosophical consensus in decades."[41] In this respect, scholars have been searching for a more practical and realistic program that could move beyond the errors of foundationalism. One such move is the adoption of realist coherentism. Stanley Grenz explains. "At the heart of coherentism is the suggestion that the justification of a belief lies in its 'fit' with other held beliefs; hence, justification entails 'inclusion within a coherent system,' to cite the words of philosopher Arthur Kenyon Rogers."[42] Does this mean that we should discard our foundational faith and follow coherentism? If there is no epistemological base to which faith can stand, how can we say that our faith in God is sure and secure?

The answer to these questions leads to our second point: the personal dimension of faith. After the demise of foundationalism, scientific theologians endeavored to define "faith" that is more in tuned with a postmodern inclusion of personal factors in the way we understand the nature of our epistemic structure. For instance, Michael Polanyi identified an epistemic category in the name of personal knowledge, which clarifies the role of faith in science. Colin Weightman lists three main features of Polanyi's personal knowledge: (1) rational activities are more than logical or explicit—they are more tacit and

---

[40] Stanley Brian Stratton, "Coherence, Consonance, and Conversation: Interaction of Theology and Natural Science in the Quest for a Unified World-View" (Ph.D. diss., Princeton Theological Seminary, 1997), 317–19.

[41] Merold Westphal, "A Reader's Guide to 'Reformed Epistemology,'" *Perspectives* 7/9 (1992): 10–11.

[42] Stanley J. Grenz, *Renewing the Center: Evangelical Theology in a Post-Theological Era* (Grand Rapids: Baker Academics, 2006), 199.

16

implicit in nature; (2) all knowledge is cast upon a fiduciary framework; and (3) although there is no ground for knowledge, the community of faith plays a critical role as the norm for the determination of truth.[43]

However, the setback of the post-critical drive for personal knowledge is the introduction of a new dichotomy—e.g., the category of impersonal rationality versus personal rationality. A good example is illustrated in Thomas Torrance's differentiation of number rationality and word rationality. For Torrance, impersonal knowledge is associated with number rationality, that is, scientific operations that strictly deal with the patterns and orders of nature, whereas personal knowledge is related to word rationality that deals with attaching words and concepts to the brute facts of life. According to Torrance, number rationality is impersonal, inferior to that of word rationality, for our dealing with number thrives only in the abstract, formal, and non-real realm of human imagination (e.g., mathematics). By contrast, word rationality is personal because of its "relational" and "real" potentiality. More clearly, word rationality has the capacity to not only perform the rigorous investigation of nature as it is made known through the compelling claims of reality without projecting our knowledge into it, but also penetrate deep into the meta-scientific level through human intuition that reaches the threshold of the ultimate intelligible ground of the universe even reaching out to the realm of *theologia*.[44] Hence, word rationality is based on personal commitment that has to do with evaluative and judgment making processes and number rationality on the impersonal speculation that has to do with making brute mechanical calculations. But the problem here is that once again, there seems to be a disconnection between impersonal and personal ways of knowing. The matters of faith could then be once again put under the rubric of

---

[43] Colin Weightman, *Theology in a Polanyian Universe: The Theology of Thomas Torrance* (New York: Peter Lang, 1994), 203–20. Also see Michael Polanyi, *Personal Knowledge: Towards a Post-Critical Philosophy* (Chicago: The University of Chicago Press, 1962).

[44] See Thomas F. Torrance, *Christian Theology and Scientific Culture* (New York: Oxford University Press, 1981), 109-117.

personal activities[45] and the matters of science under the rubric of impersonal activities,[46] which really defies what Polanyi had imagined.

Third, there is a question begging in the theology and science dialogue: "is religious faith really explainable in terms of scientific rationality?" Faith in a Christian term really has to do with religious conversion more so than the scientific way of knowing some reality out there. The Christian commitment is to the saving faith given to the believers of Jesus Christ by the power of the Holy Spirit sent by the Father, not just about putting our trust in the effectiveness and fruitfulness of scientific rationality. Even if we identify "faith" as a key rational framework upon which both theology and science operate, can we really make a connection between them without destroying the integrity of Christian faith? What is the precise relationship between "faith" operating in science and "faith" in theology? There have been some attempts to clear the fuzziness in this area,[47] but it would help the theology and science dialogue if we justify why faith in theology and faith in science are correlatable despite their differences.

As we shall see, the bottom line for this discussion has to do with the way we understand the faith-reason relationship. How are they

---

[45] E.g., faith is pragmatic (Niebuhr), faith is an existential decision (Bultmann), faith is a deep sense of sorrow (Farley), and faith is experiential (Smith). Cf. Richard H. Niebuhr, *The Meaning of Revelation* (New York: MacMillan), 77; Rudolf Bultmann, *Existence and Faith*, trans. Schubert M. Ogden (London: Hodder and Stroughton, 1961); Wendy Farley, *Tragic Vision and Divine Compassion: A Contemporary Theodicy* (Louisville: Westminster John Knox, 1990), 133; Wilfred Cantwell Smith, *Faith and Belief* (Princeton: Princeton University Press, 1979), 12.

[46] There is a growing movement in the world of mathematics that looks at the idea that mathematics, too, has a personal dimension. For more details, see Philip J. Davis and Reuben Hersh, *The Mathematical Experience* (New York: Houghton Mifflin Company, 1998); Reuben Hersh, *What is Mathematics, Really?* (Oxford: Oxford University Press, 1997); Morris Kline, *Mathematics and the Search for Knowledge* (Oxford: Oxford University Press, 1985).

[47] For example, see Alister E. McGrath, *The Foundations of Dialogue in Science and Religion* (Malden: Blackwell, 1998); Bernard Lonergan, *Insight: A Study of Human Understanding* (Toronto: University of Toronto Press, 1992); Wentzel Van Huyssteen, *Theology and the Justification of Faith: Constructing Theories in Systematic Theology* (Grand Rapids: Eerdmans, 1988); and Thomas F. Torrance, ed., *Belief in Science and Christian Life: The Relevance of Michael Polanyi's Thought for Christian Faith and Life* (Edinburgh: Handsel, 1980).

related? Can we conceive them without marginalizing one at the expense of the other? How should we define faith rationality in the post-modern scientific context? We will address these questions and more in Chapter Three.

The Divine Action Project

Finally, we come to the most controversial topic, the divine action project (DAP). With a heightened enthusiasm, in the last few decades, those who are engaged in the theology and science dialogue have been probing into the fundamental patterns of the divine action. They are dealing with a simple question: how does God act in this world? Although the question seems simple, it still haunts scientists and theologians today as it did in the early years of Christianity. What is the causal joint that connects God and the processes of nature? How is it that an infinite God could mingle with finite entities? What is the direct consequence of God influencing the world? Is God affected by the world? These intractable questions are just but a few that have come up in the contemporary dialogue between theology and science.

The difficulty of addressing these questions has not impeded the progress of interdisciplinary efforts, however. In fact, what we see is the opposite happening. The accumulation of various views on the divine action actually is drawing more attention from scholars from all walks of life.[48] Just as there is biodiversity in this world that is responsible for

---

[48] I present a small portion of the vast and manifold literature on the topic of divine action, which provides a good starting point to read about this topic. Ted Peters and Nathan Hallanger, eds. *God's Action in Nature's World: Essays in Honour of Robert John Russell* (London: Routledge, 2016); Louise Hickman, *Chance or Providence: Religious Perspectives on Divine Action* (Newcastle: Cambridge Scholars Publishing, 2014); Michael J. Dodds, *Unlocking Divine Action: Contemporary Science and Thomas Aquinas* (Washington, D.C.: The Catholic University Press of America, 2012); Denis Edwards, *How God Acts: Creation, Redemption, and Special Divine Action* (Minneapolis: Fortress, 2012); Christopher Southgate, ed., *God, Humanity and the Cosmos: A Textbook in Science and Religion* (New York: T&T Clark, 2011); Amos Yong, *The Spirit of Creation: Modern Science and Divine Action in the Pentecostal-Charismatic Imagination* (Grand Rapids: Eerdmans, 2011); F. LeRon Shults, Nancey Murphy and Robert John Russell, eds. *Philosophy, Science and Divine Action* (Boston: Brill, 2009); Philip Clayton, ed., *The Oxford Handbook of Religion and Science* (Oxford: Oxford University Press, 2008); Alister E. McGrath, *The Open Secret: A New Vision for Natural Theology* (Oxford: Blackwell, 2008); Keith Ward, *Divine Action:*

the emergence of life, the diverse approach to the problem of divine action has become the driving force for the theology and science interface. It has really brought a new life to the interdisciplinary project. In this action-packed camp, I found three main approaches that may explain the nature and the goal of the current approaches to the DAP. Of course, the goal here is not to provide an exhaustive account of the project, but as an introduction to the movement, I provide three of the most relevant methods to highlight the key issues and debates that are still ongoing today.

First, interdisciplinary scholars are dealing with the question of ontological indeterminacy. Traditionally, the typical understanding of nature was that it functions like a self-perpetuating clock, a well-made machine that has the ability to sustain itself. The intricate network of different systems in this cosmos was found to be marching to the heartbeat of the cosmos called the laws of nature. For this reason, the 18th-century scientist Pierre-Simon Laplace unapologetically declared that the world is fully deterministic, operating based on the set of given laws.[49] Hence, for Laplace, if we gain enough knowledge about the patterns and rules of the world's mechanism, we would be able to figure out the nature of all things.

However, the days of determinism are behind us. Contemporary interdisciplinary scholars no longer adhere to such a naïve view of the world. It is because, in the wake of quantum leaps and chaos theories,

---

Examining God's Role in an Open and Emergent Universe (West Conshohocken: Templeton Press, 2007); Philip Clayton, "Wildman's Kantian Skepticism: A Rubicon for the Divine Action Debate," *Theology and Science* 2/2 (2004): 186–190; Wesley Wildman, "Divine Action Project, 1988-2003," in *Theology and Science* 2/1 (2004): 31-75; Thomas F. Tracy, "Scientific Perspectives on Divine Action? Mapping the Options," *Theology and Science* 2/2 (2004): 196-201; Nicholas Saunders, *Divine Action and Modern Science* (New York: Cambridge University Press, 2002); Ted Peters, *Playing God: Genetic Determinism and Human Freedom* (London: Routledge, 1997); Robert John Russell, Nancey Murphy, and Arthur R. Peacocke, eds. *Chaos Complexity: Scientific Perspectives on Divine Action* (Notre Dame: University of Notre Dame Press, 1996); Arthur Peacocke, *Theology for the Scientific Age* (London: SCM Press, 1993); Nancey Murphy, *Theology in the Age of Scientific Reasoning* (Ithaca: Cornell University Press, 1990); John Polkinghorne, *Science and Providence* (London: SPCK, 1989).

[49] Roger Hahn, *Pierre Simon Laplace, 1749-1827: A Determined Scientist* (Cambridge: Harvard University Press, 2005), 168-180.

science has now moved into the territory of the world that is more in tune with indeterminate systems that exist within the regular patterns of nature. The divine action project follows suit. For instance, scholars like Robert Russell and Kirk Wegter-McNelly investigated the quantum world and found out that there is an "ontological" hole[50] that may reveal the possibility of the area in which God is working. Such an ontological gap is a necessary component for the divine action to occur, since, as the first law of thermodynamics implies, in a closed system, God cannot intervene, for he will introduce "new" energy that does not belong to the system of this world. God can act within this world only if the ontological system of this universe is in some way "open" to receive him. Hence, scholars like Russell and Wegter-McNelly have located God in the quantum world,[51] for the quantum indeterminacy allows God to interact with the world without destroying the integrity of natural processes.

There is more than one way to speak of ontological indeterminacy. As an example, John Polkinghorne also found a way for God to interact with this world in a non-interventionist fashion.[52] Because of his unique approach, he is called a non-interventionist. Non-interventionism does not have the burden to answer Hume's criticism, which says that God's special action in this world necessarily violates the laws of nature. If we assume that the world is ontologically open, then there is no need for God to intrude upon and violate the laws of nature. He can interact with

---

[50] This is different from "the God of the gap" problem. The God of the gap problem has to do with our limited knowledge, whereas ontological indeterminacy has to do with the open feature of the world, which is often believed to be constituted by the field of relations rather than the accumulation of individualized entities.

[51] For more details, see Robert J. Russell, "Divine Action and Quantum Mechanics: A Fresh Assessment" in *Quantum Mechanics: Scientific Perspectives on Divine Action*, ed. Robert J. Russell, K. Wegter-McNelly and John Polkinghorne (Vatican City and Berkeley: Vatican Observatory and Center for Theology and the Natural Sciences, 2001), 293-328; and Kirk Wegter-McNelly, *The Entangled God: Divine Relationality and Quantum Physics* (New York: Routledge, 2011).

[52] Rather than tackling the micro-world of the quanta, Polkinghorne develops his idea based on large-scale systems. He relies on the chaos theory to support his understanding of ontological indeterminacy. For more details, see John Polkinghorne, "Chaos Theory and Divine Action," in *Religion and Science: History, Method and Dialogue*, ed. W. M. Richardson and W. J. Wildman (London: Routledge, 1996), 243-52.

the world in a special way without having to suspend the laws of nature. Although the metaphysical view of ontological indeterminacy could define how God acts in this world without violating the laws of nature, it comes with a problem of its own.

The problem with this approach is that, due to the excessive attention given to the "indeterminate" nature of the world and God's involvement with presumed indeterminate systems of our cosmos, God is necessarily seen as indeterministic. This is the issue brought up by Brian Austin.[53] He believes that if God acts at the quantum level, because quantum phenomena are indetermined and God is mingled with them, God may not fully know the outcome of the quantum effects. God may know what happened in the past and present without a gap, but he could have limited knowledge of the future, because of his restricted action in the quantum world, which can be calculated only in terms of probabilities. But how could this be? Is not our God omniscient, immutable, and all-powerful? Although not all scholars run into the problem of mixing God's immutability and the world's changeableness, it is incumbent upon those who are involved with the divine action project to think deeper about the paradox of God's determinism in principle and his action with the world which are indeterministic in praxis.

Another way to look at the way God acts in this world is via the conceptual framework of "double agency." What is "double agency"? The controversial view of double agency asserts that "there is a certain class of events in which divine and natural causality are simultaneously active."[54] Such a theory is well depicted by Austin Farrer.[55] In essence, the main tenet of Farrer's double agency pivots on God's action as the primary cause and all other events as the secondary cause, to which the

---

[53] Brian D. Austin, "Randomness, Omniscience, and Divine Action," in *Facets of Faith and Science*, vol. 4, ed. Jitse Van Der Meer (New York: University Press of America, 1997), 41-56.

[54] Nicholas Saunders, *Divine Action and Modern Science* (New York: Cambridge University Press, 2002), 35.

[55] Brian Hebblethwaite, *The Philosophical Theology of Austin Farrer* (Leuven: Peeters, 2007), 74.

primary cause is mediated. Therefore, nothing in this world is untouched by God. God acts as the primary cause that incites the secondary cause in the creaturely things, without overpowering their freedom.

There are two key advantages to thinking God's action in this way. First, God's activity is always mediated. His action is never immediate or direct. For this reason, God's transcendence is always preserved. There is no need for God to be directly affected or influenced by the things of this world. Second, God's action can be both personal and impersonal. God's action is personal because his value-driven activity can be achieved by working through human agencies. At the same time, God's action is impersonal because his purpose-driven activity can be achieved by luring the natural movement to its ultimate aim, the union with God. What this double agency theory has achieved is the promotion of cooperative efforts between God and creaturely things.

This approach, however, is also hampered by theological problems. Immediately, I see the problem of discernment. To which action can we attribute to God if we say that God and creatures are co-operating always? How can we tell the difference? Does not this double agency defy the purpose of the divine action project? Does not the divine action project exist for the sake of discerning God's particular action in this world? In what ways can we attribute to nature its own processes?

The issue with the double agency theory has to do with identifying the causal joint. This is clearly exemplified in Farrer's work. He understood that God and creatures can cooperate via the principle of double agency, but he could not go any further and explain the precise causal relationship between God and creatures. Polkinghorne writes in this regard:

> The secondary web of created causality is treated as being complete and undriven. Yet the primary causality of God is supposed nevertheless to be ineffably at work in and through these created causalities. How this is so is not explained. Indeed Farrer would regard it as risking monstrosity and confusion if

one were to attempt to discern the "causal joint" by which divine providence acts.[56]

Due to the silence on the matters of the causal joint, the principle of double agency is unable to flesh out clearly the independent-dependent relationship between God and creatures. The burden is on the double agency advocates to answer these difficult questions: in what respect that creatures are free when all things lie within the sphere of God's providential act? Could not creaturely things act on their own even though they are within God's providential care? What aspect of human action is "free"? What aspect of the natural order is "free"? It is not clear to me how these questions can be answered without really digging deep into the matter of the "causal joint."

Going further, understanding the importance of addressing the causal joint dilemma exposed by the double agency and other divine action projects, interdisciplinary scholars have turned to the mind-body analogy. The mind-body analogy takes many shapes and forms so there is an inherent limitation in our attempt to find a one-size-fits-all description. So, it is better for this survey to detail the analogy by introducing a representative figure, Arthur Peacocke, who has taken this analogy seriously. For Peacocke, the mind-body analogy is fitting for the discussion of the divine action project because it explains God's bottom-up and top-down causality. Peacocke without hesitation likens God to the human person.[57] Like a human mind that emerges from the lower physical activities of the brain but exerts a top-down influence on the brain, God functions as the highest emergent property of the cosmos, exerting top-down influence upon the world by feeding God's own information to the physical system. So God is working bottom-up and

---

[56] John Polkinghorne, "The Metaphysics of Divine Action," in *Philosophy, Science and Divine Action*, eds. F. LeRon Shults, Nancey Murphy and Robert John Russell (Boston: Brill, 2009), 101.

[57] Arthur Peacocke, *Creation and the World of Science: The Reshaping of Belief* (Oxford: Oxford University Press, 2004), 133-138.

top-down as "the immanent creator creating in and through the processes of the natural order."[58]

The obvious shortcoming for this analogy is that, because God is pressed too close to immanentism, God remains captivated by the world, and because God exerts top-down influence at the mental level, God's action is always mediated through psychological activities, which then finally touches upon the physical realm. In order for the mind-body analogy to work, God must be reliant upon something that is psychological or physical, which goes against the grain of Christian faith. Also, the mind-body analogy comes with heavy baggage. Since it is a derivative of the theory of evolution, it has to address the issues of evolution such as the tension between God's planned creative activity and the self-reciprocating, random selection of evolution.

In sum, from this brief survey, we can see that there are several key unresolved tensions associated with the divine action project—e.g., determinism and indeterminacy, transcendence and immanence, freedom and providence, and top-down influence and bottom-up emergence. Also, from a theological perspective, there is a lack of viewing God's action in terms of his supernatural activities.[59] Part of the reason for this is that theology is more attuned to science rather than science to theology. In other words, in the theology and science interface, the priority is given to scientific data rather than theological doctrines. However, failure to acknowledge the role of God's supernatural acts could lead to devastating effects for Christian faith, since Christianity is supported by the great pillars of God's miracles. For this reason, I will tackle the issues of the divine action project in Chapter Four from the vantage point of God working in the world extraordinarily and miraculously.

---

[58] Arthur Peacocke, "Articulating God's Presence in and to the World Unveiled by the Sciences," in *In Whom We Live and Move and Have Our Being: Panentheistic Reflections on God's Presence in a Scientific World* (Grand Rapids: Eerdmans, 2004), 144.

[59] This is one of John Polkinghorne's insightful evaluations of the current status of the theology and science dialogue. His efforts to compensate this shortcoming are clearly visible in his Gifford Lectures. For more details, see John Polkinghorne, *The Faith of a Physicist* (Princeton: Princeton University Press, 1994).

Chapter Divisions

Taking these challenges seriously, I have set the book into four stand-alone chapters, each with its own thesis. Thus, the book has four specific aims. The first chapter treats the issue of naturalism, which is, in my judgment, the biggest obstacle for Christian theology. There have been many different ways of handling naturalism by theo-scientific scholars, but most of them joined hands with naturalists, and for this reason, I take issue with their approaches and lay a new trajectory for developing a theology of nature. The thesis of this chapter is that the concept of the accommodating absolute is a better metaphysical alternative to natural theology and theistic naturalism because it recognizes the dynamic interplay of God, humanity, and nature, without marginalizing the absoluteness of God and the contingency of nature.

For this reason, the first chapter becomes the starting point for rethinking the current methods of interfacing theology and science and raises the question of whether a theological appeal to naturalism is the proper way to do interdisciplinary studies. Furthermore, this chapter lays out the preliminary contours of open system metaphysics that forms the basis for the open-ended approach to interfacing theology and science.

The second chapter deals with the issues of relating theological realism to scientific realism. Here, I argue against those who try to cordon off theological realism from scientific realism. What we need to know here is that theological realism should never be equated with absolutism or fideism; rather, we should search for a new way of configuring theological realism that avoids the category of absolutism and fideism. In this respect, I claim that theological realism is correlatable to scientific realism because it meets the demand of underdeterminism when we re-appropriate theological realism by way of metascience. An open-ended approach of metascience becomes the methodological key for this chapter to safeguard Christian understanding of God as theology engages science in a holistic manner.

When we come to the third chapter, I hash out the false dichotomy between faith and reason and demonstrate why these two categories are not entirely antithetical to one another. I critically review the historical misunderstanding of the relationship between faith and reason that led to false dichotomization—i.e., faith is subjective and reason is objective. I defend the thesis that they are not mutually exclusive but complementary because faith forms the basis for "third rationality." In this way, I weave the two threads of objectivity (first rationality) and subjectivity (second rationality) into a single category of faith (third rationality) without giving up either objectivity or subjectivity. Here, we accomplish for the book the effectiveness of an open-ended approach that does not marginalize theological rationality at the expense of scientific rationality.

Finally, the fourth chapter assesses the problems associated with biblical miracles. Here, I defend the claim that miracles are a vital part of the divine action project and that they do not hinder the integrity of the theology and science interface because the possibility of miracles clears the naturalistic path all the while laying a new trajectory for open system metaphysics. Thus, the final chapter combines the methodological schema we have developed in the previous chapters and effectively fuse them to show that theology and science can interface without marginalizing the core beliefs of Christian faith. With the understanding that we have an open system of God, humanity, and nature, interacting with one another based on its own laws and intentions, we can safely move away from the myopic vision of naturalism to the wider scope of the metaphysical framework of open systems.

Although we have four independent chapters, nevertheless, there is a common thread that runs through all four chapters. That is, the two cultural forces of theology and science can be interlaced without marginalizing the distinct contribution from each of these disciplines when we apply open system metaphysics. Since I am writing the book from the vantage point of theology rather than science, I pay close attention to the preservation of key features of Christian theology such as God's absolute transcendence and his miraculous supernatural interventions, all the while modifying traditional theological themes in light of new scientific developments. I stand on the firm conviction that we can talk about God's being and act intellectually in this scientific age without giving up the classical doctrine of God, and in order to sustain this conviction, I pursue an interdisciplinary method with an open-ended metaphysical framework upon which Christians in the 21st-century can rethink about the nature and function of the theology and science interface.

Chapter One

Transcending Naturalism:
Re-visioning the Accommodating Absolute
and the Contingency of Nature

We rarely see nature. We live in it but do not actually appreciate its providence and beauty. American naturalist Ralph W. Emerson laments, "To speak truly, few adult persons can see nature. Most persons do not see the sun. At least they have a very superficial seeing."[1] But when we do see nature, Emerson guarantees that there would be a dramatic change in our lives. Like him, we will be able to see something new. He testifies, "In the wilderness, I find something more dear and connate than in streets or villages. In the tranquil landscape, and especially in the distant line of the horizon, man beholds somewhat as beautiful as his own nature."[2] Similarly, another American naturalist John Muir declares, "In every walk with nature, one receives far more than nature."[3] Muir contends that by gazing upon the green, yellow and red of the flowers that paint the landscape of the wilderness, we can only appreciate the majesty and grandeur of nature that transcends the finitude of human intelligibility. It is true. Even in darkness, the beauty of nature is overwhelming. Out in the field, away from the bright lights of the busy urban environment, it pays to look up and survey the sky. It is breathtaking to see the majestic display of starry hosts in the Milky Way. To imagine that there are billions of more galaxies like ours is mindboggling.

The problem as seen by many naturalists today is the lack of appreciation of nature. How can we not see the beauty and glory of nature? Why are we destroying the natural environment? Is human

---

[1] Ralph Waldo Emerson, *Nature* (Boston: James Munroe and Company, 1849), 7.

[2] Ibid., 8.

[3] John Muir, *Steep Trails* (Boston: Houghton Mifflin Company, 1918), 128.

progress more important than the preservation of nature? Religion is not helpful in this regard. In fact, theists seem to be the chief villains who have ruthlessly cut down the trees in the forest to build God's sanctuary and killed the animals to offer them as sacrifices so that their deity can be pacified. Consequently, environmentalist Lynn White noted that it was Christianity that planted in the mind of the commoners the belief that nature is nothing more than a footstool for man and God. Man was given a special privilege like God to put nature under his dominion.[4] As a result, man armed with the new power of machines—a byproduct of the Industrial Revolution—sought to destroy and exploit nature, which was deemed inferior and subservient to man.

Many theists in the contemporary era scrambled to diffuse the negative view of Christianity like that of White's claim and huddled up to form an alliance with naturalists to develop what I call "naturalistic theology."[5] Naturalistic theology is a contemporary form of natural theology, which relies more on the natural processes to reconfigure old theological themes such as the doctrine of God and less on biblical exegesis and traditional doctrinal formulations to do theology. The main objective of naturalistic theology is to plug the gap between God and nature, and as a result, theology that is done from the vantage point of naturalistic theology conflates God and nature into a unified whole. With this approach, many questions come to the fore. Is it proper to reformulate our understanding of God based on the naturalistic worldview? What ideas about the God of the Bible are commensurable with naturalism, if any? Can we preserve God's transcendence all the

---

[4] Lynn T. White, "The Historical Roots of Our Ecologic Crisis," in *Ecology and Religion in History*, ed. David Spring and Eileen Spring (New York: Harper and Row, 1974), 155. Also see Lynn T. White, *Medieval Technology and Social Change* (Oxford University Press, 1962).

[5] In this chapter and the following chapters, I use the terms "naturalistic theology" and "natural theology" interchangeably, although there is a slight difference. Natural theology in a traditional sense seeks the knowledge of God based solely on human reason without the aid of God's revelation. Naturalistic theology is a way to develop the doctrine of God based on naturalistic thinking such as religious naturalism and panentheism. Since naturalistic theology in a broad sense seeks to explain God based on what we know of nature, it qualifies as a modern form of natural theology.

while working within the frame of naturalistic metaphysics? What does it mean to be religious in a naturalistic society?

These are the kinds of questions that I am going to address in this chapter, and at the end, I will suggest my own way to cope with the dominance of naturalistic worldview in the way we interface theology and science by moving away from the contemporary agenda of naturalistic theology without marginalizing our love of nature. To be concise, I defend the claim that a theology of nature grounded in the interplay of the accommodating absolute and the contingency of nature saves God from being conflated with nature and saves nature from unwarranted exploitation. In order to support my claim, I first review the current landscape of naturalism and critically evaluate various contemporary theistic models that are built upon it. I close the chapter with my own model that speaks for the accommodating absolute as a way to interface theology and science without marginalizing God or nature.

Naturalism

I begin with a definition of naturalism to clearly outline the premise of our discussion, for the scope of naturalism is far and wide, and we can quickly get lost in the jungle of modern naturalism. For this purpose, I will use J. P. Moreland's four-point assessment of naturalism as the guiding template for our discussion and add my own commentary to highlight the key characteristics of naturalism. Moreland's work represents an honest evaluation of naturalism, even though he is highly critical of its methodological ground. His thorough analysis from a philosophical standpoint also helps us see the core beliefs of naturalistic thinkers.

Moreland's work on naturalism is essentially a critical analysis of well-known naturalists such as John Searle and Thomas O'Connor. In reviewing O'Connor's monograph *Persons and Causes*, Moreland suggests four main points that define naturalism: (1) physics is the basic level of reality; (2) all particulars are physical objects; (3) there are genuine emergent properties; (4) there is a causal unity in nature.[6] This list provides for me a starting point to delve deeper into the problems associated with naturalism. What follows is my own way of unpacking the significance of these four beliefs of naturalism.

The first proposition of naturalism is as follows: "physics is the basic level of reality." What this means is that every complex entity (e.g., force) can be understood as a combination of simpler material entities (e.g., the interaction between particles). Based on this principle, if we were to investigate the fundamental structure of reality, we would find only observable entities. If we find anything other than observable entities, naturalists would conclude that what they are seeing is either a theoretical entity that is not "real" or an emergent property of the material reality that has yet to be explained by natural scientists. Hence, scientific naturalism tends to rely on the observable form of empiricism to explain what goes on in nature without any recourse to a non-physical science such as religious or metascientific studies.

Because of the fact that matter determines reality, subjectivity is quickly dismissed as the chief foe of science. For instance, a well-known scientist, B. F. Skinner, stated that human "feeling" has no place in the scientific laboratory and requested his colleagues to record observations based on strict objectivity.[7] Likewise, a renowned empiricist, Rudolf Carnap, was extremely skeptical of the subjective intrusion into empirical studies. For him, what leads us to truth is not emotion, faith, or feeling, but the determinacy of logic and mathematics.[8] John Stuart Mill's criterion for science is another good example. According to Mill,

---

[6] J. P. Moreland, "The Argument from Consciousness" in *The Blackwell Companion to Natural Theology*, ed. William Lane Craig and J. P. Moreland (Malden: Wiley-Blackwell, 2012), 313-314.

[7] David A. Lieberman, "Behaviorism and the Mind: A (Limited) Call for a Return to Introspection," *American Psychologist* 34/4 (1979): 319-333.

[8] Michael Friedman, *Reconsidering Logical Positivism* (New York: Cambridge University Press, 1999), 166- 171.

the unobservable, which is the construct of the human mind, cannot be the substance of the observable. Only the observable explains nature.[9]

The second proposition states that "all particulars are physical objects." For this reason, naturalists follow the way of monism both ontologically and methodologically. Ontological monism is grounded upon the belief that the world is constitutive of a single substance. Spinoza makes this claim succinctly. "In the universe, there is only one substance."[10] For naturalists, this one substance is a physical entity often called "matter." Moreland agrees and says that for naturalists everything is "fundamentally matter, most likely, elementary 'particles' (whether taken as points of potentiality, centers of mass/energy, units of spatially extended stuff/waves)."[11] Because of the monistic tendency, naturalists pursue the "grand story" in which all other stories fit. There is no room for non-natural explanations because, for them, nature sufficiently covers the whole territory of the universe and all that it contains.

Thus, methodologically, naturalism always begins with a basic level of physical phenomena and moves upward to the complex level of theoretical data. Even at the theoretical level, the physical pattern of naturalism configures all dimensions of reality in a completely closed system of physics, and the only admissible evidence is empirical data that are dependent on or determined by the physical objects in nature. At last, methodological monism in the modern era prepared the way for standardized measurements and scientific tests, which took the center stage as the arbiter of truth.

The third proposition denotes that "there are genuine emergent properties." Not all scientific materialists believe that this is true, but for scholars like Thomas O'Connor accept the claim that theoretical entities such as human consciousness may emerge, which cannot be fully

---

[9] Philipp Frank, *Philosophy of Science: The Link between Science and Philosophy* (Mineola: Dover, 2004), 350.

[10] Baruch Spinoza, *Ethics*, trans. Samuel Shirley, ed. Michael L. Morgan (Indianapolis: Hackett, 2002), 224.

[11] Moreland, "The Argument from Consciousness," 287.

explained by the underlying basic level of physical activities. There is a catch. The emergence of a complex entity nonetheless came about through a chain of physical events, in which subatomic entities at the micro level combine to form increasingly complex aggregates at the macro level. Hence, an explanation of the mental entity such as human consciousness cannot be admitted by overriding its physical correlates (e.g., the human brain); rather, human consciousness and its supervenient actions must be described in terms of brain activities.

In the mind and body problem, naturalists have no problem to form a general tenor stating that brain processes cause mental processes, not vice versa. A staunch naturalist John Searle confirms this idea as he states that "consciousness is a causally emergent property of systems. It is an emergent feature of certain systems of neurons in the same way that solidity and liquidity are emergent features of systems of molecules."[12] Consciousness is, therefore, not an exceptional emergent event, but a byproduct of an ordinary natural evolution that accords with the property of nature. Similarly, taking the principle of Occam's Razor seriously, philosopher Jerry Fodor notes that we should explain the higher-level occurrences like psycho-social activities simply by referring to more manageable concepts in the underlying physics.[13] If we can avoid the Gordian Knot of arguing from consciousness, we can certainly do away with the confusion of dealing with the unknown variables embedded in the mental processes of human life. He is essentially saying that we must move from what is knowable to what is unknowable, rather than to start from what is unknowable and fall into the error of abstraction and subjectivism. But by doing this, would not the unknowable be reduced to the knowable?

The last proposition to consider is the following: "there is a causal unity in nature." Moreland speaks of the naturalistic tendency to construct a "grand story." Again, this grand story is none other than an attempt to explain away how everything came to be as it is spelled out

---

[12] John R. Searle, *The Rediscovery of the Mind* (Cambridge: The MIT Press, 1992), 112.

[13] Jerry A. Fodor, "Making Mind Matter More," in *A Theory of Content and Other Essays* (Cambridge: MIT Press, 1990), 137-160.

purely in terms of a natural-event causality of physics, chemistry, and biology. Within a single paradigm of scientific naturalism, naturalists are optimistic that we can predict the future accurately as we can explain what took place in the past. As we close the ontological and epistemological gap by way of scientific advancements, the world we see will be more and more clear and precise. The epistemic cloud will be removed, and efficient causality will be sufficient and proficient to explain successfully the properties and behaviors of nature.

With this proposal, the only allowable explanations would be mechanical causality that reduces all events including the teleological operations of the mind to a set of probable transactions between physical entities. For this reason, Barry Stroud points to the fact that not only teleological causation but also supernaturalism has no place in science.[14] For him, no agent who stands outside of nature can be the cause of the natural event. Nature is all that there is. Gordon Kaufman with great erudition mounts a similar argument as he states that the scientific method depends on the web of interrelated events that essentially take place within a self-contained whole, and as a result, the primitive understanding of God's action denoted in the Bible no longer makes sense to the audience living in the scientific world.[15] Indeed, if we accept the scientific understanding of the world as a unified network of natural cause and effect, then there is no room for God to affect the course of events in nature. We can only conclude that nature is self-sufficient.

With the risk of oversimplification, these four propositions of naturalism unveil the key components of naturalism. Based on this, we are now in the position to review both the positive and negative responses to naturalism. I will begin with positive responses, which will be followed by negative responses and add my own critical analysis for each of these responses.

---

[14] Barry Stroud, "The Charm of Naturalism," in *Proceedings and Addresses of the American Philosophical Association*, 70: 43-55.

[15] Gordon D. Kaufman, *God the Problem* (Cambridge: Harvard University Press, 1972), 10-15.

New Atheism

One of the chief beneficiaries of naturalism is atheism. Although atheistic philosophers in antiquity such as Epicurus countered theism based on the tenets of natural philosophy, the study of nature was for the ancient philosophers in many ways coincided with the study of God.[16] For ancient philosophers such as Thales, Plato, and Aristotle, as well as modern natural philosophers such as Descartes, Spinoza, and Hegel, nature was the primer that decoded both essence and the functionality of God. For this reason, the strongest argument against theism was offered on the ground of political or moral reasons rather than naturalistic sentiments.[17] In this respect, the so-called New Atheism that is on the rise is different than its predecessors. What stands out the most is its adherence to scientific naturalism. Armed with the view that nature reveals nothing but itself, contemporary atheists have plenty of things to say against theism solely on the account of natural phenomena. Nature is no longer a pawn for theism. It is now a centerpiece for atheists who are ready to dismiss completely not only the idea of God but the belief in God vis-à-vis scientific naturalism.

The fundamental assumption that atheists have is that there is no good reason for us to have any other interpretation than that of science.[18] The dominance of science in the modern world and its successful programs that gave rise to the technological advancements, which in turn, improved the way we live by solving many difficult issues that our ancestors could not, such as medical problems, became the standard of measurement that decisively sorts out fact from fiction. For these new atheists, the religious society that reigned for the last several thousand years has been dethroned and supplanted by the advanced technological culture. Thus, it would be unacceptable for atheists to

---

[16] Edward Grant, "Aristotle and Aristotelianism," in *Science and Religion: A Historical Introduction*, ed. Gary B. Ferngren (Baltimore: The John Hopkins University Press, 2002), 33-46.

[17] For a good historical review from this aspect, see Werner Jaeger, *Paideia: The Ideals of Greek Culture*, vol. 1, trans. Gilbert Highet (New York: Oxford University Press, 1965).

[18] E.g., Wilfred Sellars, *Science, Perception, and Reality* (London: Routledge, 1963), 173. Sellars claims that to describe and explain the world, science is the measure of all things.

return to the old religious way of life; religion simply gets in the way of the progress of human intelligence.

In this light, an atheist scholar, Lawrence Krauss, boldly declares that science has successfully disproved the existence of gods.[19] Krauss points to the fact that science has closed the "gap" on gods in such a way that more and more scientific discoveries are replacing what was once deemed the act of God. Indeed, countering the Christian worldview, modern science has been explaining natural phenomena without the aid of theistic arguments. Thus, what has taken place is the systematic removal of the God-factor in the name of science. As an example, Isaac Newton found that a mass falls to the ground not because it is seeking a natural end preordained by God but because it is pulled by a force called "gravity." The theistic worldview was all the more rejected when Darwin proposed an evolutionary theory that affirmed the transmutation of species. No longer could we see life as a gift from God; rather, life is the result of a random evolutionary process. For this reason, Charles Coulson lamented that science has successfully narrowed down the God-of-the-gaps so that theology does not have any room to insert God into science in the current state of scientific affairs.[20] Thus, what has been consistently claimed thus far, as insisted by atheists like Krauss, is that science has been successful in removing God from nature as nature is revealing to be self-sufficient and self-sustaining.

However, Krauss' argument in no way disapproves God. Instead, Krauss is misdirecting his audience to the errors of black-and-white thinking. He reasons that, since science is providing a true picture of reality whereas theistic explanations are full of fictions and primitive non-scientific ideas, we have to get rid of theism altogether. This is a misguided assumption. Science does not determine "truth." Rather, scientific activities are more about explaining the way things are "as is." Hence, it is basically tentative. Its discoveries, empirical tests, and theories are provisional, always waiting for a better theory or model to

---

[19] Lawrence M. Krauss, *A Universe from Nothing: Why There is Something Rather than Nothing* (New York: Free Press, 2012), xv.

[20] Charles Coulson, *Science and Christian Belief* (London: Fontana, 1957), 41.

appear. What science guarantees is that the specific research program may be "successful" in revealing the reality of nature within certain physical and experimental constraints once scientific theories are confirmed by empirical data. In other words, scientific data are always questioned and questionable. So, going back to Krauss' argument, it would be more proper to say that science without God found a different way to explain nature provisionally, rather than science has "disproved" or "removed" God from nature altogether.

Anticipating this limitation, another atheist scholar, Christopher Hitchens, contends that unlike science theistic claims are firmly riveted to faith declarations that have no empirical basis.[21] For Hitchens, science is always underdetermined. It requires constant revisions, so it never upholds an absolutist point of view. He points out that the faith claim of religion is different than science in this respect, because the religious claim is always absolute—theists have already decided *a priori* what is true and what is false. He says that the authority of religion demands nothing but submission to its ruling that has already been decided for the public. According to Hitchens, the servility of religious people is never seen as a detriment to the free society by theists; rather, it is deceptively lauded as the highest virtue for all humanity. Science undermines this attitude and demands all ideas and concepts to be tested and criticized based on scientific evidence. For him, the resolution to religious deceptions can only be found through the exercise of evident-based rationality.

However, Hitchens is also flawed in his thinking. He finds a small portion of fundamentalistic religion in which religious precepts and beliefs are considered infallible and uncriticizable as the whole of religion. He is essentially attacking a strawman. Not all religions or religious statements are absolute. As Wolfhart Pannenberg has shown, theology and its statements are and should be criticizable and underdetermined.[22] To speak for Christian theology, there has been

---

[21] Christopher Hitchens, *God Is Not Great: How Religion Poisons Everything* (New York: Twelve, 2009), 5, 47.

[22] Wolfhart Pannenberg, *The Historicity of Nature: Essays on Science and Theology*, ed. Niels Henrik Gregersen (West Conshohocken: Templeton Foundation Press, 2008), 8. He

more than one way to interpret theological themes such as the doctrine of God, and many theological models have been discarded and modified during the long span of Christian history due to a great circle of theological critics who have scrutinized the viability of every theological statement. The road to a successful theological paradigm is never clean and tidy. Like science, it is strewn with unwanted theories and models that have been rejected by the church as a whole.

Going further, ignoring the rigors of theological science and its academic efforts, a well-known British atheist, Peter Atkins, accuses theists of being lazy.[23] According to Atkins, Christians are lazy because they do not search for answers to difficult problems that nature imposes upon us. Rather, they conveniently accept what is given to them by religious authority and succumb to the incredible explanations that defy the results of the hard-working scientists. Atkins asserts that the sweat and tear that goes into extracting solid evidence from nature is completely neglected. According to Atkins, theists revert to the God-explanations which are so simple and naïve that they explain nothing. He dismisses theological explanations as meaningless and the work of great theologians such as Augustine a complete waste of time.

As John Lennox faithfully articulates, Christian scholars are not lazy.[24] They do not look for an easy way out to sidestep the insoluble scientific or theological problems. Theologians at least in the academic field are working hard to resolve various conundrums that we face today whether they are scientific, social, or political problems. Indeed, as Lennox has pointed out, theology is not about writing a simple made-up story that dismisses the scientific discoveries, nor is it adversely competing with science to cancel out its claims. Rather, theology like

---

writes in this regard. "Therefore, each attempt at the systematic presentation of the Christian doctrine remains a hypothetical reconstruction of the universal coherence of the phenomena of God's creation with the theological assumptions concerning the Creator."

[23] Peter Atkins, "Atheism and Science," in *The Oxford Handbook of Religion and Science*, ed. Philip Clayton and Zachary Simpson (Oxford: Oxford University Press, 2006), 114. Also see a debate between Peter Atkins and John Lennox, accessed February 17, 2017, https://www.youtube.com/watch?v=5gMS7WTHnho.

[24] For John Lennox's reply to Peter Atkins' claim of the laziness of Christianity, see https://www.youtube.com/watch?v=5gMS7WTHnho.

science searches for better answers to explain how and why things are as what they are. Simply put, theology puts real efforts into finding out the answer to why and how questions as much as science, striving toward the good, beauty, and justice. In my judgment, Atkins' fault lies in his singular way of looking at the world. He takes the plumb line of materialism and measures all things based on his narrow view of naturalism. Since he comes to the table already assuming that there is no other meaningful explanation than naturalism, he is in a sense an atheistic fundamentalist that upholds an absolutist and totalitarian view of nature. Totalitarianism or absolutism is what the theology and science interface is fighting against. Alister McGrath once said that the recent efforts of the theology and science dialogue clarify one truth about the responsibilities of scientists and theologians—that neither theists nor non-theists will ever find *the* one single answer to all our problems and only by co-operative endeavors can we see any hope of shedding light upon many unknowns in our world.

From a brief analysis of atheistic arguments, what I can see is that atheists are trapped in a closed system of naturalism. For them, theism is not an option, not because they can disapprove the existence of God, but because of their presumption that God is not in the natural equation. This argument is commonly found in the atheistic disputations of theism. The most common way that atheists argue takes the logic that, if God exists at all, then he must be a supernatural being, and for this reason, God cannot be associated with nature, because by definition, the supernatural character of God, that is, his timelessness and eternity, has to be beyond this world. This type of reasoning rejects theism *a priori*. It gives no room for a theistic way to see the world.

To be sure, I am not stating that atheists should not bring up anti-theistic theories about nature or culture. They have the right to present their theories, and as theists, we should at least consider and review their critical outlook of theism. The fallacy I see however is that these proposals are solely based on naturalistic reductionism. Naturalism by definition omits supernaturalism. Such omission automatically rejects divine causality. So, there is no way for theists to convince atheists that the God-explanation is one of the many possible ways of depicting the world in which we live. This dilemma resembles Plato's Allegory of the Cave. If our cognition is restricted to see only one thing that relies on our sense experience, like seeing the shadow of the real on the wall of the closed cave, we will never be able to see what lies "behind" the shadow. If we assume that there is nothing more than nature itself and start with this premise and refuse to search for the possibility of finding something more than what nature is all about, we have stopped ourselves short of many different ways of looking at the world. Surely, there are naturalists who say that the study of nature requires multilevel rational activities,[25] but an atheistic agenda seems to defy this argument as they refuse to include or even entertain the possibility of the God-factor. The only agenda that is feasible for atheism then is to supplant all theistic claims and replace it with "pure" naturalistic creeds that have the potential to eliminate every category that is associated with theism.

Strong Physicalism

A similar sort of ideology is put forth by the proponents of strong physicalism. Physicalists may not call themselves an atheist for they do not attack theistic questions head-on, but due to their incessant effort to explain away the mental events as an auxiliary or emergent property of the physical, they have allied with atheists to repudiate all possibilities of a teleological or personal causality that may support the fine-tuning or intelligent design arguments.[26] As Jaewon Kim notes, "no serious physicalist could accept" that "any complete explanatory theory of the physical domain must invoke nonphysical causal agents."[27] For this reason, physicalists plant their feet firmly in the soil of naturalism and seek to reconstruct our understanding of consciousness in terms of how the human mind can be captured by an account of physical entities.

---

[25] E.g., Michael Lockwood, *Mind, Brain, and the Quantum: The Compound "I"* (Malden: Blackwell, 1991). He is a materialist but not a reductionist.

[26] Incidentally, the fine-tuning and intelligent design arguments are commonly used by theists such as Frank Turek, Hugh Ross, and Craig Lane William.

[27] Jaewon Kim, *Mind in a Physical World: An Essay on the Mind-Body Problem and Mental Causation* (Cambridge: MIT Press, 1998), 40.

Essentially, physicalists reduce consciousness to the physical processes of the brain. For instance, according to Searle, consciousness is a property of the brain, not a "stuff" of its own. If there is no connection between mind and brain, a hole would be created in the seamless outworking of nature, and as contended by William Lyons, the hole will be filled in by non-physicalists with a fictional entity like the soul that is purported to exist beyond this world.[28] In order to prevent the intrusion of non-science, the advocates of physicalism seek to account for the emergence of consciousness in terms of basic physical entities, and in this way, the serious metaphysics of physicalism is inherently reductionistic. Paul Churchland seems to agree:

> The important point about the standard evolutionary theory is that the human species and all of its features are the wholly physical outcome of a purely physical process...If this is the correct account of our origins, then there seems neither need, nor room, to fit any nonphysical substances or properties into our theoretical account of ourselves. We are creatures of matter.[29]

In this case, "matter" stands over against "mind."

Consequently, one of the most effective arsenals that physicalists use to counter the detractors of physicalism is the theory of emergence. There are several types of emergence, but to stay within our premise, we focus on two main parts of the theory: strong and weak emergence. The former denotes the emergence of a novel phenomenon such as consciousness from its subvenient base (e.g., brain) that is irreducible to its lower level activities. The latter depicts the emergence of an unpredictable phenomenon from the subvenient base, but this novel event is reducible and falls under strict mechanisms of the lower level systems. Physicalists normally accept some form of weak emergence but deny strong emergence, for it would open up a door to an ontological autonomy of the higher-level phenomena that are distinct from the

---

[28] William Lyons, "Introduction" in *Modern Philosophy of Mind* (London: Everyman, 1995), xiv-iv.

[29] Paul M. Churchland, *Matter and Consciousness* (Cambridge: MIT Press, 1984), 21.

lower level activities. In this respect, Brian McLaughlin argues that there is "not a scintilla of evidence"[30] of strong emergence found in this world.

These reductive physicalists are fond of weak emergence since they can explain the problematic property of the human mind in terms of purely physical activities. If we understand that a complex whole can emerge from simpler parts, we can learn about human consciousness from studying its source, namely, the underlying physical make-up of the mind, which is our brain. John Searle uses a helpful analogy here. He likens the study of consciousness as the study of the relationship between solidity and liquidity.[31] From the base structure of solidity emerges liquidity, and although liquidity has a different property than that of solidity, they are nonetheless of the same physical structure. Moreland has rebutted Searle's argument most extensively. I will review Moreland's rebuttal of Searle's argument later, but it suffices to say that Searle's analogy does little justice to "consciousness," which is for sure not a physical object like a "liquid." We can see a clear continuity between solid and liquid despite the fact that they have two different properties. The former can be described as a group of tightly packed particles, and the latter, as more loosely packed particles. However, we cannot say the same regarding consciousness. Can we really say that consciousness is formed by "loosely" packed particles? Though there are a few scientists who are tempted to say that consciousness is some form of energy, there is no empirical evidence that consciousness has any "physical" properties of energy. In my judgment, consciousness is not a physical object albeit it is correlated to brain activities. I will explain more in detail in the second section.

The problem of physicalism is not just related to ontology. It also has an epistemological significance, according to Frank Jackson.[32] For him, physicalism is nothing but recourse to an assumed superiority of naturalist epistemology. What happens when there is a puzzling

---

[30] Brian P. McLaughlin, "The Rise and Fall of British Emergentism" in *Emergence or Reduction? Essays on the Prospect of a Nonreductive Physicalism*, ed. Ansgar Beckerman, et al. (Berlin: Walter de Gruyter, 1992), 55.

[31] Moreland, "The Argument from Consciousness," 309.

[32] Ibid., 287.

phenomenon that does not coincide with a naturalist view? Jackson says that physicalists resort to a closed causality of naturalism and begin to systematically prune away non-scientific explanations and reconstruct them with physical scientific theories. The epistemic standing of any other sciences that are nonphysical in nature is deemed inferior to physicalism and does not merit full credence. Thus, as a natural consequence, physicalists take a skeptical stance when it comes to the claims of our knowledge of reality that are non-physical in nature. In short, "the elevated or exhaustive scientific knowledge entails that either the only explanations that count or the ones with superior, unqualified acceptance are those employed in the hard sciences."[33]

In the end, such physicalist reductionism once again has drawn a line between what is real and what is a mere appearance of the real. What is real for physicalists is matter. Nothing exists over and above physical entities. Non-physical entities such as consciousness are simply epiphenomenal, a mere appearance of physical functions. In this way, mental events are treated as shadows of the physical. Had they been otherwise, they would violate the completeness theorem of physics and the closed causality of nature. As a result, the logic of physicalism cannot let scientists move beyond the world of physics, and despite the fact that physicalism is severely limited in describing what consciousness is all about, physicalists refuse to proceed any further except to search for answers only in the physical arena. Moreover, because consciousness is described only with physical metaphors, the real-life events of mental activities such as the first-person perspective are treated as inferior to the third person perspective and the whole question of the possibility of the non-physical influencing the physical evaporates as meaningless conjectures. If the claims of physical reductionism are true, they would devastate not only anti-physicalism such as panpsychism, but more importantly, theistic emergentism and its belief that God as the absolute personal agent asserts a top-down influence upon nature. Anticipating such shortcomings, both non-physicalists and theists levy strong criticisms against physicalism and suggest their own way to frame the

---

[33] Ibid., 284.

matter-mind relationship. This impetus has given theologians the reason to reformulate the old theological paradigms and begin to think of God's being and act in terms of how he is influenced by nature. The two exemplary cases are panpsychism and panentheism. What follows is my critical interaction with panpsychism and panentheism to set up for the final section that outlines my own proposal to reconcile the differences between God and nature.

Panpsychism

There is a growing interest in the field of philosophy that treats a fairly unknown territory of panpsychism. Although a variety of panpsychism is extensive, [34] it can be treated within a manageable context of speculative realism since what I am looking for is its relationship to naturalism. So, the main task for this section is to identify the chain of the relationship between speculative realism, naturalism, and panpsychism, and how panpsychism in relation to nature has overturned the main tenets of physicalist reductionism. I will add my own critical analysis so that the reader will know whether panpsychists' counterargument to physicalism is acceptable or not.

The first task then is to assess the key assumptions of speculative realism. Speculative realism often falls under the banner of what is normally labeled as "new materialism" or "continental realism," with which a new breed of maverick philosophers are equipped to fight against the main currents of modern philosophy of what Quentin Meillassoux calls "correlationism." [35] According to Meillassoux, the philosophical syndrome of correlationism from which most of the contemporary scholars are suffering testifies to the idea that thinking and being cannot be understood apart from one another. These two components of nature have to be correlated; otherwise, we will return

---

[34] For a good synopsis of different kinds of panpsychism, see David S. Clarke, *Panpsychism and the Religious Attitude* (New York: State University of New York, 2003).

[35] Quentin Meillassoux, *After Finitude: An Essay on the Necessity of Contingency*, trans. Ray Brassier (New York: Continuum, 2008), 5.

to the error of naïve realism on the one hand, and the error of non-cognitivism, on the other hand.

In order to remedy the ills of correlationism, speculative realists question the viability of anthropocentrism, which has been the dominant theme of Western philosophy. Why do we need to seek the world from our point of view? Even if we say that there is no such thing as a view from nowhere, can we see the world without prioritizing the subject over the object? Why must our view always take precedence over against the thing-in-itself? Is there any way that we can free the thing-in-itself from the fetters of anthropocentrism? This is precisely what Eugene Thacker has searched for and he found the answer in the world-without-us.[36] The world-without-us is a view that does not start from human-centeredness. It is a view that is based on the inspection of the world itself; therefore, it is not amenable to our concerns.

If we seek the real without looking through our lens, what is left is the real that far exceeds our symbolization. Steven Shaviro says the same thing when he notes, "Things are active and interactive far beyond any measure of their presence to us."[37] If reality far exceeds our rational attempt to capture it, then our cognitive representation of the real always falls short, thereby untenable to read the real from our perspective only. The only recourse then, like what Thacker has done, is to overturn the Kantian program that does not privilege human rationality over against the thing-in-itself.

Once we turn the table around, we can dismiss Kant's dictum that the thing-in-itself cannot be known. Contra Kant, Thacker declares that the thing-in-itself can be known, though in a speculative realist sense. To know in the Kantian way is to know by way of our own concern. But to know in the speculative realist way is to know by way of speculation, that is, excluding our concerns to include the concerns of the thing-in-itself. How is this possible? Is it not that from Descartes to Kant, our

---

[36] Eugene Thacker, *In the Dust of This Planet: Horror of Philosophy*, vol. 1 (Alresford: Zero, 2011), 5.

[37] Steven Shaviro, *The Universe of Things: On Speculative Realism* (Minneapolis: University of Minnesota Press, 2014), 49.

knowledge of reality is obtained and obtainable only through a representation that arises from the human mind? How can we see intentionality without an intentional subject? The object itself cannot think. It needs a thinker.

In George Molnar's case, this is not a difficult problem to solve, since he believes that the object does not need a thinker because it has its own intentionality. In fact, the object has what he calls "physical intentionality." [38] In other words, intentionality is not an exclusive category belonging to the human agent only. We are not exceptional in this respect. Intentionality is also part of the physical make-up of this world. For Molnar, we do not need to demarcate and draw a line between what is psychic and what is physical. They are two sides of the same coin. Although Molnar himself does not embrace panpsychism, the idea of the ubiquity of thought existing everywhere even in the world of physics provides a healthy springboard for speculative realists to adopt panpsychism.

Before we move onto the discussion of panpsychism, we need to understand the opposing group of speculative realists who do not follow the way that leads to panpsychism. As we have seen, panpsychists have found a new avenue to retrieve realism that deprivileges anthropocentrism. After overturning the previous method of subordinating the thing-in-itself to the thinker, speculative realists are left with two options. On the one hand, they have the option to articulate the thing-in-itself without any involvement of subjectivity. That is, they can suppress the subject for the sake of the object. On the other hand, they have the option to articulate the thing-in-itself without suppressing the subject; rather, they can include the subjectivity to all things, including non-organic matters. The former underwrites eliminationism and the latter panpsychism. The burden is actually heavier for panpsychists because they have to show why it is necessary to keep subjectivity alive, when it is simpler to dismiss subjectivity altogether.

---

[38] George Molnar, *Powers: A Study in Metaphysics* (Oxford: Oxford University Press, 2003), 61.

Indeed, as Meillassoux contends, if the subject is problematic, it seems logical to purge subjectivity altogether and say that reality is entirely a-subjective.[39] If the subjective view was problematic from the time of Descartes, what is the reason for keeping it? Thus, we have a new view of physicalism. A new view of physicalism, promoted by eliminists, now allows us to think of the world essentially unaffected by our own conception of it. This is a radical move. Granted that all realists think that the world exists independent of our mind, eliminists now want to speak for the world without a thinker. For Meillassoux, the world without a thinker must be impassive, unaffected, lifeless, and unconcerned. The existence is purely physical. For this reason, Meillassoux could only see the world in terms of brute physicality, in which only physical science has the right to give us the true picture of reality that is purely external, structural, and corporeal.

Such physical reductionism is not acceptable to panpsychists, and they part with a pick-and-choose attitude of eliminists. When we pit the psychic against the physical, we have no choice but to follow a dismissive strategy and pick one at the expense of the other. Panpsychists do not wish to fall into this trap of eliminationism that forces them to partition the world into neatly divisible compartments. Rather, they want to lay an entirely different trajectory for the contemporary philosophy of realism. They conceive of reality in terms of a dual polarity consisting of the physical and psychical. In this way, they do not need to privilege one over against the other.

For instance, Shaviro, drawing upon Whiteheadian metaphysics, argues that every actual entity has a dual polarity, one physical and another psychic, as fact and value cannot be neatly separated. He explains Whitehead's aestheticized account of ethics. "He [Whitehead] insists that fact and value cannot be cleanly separated. They are always intimately entwined, since value is intrinsic to existence."[40] Because "value" belongs to each entity, we cannot "deface the value experience

---

[39] Meillassoux, *After Finitude*, 38.

[40] Shaviro, *The Universe of Things*, 24.

which is the very essence of the universe."[41] The significance of this argument squarely confronts us when we listen to Jane Bennett. She says that each entity has the potential to display "a positive, productive power of their own."[42] Unless we shift our focus from "conglomerates of human designs and practices," we cannot discern "the active role of nonhuman materials in public life."[43] In this way, we are now ready to authenticate our inner experience over against the experience that comes from the external to us. The inner and outer or private and public dimensions of reality are intimately linked, and due to this linkage, every entity has the power to relate to one another.

Therefore, panpsychists believe that, due to this bipolarity inherent in every entity, whether organic or non-organic, everything in this world has the potential to sustain a relationship of not only object-to-object but also subject-to-subject. The subject-to-subject experience, therefore, is not a rational experience that takes the form of the Cartesian cogito. Rather, it is a "precognitive, prereflective, and aesthetic mode of subjectivity."[44] This, of course, is not a sophisticated exhibition of subjectivity. It is a down-to-earth, value-seeking process of each entity, which functions like a "blind emotion" that looks very much like random events to us.[45] As Molnar has argued, such a rudimentary form of experience does not give us the right to dismiss intentionality that belongs to the physical units in nature.

In this respect, panpsychists can make the bold claim that thought is a fundamental property of matter itself. Galen Strawson, a chief proponent of panpsychism, argues that thinking happens not just in us but everywhere.[46] Thought extends all the way down and all the way up.

---

[41] Alfred North Whitehead, *Modes of Thought* (New York: The Free Press, 1968), 111.

[42] Jane Bennett, *Vibrant Matter: A Political Ecology of Things* (Durham: Duke University Press, 2010), 1.

[43] Ibid., 1-2.

[44] Shaviro, *The Universe of Things*, 21.

[45] Ibid., 79.

[46] Galen Strawson, "Realistic Monism: Why Physicalism Entails Panpsychism," in *Consciousness and Its Place in Nature: Does Physicalism Entail Panpsychism?* (Exeter, Imprint Academic, 2006), 3-31.

What this means is that our mind is not an emergent property. Strawson, like Moreland, contends that experiential phenomena cannot emerge from non-experiential phenomena. There is no bridge that can connect the two. Moreover, contra Meillassoux, Strawson insists that thought does not arise *ex machina*. [47] Clearly, Strawson is arguing against emergentism. For him, he does not need a magic wand of emergence to make thought appear from nowhere or from the subvenient level of the physical. Reality is already experiential. Mind is intrinsic to reality. It exists for itself. This is where panpsychists stand.

The idea of dipolar realism put forth by panpsychism is not new[48] but modern panpsychists' re-appropriation of dipolar realism is innovative, for it provides a good alternative to correlationism on the one hand, and physicalism on the other, without marginalizing the naturalistic vision of which we all need to take seriously. For this reason, there have been many theistic scholars attempting to develop a reformulated understanding of God based on the panpsychic approach to reality. Contemporary scholars like Pierre Teilhard de Chardin, John Cobb, and Stuart Kauffmann, all fit into this category. The main tenet of their theology is well summarized by John Cooper. Panpsychic theology is "the view that 'everything is soul,' a Life Force that is conscious in higher beings,"[49] and "this basic reality is God."[50] In view of panpsychic theology, the soul of the cosmic God is commonly rendered as the supermaterial bound up with nature. For this reason, like nature, God grows, matures, and undergoes process indefinitely, so God is none other than infinite possibilities of the world. Instead of picturing God based on substance metaphysics, panpsychic theologians depend on subjective metaphysics, and as a result, God has shifted from an immutable being to a changeable subject who creates and recreates in the matrix of an indeterminate, organic system of life. In this way,

---

[47] Ibid., 19.

[48] Spinoza had this idea, but Schelling and Hegel in their own ways worked with this idea most explicitly. For more details, see John Cooper, *Panentheism: The Other God of the Philosophers—From Plato to the Present* (Grand Rapids: Baker, 2006).

[49] Ibid., 121.

[50] Ibid., 140.

panpsychic theologians have succeeded in the unification of God and nature as the manifestation of all events in the world. God is no longer seen as the absolute being but an entity that is in the process of becoming, just like any other natural events in the world, albeit growing indefinitely.

For this reason, although panpsychism is a metaphysical innovation that has the potential to fight off the encroachment of physicalism, I cannot wholeheartedly agree with their program. The first thing that comes to my mind is their unsuccessful effort to move away from correlationism. Although they tried to preserve both subjectivity and objectivity, due to their persistent emphasis on the universality of thought, they have subsumed the thing-in-itself to mentality. Purposefully or not, they have subjectified the thing-in-itself to the point where the object is, seemingly, vanished to nothingness. Because of this weakness, I do not think they are successful in providing us with a better alternative to correlationism.

The second troubling aspect is an unresolved tension between subjective dualism and ontological monism. Concerning subjective dualism, panpsychists have created an unbridgeable gap between matter and thought, for they assume that matter cannot produce thought; only thought produces thought.[51] In this way, thought becomes the undergirding matrix that determines all occurrences in the world, even physical events. By contrast, regarding ontological monism, they have conflated matter and thought into a nondivisible whole. Although matter and thought have two distinct properties, for panpsychists, matter becomes another form of thought. Again, I do not see this move as a better alternative to correlationalism.

The third and the most important point from a Christian theistic perspective is the treatment of God in terms of panpsychism. The proponents of panpsychism work very hard to avoid a pick-and-choose method by sidestepping the correlationist anthropic association

---

[51] If matter produces thought, then panpsychists have to accept emergentism, because emergentists have argued that the mind is the byproduct of brain activities (its physical base). Oddly, not many panpsychists side with emergentism.

between thought and reality. However, this new metaphysical view they present subsumes God under the category of the mind. They have changed the essence of God, from his immutability and absoluteness in his own uncreated existence to his changeability and creativity as he has turned into the Cosmic Mind.[52] This is partly so because, as John Cooper has insightfully argued, panpsychists do not deal with the immutable absolute. Like any other naturalists, panpsychists value highly the principle of creativity and change. For them, this is what nature reveals, and since God is the underlying matrix of nature, God's essence must be the same, changing and creative, albeit infinitely so. For panpsychists, once we introduce the concept of the divine absolute, they worry that we will eventually revert to literalism and treat the thing-in-itself as the absolute, rather than metaphorically in the form of aesthetic causality. They do not want us to think outside our own thought. However, what panpsychists are confused with is the difference between the absolute and absolutism. The proffer of the absolute does not follow absolutism. Indeed, we need to worry about the contamination of absolutism, that is, fundamentalistic thinking that privileges one dogma over the other voices while rejecting the rest as an inferior form of truth claims. However, the inclusion of the absolute does not necessarily entail absolutism. There is an inevitable gap between the absolute and absolutism just like the gap between God and our knowledge of God.

For theological and philosophical reasons, I do not feel that contemporary panpsychism is a good alternative to correlationism. I suggest that we stay with correlationism because it does not walk away from the fact that we need both the knower and the known in making sense of the world itself. We cannot prefer one at the expense of the other. Rather, everything in this world has to be correlated in some respect in order to find the meaning that lies beneath the appearance of the real. We cannot say that an entity is completely independent or entirely dependent. Perhaps, the best way to conceive the world is by

---

[52] E.g., Stuart Kauffman, "Cosmic Mind?" *Theology and Science* 14/1 (2016): 36-47. Kauffman proposes panpsychic metaphysics to flesh out the basic structures of reality, including God. Also see Ted Peters critical review of Kauffman's proposal. Ted Peters, "The Cosmic Mind: Entanglement over Physics, Panpsychism, and the Trinity," *Theology and Science* 14/1 (2016): 1-5.

recognizing the duality of independence and dependence. Substance dualists precisely had taken such a route and tried to account for the independent and dependent nature of consciousness.

Substance Dualism

At last, we come back to Moreland's work and his substance dualism. To counter physicalism like the proponents of panpsychism, Moreland proposes his own theory, which is drastically different from panpsychism, by re-appropriating the old metaphysics of substance dualism.[53] Based on substance dualism, Moreland has painstakingly worked out the details of why physicalism fails to be the overarching explanatory rubric for today's scientific world. Let me introduce several key points he has brought up against physicalism.

Moreland claims that, in this world, there is always something more than the physical. When we see nature, we do not see nature only. We always see and conceive something more than nature. How do we know that this is true? We know this because of our conscious awareness of the self, and the self which exists in this world is not constraint by the spatiotemporal dimensions of this world. Moreland writes,

> These two facts—I am the owner of my experiences, and I am an enduring self—show that I am identical to my experiences. I am the conscious thing that has them. And arguably, I am also aware of myself as a simple, uncomposed and spatially unextended center of consciousness.[54]

What this means is that, for Moreland, there is a stark difference between the physical properties of the brain and the mental properties

---

[53] Moreland has published several books on this topic. Cf. J. P. Moreland, *The Soul: How We Know It's Real and Why It Matters?* (Chicago: Moody, 2014); *Consciousness and the Existence of God: A Theistic Argument* (New York: Routledge, 2008); *The Recalcitrant Imago Dei: Human Persons and the Failure of Naturalism* (London: SCM, 2009). For a brief analysis, see J. P. Moreland, "The Argument from Consciousness" in *The Blackwell Companion to Natural Theology*, ed. William Lane Craig and J. P. Moreland (Malden: Wiley-Blackwell, 2012), 282-343.

[54] Moreland, *The Recalcitrant Imago Dei*, 72.

of the self. For Moreland, they are mutually exclusive. They cannot be of the same kind because physical properties belong to the spatiotemporal world such as chemical reactions while mental properties such as the awareness of "I" are timeless and spaceless. Surely, we can conceive of "I" of the past and future without leaving the present. For a physical object, this is impossible.

Because of the distinct qualities of consciousness, Moreland argues that consciousness has its own causality that need not be dependent upon natural causality. Moreland distinguishes two types of causality, one efficient and other personal. The former he denotes as an event-event causation "in which everything would be exhaustively described from a third-person point of view in terms of objects, properties, processes, and their spatiotemporal locations."[55] The latter denotes a belief-desire causation which conveys a libertarian account of freedom of the will. He gives an insightful illustration. On the one hand, the event-event causation explains the boiling water in this way: "The water boiled because it was heated."[56] In this case, the boiling water can be explained as the transfer of heat energy between water in the kettle and the heating source upon which it stands. On the other hand, the belief-desire causation explains the boiling water in this way. "Smith went to the kitchen because he wanted to get coffee."[57] The water is boiling not just because of an efficient cause, but because of a personal goal, that is, to make a cup of coffee. Both explanations are genuinely effective in describing the boiling water. The key point that Moreland wants to make here is that the physical causality cannot explain why the water is being heated. It only tells that it is boiling due to a heat transfer. It cannot tell us why the water had to be heated in the first place. What is missing is the top-down influence of the mind upon physical processes. Does this mean that Moreland is siding with emergentism?

It seems that Moreland is not completely dismissing the theory of emergence, since he accepts some aspects of strong emergentism. What

---

[55] Moreland, *The Soul*, 121.

[56] Moreland, *The Recalcitrant Imago Dei*, 48.

[57] Ibid.

is certain is that Moreland dismisses weak emergence. For him, although consciousness may influence physical processes at the subvenient level, it is a novel phenomenon that is entirely different from physical events. Thus, according to Moreland, the human mind cannot be reduced to the physical components of the brain. Although "mind" and "brain" are two separate entities, Moreland does not hesitate to say that they are related in many ways. How are they related? They are not related bottom-up. From a substance dualistic perspective, Moreland believes that mind and brain are related top-down only. It is the personal agency—in Moreland's language, a personal agency is the self—who possesses the thought and asserts influence upon the brain to churn out the necessary physical processes whether consciously or subconsciously. For Moreland, a thinker precedes thought, never vice versa. If we follow the way of weak emergence, the physical process will give rise to thought, and thought finds its way into the person—that is, thought precedes the thinker, which is absurd for Moreland.

Although I agree with Moreland's dictum that a thinker precedes thought, the difficulty I have with Moreland's argument is his insistence that the mind asserts influence upon the brain more so than the brain on the mind. Neuroscience in the contemporary world has repeatedly shown that the brain affects the mind and is responsible for the critical functions of our consciousness. A simple example is the effect of a chemical imbalance in our brain that produces various levels of phobia and hallucinations. [58] Due to the complex entanglement between consciousness and the brain, it is more feasible to conceive the mind and body relationship in terms of the mutual interaction between the two. Although Moreland is right to say that the theory of emergence does not explain the mental events, it is wrong to dismiss entirely the possibility that some portion of our mental activities owes its process to the neurons in the cerebral cortex.

Going back to Moreland's work, his argument rests on the denial of the Indiscernibility of Identicals. This principle basically states that if two entities are identical, then they must share all properties without

---

[58] Churchland, *Matter and Consciousness*, 30.

remainder. Hence, if the two mental events are identical or essentially a derivative of the brain, they must have the same property of the physical. However, Moreland sees that, as the first-person perspective and the third perspective are completely divergent, mental properties and physical properties do not match, nor do they align with each other. This misalignment is a clear telltale sign for Moreland to see soul and body as two different particulars acting upon the world with its own unique causality. The separation of soul and body permits Moreland to sever the dead weight of physicalism and move into the world of theism.

Moreland contends that since physicalism has no good explanation for the existence of consciousness and that the mental state does not emerge from the physical, the only possible means of locating the origin of consciousness is God, namely, the Christian triune God. He makes a huge jump from the argument from consciousness to the God existing in three persons. How are they connected, if at all? Why is it that the only alternative to physicalism is trinitarian theism? Could it be that the mind underwrites matter and that matter is just a manifestation of the mind, as declared by panpsychists? The connection between the mind and the triune God seems too far-fetched to be taken at face value. As a matter of fact, Moreland is creating a false dichotomy. He is asking to choose one between two options: physicalism or substance dualism (which guarantees for him to lead to theism). These two options are assumed to be mutually exclusive, and at the same time, they are only two viable options for today's apologetics, which is not true. As we will see below, there are scholars such as religious naturalists and panentheists who are building theism upon the foundation of naturalism.

Most troubling is the fact that he is committing the fault of naturalistic theology because he is reading Christian theology based on our understanding of consciousness. If we follow Moreland's pattern, we cannot guarantee that we arrive at the God of the Bible, because from the argument of consciousness to theism does not necessarily end up in the arms of the trinitarian God, as I have shown via the discussion of panpsychism. Even if it may lead to a theistic vision, what guarantee is there that such a theistic vision is not polytheistic? Why does it have to be a Christian God? There is no guarantee that this personal god is the God of the Bible. What guarantees the connection between the God of creation and the God of the Bible is the God of redemption that is clearly revealed through Jesus Christ in the power of the Holy Spirit sent by the Father. This revealed theology, which is unique to Christianity, cannot be gleaned from natural knowledge, and it would be wrong for any scholars to extrapolate the God of the Trinity without the aid of revelation.

In this respect, Moreland's argument from consciousness demonstrates the limitation of naturalistic theology. We may start with the first-person perspective of the self as the proof of the existence of the personal agent in this world, but the origin of the person, whether it be natural or non-natural, could not guarantee the existence of the triune God. Even if we base our argument on the concept of contingency, that is, all existence is depended upon God, we cannot say that this God is the God of Christianity. By the principle of underdetermination, such a theistic vision can be explained in many different ways, as we can use different names to describe the deity such as Allah or Kami. On a positive note, however, Moreland's argument from consciousness does provide a way to show that there is something more than what physicalism can reveal. We cannot omit or neglect personal causation, which is so influential in our day to day life. To write off the personal agency as a mere epiphenomenon of the underlying physical systems is to misrepresent the independent status of the mental events that have the potential to assert top-down influence upon the physical.

Moreland's dualism is not the only alternative to a theistic response to physicalism in particular or naturalism in general. Rather than pitting naturalism against theism, there have been many attempts to put them together as a unified whole. The most innovative way to reconcile the difference between theism and naturalism is the presentation of religious naturalism, on the one hand, and panentheism, on the other. There is a common denominator that links the two as they both depend on the methodology of naturalism. However, they diverge insofar as how God is treated. Here, I offer a brief account of religious naturalism and panentheism respectively, followed by a critical evaluation that may shed light on their areas of shortcomings.

Religious Naturalism

From a theistic perspective, religious naturalists' proposal marks a monumental shift in the way we perceive God, religion, and nature. Traditionally, God has been conceived as the ultimate being that is responsible for the existence of the universe and everything in it. This ultimate being is not of this world. Ted Peters succinctly summarizes. "Underneath or above what we see and hear is a transcendent yet present reality that is suprasensory, supranatural, spiritual, and divine or all of these."[59] Moreover, according to Christian biblical narratives, by God's grace, he has freely entered into the sphere of his own creation to interact with the finite creatures. In this way, God guides, nurtures, and provides what he has created. It is the God of eternity who stands above and beyond this world, reaching down to the finite to provide what is necessary and sufficient for creatures to live and have their existence.

However, the proponents of religious naturalism are not satisfied with the traditional theistic claims. They do not wish to be stagnant and riveted to old theistic paradigms. They want to move forward and follow the ways of modern science rather than adhere to the obsolete stories of the past. For them, the religion of the past cannot speak to emerging generations. Nor can it solve current problems that the technological society is facing. As Jerome Stone contends, religious naturalists boldly took the next step to fly away from the nest of their ancestors and locate a new home in the naturalistic realm.[60] According to Stone, it is a courageous move on the part of religious naturalists who have earned their independence which granted them to explore and

---

[59] Ted Peters, *God—The Word's Future: Systematic Theology for a Postmodern Era* (Minneapolis: Fortress, 1992), 83.

[60] Jerome Stone, *Religious Naturalism Today: The Rebirth of a Forgotten Alternative* (Albany: State University of New York Press, 2008), 1-4.

venture into the world of nature as more mature individuals than those who are still drinking the milk from the authority of the old paradigm.

Despite the fact that religious naturalists have some misgivings about religion as a whole, they refuse to eliminate it like physicalism. Rather, they take religion and its primary themes very seriously, such as "reverence," "grace," and "transcendence." There is a catch, however. They do not want to commit the error of absolutism and see the world as a single divine system without any regard for the natural order. So, they have a burden. They need to wed together two seemingly antithetical components of our culture: one religion and other naturalism. Religion, of course, stands on the conviction that there is something more than nature, whereas naturalism upholds the belief that there is nothing but nature. Religious naturalists in their own way have come up with many ingenious ways to reconcile this difference, but despite a variety of methodology, with careful analysis, we can discern a few similar characteristics that underwrite religious naturalism.

The first component that I want to mention is their incessant effort to synthesize religion and nature without succumbing to any type of reductionism. Religious naturalist Willem Drees explains why this is the case. "Naturalism cannot be articulated from a fundamental ontology upwards. Nor does it imply that all phenomena can be described in terms of physics and chemistry. This is so because our knowledge has not yet reached rock bottom."[61] What Drees is implying here is that no single epistemic system has the ability to explain "everything." They are willing to live with limit questions and accept them as a lived fact. Physical reductionism is, therefore, not accepted. A religious naturalist, Ursula Goodenough, notes that a sense of awe and veneration that we carry toward nature cannot be simplified in terms of cell mechanisms no less than Mozart's sonata being reduced to blobs of ink on a piece of paper.[62] For religious naturalists, a sense of "mystery" always relativizes our tendency to absolutize or reduce the complexity of nature into a

---

[61] Willem B. Drees, "Should Religious Naturalists Promote a Naturalistic Religion?" *Zygon* 33/4 (1998), 619.

[62] Ursula Goodenough, *The Sacred Depths of Nature* (New York: Oxford University Press, 1998), 34.

single matrix, whether it be theism or physicalism. Mystery only permits the correlation of the two.

Because of religious naturalists attempt to combine the two antithetical components of life, they are susceptible to the Hegelian principle of synthesis. In other words, the merger of religion and naturalism ought to produce a totally different entity that neither follows the way of naturalism nor religious beliefs. Did it actually produce a new form of naturalism and religion? Yes, it did. The scope of religious naturalism no longer resides in the territory of strict naturalism as it was defined by Moreland in the previous section. There are several modifications, and one of them is an anti-reductionistic tendency, which is a huge plus for the theology and science interface. Within the context of religious naturalism, there is no need to pit mind against matter, subject against object, or empiricism against valued tainted "faith." They are all legitimate players who compete for a better knowledge of the world we inhabit.

Moreover, naturalism is no longer dependent upon a closed system of efficient causality. Cross-fertilized with a religious mindset, religious naturalism is articulated from the standpoint of emergentism. Willem Drees notes in this regard. "A [religious] naturalist can also maintain that there are genuinely new objects with new properties, even though they have arisen out of other objects."[63] In this light, emergent novel entities such as "consciousness" carry in its own right a system of phenomena and thought that may not be explainable in terms of lower level physical activities. In this respect, they are willing to leave behind weak emergence to explore the world of strong emergence.

This does not mean that nature was deprivileged in the hands of religious naturalists. Rather, the importance of nature is all the more emphasized. Like Arthur Danto's famous quote which says that nothing "exists or could any entities or events exist which lie, in principle, beyond the scope of scientific explanation,"[64] religious naturalism is

---

[63] Drees, "Religious Naturalists," 619.

[64] Arthur C. Danto, "Naturalism" in *The Encyclopedia of Philosophy*, ed. Paul Edwards (New York: Macmillan, 1967), 448.

empirically oriented, insisting that the answer lies not in the supernatural or philosophical, but in the thorough examination of the physical. More clearly, "religious naturalists are those who find in the natural world (usually construed as including culture and history) inspiration and resources for their religious and spiritual life."[65] Simply put, religious naturalists appreciate the concrete particulars, for they designate the specific "form" to the "formless."

Regarding religious modifications, there are plenty of noticeable changes that are much more visible and conspicuous than that of naturalistic modifications. Due to limited space, I mention three here. First, the language of absolutism that is associated with the traditional theism has been eliminated along with the naming of God. For instance, Stone considers absolutism a sin of idolatry.[66] It commits the greatest travesty of absolutizing the finite. In this respect, religious naturalists part their way with panentheism or pantheism. Also, the naming of God is dismissed since there is no infinite "ontological" ground to which they can refer. Instead, they use words like "mystery," "sacrality," or "ultimate" as its substitution, for God can only be spoken conceptually and symbolically.

Second, the concept of supernaturalism finds no place in religious naturalism. Stone notes in this regard by saying that "everything must be rethought in response to our knowledge of how deeply we are rooted in natural processes."[67] If nature can speak to us of everything that we ought to know, then there is no need to refer ourselves to the ambiguous figure of the supernatural. Stone further adds in this regard, "There is no God to cling to. We cannot take refuge in God's will to make sense of it all or rely on God to save us. It is our responsibility to strengthen the levees and prepare for emergencies. It is our job to comfort the bereaved. It is our job to resist genocide and to remember those who perished."[68] Very similar to Peter Atkins' accusation of religious laziness, Stone

---

[65] Stone, *Religious Naturalism Today*, 13.

[66] Ibid., 229.

[67] Ibid., ix.

[68] Ibid., 228.

perpetuates the idea that we humans ought to do the things on our own without lazily relying upon the more powerful figure who does not reside in the same location as we do.

Third, the key religious themes have been reinterpreted in light of the new naturalistic vision of the world. For instance, the term "grace" has been transformed from God's free gift from on high to a natural ability to revere, love, and respect. [69] Likewise, the concept of transcendence no longer refers to God's power of omnipotence but human beings' ability to challenge the standing norms. It is also our creative power that "arises from our experiences and at the same time offers a map for exploring experience further."[70] Moreover, the key Christian concept of immortality is redefined as the survival of our cultural, biological, and physical information in this world long after the terminus of individual existence. In short, although religious naturalists are ready to admit that there is something more than nature, they allow themselves to see religion only through the lens of nature.

From a Christian theological perspective, religious naturalism is a hard pill to swallow. For one thing, they uphold atheistic beliefs, even though they are not professing atheists. It is understandable that they want to relate God to the scientific culture, but we cannot allow this correlation to happen for the sake of upholding an empirical view of the world that completely press theology to the level of science. This type of argument denies a unique role for theology. Theology studies God. In other words, God is the object of theological reflections. It is true to say that theology attempts to explicate the things we experience and relate them to particular religious feelings and beliefs. But this is not the chief aim of theology. As Stanley Grenz and Roger Olson succinctly note, "theology seeks to understand God's being, God's nature and God's relationship to the world."[71] In brief, theology is a quest to gain a special

---

[69] Ibid., 85.

[70] Ibid., 144.

[71] Stanley J. Grenz and Roger E. Olson, *Who Needs Theology?: An Invitation to the Study of God* (Downers Grove: Intervarsity Press, 1996), 38.

understanding of God's reality, not just about the concept of God or our religious inclinations concerning a variety of symbols of God.

The second problem I see is that they have pantheistic tendencies even though they are not pantheists. They find divine qualities such as "grace" "reverence" "mystery" "awe and wonder" and "transcendence" in nature without a specific reference to a supernatural being. Although these concepts are applicable to nature as well as a divine figure, because they have removed God (or a supernatural entity like God) from nature, it seems that nature has taken the place of the supernatural and it serves as the point of entry to the mystical and transcendence. As a result, the denial of the supernatural creates a false escape from physicalism. There is no actual transcendence. Rather, it moves in a vicious circle that keeps coming back to where it started, that is, nature.

What follows then is naturalistic reductionism. Religious naturalists do not follow strict physicalist reductionism, but they have strong naturalistic tendencies that religious attitude is almost reduced to simple naturalism. Their aim is to make sense of religion in the contemporary scientific context, so although they do not employ a strict scientific methodology to explain our religious attitude, they take empirical inquiries seriously, and most of their insights are informed by the best sciences available. At this point, we may ask, what about theological explanations? What about theological answers to scientific questions? These concerns are rejected because they do not meet the requirements of empirical science. Once again, theistic beliefs and explanations were pruned away even before they can set foot on the stage of religious naturalism. Naturalistic theists, therefore, are inclined to follow the ways of panentheism more so than religious naturalism.

Panentheism

A new breed of Christian scholars who are interested in the interface of theology and science in the name of panentheism has emerged in the last century. John Cooper has identified a large flock of panentheists that thrive in the contemporary theological camps. [72] Apparently, panentheism is attracting contemporary theological scholars and the number is increasing. As Cooper rightly notes, panentheism is not a new theo-philosophical ideal. Panentheism has been with us for centuries. However, modern panentheism has taken a new look as it metamorphosed into a grand philosophical rubric that has put two main forces of our culture, science and theology, under its own canopy. Panentheism indeed has become the driving force for contemporary interdisciplinary studies.

What is panentheism? Before we address this question, as Cooper reminds us, we need to understand that there is a problem of definition.[73] Panentheism, like any other philosophical concept, is very elusive. There is no general consensus as to what it is or what it stands for. The problem is all the more amplified due to the fact that panentheists rarely give a clear definition when the term is used. To make things a bit more definitive, Michael Brierley has provided a starting point for us to think more clearly about panentheism.[74] He gives us several different ways of perceiving what panentheism is all about, and for this reason, I take his working definition as the point of departure here.

According to Brierley, we can peek into the unknown territory of panentheism by breaking down the term "pan-en-theism" into three parts.[75] The prefix "pan" stands for "all." The preposition "en" stands for "in." Finally, the root word, "theism" stands for the belief in God. Thus, combing all these terms, we can see that panentheism denotes the belief that all things are in God and God is in all things. This is not the end of the story for panentheism. Pantheism also notes the same idea

---

[72] Cf. John W. Cooper, *Panentheism—the Other God of the Philosophers: From Plato to the Present* (Grand Rapids: Baker, 2013). He has tied the modernist panentheistic philosophy such as Hegel and Schelling to the contemporary Christian scholars such as Philip Clayton and Wolfhart Pannenberg.

[73] Ibid., 27.

[74] Michael W. Brierley, "The Potential of Panentheism for Dialogue between Science and Religion" in *The Oxford Handbook of Religion and Science*, ed. Philip Clayton and Zachary Simpson (New York: Oxford University Press, 2006), 635-651.

[75] Ibid., 636.

that God is totally coterminous with everything in this world. However, panentheism is differentiated from pantheism by noting that God is not entirely exhausted by the world. God is bigger than the world. Hence, panentheism recognizes the transcendental pole of God, although God is present to the world immanently.

Furthermore, Brierley notes that panentheism can be differentiated from classical theism in several ways.[76] First, whereas classical theism begins with the idea that there is a gap between God and the world, panentheism denies this claim and states that there is no gap between God and the world. In a panentheistic world, God is present everywhere. We may refer to the classical theistic concept of omnipresence, which denotes a similar idea. However, they are not the same. In classical theism, although God can be everywhere, it does not entail necessarily that God is indeed everywhere. God is capable of being everywhere, but he is not necessarily tied to the cosmos in such a way that God and creation are not differentiable. By contrast, panentheism is underwritten by the notion that God is necessarily everywhere because the world is in God without remainder. This is not a condition but a brute fact for panentheism.

Second and following from the first, God arises from within, never comes from above or from outside. In classical theism, God intervenes in the affairs of the world as he intrudes from above. Panentheism goes against the grain of classical theism once again as it denies any intrusion of God from above. God does not need to break into the natural flow of the cosmos. There is no need for a suspension of natural laws. God does not need to interrupt because he is already in the world. In this respect, God and the cosmos are intricately and inextricably intertwined.

Third, because God is thoroughly intermingled with the world, there is a bilateral influence between God and the cosmos. Ignoring classical theistic concepts such as immutability or impassibility of God, panentheists are convinced that God is changeable and passible. God is, in some aspects, dependent on the world and the things that take place in the world. The world may not completely change or affect God

---

[76] Ibid., 636-638.

because of his transcendence, but due to mutual coinherence between God and cosmos, it is possible for God to be affected by worldly events.

From this brief analysis, we can see that panentheism has significantly changed the view of classical theism. As Brierley has shown, the corrective to classical theism vis-à-vis panentheism results in a holistic vision that allows us to see the intimate connection between God and the world. Panentheism, without erasing the difference between God and the world, pushed the two entities so closely that there is no need to see them with two different lenses. Panentheism is a single theo-philosophical matrix upon which we can see God and nature at the same time, without marginalizing one at the expense of the other.

Such a grand scheme is not without a problem. Immediately, I see the problem of natural theology. The error of natural theology is well identified by Karl Barth. He argues that we cannot come to God on our own because of the infinite qualitative distinction between God and his creation.[77] Because of this gap, we cannot say that nature is in God and God in nature. However, in the panentheistic world, this gap between God and nature is missing. For instance, Philip Clayton builds the case for panentheism based on the theory of emergence and finds God everywhere. This is analogous to the mind-body relationship. As the mind is an emergent phenomenon of the brain all the while the mind asserts top-down influence upon the brain, there is a co-dependence between God and the cosmos. Although Clayton does not push emergentism to its limit by saying that God is an emergent property from nature, he nonetheless is hard-pressed to say that "God depends on the world because the nature of God's actual experience depends on interactions with finite creatures like ourselves."[78] Clayton's conclusion of God's dependence on the world comes from the theory of emergence, not from "revelation." The danger here is well explained by Roger Trigg who notes that "natural theology should not be regarded as a substitute

---

[77] Karl Barth, *Church Dogmatics*, (Edinburgh: T. & T. Clark, 1957), 2/57-58.

[78] Philip Clayton, "Panentheism in Metaphysical and Scientific Perspective," in *In Whom We Live and Move and Have Our Being: Panentheistic Reflections on God's Presence in a Scientific World*, eds. Philip Clayton and Arthur Peacocke (Grand Rapids: Eerdmans, 2004), 83.

for any particular revelation."[79] Clayton seems to commit the fault that Trigg has identified since Clayton's emergentist paradigm has become the overriding principle of the revelation-based theology of classical theism. It is acceptable to use emergentism as a supplementary concept to revelation, but it cannot be the determining concept for God's act and being in this world.

Moreover, there is the issue of necessity introduced in the way God acts in the world. Process panentheism is a good example. A process theologian, Joseph Bracken, not only commits the fault of natural theology like Clayton, but also introduces a naturalistic necessity in God. For Bracken, God necessarily exists as the field of social activity. According to Bracken, "the three divine persons of the Christian doctrine of the Trinity co-constitute an all-inclusive divine field of activity which simultaneously serves as the 'matrix' or womb of creation."[80] He further adds, "For creation, in terms of this scheme, is at every moment emergent out of the divine matrix, existing in its own right here and now, and yet continually being incorporated into the communitarian life of the three divine persons as its ultimate salvation or self-fulfillment." [81] Anticipating his critics, Bracken assuages his readers that the "field" concept is only a symbolic representation of the God-world relationship and that it should not be taken literally.

Even if we take his advice and treat the divine field of activity as a symbolic model of divine action in this world, due to the fact that it has penetrated even to the inner life of God (e.g., the trinitarian relationship of God), it has inadvertently determined the ontological make-up of God. God is now seen as a society, a community of being. On the surface, the communitarian metaphor may be a better alternative to the outdated Aristotelian notion of pure actuality; however, because he reads metaphysics into theology, he makes the same mistake as his

---

[79] Roger Trigg, *Rationality and Religion: Does Faith Need Reason?* (Malden: Wiley-Blackwell, 1998), 181.

[80] Joseph Bracken, "Panentheism: A Field-Oriented Approach," in *In Whom We Live and Move and Have Our Being: Panentheistic Reflections on God's Presence in a Scientific World*, eds. Philip Clayton and Arthur Peacocke (Grand Rapids: Eerdmans, 2004), 212.

[81] Ibid.

predecessors by adding necessity to God. We cannot say that God is by nature communitarian. If we accept this claim, we are certainly confining God to a place, time, or culture that identifies the particular characteristics of a community. God then becomes relative.

Consequently, God cannot be socially determined. Sociality by definition defies the absoluteness of God. Society is a contingent event. It depends on the ongoing drama of different relations in this world. Nor can God's inner life be sustained by political factors such as economic or power struggles that the idea of community carries. There is no conflict in God. Nor is God intersubjective (e.g., socially equal and co-dependent to what is external to him) as claimed by many socialists like Marxists. God does not exist to satisfy the aspiration of social existentialists who want to promote egalitarianism and pan-sociality by reading socialism into God himself. The interior life of God is co-operative because of his absolute uncreated existence, not because he is "communitarian" in a creaturely sense. Indeed, we can express God's relationship in terms of communitarian language, but we proceed to do this analogically only after recognizing God's absoluteness.

Furthermore, if we say that God is inherently communitarian by nature, then creation becomes a necessary component in God's life because God has to relate to what is "other" than himself.[82] God has created the world *ex nihilo* in his freedom, not out of necessity. The fallacy that panentheists adhere to is that they invent new metaphors that portray the world as one part of God (e.g., the universe as the body of God) in order to show that God and the universe are linked without a gap. Even if we say that God and the world have a bilateral relationship, we do not have to show that the universe is a "member" of God. God and the world can affect one another in their mutual participation while maintaining their distinct qualities (e.g., God as an uncreated entity and the world as a created thing). This means that we do not naturally belong to God. We are partakers in God's life because of God's outreach (via grace). God in this sense is a gift to us. What was

---

[82] Martin Buber's theory of relationship affirms that the I-Thou relationship necessarily requires the two distinct elements, that is, "I" and "Thou." See Martin Buber, *I and Thou*, trans. Walter Kaufmann (New York: Touchstone, 1970).

not possible in our end has made possible because of God's free act of self-giving. This is the crux of Christian attestation of the gospel. In other words, our participation in God is not intrinsic to God. For this reason, God has to come to us first in order for us to have any relationship with him. This theological "gap" has to be recognized. Without such a gap, we will be lost and unable to discern natural phenomena from the divine action. In the end, panentheism may have gone too far ahead of itself and left behind valuable resources of the Christian past.

In sum, for the sake of an interdisciplinary effort, naturalistic theology such as panpsychism, religious naturalism, substance dualism, and panentheism became the primary metaphysical and theistic themes with which interdisciplinarity have been emphasized. However, these naturalistic paradigms fail to do full justice to the traditional theological paradigms. From a Christian perspective, we also need to consider our inherited theological themes such as the doctrine of the Trinity as a way to preserve the identity of Christianity and its core beliefs. What is most troubling is that the new programs that have been examined in this chapter seem to serve under the dominance of naturalism more so than making God's revelation and the biblical principle relevant to the public. In order to fill this lacuna, in the following section, I propose a theology of nature that is more feasible to the Christian way of thinking about nature.

The Accommodating Absolute and the Contingency of Nature

A brief survey of the modernist entanglement with nature reveals the fact that there have been many innovative attempts to replace classical theism with naturalistic theism. However, introducing naturalism to the theological arena is quite dangerous. What I am talking about here is the danger of naturalistic reductionism and absolutism. Naturalistic reductionism presses upon us to reduce all elements in the world to a single category of nature. Theological categories such as God's being and act are fleshed out under a single matrix of nature. Similarly, naturalistic absolutism grips us so hard that it does not allow us to see anything else but nature, even at the expense of God's own absolute essence. Due to these dangers, especially as Christians, we must rethink the God-nature relationship. To merge three highly volatile categories, God, man, and nature, we cannot simply depend on naturalistic assumptions to make this connection happen. We have to rely on a more holistic and broader theo-philosophical catalyst that does not marginalize the essence of Christian God as theology is interfaced with science.

Thus, in this section, I introduce the concept of the accommodating absolute, and its cognate, the contingency of nature which is underwritten by open system metaphysics. Since they derive from trinitarian metaphysics, I will highlight key features of the doctrine of the Trinity. Due to Thomas Torrance's extensive study in this area, I draw upon Torrance's work to flesh out the trinitarian metaphysical implications for our discussion of the accommodating absolute. Furthermore, since open system metaphysics is process oriented, I borrow the work of Joseph Bracken to unpack the main features of open systems. My claim here is that the theo-philosophical catalyst of trinitarian metaphysics preserves the distinct features of God and nature all the while linking them to the open world in the continuous act of accommodation. There are two key guiding questions. The first question is: what is the accommodating absolute? The second question follows from the first: what is nature?

What Is the Accommodating Absolute?

The concept of the accommodating absolute is a derivative of the doctrine of the Trinity. The doctrine of the Trinity, which is really a theo-metaphysical concept of Christian God, is a unique way to consolidate the seemingly two antithetical nature of God: his oneness existing in three distinctive persons. Torrance standing amongst the constellation of trinitarian Christian thinkers tackles this great mystery by referring to the ontological priority of God. Put pneumatologically, Torrance says that the Holy Spirit is God's own being working in nature.[83] He refers to the ancient Christian writers who testified to the ontological priority of God's being by stating that the Spirit has come to us from the being of God himself, communicating to us the knowledge of God that derives from God.[84] In other words, the Spirit is not some force or power of this world. Rather, the Spirit is God's being and act, which is external to this world. Nonetheless, by God's grace, the Spirit of God is working in this world. Furthermore, for Torrance, to know or to be acted on by the Spirit is to be concerned with the being of God himself. The Holy Spirit as the being of God is the divine reality that exists infinitely above and beyond all creatures, but at the same time, is free to be present to the creatures coming from the side of the divine for the sake of binding the creation to the Creator.[85]

What I want to focus here is Torrance's undivided attention to God's self-givenness, that is, God's being in his uncreated existence. This is the starting point to explicate the nature of the absolute. When we say that God is absolute, we mean that he is who he is in himself, a non-derivative existence that lies beyond and above nature that cannot be mixed or blended into the things of this world though he may mingle with his creation. In this respect, like Torrance, we must give credit to Barth's dialectical theology for orienting us to the proper starting point of thinking about God's absolute and wholly otherness.[86] Due to Barth's strong anti-anthropocentric sentiment, he emphasized the importance of starting with who God is and what he does for us rather than from what we can know about God or what we can do for him. Barth's denial of all forms of natural theology sustains a thesis that there is an unbridgeable gap between God and man, and that it is futile for man to think that he can comprehend God without the help of God's self-

---

[83] Thomas F. Torrance, *Theology in Reconstruction* (London: SCM Press, 1965), 209.

[84] For instance, Basil taught that it is the Spirit who can express the inexpressible for us and who can draw us to the unapproachable because the Spirit comes from God as God. Basil the Great, *De Spiritus Sanctos*, 12.28; 8.18; 18.44; 22.53.

[85] Torrance, *Theology*, 209.

[86] Torrance is in absolute agreement with Barth in this regard. Undoubtedly, the ontological dimension of God put forth by Torrance derives from the patristic writers, but it is also heavily influenced by Barth's dialectical theology.

revelation.[87] Although Barth's theological proposal may be directed against Christian scholars taking residence in the modernist camp and perhaps treating them unfairly with one giant sweeping gesture of neoorthodoxy, he nevertheless has turned our attention to the undeniable truth, the ontological gap that exists between God and man.

However, our concern for the priority of God's ontology could be problematic to a particular epistemic pattern proposed by Bernard Lonergan. Lonergan writes that "while objectivity reaches what is independent of the concrete existing subject, objectivity itself is not reached by what is independent of the concrete existing subject. On the contrary, objectivity is reached through the self-transcendence of the concrete existing subject."[88] Lonergan is essentially arguing that, like Torrance, we need to affirm the reality of God existing in its own right and safeguard his transcendence, but this ontological priority has to be turned around and ultimately follow the epistemological order that centers not on the sphere of God but the faculty of our own judgment and interpretation of God. For Lonergan, we have to reckon with the fact that theology is a second-order activity that relies more on our interpretative judgment and insight and less on the abstraction of the ontological dimension of God.

Surely, in the post-Kantian ethos, due to the inaccessible thing-in-itself, theologians scramble to construct realistic theology based on the philosophical ground of experience and creativity. In this schema, theology is underwritten by what we make of the reality at hand rather than what the reality is in and of itself. David Tracy sees this trend inevitable. He notes that all data are theory-laden because of "the fact that 'fact' means not an uninterpreted 'already-out-there-now real,' but a verified possibility."[89] This means that, unlike speculative realists, we

---

[87] Barth, *Church Dogmatics,* 2/57-58. There is an undeniable connection between Barth and Kierkegaard. Thus, Barth's dialectical theology is underwritten by Kierkegaard's famous dictum, "the infinite qualitative distinction" between man and God.

[88] Bernard Lonergan, *Method in Theology* (London: Darton, Longman, and Todd, 1972), 338.

[89] David Tracy, *Plurality and Ambiguity: Hermeneutics, Religion, Hope* (San Francisco: Harper & Row, 1987), 48.

would not be able to move outside of our own perspective of reality, including God. From this epistemic vantage point, we can only see God through the lens that is particular to our own existential situations and colors the divine reality accordingly. We have returned to the problem of correlationism again. How can we maintain the balance between the two poles of subjectivity and objectivity? Torrance is helpful in this regard.

Torrance also understands the inseparable relationship between subjectivity and objectivity, or the dialectics of the absolute and the relative, but follows a different path than either Lonergan or speculative realism. He maintains this balance by way of minimizing a subjective penetration that leads to the distortion of reality albeit not losing subjectivity altogether. Here, he recommends the scientific way of doing theology.[90] In science, according to Torrance, the proper way to relate theory and data is to think from the center in the object "out there" independent of the human mind, rather than from the center in oneself projecting one's own ideas or imagination onto the object. Translated to theology, Torrance draws attention to the concept of onto-relationality. Let me unpack this concept briefly.

According to Torrance, the doctrine of *homoousion* manifests consubstantial ontology in the Godhead and the inner enhypostatic relations that define the personhood of each member in the Trinity as one yet distinctly three. This means that the trinitarian relationship between Father, Son, and Holy Spirit reveals God existing as one being in three persons. The deployment of the trinitarian logic that has been at the heart of Christian theology accentuates the inseparability of the ontological and personal dimensions of God, which regrettably have been either completely severed as mutually exclusive categories or completely conflated into a single rubric of pan- or panen-theism, by

---

[90] Philip Clayton has taken issue with Torrance's claim of theology as science. He believes that theology can never be scientific. Theology and science can only interact on the metaphysical level. See Philip Clayton, *Adventures in the Spirit: God, World, Divine Action* (Minneapolis: Fortress, 2008), 34. What we need to understand is that Torrance never intended to conflate theology with science nor reduce theology to science. For Torrance, theology is scientific because, like any other sciences, it investigates the reality on its own terms. In other words, to be scientific means to be realistic.

modern thinkers. This move is made possible by the use of impersonal metaphors.

Indeed, the spirit of the modernist vanguard has been consistently pushing for impersonal metaphors to speak of the absoluteness of God. This trend fits nicely with the scientific age in which there is little room for God as the absolute person freely interacting with his creatures. Broadly, there have been two ways to deal with the personhood of God in the philosophical-scientific world. I refer to two key German idealists: J. G. Fichte and G. W. F. Hegel. On the one hand, Fichte argued that God cannot be a person, for if he were so he would not be an absolutely infinite being. Fichte essentially identified "person" as a self-conscious being who always "presupposes the existence of another, from whom one distinguishes oneself, thus becoming conscious of self."[91] With this definition, Fichte simply denied the personhood of God due to the fact that God who is absolutely infinite could not have any other being from whom to distinguish himself. On the other hand, Hegel, since all reality is active and dynamic, refused to correlate God to Aristotle's notion of pure actuality, a static and timeless absolute being. Hence, for Hegel, the divine Spirit cannot be a static substance, but an active "spirit" which is constituted by a process or an activity of this world.[92] In the end, although both Fichte and Hegel brought a new idea about God that defied divine personalization and pure actuality, respectively, their understanding of God could be reckoned only as the "God of the philosophers." In short, with the help of modern philosophy, the

---

[91] Najib George Award, *Persons in Relation: An Essay on the Trinity and Ontology* (Minneapolis: Fortress, 2014), 40. For a similar argument, see Martin Buber's work, *I and Thou*.

[92] Hegel, *The Phenomenology of Mind* (New York: Harper and Row, 1967), 86.

Christian God of the absolute has turned into either an impersonal God[93] or an "infinite" process[94] that undergirds all other processes in the world.

Is there a way to avoid either dualistic metaphysics (e.g., Fichte), or monistic metaphysics (e.g., Hegel)? Is there any way to merge God's absolute singleness and three distinct personalities? Is there any way to reconcile the ontological and personal dimensions of God? Torrance's answer is affirmative and turns our attention to the trinitarian logic, that is, the affirmation of God's ontological and personal nature, or in his own neologism, God's "onto-relational" personhood.[95] There have been some vague speculations as to what this means, but in my own view, Torrance is simply pointing to the trinitarian logic that Father, Son, and Holy Spirit, are at once "Trinity in Unity and Unity in Trinity."[96] What Torrance wants to emphasize here is that God's oneness and threeness can never be separated. God is one and at the same time three. It follows then that God's relationship is ontological because he is related as he in himself. Even in his relationship to the other, he never becomes something that he is not. He remains who he is in his relationship to the other. Thus, starting with this logic prevents the reading of the philosophy of personhood into God all the while affirming the inseparability between what God is in himself (e.g., God's absoluteness as one single essence) and what he does in the world as himself (e.g., God's accommodation in the form of three persons).

So, I appeal to the same logic. In order to avoid theology being entirely subsumed under or controlled by the erroneous naturalistic metaphysics, we need to think of God's accommodation in light of God's action that moves from the absolute to the relationality (e.g., God

---

[93] Paul Tillich and Wesley Wildman are two good examples. See Paul Tillich, *Courage to Be* (New Haven: Yale University Press, 1952) and Wesley J. Wildman, *Science and Religious Anthropology: A Spiritually Evocative Naturalist Interpretation of Human Life* (New York: Routledge, 2016).

[94] For instance, see John B. Cobb, *God and the World* (Eugene: Wipf and Stock, 1998) and Joseph A. Bracken, *The One and the Many: A Contemporary Reconstruction of the God-World Relationship* (Grand Rapids: Eerdmans, 2001).

[95] Thomas F. Torrance, *The Christian Doctrine of God, One Being Three Persons* (Edinburgh: T&T Clark, 1996), 157.

[96] Ibid., 168.

moving *ad extra* to the world) and from the relationality to the absolute (e.g., God moving *ad intra* to himself). In this way, we can see that God has the power to be himself in an absolute sense and at the same time God has the power to relate to the other *as himself* relatively. Even in our construction of the secondary language of God, we must first pay respect to the ontological dimension of God (e.g., God as the absolute being) and resist the temptation to see God merely in terms of the symbolic construction of the human imagination (e.g., God as the relative being). Theological creativity is important for sure and we should not deny its critical role in the development of an interdisciplinary method by relying on naturalistic metaphysics like process metaphysics or emergentism, but we should not promote it at the expense of marginalizing God's ontological priority.[97] Because God is absolute, it is wrong to say that he is contingent upon man's creativity. On the contrary, because of the accommodating God, who has come to us as he in himself and communicates to us the things of God as God, he relativizes all other realities, even to the point of utterly constituting natural existence and human cognition as a fleeting entity that has no ground in and of itself.

Before I move forward, I need to add that, even though the idea of the absolute informed by the trinitarian logic is innovative, it does carry the old philosophical residue. After all, trinitarian theology is heavily colored by Greek philosophy. For this reason, drawing upon the old metaphysics, I can say, at least, that what is absolute must be completely unique and distinct that does not depend on anything else but itself. What we can see here is that God's absoluteness carries a sense of unity, totality, indivisibility, and immutability. What is new then? The novelty is emphasized by the modifier, "accommodating." [98] There is a

---

[97] For more details, see my upcoming book, *The Order of God*, which will be published shortly.

[98] The idea of accommodation is not new. I borrowed the concept from T.F. Torrance, who in turn, drew upon patristic writers and the Reformers. Torrance, *Theology in Reconstruction*, 70. He writes, "The doctrine of accommodation, i.e., that God condescends to our ignorance, and lets himself down to us in our littleness, adapting himself to our knowing that he may adapt us to himself. Thus God so objectifies himself for us in the incarnation that far from negating, he rather posits and fulfils our subjectivity in Christ." To add, the theory of accommodation is different from the concept of kenosis. The kenosis

potentiality in God to move *ad extra* and reach out to what does not belong to him as in the case of God's *creatio ex nihilo* and the event of the Incarnation. In other words, the absolute does not necessarily have to be exclusive, isolated, or totalizing because God is able to accommodate multiplicity, divisibility, and changeability. In this respect, the trinitarian metaphysics of one-and-the-many resonates with the call to preserve the unity in the midst of diversity, recognizing both the importance of maintaining plurality and individuality without marginalizing one at the expense of the other. Thus, the addition of the term "accommodating" emphasizes the theological need to jettison any form of absolutism or solipsism, even though we are dealing with the reality of the absolute. In sum, the accommodating absolute has the power-to-be-itself and the power-to-relate-itself-to-the-other-as-itself.

What Is Nature?

Having laid a workable pattern for the accommodating absolute, we can now address the question, what is nature? More specifically, how do we conceive of nature when God the absolute is accommodated to nature? We have seen that to begin with the concept of the accommodating absolute is to locate the point of departure for understanding God in God himself, in his power-to-be-himself and power-to-be-related-to-the-other-as-himself. In this way, the argument from the absolute avoids natural theology such as the argument from nature (e.g., naturalistic theology) or the argument from consciousness (e.g., panpsychism or substance dualism). Christian theology thus starts with the absolute, namely, in God's own existence as he in himself. There is no qualifier other than God's trinitarian relationship that is needed to identify God. God is unique as it was declared, "I am who I am" (Ex. 3:14). If we see God as the absolute, it follows that nature or anything that is in nature

---

theory points to the idea that a certain quality of God is limited when he relates to us, as in the case of Jesus becoming incarnate. I do not follow this line of reasoning, because it may mislead to think that God is restricted to some extent by the variants of this world. This type of error stems from what Torrance calls the "container mode" of thinking. We cannot put the infinite God into the box of a finite matrix and assume that because God is operating in the finite matrix, his functionality is limited.

is not the absolute. They are contingent. The contingency of nature in relationship to the accommodating absolute can be flesh out further in terms of open system metaphysics.

Open System Metaphysics

In order to define the key characteristics of open system metaphysics, very briefly, I draw upon Joseph Bracken's contribution to process metaphysics.[99] Bracken's main task is to bring together Whiteheadian forms of thought and Roman Catholic understanding of the God, man, and nature relationship. So, his starting point is the Whiteheadian metaphysics of "process." What is process metaphysics? In short, process metaphysics focuses on what is changing rather than what is fixed or immutable. So, to tease out the ontology of "being," unlike an old-fashioned medieval scholar, Bracken confirms the process metaphysical dictum: "being is in the becoming." From a process perspective, "being" is nothing less than a changing entity, always transforming into something different or something more complex and higher in form. So, as contended by Bracken, since nothing in this world is fixed or closed, the things in this world must exist as interrelated, open systems, interacting with one another, advancing and growing *ad infinitum*. What happens to all these individual actual occasions in the process of becoming? Bracken takes a step further and brings up Whitehead's idea of society.[100] According to Bracken, propelled by the strong force of creativity, the actual occasions aggregate and form many different societies. Some societies can be just plainly physical or mental, while other societies are constituted by both. Bracken even speaks of

---

[99] For more details about Bracken's work on locating areas of intersection between theology and science based on open system metaphysics, see Joseph Bracken, *The World in the Trinity: Open-Ended Systems in Science and Religion* (Minneapolis: Fortress, 2014); *Subjectivity, Objectivity, and Intersubjectivity: A New Paradigm for Religion and Science* (Conshohocken: Templeton Foundation Press, 2009).

[100] Although Bracken uses the term "society" and "system" interchangeably, he prefers to use "society" rather than "system." By contrast, I prefer the language of "system" for it is more attuned to the theology and science dialogue. The term "society" can be mistaken for focusing primarily on human society rather than a cosmic vision of different systems at play (e.g., God, humanity, and nature).

God as a divine field of activity, a unique form of society that is infinitely greater than all other societies. [101] Thus, a society is essentially an accumulation of the common form of actual occasions that solidify into well recognizable systems, such as nature, human society, and God.

There are two key implications of Bracken's process metaphysics that underwrite the main features of open system metaphysics. First, the world is constituted by many societies with their own distinctive causality, intentionality, and ontological status.[102] Although there is a common element of form that could be shared by different fields of activity, the principle of supervenience applies to open systems in such a way that higher-level properties emerge from lower-level entities whereas higher-level entities exist as distinct systems from lower-level entities. For instance, in the mind-body relationship, "the mind should be understood, rather, as an enduring intentional field of activity constituted by the ordered succession of those same higher-level, strictly mental actual occasions"[103] despite the possibility that the mind emerges from brain activities. Put differently, causality, intentionality, or the ontological make-up of human consciousness cannot be explained away by causality, intentionality, or the ontological make-up of the brain.[104]

For a divine matrix, which is the highest and pre-existent system antecedent to all other worldly systems, there is also unique and distinctive causality, intentionality, and ontological status, which must be distinguished from the natural and personal systems. To borrow

---

[101] Joseph A. Bracken, *The One in the Many: A Contemporary Reconstruction of the God-World Relationship* (Grand Rapids: Eerdmans, 2001), 172-174.

[102] Joseph A. Bracken, "Creatio Ex Nihilo: A Field-Oriented Approach," *Dialog: A Journal of Theology* 44/3 (2005), 246-249.

[103] Joseph A. Bracken, "Supervenience: Two Proposals," *Zygon* 36/1 (2001), 145.

[104] To note, the mind and body analogy has to be well qualified. For instance, like J.P. Moreland, I cannot agree that an immaterial system like "consciousness" is derived entirely from the physical. Even if we say that consciousness emerges from the physical, the movement from the physical to the spiritual must include a non-reducible transcendent factor—what I call, a divine spiritual factor—that asserts top-down influences upon the entirety of the bio-physical system to bring about a novel spiritual entity. I will discuss more about the divine spiritual factor later in this section in terms of the action of the Holy Spirit, but it suffices to say that the divine spiritual system is involved in the formation and reformation of creative spirituality. In this respect, there is no pure natural "self-transcendence."

Bracken's logic, there are at least three unique qualities of the divine matrix: (1) God is present in a creature not as part of its essence, nor as one of its accidental modifications, but as an agent is present to that upon which it acts; (2) It is necessary that God be intimately present to it as its ongoing cause of being, as long as the creature exists; and (3) God is everywhere in creation first through his essence as the cause of the existence and activity of creatures, then through his presence since all creatures are present to his knowledge and love, and finally through his power insofar as all creatures are subject to his power. [105] This explanation highlights the fact that, although God is related to the world, God and the world are distinct from one another, and the world is made to be dependent and yet independent from God, all the while God continues to "lure" them to the final telos, that is, the development of a massive single society in God.

Note that Bracken's multiple systems theory is different from that of naturalistic theology. Theistic naturalists too pointed out that nature manifests itself in many different ways like thought and matter, which is a clear sign that they have conformed to a multiple systems theory. Like Bracken, their three primary systems are God, humanity, and nature. But ultimately, for theistic naturalists, the triad is just an expression of one and the same substance, namely, nature itself. Hence, the differentiation in the world, whether physical, personal, or divine, in its finite mode of being, is just a matter of the temporal appearance of one substance (e.g., nature). Hence, even if they talk about three primary systems of God, humanity, and nature, these categories in principle have been blended without differentiation as a monistic system of nature. The result is that we have to see God, humanity, and nature, all being contained in the same matrix that adheres to a common intellectual principle, whether it be physicalism, panentheism, or panpsychism.

Thus, in light of Bracken's theory of society, we cannot really credit theistic naturalists' dual-aspect monism for advancing the cause of distinct, multiple systems theory. In order for the multiple systems

---

[105] Bracken, "Creatio Ex Nihilo," 247.

theory to work, we have to recognize that there are distinct features, which are not reducible to other systems completely. This means that the multiple systems theory rejects all monistic metaphysics. For this reason, from a multiple systems theory perspective, it is naïve to say that there is a one-to-one correspondence between any two distinct systems—e.g., the correspondence between God and nature, although there are scholars who are optimistic that one day, we can find a one-size-fits-all theory that may harmonize all theories, which in my judgment, is highly doubtful.

The point here is that the multiple systems theory is another option that we can use as the underlying philosophical frame of reference for theology in lieu of a single system theory of naturalism. Based on a more nuanced scientific understanding of the world, we can say that the multiple systems theory better recognizes the true landscape of how the universe is operating. Undoubtedly, science recognizes not only one system but multiple systems at work that drive the engine of the cosmos. There is even a theory that purports that our universe is connected to the multiverse that is constituted by an infinite number of universes. As a result, theologically, we can confirm that the three main categories of Bracken's philosophy, that is, God, humanity, and nature, as a minimum requirement for the multiple systems theory, existing as distinct systems having their own set of laws and ontological particulars that may or may not correspond with other systems.

Second, although the world is made up of distinct, multiple systems, they are nonetheless intersubjectively relatable. This is the core of Bracken's message. Bracken believes that each system is a society within the network of many different societies and sub-societies, working together as one giant cooperative system, and as a result, there exists an intrinsic form of relationality that frames the entire structure of our universe. What is apparent for Bracken is that this intrinsic form of relationality derives from the divine matrix, as the power to relate himself to the other. In this regard, he notes that,

> the reality of God does not in any sense emerge from the field
> of activity proper to the world, but, quite the contrary, the
> reality of this world must necessarily emerge from the field of

activity proper to the three divine persons in their dynamic interrelation… [because] God is not emergent from the world but always ontologically prior to it.[106]

This is understandable for Bracken is coming from a panentheistic school, especially influenced by Whiteheadian process metaphysics, so there is no reason for him to say that different systems ought to be isolated from one another.

What we can learn from Bracken is that intersubjectivity is an innate feature of nature. Bracken is not hesitant to say that within hierarchically structured fields of activity, the world consists of different societies, such as "societies of atomic and molecular actual occasions,"[107] plant and animal life, and human species with a well-developed brain and nervous system. As we can clearly see from the make-up of cosmic systems, from subatomic activities to human social processes, all are interrelated and co-operating. Indeed, from the actual occasions of subatomic activities that connect the space and time in the far reaches of cosmos, a field of forces produces elemental particles. Elemental particles then interact with each other and produce the ingredients of life, such as water by pairing up two atoms of oxygen with one atom of hydrogen, and from the hydraulic ecosystem comes the source of life. For this reason, open system metaphysics is back-up by a well-nuanced scientific understanding of nature.

Bracken's common parlance of "field" all the more highlights the intersubjectivity of open systems. For Bracken, a field of activity is a society made up of cooperative networks. Bracken's society, therefore, is constituted by not only its own rules and ontological make-up, but also its intention to relate to other systems. This relational impetus is the energy of process that leads to an ontological transformation moving beyond the constraints of individuality to higher fields of social activity. Bracken terms this system a structured society—e.g., each society having the freedom to be creative and relational for its own sake.[108] For

---

[106] Bracken, "Supervenience," 148-149.
[107] Bracken, "Creatio Ex Nihilo," 248.
[108] Ibid.

Bracken, changeability or "the process of becoming" is more important than being static. In this respect, libertarian intentionality is a non-negotiable category for Bracken.

All is good if we follow the metaphysical assumption of process philosophy. I approve of Bracken's reliance on Whiteheadian process metaphysics to underwrite the main features of open systems metaphysics, but I part with Bracken as he applies process metaphysics to develop a process theology. Let me mention three critical comments here. My first critical comment has to do with Bracken's unwarranted reading of process into God. It is one thing to say that multiple systems in this world are undergoing changes in their own unique ways, but it is another thing to assert that the same type of change applies to God. We have to give Bracken the credit for modifying Whitehead's purely naturalistic philosophy by claiming that the process of this world does not make God inter-relational; rather, the process in God is the root of the process in this world. He has turned the table around. The root of change is not nature but God's power to relate himself to the other. The change of order, however, makes no difference. God is already prejudged to be in the process of becoming. Why is God the God of process? Where does he find this idea? I cannot but trace this idea back to process metaphysics. Bracken's lens has been already tainted by process metaphysics and committed the fault of omitting the final and the most important aspect of God's accommodation—God accommodates nature not just as the power to relate himself to the other, but also the power to relate himself to the other *as himself.*

I cannot say that the God of process is the God of Christianity. From a biblical perspective, God does not change (e.g., Mal. 3:6, Ps. 33:11, Heb. 6:17). If he does, he is no different than any other system in this world. The question naturally follows. How is it that God can intersubjectively interact with different systems in this world if he is not changed by it? Is he not enriched by his interaction with what he has created? To answer this question, as an illustration, let us turn to the concept of infinity.[109] The property of infinity is unique in that whatever is added

---

[109] The analogy of the infinite given here is metaphysical and theological, not mathematical. In mathematics, the infinite could be interpreted as a set that consists of

to "enrich" it, it still remains infinite. So, when a finite number of items are added to what is infinite, it still remains infinite. Even if infinitely many finite items are added to the existing infinity, the property of infinity does not change to something that is finite. In short, although God may interact with the finite process of this world, God does not become something that he is not. God remains as the absolute being, unchangeable in essence and being even though he interacts with and is affected by the creative process in this world. Of course, this does not mean that God cannot experience change. He does, as he interacts with his creation. However, we can describe God's experience as God's accommodation, never incurring God's ontological or essential change.

The second comment that I want to make is that God should not be considered as the all-embracing matrix in which everything exists. I agree with Bracken and admit that God's outreach can penetrate every corner of our being as well as the far reaches of heaven, seeking out even the remotest area of the quantum world. However, God's universal outreach does not mean that God is the underlying matrix from which the "stuff" emerges. I have to part with Bracken here because it is too immanentistic. Once again, what we have to realize is that the starting point of theology must always be the Kierkegaardian principle, namely, the recognition of an infinitely qualitative gap dividing the line between God and the world. From a Christian perspective, the gap can only be bridged by God's initiation, namely, via his free offer of grace, and only when we accept God's free invitation in and through Jesus Christ, the gap is finally closed and we live and breathe in God by the indwelling of the Holy Spirit. What I fear is that, without respecting the pre-existing gap between God and the world, God's transcendence is marginalized. Granted that Bracken's God is not an emergent entity having its root in nature, nonetheless, his God is too imminent, for God is never seen as a separate entity from that of the worldly systems. The world seems to be always "in" God, though God is more than the world. If the world is

---

infinitely many finite items (e.g., a set of all natural numbers). God is not an accumulation of infinitely many finite items. His infinity is non-derivative. He is in himself infinite.

always in God, why is there any need for God to "sacrifice" himself and bring the lost to himself in and through Christ and the Spirit?

The third and final comment has to do with the necessity of relations. I have already mentioned this aspect in the previous section, so it suffices to say that, it is wrong for Bracken to turn relationality into the primary matrix upon which all systems, including God, are made to cross-fertilize with one another. If we follow this logic, we cannot but make relationality a necessity category for existence. For me, relationality is not a necessity but a potentiality. Systems have the freedom to either relate or isolate themselves from one another. If there is genuine intentionality in each system, then there must be genuine freedom that corresponds to two types of intentionality: rejection and acceptance.[110] In other words, not every system is cooperative. For this reason, there is always a possibility of isolation, division, and conflict. We cannot deny free will exacting libertarian agents to be selfish and reduce the whole into mutually exclusive parts and seek for a self-sustaining system, refusing to participate in the reciprocal society. But this begs the question. Why is it that a cooperative system is sustained when there are fields of activity that may defy it?

In my judgment, any trace of a cooperative effort, the sustenance of intersubjectivity, or the promotion of reconciliation is a sign of "sacrificial" systems. Cooperation is not "cheap" or simply "given." It requires "sacrifice."[111] To speak in terms of energy, some positive energy has to counter negative energy that tends to bring about decay and death. The equilibrium is maintained because positive energy has been

---

[110] Whitehead's societal paradigm also takes into consideration the negative and positive behaviors of a society. However, for Whitehead (and Bracken), despite the rejection and isolation, the progress will continue and the good will emerge from the onward march of evolution. This is not a Christian view of the cosmic process, for it is overly optimistic. For Christians, the old world will pass away and God will disrupt this process of entropic cosmos and turn it into "new heaven and new earth" at the eschaton. Thus, the optimism does not come from the worldly process but from God's eschatological disruption.

[111] This is the point made specifically by Bonhoeffer when he spoke of "cheap grace." He writes, "Cheap grace is the preaching of forgiveness without requiring repentance, baptism without church discipline, communion without confession, absolution without personal confession. Cheap grace is grace without discipleship, grace without the cross, grace without Jesus Christ, living and incarnate." Dietrich Bonhoeffer, *The Cost of Discipleship* (New York: Touchstone, 1995), 44-45.

spent to counter negative energy. This means that the price paid for cooperation is the sacrifice made by each participating system, putting out its own positive energy, the power to relate rather than the power to isolate. Each system sacrifices the part of itself for the sake of the whole. The cooperative effort thus demands the participation and sacrifice of God, humanity, and nature, all working together as a unitive force for the sake of maintaining a holistic society.

In sum, as long as we do not read process into God, we are ready to apply open system metaphysics to our discussion of nature. There are three key implications of open system metaphysics for our understanding of nature. First, nature operates as a distinct system that is simultaneously independent and dependent upon the divine matrix. For this reason, nature and everything in it must be conceived as contingent entities. In Christian language, they are created entities. Because they are created entities, it is not proper to prescribe God in terms of nature or any events that occur in nature such as process, creativity, or a field of relations. Any attempt to do so falls short of reaching the absolute. By definition, God's power to be himself and his power to be related to the other as himself is the only qualifier of the absolute. In this respect, we cannot endorse any form of natural theology that marginalizes the absoluteness of God, which includes but not limited to theistic or religious naturalism, materialism, panentheism, and panpsychism.

Second, the multifaceted system of nature is potentially cooperative and accommodatable. They have the potential to open themselves to the others as they are guided by the accommodating power of the divine matrix. Of course, some natural systems do isolate and divide, unwilling to cooperate with God and with each other; however, God's continual embrace and healing of estrangement and alienation lure all systems to visit the "outdoors" and explore each other's systems and societies. What we need is to rethink the accommodating extension of nature in light of exploration. As God in his cooperative spirit left his home and ventured into the outdoor, nature also does the same. In nature, there is always a movement of *ad extra*. The societal visitation is nature's transcendental extension for the purpose of interacting with not only other natural systems like human society, but also the divine system by "not assuming another identity, but attempting to give voice to difference as authentically as possible."[112] In other words, in nature, many systems such as God, humanity, and nature accommodate one another, co-inhabiting in the space and time continuum as the explorers of the outdoor.

Third, because of the open-endedness of nature, it is also capable of accommodating God. More clearly, nature has the potential to receive God's offer of himself and work as partners to bring about new existential situations. This does not mean that nature has the power to relate itself to God on its own; rather, as a contingent entity, nature is open to receive God only because God has initiated his visitation to nature. As Jerome Stone has pointed out, nature's transcendence is always relative, never absolute.[113] Hence, the sense of wonder and mystery that nature invokes is just a pointer to the God of the absolute, who has open up the path to ultimate transcendence through his two hands, namely, the Son and the Spirit. This ultimate transcendence, in turn, fuels the propagation of religious consciousness of what Heidegger calls, "the quest for the sacred."[114]

Before I conclude, I reiterate here that the yearning for the sacred does not guarantee access to the God of Christianity. Contra Schleiermacher, I cannot equate religious consciousness to God-consciousness univocally. He writes, "Now this is just what is principally meant by the formula which says that to feel oneself absolutely dependent and to be conscious of being in relation with God are one and the same thing; and the reason that absolute dependence is

---

[112] Lisa L. Stenmark, "Going Public: Feminist Epistemologies, Hannah Arendt, and the Science-and-Religion Discourse," in *The Oxford Handbook of Religion and Science*, ed. Philip Clayton and Zachary Simpson (Oxford: Oxford University Press, 2006), 833.

[113] Stone, *Religious Naturalism Today*, 145. He adds that "as a counter to fanaticism and superstition, the sacred is not to be walled off from questioning, criticism, and rational-empirical inquiry."

[114] Frank Schalow, *Heidegger and the Quest for the Sacred: From Thought to the Sanctuary of Faith* (London: Springer, 2001), 1. Surely, Heidegger's quest for the sacred is nothing like that of Christians, but a correlation can be made albeit analogically due to God's act of accommodation.

the fundamental relation which must include all others in itself."[115] As John Cobb has reminded us, religious consciousness is always plural.[116] It does not necessarily converge on a single religious matrix. Because of the divergent output coming from religious consciousness, we have religious pluralism. Unlike Schleiermacher, I can only see "feeling of absolute dependence" as a pointer to God, not our intrinsic ontological connection to the absolute Creator. God as the absolute cannot be captured by mere religious feeling.

However, knowing that nature has the potential to accommodate God, we can say that religious consciousness is a rung in the ladder that reaches into the absoluteness of God. Though implicit and fallible, it is a companion to God and God uses it as one of his key signposts on the road to his kingdom. Thomas Torrance is right to note that the intelligibility of nature may be regarded as something like the "signature of the Creator in the depths of contingent being."[117] If we pay close attention to the intelligibility of nature with respect, reverence, and admiration, perhaps, we will be able to take a glimpse of the absolute behind the walls of nature. To see God with clarity, however, we need the final piece of God's ultimate accommodation, that is, his self-givenness in and through Jesus Christ, the Incarnation and the sacrificial death of the Son for the life of the many.

With this final piece of the puzzle in place, we can see the whole picture of the God-nature relationship, the unity of the creator God and the saving God as one single continuum of the accommodating absolute. In this regard, Eastern Orthodox theologian John Chryssavgis writes,

Our relationship with the heavens above depends on our relationship with the earth below. Accordingly, our recognition of grace and repentance from sin does not consist in denying or

---

[115] Friedrich Schleiermacher, *The Christian Faith* (New York: T&T Clark, 1999), 17.

[116] John B. Cobb, Jr. *Christ in a Pluralistic Age* (Eugene: Wipf and Stock, 1998), 58.

[117] Thomas F. Torrance, *Divine and Contingent Order* (Edinburgh: T&T Clark, 1998), 73.

doing away with the world; it consists rather in accepting and esteeming the world for what it is.[118]

This is so because, by way of God *ad extra*, God encounters nature humbly offering himself to nature as himself, and by way of God *ad intra*, God brings nature to himself extraordinarily transforming the world for the sake of the renewal of life. God's dual movement can also be translated into God working within nature in his immanence and God working without nature in his transcendence. Top-down and bottom-up movements of God are not dichotomized, however, for there is no sharp line of demarcation between the two from the vantage point of his accommodation. This is the combination of God's visitation to the outdoor (the accommodating absolute) and nature providing enough space for God (the accommodated nature) to interact with various natural systems upon which we can build our understanding of the God-nature relationship.

Concluding Remarks

In the opening chapter of the *Blackwell Companion to Natural Theology*, one of the authors, Charles Taliaferro, presents a sophisticated defense for natural theology. He is so optimistic about natural theology that he finds no other way to do theology in the contemporary setting. He argues that the knowledge of God is accessible to all rational beings without recourse to any special revelation and that the existence of God is provable based solely on natural evidence. Bernard Ramm who had taken a similar path decided to change his mind during the middle of his academic career. Early on in his life, Ramm passionately searched for innovative ways to interface theology and science, which propelled him to become a Christian apologist defending his faith based on modern scientifically oriented knowledge. He searched for new evidence in the world of science that may prove those facts that have been narrated in the Bible. However, Ramm quickly realized that the historical dimension of the Bible cannot easily be reconciled or proved by natural

---

[118] John Chryssavgis, "Sin and Grace—An Orthodox Perspective," *Colloquium* 26/2 (1994), 86.

evidence. He thus reverted back to the idea of full spiritual certitude which comes from the persuasion of the Holy Spirit. He comments, "The Christian apologist then says that spiritually, inwardly, convictionally, he rests his faith in full certitude; in reference to the objective historical, factual, etc., basis of the Christian revelation, he believes with a high degree of probability."[119] Ramm's change of mind is not a sign of his academic weakness but an affirmation of the limitation of natural theology and the need of "revelation" to complete the construction of a theology of nature. This thesis is the crux of my argument in this chapter.

What I wanted to show essentially is that theology's engagement with naturalism ought to be done judiciously. One wrong step would throw off the intricate balance between God, man, and nature, tipping the scale to the side of nature. Nature must be embraced by theology, but naturalism must be transcended. Although naturalism is the dominant force in today's scientific culture, we cannot let it be the overarching frame upon which all other frames are built. We cannot let naturalism play the role of a dictator and fall into the pit of totalitarianism. Even if naturalism is modified in such a way that theism is fitted into its overarching naturalistic vision like panentheism or religious naturalism, we would still be confined by a narrow view of nature. The interplay of theism and naturalism should permit theism to transcend naturalism without completely leaving behind nature.

I am against naturalism but I am not against nature. The two must be distinguished. Naturalism is one view of nature, while nature is an ontological subvenient base of the world as a whole. Nature is outdoor, which is open to everyone. The only requirement is to take courage and make the first step into the world of the wild. Theists, therefore, can become naturalists, without succumbing to naturalism. If we give into naturalism, as many contemporary scholars who are working within the confines of naturalism have done, it is easy to assign "nature" to the same status as that of God. It can be treated as absolute. Nature is certainly not absolute. Whenever we exalt nature above and beyond

---

[119] Bernard L. Ramm, *The God Who Makes a Difference: A Christian Appeal to Reason* (Waco: Word Books, 1972), 73.

what it really is, there is a danger of falling into the pit of absolutism, thinking that nature is no different from God the absolute.

For this reason, I eschew any attempt to rely on natural theology. At the most, the argument from nature to God help theism only relatively, particularly due to the fact that we can ascend from nature only up to religious naturalism. Religious naturalism, in turn, does not guarantee a theistic affirmation whether it is the God of creation or the human affection directed toward nature that we are endorsing. Nature in this respect is only a pointer to God, not a determinate category of God. What we need to remember is that nature is not absolute. Rather, it is merely a contingent reality, and in its contingency, it implicitly reveals the source of transcendence via our religious consciousness.

This implies that the absolute has to come from beyond nature and intersect with it. For this reason, the explicit expression of God is needed to supplement the implicit inference to God from nature, which basically functions as a pointer to God. From a Christian perspective, I feel that there is no other explicit expression than what is known in and through Jesus Christ and the Holy Spirit sent by the Father. God's self-revelation in Jesus Christ through the Spirit explicitly reveals the trinitarian ontology of God. And on the basis of the trinitarian relationship of God, we can safely move to the metaphysics of the co-operative absolute by which the absolute and the contingent can be interwoven into a non-exclusive whole.

As we proceed to the next chapter, the renewed understanding of the God-nature relationship will help us rethink about the way we relate theology and science. The key motif that we need to keep in mind for this work is that interdisciplinarity should not fall into either the error of absolutism or the error of exclusivism. The former allows one to be subsumed under the other and the latter allows one to be completely separated from the other. Neither of these options is appropriate for our interdisciplinary effort. Thus, we tackle similar problems in the next chapter, as we deal with the issue of the relationship between theological realism and scientific realism.

Chapter Two

Correlating Theological Realism with Scientific Realism by Way of Metascience

Plato taught that nothing perfect exists in the world in which we live. What we see in this world is just a shadow of the Ideal. Moreover, he believed that the Ideal, or what is perfect, is not of this world; it is transcendent, although it forms the basis of our transient reality. This ancient dualism stuck in the minds of Western philosophers of the past and the present and finally became the most problematic area for theology and science as reality in this world has been identified in two distinct ways. In the realm of science, the scientific theories of nature reveal approximately or "imperfectly" the fundamental properties of reality, whereas, in theology, God as the perfect being not only reveals the true nature of reality but also determines its very existence and telos. God as the all-determining reality, however, is not included in the discussion of science, for the impeccable status of God's reality is treated as non-being. If God exists at all, he could never be equated or treated like the things in this world. Thus, what we have is non-mutually inclusive realities, the reality of God on the one hand, and the reality of nature (and everything in it), on the other hand. Can these two seemingly incommensurable realities be related? Or from a metaphysical point of view, can our two realist positions of theology and science be related? This is the key question that confronts us when we attempt to cross-fertilize theology and science, and thus, we must check to see if theological realism and scientific realism are correlatable, and if so, in what ways this correlation can be achieved. The thesis of this chapter is that indeed theological realism and scientific realism, though discontinuous at their particular levels of discussion, are relatable.

In order to defend this claim, I show first that realism is still a viable option even with the consistent opposition from antirealists. In dialogue with Bas C. van Fraassen and Ernan McMullin—the former an antirealist and the latter a realist—I demonstrate that scientific realism, though distinctly modified from classical metaphysical realism, is still a viable option for science today. Second, I deal with the problem of commensurability between scientific realism and theological realism. Obviously, science and theology are different in many aspects, especially in the way they validate and explain the realities being investigated. For this reason, Andrew Moore claims that theology and science are incommensurable realistically. I counter his position by interacting with Wolfhart Pannenberg who has provided a way to correlate theological realism and scientific realism albeit in a general sense. I conclude with a detailed description of the metascientific method and state that theological realism and scientific realism are relatable by way of metascience.

The Viability of Realism

There is a rumor brewing in the world of science. This rumor is about the demise of realism.[1] Why is this rumor significant? It is a telltale sign that the attention of scientists may have shifted from realism to antirealism. From Plato down to Bacon, the long history of the Western world enjoyed a realist paradigm and believed that "matter" existed independent of the mind and exerted its own power of existence and pattern upon the knower. Such a strong realist paradigm held its ground even at the onslaught of the so-called turn to the subject that started with Immanuel Kant[2] and followed through by the Romantic writers. However, this received view did not last long; rather, it soon began to falter as postmodernist thinkers came onto the scene with the idea that a mind independent thing really does not exist. This is especially true for social constructivists. As Peter Berger notes, constructivism reclaims

---

[1] See Larry Laudan, *Science and Relativism: Some Key Controversies in the Philosophy of Science* (Chicago: University of Chicago Press, 1990). At one place, he writes, "Most of us relativists reject the notion of progress because the two well-known accounts of scientific progress—associated with positivism and realism respectively—have been dismal failure."

[2] Perhaps, Kant himself carried a realist tendency despite his incessant effort to move away from it. Lucy Allais may be right to say that "Kant's position is a careful combination of realism and idealism." Lucy Allais, *Manifest Reality: Kant's Idealism and His Realism* (Oxford: Oxford University Press, 2015), 11.

the world we know in light of our creativity rather than as a passive reception of reality "out there."[3] Even scientific theories are thought to be non-referential. As John Dewey unequivocally notes, scientific theories may be just simple tools of the trade that help us predict certain aspects of future events, never fleshing out what reality is all about.[4] According to Dewey, the property of reality has never been clearly justified or extended by working scientists. What was clarified is our ability to make sense of the world in which we live. The echoes of this antirealist claim can also be detected by quantum physicists. For them, quantum physics has revealed that mind is, indeed, over matter.

Quantum physics provided a completely different picture of the world that we have inherited from classical physics. Classical physicists such as Descartes and Newton thought about matter atomistically, and for this reason, they could only explain the interaction between two objects in terms of discrete science. That is, matter was believed to be made up of stuff that interacted with one another like billiard balls. In this schema, particles could move only in one direction. This implies that the result of measurements had to be consistent across space and time. We could predict the position of an object once we know its initial condition and trajectory, for it could not be following two lines of the trajectory at the same time. In this light, Pierre-Simon Laplace boldly declared that the whole universe was deterministic. He felt that every event and occasion in this world could be calculated with given initial conditions, because the universe follows a set of determined trajectories and patterns that are discernible through mathematical manipulations. However, the theory of quantum mechanics overturned this classical theory of inertia.

Essentially, in the quantum world, subatomic particles do not move or behave the way classical physics had predicted. A simple experiment proves this point. When subatomic particles are emitted to a double slit apparatus, they create an interference pattern on the detecting wall

---

[3] Peter Berger, *The Sacred Canopy. Elements of a Sociological Theory of Religion* (Garden City: Doubleday, 1967), 3–5.

[4] Cf. John Dewey, *The Later Works, 1925-1953*, ed. Jo Ann Boydston (Carbondale: Southern Illinois University Press).

behind the slit.[5] The first thing that scientists recognized from this experiment was that subatomic particles such as electrons behaved like waves. This is completely at odds with classical physics. In classical physics, discrete objects do not cause interference. Only can a stream of waves perform such a feat. All objects were supposed to travel in a well-defined single trajectory. An object in discrete terms cannot be traveling like a wave, for its final position supposedly occupies a single, fixed location, not a wide range of different positions in space. How could this be? Is matter really something unreal? This behavior was so puzzling that Niels Bohr lamented, "Anyone who is not shocked by the quantum theory has not understood it." [6] The wave character of subatomic particles was not the only surprise. It led to many different novel ideas about reality.

For one thing, the location where these particles accumulate had to be random. There is no known way to predict the behavior of quanta other than statistically show where these particles may end up on the screen. Simply put, a single particle is located in terms of mathematical probability along the line of a wave curve. This means that the underlying structure of quantum reality is nothing more than a mathematical probability. For this reason, Arthur Compton notes, "For me, the important thing about quantum mechanics is the equations, the mathematics." [7] Quantum reality is thus not entirely physical or deterministic; rather, it is mathematical and probabilistic, which forces us to abandon the notion of a concrete form of matter in time and space. Instead, we must talk about them in terms of a mathematically induced theoretical *structure*, an alternative configuration of reality.

However, there is a possibility that mathematical randomness might just be due to an unknown underlying real physical property that we

---

[5] A concise description of double slit experiment can be found in John Polkinghorne's *Science and Theology*. He also explains the quantum theory in layman's term. See John Polkinghorne, *Science and Theology: An Introduction* (Minneapolis: Fortress, 1998), 25-40.

[6] This was cited from Gary Bowman's work. See Gary Bowman, *Essential Quantum Mechanics* (New York: Oxford University Press, 2008), 172.

[7] Arthur Compton, "Foreword" in Werner Heisenberg's *The Physical Principles of the Quantum Theory* (Chicago: University of Chicago, 1930).

just have not measured it properly. In order to eliminate this possibility, scientists set up an experiment that could track the path of a subatomic particle. Which of the two slits did it go through on its way to the screen? It should be simple enough to answer this question. We can add detectors to the double slits apparatus and see which one of the two slits a particle may pass through. It turns out that, when we conduct this experiment, the interference pattern goes away. A wave function is no longer detected. This is an inherent feature of quantum mechanics. Any modification we make to the experiment destroys the interference. In essence, when a measuring device is added, the probability wave collapses and the location of the particle no longer follows a wave pattern. The introduction of an observer to the quantum equation profoundly alters the nature of quantum reality. The reality seems to be in some sense determined by the observer. Berkeley's prediction perhaps came true. "To be is to be perceived."[8] Reality is proven to have a tangible, fixed existence only when it is observed. Without observation, it remains a probability that is only mathematically describable.

From a quantum perspective, the existence of subatomic particles which underlie all concrete objects in this world is indeterminable in itself. It appears that the subatomic particles come into existence only when they are looked upon. Otherwise, they may not exist at all, or at most, they exist as mere mathematical objects of probability. With this experimental confirmation in mind, physicists such as John Wheeler quipped that "no elementary phenomenon is a phenomenon until it is an observed phenomenon."[9] He may be right. Reality is not only mind-dependent but also mind-determined. Perhaps, matter is a derivative of the mind. Eugene Wigner supports the same idea, saying that "the very study of the external world led to the conclusion that the content of the consciousness is an ultimate reality."[10] From a quantum perspective, the

---

[8] Cited from Georges Dicker's Berkeley's Idealism. See Georges Dicker, *Berkeley's Idealism: A Critical Examination* (New York: Oxford University Press, 2011), 3.

[9] John Wheeler, *Quantum Theory and Measurement* (Princeton: Princeton University Press, 1983), 195.

[10] Eugene Wigner, *Symmetries and Reflections: Scientific Essays of Eugene P. Wigner* (Woodbridge: Ox Bow Press, 1979), 172.

world could not have been made up of things that bump into each other like billiard balls. In fact, they are nothing but possibilities, that is, the possibilities of perception.

The extraordinary features of quantum theory may have shattered the traditional creed of realism. We can no longer say that the reality of science is mind-independent. As Wigner has noted, "The laws of quantum mechanics itself cannot be formulated ... without recourse to the concept of consciousness."[11] Reality is found to be thoroughly mind-dependent. Hence, Georg Süßmann writes, "Thus, the material of all things appears to be as if crafted out of thought."[12] Does this mean that realism is no longer relevant in the world of science? Has the truth-seeking method of science moved into the world of subjectivism, leaving behind the world of objects and objectivity? Is realism dead and no longer sustainable in the post-quantum world? Scholars such as Bas C. van Fraassen believe that science or what scientific theories purport to address cannot follow the old realist way of thinking and they come up with an "antirealist" position. As a way to highlight the claims of antirealism, I evaluate the arguments presented by van Fraassen, a significant figure in the antirealist camp.[13]

Van Fraassen's Antirealism:
The Demand for Empirical Adequacy

Van Fraassen's antirealist project should not be explicitly categorized as an attempt to completely overthrow realism in general or scientific realism in particular. Rather, he aims to reinterpret realism in terms of

---

[11] Eugene Wigner, "The Probability of the Existence of a Self-Reproducing Unit," in *The Logic of Personal Knowledge: Essays Presented to Michael Polanyi on his Seventieth Birthday, 11th March 1961* (London: Routledge and Paul, 1961), 232.

[12] Cited from Wolfhart Pannenberg, *The Historicity of Nature: Essays on Science and Theology* (West Conshohocken: Templeton, 2008), 114.

[13] For other key figures in the scientific antirealist camp, see Larry Laudan and Arthur Fine. Cf. Larry Laudan, *Science and Relativism: Some Key Controversies in the Philosophy of Science* (Chicago: The University of Chicago Press, 1990); and Arthur Fine, *The Shaky Game: The Shaky Game: Einstein Realism and the Quantum Theory* (Chicago: The University of Chicago Press, 1996).

scientific empiricism, which in his opinion is a better alternative than that of a metaphysical realist account of what science is all about. In van Fraassen's assessment of the current status of realism in science, there are two major deficiencies. First, scientific realists believe that they can "give us, in its theories, a literally true story of what the world is like."[14] This is unacceptable to him. His disapproval comes as no surprise since no one in science, after the advent of new physics, can claim the theory's ability to depict absolutely perfect knowledge of the world. Reality can only be interpreted partially, at best, with a high degree of probability. Due to the ontic and epistemic limitations, we cannot say that scientific theories are reproducing the exact picture of the world. This position reminds of Plato's dilemma. We can only see the things in this world partially and imperfectly. Van Fraassen's philosophical corollary comes very close to the Platonic lament about the appearance of reality.

His second point denotes that it is not possible for scientists to say that "acceptance of a scientific theory involves the belief that it is true."[15] For van Fraassen, science is not in the business of "believing" some statements to be "true" or "real." Science's main task is to empirically justify each theory based on observable data. If we were to say that science operates based on "beliefs," scientific theories once again stake a territory on absolutism or dogmatism. For van Fraassen, this attitude is unrealistic; it is like chasing after rainbows. In pragmatic terms, science always allows a degree of uncertainty when they operate. All theories in this way are tentative, never absolute. It requires a continual modification to give a better picture of reality we experience every day.

What is the alternative then? Gladly, van Fraassen proposes a new direction to think about the way science approaches reality. He argues that "the language of science should be literally construed, but its theories need not be true to be good."[16] Van Fraassen's language is not clear insofar as what constitutes "literally construed" but, from the

---

[14] Bas C. van Fraassen, "To Save the Phenomena," in *Scientific Realism*, ed. Jarrett Leplin (Berkeley: University of California, 1984), 250.

[15] Ibid.

[16] Ibid., 251.

context, it is safe to say that he is emphasizing the difference between the metaphorical and non-metaphorical language of science. This differentiation becomes a critical point of departure for McMullin as we will see later, but for now, it suffices to say that van Fraassen wants to keep a safe distance away from poetic language and concentrate on the precise and accurate depiction of scientific language. Because of the fact that scientific theories do not construct reality truthfully (e.g., as an absolutely true representation of reality) or faithfully (e.g., the belief in the real), "science aims to give us theories which are empirically adequate; acceptance of a theory involves a belief only that it is empirically adequate."[17] Here, van Fraassen has found a new way to insert the language of "belief" in science, albeit he has nuanced differently than realists such as Wilfrid Sellar and Grover Maxwell.[18] For Sellar and Grover, we cannot draw a non-arbitrary line between belief and fact, because all language is theory-laden. However, for van Fraassen, this differentiation is possible because of his demand for empirical adequacy.

What is the criterion for empirical adequacy? He notes that "a theory is empirically adequate exactly if what it says about the observable things and events in this world is true—exactly if it 'saves the phenomena.'"[19] He adds, "I must emphasize that this refers to all the phenomena."[20] This statement requires a further explanation. What van Fraassen is saying here is that empirical adequacy can be explained in terms of what is observable. This seems to echo the words of W. V. Quine who said that natural science is "not in need of any justification beyond observation and the hypothetical-deductive method." [21] Following Quine, he has rejected all scientific theoretical entities such as electrons as unobservable. For this reason, he calls his philosophical position, "constructive empiricism."[22] Underwritten by a constructive

---

[17] Bas C. van Fraassen, *The Scientific Image* (Oxford: Clarendon, 1980), 12.

[18] Ibid., 33, 59.

[19] Ibid., 12.

[20] Ibid.

[21] W.V. Quine, *Theories and Things* (Cambridge: Harvard University Press, 1981), 72.

[22] Ibid., 5-6.

empiricist outlook, he sorts out those things that are "physically" ascertainable and those that are "theoretically" abstracted. As an example, it is empirically not adequate to say that there exists an electron, because we cannot "see" it or experience it directly. If such physical inaccessibility to the subatomic world qualifies empirical inadequacy, then could we say that the planet Jupiter is not real, for we cannot get there at the moment? Van Fraassen understands that it is notoriously difficult to delineate what is observable and what is not, but he is convinced that human's observable capacity can discern which can be describable *in principle* and which cannot. Hence, Jupiter is observable in principle due to the fact that we can get there if we set out to do so.

As we can see, van Fraassen stands firm on the conviction that he can draw a line between what is observable and what is not observable. He wants to preserve this distinction because, as we have seen, in the wake of quantum physics, there is a blurry line between what is real and what is of the mind. If we fail to distinguish the two, we would include in the set of all real entities the theoretical objects such as mathematical probabilities, mythology, or even gods that do not have any connection with empirical phenomena. Although there are many scholars like Philip Kitcher who are not convinced that such demarcation is possible, again, like Plato, van Fraassen is never hesitant to draw a line between what is real and what is merely apparent, and in his case, what is apparent is theoretical entities that are "unobservable."

Moreover, he goes on to say that empirical adequacy is universally applicable. In other words, empirical adequacy has to be true in principle for all cases. For instance, if an electron is real, it must be real not only 50% of the time, but always so. Reality cannot exist as a mere probability. Despite the fact that the experiment may be able to show that an electron behaves like a particle once a measuring device is set in place, its position cannot be ascertained by the experiment in all instances. When a quantum eraser is introduced, for instance, the positions of electrons revert to a wave function and produce interference.[23] In this situation, the experiment reveals that, even with a measuring device in place, electrons behave more like a wave function rather than a particle. Hence, for van Fraassen, electrons are not "real."

As a realist, I applaud van Fraassen's bold attempt to save science from spiraling into the abyss of subjectivism. He has turned the table around and put matter over mind. Indeed, he correctly asserts that it is our experience with the physical that underwrites scientific realism. Van Fraassen thus essentially is teaching us that we as scientists have a job to do, that is, we have to sort out what is real and what is not real. According to van Fraassen, such classification can be accomplished by performing experiments that verify the scientific theory of its empirical fittingness, that is, a scientific way of meeting the demand of empirical adequacy. Although scientific experiments do not give us the true picture of reality "as is," they nonetheless provide sufficient fit in the proximity of what the reality actually is. Thus, all scientific theories are hypothetical that need to be grounded on experimental results. From this idea, we find the demarcation between the observable and the unobservable.

Based on this analysis, we can conclude that van Fraassen is a realist when it comes to his argument for the observable that sustains scientific realism. What is remarkable is that his realism is starkly different from the past. Hillary Putnam's succinct definition of the traditional understanding of realism is helpful here to identify the key features of the received view of the old realist paradigm. "The world consists of some fixed totality of mind-independent objects. There is exactly one true and complete description of 'the way the world is.' Truth involves some sort of correspondence relation between words or thought-signs and external things and sets of things."[24] If this is indeed the old view, van Fraassen now shows a different kind of realism. The scientific realism of today does not follow a belief that there is "some fixed totality of mind-independent objects." Rather, there are many different ways of

---

[23] This was not argued explicitly by van Fraassen. But it proves his point. A detailed but simple explanation of the quantum eraser, see http://grad.physics.sunysb.edu/~amarch.

[24] Hilary Putnam, *Reason, Truth and History* (Cambridge: Cambridge University Press, 1981), 49.

ascertaining the property of an object through the correlation of theory-making and the thing-in-itself. Furthermore, thought-signs and sets of things do not correspond to one another absolutely or completely. Rather, they are related only when there is an empirical warrant.

However, he is not a realist when it comes to his argument against the unobservable which, according to van Fraassen, has the potential to undermine the reality that science is dealing with. For this reason, he is rightfully labeled as an antirealist. As far as the cross-fertilization of theology and science is concerned, van Fraassen's proposal cannot work since it defies the realist position for the unobservable. One obvious reason is that theological realism involves a massive array of the unobservable. Theological realism does not limit itself to the physical or the observable. It deals with the entities that cannot simply be captured by the physical description of the world. Hence, from a theological point of view, we have to ask the question of the viability of van Fraassen's work that excludes the unobservable. For this project, we turn now to Ernan McMullin. Against the anti-realist claim of van Fraassen, McMullin brings to the fore his own view of why scientific realism is viable for today's science.

McMullin and Scientific Realism

McMullin is a staunch realist. His realist stance derives from not only the study of scientific philosophy but more importantly the study of the history of science. The historical approach to the study of science is not unique to McMullin's work. Already such an approach was visible in the work of philosophers of science such as Thomas Kuhn and Imre Lakatos. However, McMullin's work is unique in that, unlike his predecessors, he argues for a progressive nature of scientific realism, as opposed to the Kuhn's paradigm shift theory. According to McMullin, historical records show that scientific theories provide a progressive and yet tentative account of the physical world. In this light, McMullin defines scientific realism as "the long-term success of a scientific theory [giving] reason to believe that something like the entities and structure postulated by the theory actually exists."[25] Based upon his historical view of scientific progress, McMullin sets out to defend his realist stance against anti-realist claims. Before we review McMullin's argument against anti-realism, we need to identify the key characteristics of his view of scientific realism. I will do this by basing upon McMullin's own definition of scientific realism.

The first concept that that needs to be emphasized is the phrase, "something like the entities and structure postulated by the theories actually exists." It sounds like McMullin is pitching his tent in the camp of old metaphysical realism and adhere to some form of the correspondence theory of truth. This is not the case. In the past, correspondence with reality means that our abstract concepts or mathematical theories unveil in a logical manner the full scope of the reality in question. There was a sense of direct or logical correspondence between empirical data and theoretical constructs hypothetically employed by scientists. McMullin is not arguing for this cause. He diverges from classical metaphysics because he does not believe that the empirical entities can be precisely described by the scientific theories. Rather, our knowledge of reality is always tentative and progressive.

Indeed, there are certain things that we can discern via our senses in our empirical studies of the reality in question. In this respect, McMullin is not too far from where van Fraassen stands. Had he not moved on at this point, McMullin and van Fraassen would have been allies, but McMullin goes beyond van Fraassen and says that historically science is never satisfied with its immediate empirical data. It continues to search for "more" and even conjure up imaginative ideas for a better theory that would lead science to a greater understanding of the reality in question. Scientists constantly search for a grander view of the world, and for this reason, science always demands additional data either to sustain their existing scientific theories or to introduce a new theory that may expand and improve old ideas.

---

[25] Ernan McMullin, "A Case for Scientific Realism," in *Scientific Realism*, ed. Jarrett Leplin (Berkeley: University of California, 1984), 26.

Hence, the next phrase "the long-term success of a scientific theory" becomes important to McMullin's theory of scientific realism. McMullin's concept of a "long-term success" is tied to a key philosophical idea to which I refer here as retroduction that is sustained by metaphorical extensions and fertility. What follows is an illustration that shows the outworking of retroduction. Let say a ring came out of the finger. However, with a quick glance, it is nowhere to be found. If we were to investigate this problem empirically, we would test to see where the ring might have fallen by duplicating the event. So, we take a similar ring and let it freefall to the ground and check the location of its fall. Several repeated experiments will give us a well-defined range of the falling ring. With this experimental prediction, the ring should have been found, for argument's sake, within 10 feet from where it has dropped. However, even with a thorough search, the ring is not found within this range. What else can we do?

According to McMullin, this is the end of the road as far as van Fraassen's method of science is concerned. However, in a real-life setting, due to the complexity of real-life situations, simple direct empirical testing would not give us all the answers. The complexity of real-life situations demands our metaphorical extension. In other words, scientists begin to imagine other possibilities. Going back to the illustration, in order to continue our search, we look for more data. For this purpose, we could rightfully introduce a new theory, postulating that the ring may have "flown away." This is a "flying ring" theory. It sounds absurd to say that the ring flies away to some odd place farther than we could ever imagine. Although absurd, a "flying ring" is a metaphor that has been concocted to describe this unexplainable situation. Although such a metaphor defies the appearance of any real ring that we know, it becomes a new impetus to think broadly about the situation and perform different tests that may well prove the flying ring hypothesis. At last, one experiment shows that the ring can indeed "fly" if it is hit by something hard like a rock. More clearly, if a ring falls on a rock, it could literally "fly" away to a distant place.

In this illustration, there are at least two additional scientific criteria that move beyond van Fraassen's demand for empirical adequacy: a metaphorical extension and fertility. According to McMullin, scientific theories are not just propositional but also metaphorical. He writes, "The metaphor is helping to illustrate something that is not well understood in advance, perhaps, some aspect of human life that we find genuinely puzzling or frightening or mysterious. The manner in which such metaphors work is by tentative suggestion."[26] Will not the use of metaphor marginalize the precise account of reality that science enjoys? This is Michael Bradie's argument against McMullin. [27] Answering Bradie's criticism, McMullin assures his critics that the use of a metaphorical extension does not erase the precise language of science, for when it is accepted, it will be supported by new evidence. In the case of the flying ring, it is shown that the anomaly of locating the ring far away from its predicted range was supported by new evidence. The initial freefall data did not work, but a ring falling on the hard rock with a sufficient force explains the ring being located far away from the original predicted location. Likewise, McMullin argues that "there are structural continuities from one stage to the next, even though there are also important structural modifications." [28] In other words, science makes a huge leap and progresses from its previous understanding of empirical particularity by way of metaphorical generality, and even in this great leap of scientific advancement, scientific theories nonetheless always refer back to reality. For McMullin, it is the underlying reality that allows us to see both particular areas as well as greater depths of the physical property in a general sense.

This is not all. Speaking of the wider view of reality, the next point that McMullin brings up is the issue of fertility. Drawing upon Thomas Kuhn's interpretation of science, McMullin argues that the success and acceptance of scientific theories always rely on the scientific requirement of fertility. Fertility, in brief, concerns the future promise of scientific research. Thomas Nickles succinctly writes, "For something to gain the status of an exemplar multiple scientists have to judge it a valuable

---

[26] McMullin, "A Case for Scientific Realism," 31.

[27] Michael Bradie, "Models, Metaphors and Scientific Realism," *Nature and System* 2 (1980): 3-20.

[28] McMullin, "A Case for Scientific Realism," 33.

guide to their planned future work. Being models to emulate, exemplars possess a forward-looking, normative component."[29] If the theory does not lead to further studies, it may run out of steam quickly, and scientists presume that it has exhausted its full potential and discard it in light of other competing theories. For this reason, fertility is connected to the use of metaphors. Metaphors open up to a vast array of different possibilities, and as a result, the metaphorical extension of scientific theories leads to more passionate research programs even though it may be "badly undeveloped, unorthodox, even crazy-looking new approach with a slim record of success."[30] McMullin similarly notes, "Fertility is usually equated with the ability to make novel predictions. A good theory is expected to predict novel phenomena, that is, phenomena that were not part of the set to be explained."[31] In the case of the flying ring, the impetus to look for other possibilities came not from a normal experiment, but from a conception of an extraordinary concept called the "flying ring." What McMullin wants to add to this idea is that novel predictions normally emerge by integrating various levels of scientific activities such as experimental tests, interpretations of observed data, and imaginative metaphorical extensions. In this respect, retroduction suggests a new way of looking at reality out there. It is a way to access many different possibilities that could interpret reality comprehensively. If we are stuck with the demand for empirical adequacy, reality will be looked upon too narrowly and puff out the spirit of scientific explorations, and according to McMullin, this is not what science is all about.

Thus, according to McMullin, science essentially is underwritten by "the long-term success of a scientific theory." In other words, the success of a scientific theory is guaranteed not simply by meeting the immediate demands of empirical adequacy. It needs to show that it is meaningful and valuable to the scientific community in the long run, all the while

---

[29] Thomas Nickles, "Some Puzzles about Kuhn's Exemplars," in *Kuhn's The Structure of Scientific Revolutions Revisited*, eds. Vasso Kindi and Theodore Arabatzis (New York: Routledge, 2012), 129.

[30] Ibid., 129.

[31] McMullin, "A Case for Scientific Realism," 30.

continuously useful in showing that "something like the entities and structure postulated by theories actually exists." Scientific investigations never rest on a single paradigm or theory due to the fact that no immediate physical depiction is sufficient to explain the theoretical. Even without empirical support, scientists move forward, and based on their imaginative generalization, they explore the territory of unobservable causality, giving rise to tentative ontological statements.

One thing to note before we move on is that McMullin's theory of retroduction seems to be at odds with Kuhn's theory of science. According to Kuhn, there are two basic activities associated with scientific theory development. On the one hand, within the realm of normal science, scientists solve problems, develop theories, and manipulate previous scientific systems, relying on the accepted paradigms within a specific community. On the other hand, science advances as scientists encounter anomalies that could not be explained within existing paradigms. Such anomalies become the source of the scientific crisis that ultimately leads to the re-formulation and extension of existing paradigms. Simply put, science progresses by overturning the previous ideas, not by "the long-term success of a scientific theory."

However, McMullin argues against Kuhn's theory by looking at Newton's work. According to McMullin, the concept of "force" was treated rigorously by Newton. Indeed, Newton believed that the universe is "augmented by the presence of forces" and it provided for him "the means to make a general statement about the conformity of the physical universe."[32] What stands out for McMullin is Newton's use of the term "ether" to explain the nature of various forces at work. Borrowing the term from his predecessor Descartes, Newton's ether carried the ancient connotation of "an imperceptible medium capable of transmitting activity and endowed with mechanical properties."[33] So, according to McMullin, ether was tied to the notion of "active principle." Newton could only imagine the world of forces working in the

---

[32] Wolfgang Vondey, "The Holy Spirit and the Physical Universe: The Impact of Scientific Paradigm Shifts on Contemporary Pneumatology," *Theological Studies* 70 (2009), 10.

[33] Ibid.

nonmaterial medium called ether that is responsible for all motion in the universe.

It turns out that Newton's ether was a hypothetical entity, and Newton's theory of motion, including his theory of gravity, has been modified by Einstein, and now, Einstein's theory of relativity is known to be a better theory than that of Newton's. In this instance, it seems that Newton's theory was overruled by the succeeding theory, which in this case is Einstein's theory of relativity. However, McMullin disagrees. He writes,

> There was no way for Newton to know that attempts to interpret force in terms of the simple ontological alternatives he posed would ultimately fail, whereas the ontology of "insensible corpuscles," which he proposes in Opticks, would prosper. Each of these ventures was "metaphysical" in the sense that no evidence then available could determine the likelihood of its ever becoming an empirically decidable issue. But it is of such ventures that science is made.[34]

In other words, Newton's theory was not a complete failure. Not only Newton's theories provided a new impetus for scientific advancements but also his metaphorical extension of "ether" led to a new discovery of the underlying ontological structure of reality called "field." The use of metaphor by Newton was not a denial of ontology but an acceptance of something that is beyond the description of his mechanical analysis. Newton's theory of the active principle tied to the notion of ether became a prototype for a new theory, that is, the field theory which was to be developed much later in the early years of the 20th century. In short, Newton's search for the further intelligibility of the active principle in terms of an ontological category of ether was not completely fruitless. It just had to wait its time for further supporting data, and meanwhile, it provided an important motivation for scientists to dig deeper into the nature of forces acting in the world. What is interesting is that Newton's science that is based on empirical data failed (e.g., unmoving space),

---

[34] McMullin, "A Case for Scientific Realism," 12.

while his imaginative theory which had no empirical basis at the time flourished (e.g., the notion of ether).

What about quantum physics? Did it not overthrow the classical view of the physical structure? McMullin admits that the laws of quantum physics have no resemblance to the laws of classical physics. However, there is still a trace of ontological continuity between the two. As the study of classical physics was propelled by inferring to the underlying structure of reality, the study of quantum physics is also propelled by the same structure of reality. It is just that subatomic structures were only "imaginable in the categories of the macro-world."[35] For this reason, according to McMullin, quantum mechanics did not overthrow classical mechanics; rather, "what is ruled out is the expectation of the micro level of the universe behaving in the classical way."[36] Like Newton's theory of ether, the empirical data of classical physics were not deep enough to explain the theoretical aspect of quantum mechanics, but nonetheless, we are describing the same reality such as light now from a different perspective than classical physics. In this respect, McMullin's analysis of science basically rests on seeking the areas of continuity between the past and the present all the while recognizing the shift from the old and the new paradigms.

So, do unobservable entities like electrons exist? Yes, they do, according to McMullin. He justifies his argument based on his own view of a realist correspondence. If classical physics is driven by the study of the underlying reality of the macro world and scientists believe that "something like the entities and structure postulated by the theories actually exists," the same could be said of quantum theories. Quantum theories are also driven by the study of the underlying reality, in this case, in the micro world instead of the macro world of classical physics, and scientists believe that "something like the entities and structure postulated by the theories actually exists," all the while it refines classical physical theories. Hence, because scientific rationality is driven

---

[35] Ibid., 14.

[36] Paul Allen, *Ernan McMullin and Critical Realism in the Science-Theology Dialogue* (Burlington: Ashgate, 2006), 65.

by the common objective, that is, the study of the underlying structure of reality, both classical and quantum theories reflect the actual underlying structure of reality in a progressive way, moving from classical to quantum levels.[37] McMullin sums up his claim:

> The sort of theory on which the realist grounds his argument is one in which an increasingly finer specification of internal structure has been obtained over a long period, in which the theoretical entities function essentially in the argument and are not simply intuitive postulations of an underlying reality, and in which the original metaphor has proved continuously fertile and capable of increasingly further extension.[38]

From a realist stance, although there are areas of discontinuity, scientific theories progress over a long period of time to increase and refine our knowledge of reality out there.

We are now ready to argue against van Fraassen's anti-realist arguments based on McMullin's theory of science. I list three major flaws in van Fraassen's evaluation of science and its realist agenda. First, scientific realism does not rely on literal statements only. Rather, it also depends on metaphorical extensions. What makes scientific theories so successful and effective? Scientific theories are successful because the scientific "model approximates sufficiently well the structures of the world that are causally responsible for the phenomena to be explained to make it profitable for the scientists to take the model's metaphoric extensions seriously."[39] Science is successful not just because its theories are forced into the Procrustean bed of empirical adequacy; rather, it is successful because scientists are relying on the complex interplay of deductive, inductive, and reductive procedures.

---

[37] McMullin, "A Case for Scientific Realism," 17. He writes, "The sort of theory on which the realist grounds his argument is one in which an increasingly finer specification of internal structure has been obtained over a long period, in which the theoretical entities function essentially in the argument and are not simply intuitive postulations of an underlying reality, and in which the original metaphor has proved continuously fertile and capable of increasingly further extension."

[38] Ibid.

[39] Ibid., 33.

Second, scientific realism is always underdetermined. Unlike what van Fraassen had claimed, scientists with a realist inclination do not have *a priori* assumption that one single theory will be able to explain the totality of reality. McMullin writes in this regard:

> Scientists have never thought themselves disqualified from pursuing one of a number of physical models (metaphysical models including) that, for the moment, appear empirically equivalent. As metaphors, these models may give rise to quite different lines of inquiry, leading eventually to their empirical separation. Or it may be that one of the alternative models appears undesirable on other grounds than immediate empirical adequacy (as action at a distance did to Newton).[40]

Because theories are metaphorical and reality always stands outside the scope of our empirical adequacy, "[t]he underdetermination of theory to data is accepted by McMillan as a feature of a theory's partial truth value," as it presents the "probability of theory revision in the course of verification."[41]

Third, both the observable and the unobservable are bracketed as an inseparably linked dual warrant for scientific realism. As McMullin has pointed out, we cannot automatically dismiss the theoretical entities as a non-viable realist category of the unobservable. In science, they are legitimate objects of study, not just because of their usefulness, but more importantly, because they reveal the deeper and broader spectrum of reality. Reality is too grand. It cannot be determined by mere empirical adequacy. It requires something more such as a metaphorical extension to capture its full scope of existence. The metaphorical extension, in turn, can stretch the theories to describe extraordinary things without the loss of their ontological status. In this respect, the unobservable entities of science cannot be described simply in terms of empirical adequacy; rather, it is imperative to know that scientists search for an underlying

---

[40] Ibid., 11.

[41] Allen, *Ernan McMullin*, 67.

structure of reality that corresponds to what the unobservable entities purport to describe.

In sum, McMullin has rebutted anti-realism based upon scientific realist categories such as retroduction and realist correspondence between theory and data. The key thesis of McMullin's retroduction is the fact that science aims to depict reality through a long-term success of scientific paradigms, and it is this reality in question that guides scientists to formulate scientific theories whether they are referenced to unobservable entities or observable entities. Granted that scientific realism proposed by McMullin successfully defeats anti-realism, does McMullin's theory of scientific realism allow us to build theological realism on the ground of scientific realism? According to McMullin, two realisms should not be correlated.

For McMullin, even if we say that theology adheres to a similar type of realism such as "critical realism," it has nothing to do with scientific realism. He makes a strong argument against Arthur Peacocke who has made such an attempt and says that "the critical realism of natural science does not, to my mind, carry over into theology." [42] In this statement, McMullin clearly lays out two reasons for his avoidance of merging scientific realism and theological realism. On the one hand, he sees that the context of justification in theology and the context of justification in science differs so much that they are not correlatable. On the other hand, he sees theology relying on a completely different type of reality than science. McMullin's rational for taking this stance is backed by his strong Augustinian theology. I will come back to the issue of verification later in the section when I argue against Andrew Moore, but for now, let us review McMullin's adoption to Augustinian theology and see why theology relies on a completely different type of reality than science.

McMullin's theology does not allow God to be associated with the temporal things in this world. In short, drawing from Augustine, McMullin believes that God is atemporal. God is not part of the world,

---

[42] See McMullin's review of Polkinghorne's "Belief in God in an Age of Science" *Commonwealth* 17 (1998), 23.

nor is the world in and of God. There is an unbridgeable gap between God and nature. McMullin appeals here to the Augustinian tradition more so than the Aristotelian tradition,[43] because the starting point for the doctrine of God is not from temporality or creatureliness but eternity or the transcendence of God. If God is atemporal, it follows that God cannot be described by or associate with anything in this world. He writes, "What one cannot say is, first, that the Christian doctrine of creation 'supports' the Big Bang model, or second, that the Big Bang model 'supports' the Christian doctrine of creation."[44] From the vantage point of God's transcendence, when we try to retrace God's creative event to some point in time, we will miss the theological fact that we are dependent on God who created the world *ex nihilo*.[45]

Here, with his understanding of the atemporality of God, McMullin is forced to draw a distinction between history and nature. For him, theological discourse deals with the interpretation of history in terms of redemptive categories whereas scientific theories deal with the explanation of reality in nature.[46] This is how McMullin differentiates theology from science; science involves natural entities, whereas theology has no demand for empirical adequacy for it deals with a supernatural entity called God. If theology has any verification procedure at all, because theology is not scientific in nature, it only pertains to the personal meaning gleaned from the study of the Bible. Paul Allen writes in this regard, "The first part of this [theological] verification process involves the uncovering of other insights, beliefs, experiences and discoveries in theological sources, primarily scripture. It is here where the very term 'creation' possesses its primary reference

---

[43] Allen, *Ernan McMullin*, 126.

[44] See McMullin, 'How Should Cosmology Relate to Theology?' in Arthur Peacocke, ed. *The Science and Theology in the Twentieth Century* (Notre Dame: University of Notre Dame Press), 39.

[45] Ernan McMullin, "Religion and Cosmology," in Norris Hetherington, ed. *Cosmology: Historical, Literary, Philosophical, Religious and Scientific Perspectives* (New York: Garland, 1993), 604.

[46] This is very similar to Oscar Cullmann's differentiation of salvation-history and general history to which salvation-history is not included. See Oscar Cullmann, *Salvation in History* (New York: Harper & Row, 1967), 135-146.

to personal meaning." [47] So, McMullin's natural theology is geared toward finding a personal significance of God's creation, rather than understanding reality itself, like science.

At this junction, I part with McMullin. I agree with McMullin that theological statements and doctrines cannot leave behind its soteriological dimensions, but I find it difficult to let theology be cut off from scientific realism. Theology from an interdisciplinary perspective cannot be reshaped and fit into a sort of personal and fideistic knowledge. This is precisely what Wolfhart Pannenberg argues against. For this reason, I bring him into the conversation and see if Pannenberg's work in the areas of interfacing theology and science can resolve the unbridgeable gap between theological realism and scientific realism created by McMullin. Before I introduce Pannenberg's work, I refer to the work of Andrew Moore at this time, because, drawing from McMullin, he has presented several key arguments against correlating the two realisms with greater details than that of McMullin. In this respect, Moore can assist in identifying key counterarguments associated with correlating two realisms to which I will respond based upon my analysis of Pannenberg's work.

Moore's Incommensurability between Two Realisms

Moore's essay begins with the assertion that, due to the recent efforts to argue for theological realism based on the defenses of critical realism in the philosophy of science, theology is in danger of losing its realist foundation. Quoting Don Cuppitt, he argues that if theological realism is dependent on scientific realism, then "the scientific derivation of which renders it [theological realism] inapplicable to expressions of Christian faith on the grounds that it will falsify what those expressions are intended to affirm."[48] Moore is drawing upon Cuppitt's anti-realistic

---

[47] Allen, *Ernan McMullin*, 160.

[48] Andrew Moore, "Theological Realism and the Observability of God," *International Journal of Systematic Theology*, 2/1 (2000): 80. Moore's argument sounds very much like the old Barth-Scholz debate. They are related because we are still talking about the demands of scientific empiricism, but the current debate has more at stake, such as the viability of using critical realism to substantiate theological realism.

statement and believes that science "sharply separates factual description from religious expression," [49] so it is not possible for theology to interface with science vis-à-vis scientific realist categories.

What is the alternative way to speak about theological realism? He sets the foundation of theological realism upon the edifice of what he calls a "dialectical fideism." He explains, "By this phrase, I mean to denote a fideism shaped by a Christian orientation to and engagement with the world which, guided by scripture and the Holy Spirit, learns to find God acting there in both judgment and grace."[50] What he is trying to say is that, drawing upon Karl Barth, theology should not be dependent upon science to configure its realist paradigm; rather, theology should stick to religious faith where the reality of God is found. In science, God is absent since he is not the object of its study. For this reason, Moore warns that if theologians follow the current trail and continue to merge the two distinct worlds, they would be eventually faced with a more serious issue of confusing God with scientific facts, which in turn, leads to a slew of irreconcilable problems such as pantheism.

Going further, he raises the problem of theological realists being unable to rebut the objections of antirealism. According to Moore, in order to counter the antirealists' objection to scientific realism, theological realists have to address three issues: observability, underdetermination, and fallibilism.

In regard to observability, Moore is not convinced that theological realism can help theological realists rebut the demand of empirical adequacy posed by the philosopher of science like van Fraassen. Moore writes, "Hypotheses and theoretical constructs serve scientists by enabling them to make accurate predictions in the realm of the observable—that is, the laboratory and its apparatus."[51] Moore is right to say that science relies heavily on the experimental data. So, in order to argue against antirealists, as Moore suggests, theological realists have

---

[49] Don Cupitt, *Taking Leave of God* (London: SCM Press, 1980), 44.

[50] Moore, "Theological Realism," 86.

[51] Ibid., 82.

to show that God can be tested. Moore says that this is impossible. "The Christian God is not an entity about whom we can construct experiments, still less a tool to be manipulated."[52] If theological realists cannot bring God into the laboratory, they have no way of rebutting the antirealist argument because scientific realists' debate is decided by experimental results.

Even if we say that God is unobservable so that he is exempt from the demands of empirical adequacy as claimed by theo-scientific scholars such as Janet Martin Soskice, Alister McGrath, and John Polkinghorne, Moore rejects any possibility for theologians importing the concept of unobservability from science to theology. He writes,

> Given their prior commitment to a realist construal of Christian faith, theological realists cannot coherently consider the empiricist objection, for, despite their readiness to talk of God as a hypothetical and unobservable entity, they neither regard his existence as hypothetical nor do most of them think that all the data of humankind's religious experiences are germane to the project of modelling God.[53]

Why is this the case? He reasons in the following way. "Even if we grant God the status of a hypothetical, unobservable entity, the Christian God is not an entity about whom we can construct experiments, still less a tool to be manipulated."[54] Even if we consider God to be unobservable, to base God's unobservability on scientific realism, it has to be supported by empirical evidence. Moore quotes McMullin to bolster his argument. "McMullin generalizes the point: theoretical expectations concerning hypothetical unobservable entities are frequently made good when 'theoretical entities previously unobserved, or in some cases even thought to be unobservable, are in fact observed [later].'"[55] Hence, he concludes that "as a result of the progressive confirmation of theories, more and more entities are shifted from the unobservable end of the

---

[52] Ibid., 87.

[53] Ibid., 86.

[54] Ibid., 87.

[55] Ibid., 92

continuum to the observable."[56] So in science, the unobservable is still required to be backed by observable data, and God who is not a part of this reality cannot be put in the same category as the scientific category of the unobservable.

Concerning the notion of underdeterminism, Moore argues that theological realist statements do not meet this criterion of scientific realism. According to Moore, nothing is absolute in science; all scientific theories are underdetermined. Moore writes,

> The difficulty here is that "there may be two or more quite distinct ... accounts of the nature of reality, which have the same empirical consequences." In other words, the same set of observations might be explained by any number of radically different and incompatible theories.[57]

Moore is once again right concerning underdeterminism in science. Indeed, "for the philosopher of science ontological component is up for grabs."[58] Moore maintains that, in contrast, theological realists dance to a different tune. Theological realists actually overdetermine their theories. He writes,

> By operating with a commitment to realism's being true of Christian faith *before* the case for theological realism has been made out, they overdetermine the interpretation of their data by their prior commitment to a particular theory. They interpret religious experience in a realist way whilst suspending the question as to whether this, rather than a naturalist, non-cognitivist account is correct.[59]

Essentially, Moore is talking about a fundamentalistic way of doing theology, in which a prior judgment or a set of creeds determines the way we view the world theologically. However, it is doubtful to say

---

[56] Ibid., 93.

[57] Ibid., 83.

[58] Ibid., 86.

[59] Ibid., 85.

that all theological realists follow a sort of absolutist rationality. I will come back to this point later.

Concerning fallibilism, Moore contends that an epistemic fallibilism is an inherent feature of scientific realism, whereas theological realism holds no such feature. He writes, "Both arguments regard scientific realism as a hypothesis which is in the process of being confirmed. It is not a settled position; it could turn out to be false. There is, therefore, a fallibilism built into scientific realism."[60] Although there are some theo-scientific scholars such as Soskice who claim to show that theological statements are fallible, Moore is not convinced that this is the case. Drawing upon Michael Durrant, he explains that the claim of theological fallibilism is "'unacceptable' since on Soskice's view presumably Christ himself might have been mistaken as to God's nature; an untenable position for any Christian theist to entertain.'"[61] Once again, in Moore's view, theological realists cannot eschew the demand of the absolutist view of their faith. According to Moore, theologians have a deep-seated commitment to faith understanding, and as such, theological data are not falsifiable like scientific theories.

In the end, Moore recommends that we ought to construct theological realism not by building analogous relationships between theological realism and scientific realism, but by way of Barthian fideism. He feels that theological realists have been mistakenly building the case of theological realism upon God's apophatic nature, or what he calls the unobservability of God. Consequently, Moore kills the analogy of "unobservability" between God's reality and the theoretic entities of science.

I do not agree with Moore's assessment of theological realism and its incommensurability to scientific realism under the headings of observability, underdeterminism, and fallibilism. In order to rebut Moore's claim, I turn to Wolfhart Pannenberg.[62]

---

[60] Ibid., 89.

[61] Ibid.

[62] Note that I agree with Pannenberg's critics such as Grenz that there are theological weak spots such as his trinitarian paradigm, but as far as his interdisciplinary method is

Pannenberg's Theology of Nature and Realist Correlation

Pannenberg is known as "one of the most significant theologians of the 20th century,"[63] and often listed as the key figure of theology in the contemporary world.[64] As Timothy Harvie notes, Pannenberg's lasting contribution to theology is "his efforts to provide a doctrinal account which does not ignore physical descriptions of reality."[65] Harvie is essentially pointing out Pannenberg's contributions to the theology and science interface. Philip Clayton also makes a similar comment as he acknowledges Pannenberg's lifelong work in the field of "religion-science."[66] Clayton as a key disciple of Pannenberg finds that it was his teacher rather than Thomas Torrance who convinced him to rethink the way we relate theology and natural sciences. Clayton feels that Torrance's theo-scientific paradigm would not have worked out for him because of his loyalty to Barthian theological programs. I would not agree with Clayton's assessment of Torrance's work, but he is right insofar as Pannenberg's effort to relate theology and science. Indeed, Pannenberg has labored most of his academic career to bridge the gap between theology and science. A symposium was held in his honor to recognize his contributions to this area of study. The title of the symposium testifies to Pannenberg's legacy: "Laying Theological Claim to Scientific Understandings."[67]

---

concerned, I find his project most comprehensive and internally coherent that it fits the bill for the clarifying the realist correlation between theology and science. For more details on Grenz's critical review of Pannenberg's work, see Stanley J. Grenz, *Reason for Hope: The Systematic Theology of Wolfhart Pannenberg* (Grand Rapids: Eerdmans, 2005).

[63] Fred Sanders, "The Strange Legacy of Theologian Wolfhart Pannenberg," September 2014 *Christianity Today*.

[64] E.g., Stanley Grenz, *20th Century Theology: God and the World in a Transitional Age* (Downers Grove: Intervarsity, 1992).

[65] Timothy Harvie, "God as a Field of Force: Pannenberg's Doctrine of the Holy Spirit," unpublished paper.

[66] Philip Clayton, "Science, Meaning, and Metaphysics: A Tribute to Wolfhart Pannenberg," *Interdisciplinary Science Reviews* 28 (2003): 237-240.

[67] Joel Haugen, "Introduction: Pannenberg's Vision of Theology and Science," in *Beginning with the End: God, Science, and Wolfhart Pannenberg*, eds. Carol Rausch Albright and Joel Haugen (Grand Rapids: Eerdmans, 2008), 1.

What is Pannenberg's key rationale for taking this route? Basically, he wants to avoid any sort of fideism, especially Barth's way of understanding theology. Pannenberg writes, "If one takes the task of theology seriously, it must be theocentric, not anthropocentric. But, then the question is whether one can get to the theocentric position simply by way of a personal decision [of faith], as Barth originally proposed."[68] Pannenberg has realized that in the name of "faith" theologians such as Erich Schaeder and Karl Barth exempted theological statements from the standard of critical inquiry. Pannenberg's objection to fideism[69] runs the same course with scientific realist's rejection of "overdetermination." As McMullin has pointed out, it is not necessary for scientists to uphold an absolutist view and attach themselves *a priori* to a selected few theories that seem appealing to them; rather, all theories are hypotheses and need further testing to unveil the hidden structures of reality. In this light, Pannenberg asserts that the rigors of science only allow theology to take criticizability, revisability, and hypothetical reasoning, as the *modus operadi* for theologians.

Thus, Pannenberg suggests that all theological claims be tested. If theology wants to function as a reasonable science, its claims must be tested like any other scientific discipline. But how we do test theological claims? He is not following the way that was recommended by John Hick or Gerhard Ebeling. The former deferred the verification of theological statements until the eschaton, for nothing in this world will be able to "verify" God, and the latter reversed Hick's agenda by allowing God to verify us as he brings humanity to the realm of truth. The first option is meaningless to Pannenberg because theology is removed from the historical event. Likewise, the second option is not acceptable because it follows the same pattern set forth by Barth—the

---

[68] Pannenberg, "The Historicity of Nature," 4.

[69] Pannenberg is not entirely against "faith" as van Huyssteen purports. He understands that faith is an indispensable ingredient for the theology-making process. Philip Hefner's assessment is more accurate in my judgment. Pannenberg preserves the core belief while keeping the auxiliary use of theological explanations as provisional. See Philip Hefner, "The Role of Science in Pannenberg's Theological Thinking," in *Beginning with the End: God, Science, and Wolfhart Pannenberg*, eds. Carol Rausch Albright and Joel Haugen (Grand Rapids: Eerdmans, 2008), 97-115.

truth statement could only end up as a dogmatic faith statement. Moving beyond these two options, Pannenberg proposes a novel idea. Theological statements should be tested hermeneutically.

For Pannenberg, all theories, including that of science, carry a hermeneutical inference. This is due to the fact that there is no such thing as a purely empirical research program that completely discloses the essence of reality by a mere presentation of objective facts. Science is always delimited by its inevitable matrix of underdetermination.[70] On account of this limitation, Pannenberg maintains that theology can propose its own interpretation of scientific data, laying theological claims upon scientific understanding. Hence, according to Pannenberg, the interpretation of scientific facts is not reserved only for scientists. Theological interpretations of scientific data can also "compete"[71] with scientific theories, though never directly but in a more general sense. The same applies to theology. Theological theories can be stated in many different ways as each theory apprehends in its own unique way the meaningfulness of the "scientific" data. What this implies is that Pannenberg is not just concerned with a linguistic exercise of theology exegeting the Bible, but more importantly, the interpretation of real events in nature grounded upon the scientific metaphorical extension. With this idea of hermeneutical testability, Pannenberg has created enough space for Christian scholars to lay their theological claim upon scientific data. Due to an inherent hermeneutical possibility in all sciences, theology has a legitimate role to interpret empirical data albeit, in a general sense, that is, by way of a hermeneutical inference.

---

[70] Note that "underdetermination" in theology is not the same as scientific underdetermination, albeit the apparent continuity between them. In science, underdetermination denotes the inadequacy of empirical verification, whereas in theology, underdetermination denotes the inadequacy of theological evidence and arguments in unveiling the full scope of God's being and act in this world.

[71] For Pannenberg, even as competing theories, they are related to one another. Lena Soler's statement about the nature of competing theories comes close to what Pannenberg is talking about here. "Competing theories are theories that must have some important common points. They must notably take some common phenomena as relevant to their field, which means that they must be connectible, at a certain level, which a set of common basic statements (in Popper's sense) and hence with some common semantic categories." Lena Soler, *Rethinking Scientific Change and Theory Comparison: Stability, Ruptures, Incommensurabilities?* (Dordrecht, Springer, 2008), 13.

An illustration is in order to show how Pannenberg's hermeneutical method can be played out. Pannenberg chooses to work with a field theory. This theory fits well with his theo-scientific paradigm because it enables him to show that the universe as a whole is undergirded by "non-embodied" causality, which in turn, explains why God is active in this world working as "spirit" all the while God's action in this world can be understood in light of natural events.[72] This is Pannenberg's way of interfacing observability (e.g., the causality of God) with unobservability (e.g., the non-embodiment of God). According to Pannenberg, in the past, the God-world relationship was conceived primarily in two ways. On the one hand, God and the world interacted in an atomistic manner, in which there is no possibility of the intermingling of the two. On the other hand, God and the world were associated ideally as God is often perceived as *Nous*, a rational principle (e.g., nonembodied causality) that has no "real" counterpart in this world. For Pannenberg, these two options create a false dichotomy. God can be both non-atomistic all the while being related empirically to nature if we consider God the Spirit as the divine field of activity.

According to Pannenberg, God can be ontologically related to the physical field because God as all-embracing reality must be connecting himself to the world and everything else in it through this irreducible unifying reality of field.[73] In this way, Pannenberg affirms the Christian tradition of the universal scope of God's economy. For Pannenberg, there is even a degree of fertility evinced by its usefulness in the study of biology and social sciences, reaffirming that the field is the underlying

---

[72] Rodney Holder makes a useful comment about theologians' use of the field theory. He writes, "[T]he field concept (as developed from Faraday onward) allows for the nonmaterial to act at a distance since fields permeate the whole of space; indeed, for Faraday the field became primary and bodies were particular concentrations of field lines. This is better for theology both from the nonmaterial aspect and because it was antireductionist, the whole now acting on the parts." He later adds about Pannenberg's use of the field theory. "Pannenberg links the dynamic work of the Holy Spirit to this concept of field, and theologically God grounds the whole of creation. Here, Hefner remarks, Pannenberg's addition to scientific knowledge is the insight that the 'largest field of all, which embraces all of reality, is God.'" Rodney Holder, *The Heaven Declare: Natural Theology and the Legacy of Karl Barth* (West Conshohocken: Templeton Press, 2012), 133-134.

[73] Wolfhart Pannenberg, "God as Spirit—and Natural Science," *Zygon* 36/4 (2001): 783-825.

structure of our existence.[74] Without a doubt, he recognizes that God is involved with everything in this world as he creates, recreates, and renews life. However, there is a catch. Scientific theories that explain the reality of field are only analogical and provisional. It cannot explain the full scope of the all-embracing reality of God. Consequently, the field theory has to move beyond science into the deeper level of theology.

In the process of appropriating field theory for the explanation of God's action in this world, Pannenberg contends that there is a semantic change from science to theology. He points out this process as he addresses Polkinghorne's criticism. Polkinghorne severely chastised Pannenberg for using the scientific concept of field as the basis for the theological development of pneumatology. According to Polkinghorne, Pannenberg has confused what is spiritual to what is natural. He writes, "It is important to note that [field] energy is not a kind of *spiritual* concept. Einstein's famous equation, $E = mc^2$, asserts the materiality of energy as much as it does the energetic character of matter."[75] In other words, when scientists refer to the concept of "field" they are not concerned with any religious spirituality or religious spiritual entity; rather, they simply refer to a physical entity called "field," "such as Maxwell's electromagnetic field" that functions like particles and matter. [76] Polkinghorne at best could grant Pannenberg to use the language of field in a metaphorical way, denoting its "extended relationality," though it may undermine the precise language of science.

Pannenberg in reaction to Polkinghorne's comment notes that,

the interpretation of the pneumatic essence of God's divinity as a field can be applied to the undivided unity of space and time that precedes all geometric description. It is thereby at the same

---

[74] Wolfhart Pannenberg "Spirit and Energy in the Phenomenology of Pierre Teilhard de Chardin" in *Beginning with the End: God, Science, and Wolfhart Pannenberg*, eds. Carol Rausch Albright and Joel Haugen (Grand Rapids: Eerdmans, 2008), 76.

[75] John Polkinghorne, "Wolfhart Pannenberg's Engagement with the Natural Sciences," *Zygon* 34 (1999), 154.

[76] Ibid.

time distinguished from physics' concepts of field but should be regarded as the precondition for them.[77]

Hence, there is a significant difference between the scientific use of field and that of theology without losing continuity between the two. Furthermore, Pannenberg says that theologians can re-appropriate the term "field" for a theological use because it is a metaphor. Although it is a metaphor, it is not a vague analogy since it has an empirical correlate. "The reason is that space is the minimal requirement for any notion of field," and "in theological use, talk of God the spirit in terms of field also implies a connection with the concepts of space and time, though different from their use in physics."[78] Hence, because both field concepts in theology and science are underwritten by reality, that is, the real relations between things in space and time, they are compatible, at least, unequivocally and non-univocally.

Despite Pannenberg's explanations, his use of a metaphorical extension moving from science to theology has been strongly opposed by contemporary scholars. [79] What seems to be troubling for contemporary scholars is that Pannenberg may have conflated theology and science into a non-distinguishable single matrix of field, and as a result, in the process of interfacing theology and science, the Christian God is explained away by our understanding of science. For instance, Michael Chiovene notes, "Because he understands God's essence to be intimately linked with [cosmic] history, it appears that Pannenberg may be compromising God's transcendent aseity."[80] Similarly, Paul Molnar suggests that Pannenberg has made "God dependent on [cosmic] history."[81] More directly, John Cooper finds Pannenberg flirting with the idea of panentheism because God has been treated as the underlying

---

[77] Pannenberg, *The Historicity of Nature*, 37.

[78] Ibid., 67.

[79] For example, see Holder, *The Heavens Declare*, 120-136.

[80] Michael L. Chiovene, *The One God: A Critically Developed Evangelical Doctrine of Trinitarian Unity* (Eugene: Pickwick, 2009), 165.

[81] Paul Molnar, "Toward a Contemporary Doctrine of the Immanent Trinity: Karl Barth and the Present Discussion," *SJT* 49 (1996), 328.

structure of nature.[82] The problem lies perhaps in Pannenberg's unique idea of God's revelation that is associated with cosmic history, so it is necessary at this point to examine more closely Pannenberg's idea of revelation.

Pannenberg's Reformulation of Revealed Theology

A close examination of Pannenberg's work reveals that Pannenberg adheres to a unique idea of revelation. In what way is Pannenberg's conception of revelation unique? If we compare the works of Pannenberg and Barth, we can see the unique features of Pannenberg's work. So allow me in this section to briefly compare the works of two theological giants in our time. I begin with Barth.

For Barth, the doctrine of revelation is closely aligned with that of Augustine. He ties the notion of God's self-revelation to Christology. In other words, God reveals himself in and through Jesus Christ. Without Jesus Christ, insists Barth, human beings are hopelessly lost and will not be able to find God nor have any knowledge of him.[83] It seems that, for Barth, Jesus Christ is the ultimate frame of reference by which God's being in act and God's act in his being are to be interpreted, and for this reason, Barth can only affirm that, because it is God who has revealed himself in Jesus, all knowledge of God should begin from God to the world, not vice versa. We can categorize Barthian understanding of revelation under the rubric of revealed theology.

There are a few salient characteristics of revealed theology. First, as Hugh Mackintosh has pointed out, the knowledge of God "comes by revelation; otherwise we should be committed to the incredible notion

---

[82] John Cooper, *Panentheism, the Other God of the Philosophers: From Plato to the Present* (Grand Rapids: Baker, 2008), 260-275.

[83] So in this regard, he denies any possibility of natural theology. Barth writes, "Natural theology is the doctrine of a union of man with God existing outside God's revelation in Jesus Christ. It works out the knowledge of God that is possible and real on the basis of this independent union with God, and its consequences for the whole relationship of God, world and man." Karl Barth, *Church Dogmatics*, ed. G.W. Bromiley and T. F. Torrance (Edinburgh: T&T Clark, 1957), 2:168.

that a man can know God without His willing to be known."[84] It is God who comes to us and reveals himself to us. We on our own cannot approach God. God, in essence, is unapproachable. It is God who has freely entered into the realm of space and time that we are now able to relate ourselves to God. Second, God's self-revelation is an act of grace. As Barth notes, it is God's free act of giving himself to us.[85] It is a gift. Although God is the object of our worship, he became a subject of our relationship. This condescension of God is well recognized through the Incarnation and the cross. The ministry of Jesus Christ is the genuine display of God's love and mercy. In his love for the lost world, the only begotten Son has sacrificed his life in exchange for eternal life for the many. Third, God's self-revelation is a miracle.[86] It is not a natural outworking of what the creation reveals. God has to come into the world not out of necessity, but out of love. The world is not an extension of God. There is an infinite qualitative difference[87] between God and the world. Hence, God's entrance into the world is not natural; rather, it is a miraculous event. It should not have happened according to the natural flow of history, but it did, and this is so because God has overcome the world. For this reason, God's revelation must be accepted in a leap of faith. The implication of Barthian revealed theology is well summarized by Stanley Grenz:

> Knowledge of God is not an innate capacity within human nature or experience, but is possible only because God graciously gives it in Jesus Christ who is both God and human. One either "sees" Jesus Christ as the Way, the Truth, and the Life, or one does not. There is no proving this truth. In fact,

---

[84] Quoted from Alister McGrath's *Christian Theology*. Alister McGrath, *Christian Theology* (Malden: Blackwell, 2007), 153.

[85] Barth, *Church Dogmatics*, 2:315.

[86] Ibid., 198.

[87] Barth writes that "if I have a system, it is limited to a recognition of what Kierkegaard called the 'infinite qualitative distinction' between time and eternity, and to my regarding this as possessing negative as well as positive significance: 'God is in heaven, and thou art on earth.' The relation between such a man and such a God, is for me the theme of the Bible and the essence of philosophy." Karl Barth, *The Epistle to the Romans*, trans. Edwyn Hoskyns (Oxford: Oxford University Press, 1933), 10.

every attempt to prove Christ borders on idolatry, for it calls
God and his revelation before the bar of human reason.[88]

This means that Barth's revealed theology completely isolates itself from
the encroachment of natural theology that we see in the modern
theological developments.[89]

Surely for Barth, there is no such thing as the "innate" knowledge of
God. We are not naturally oriented toward God. According to Barth, the
point of contact between God and human is never determined by the
human side; rather, it is God who comes to us and reveals himself to us
in and through Jesus Christ. If there is an innate knowledge of God, it is
merely a reflection of our own self. The claim of innate knowledge, in
Barth's judgment, is the fallout from modern anthropocentrism. What
we need is "a pure heart, eyes that have been opened, childlike
obedience, a life in the Spirit, and rich nourishment from Holy
Scripture."[90] For this reason, Barth unequivocally places his theology
upon the doctrine of justification by faith alone. It is by faith that we
come to Christ, not by our own merit.

---

[88] Stanley J. Grenz and Roger E. Olson, *20th Century Theology: God and the World in a Transitional Age* (Downers Grove: Intervarsity Press, 1992), 69.

[89] Barth makes a succinct counterargument about the modern theologian's tendency to wed the God of creation to creation itself. "Our first point is simply that although this new work takes place within the sphere of the creation and continuous preservation of the world, it is still a special work, and not directly coincident with the other. Nor can it be understood merely as the continuation and crown of the work of creation (as Schleiermacher would have it) although it certainly is this as well; for necessarily God the Creator is alive and active in it, continuing and completing His work. On the contrary, God so surpasses Himself in this new work that it is only here that He can really be known, as it were retrospectively, as God the Creator. Between us and God's being and action as the Creator, there stands our sin and rebellion by which we have forfeited our life as His creatures and our fellowship with Him as our Creator, and perverted our knowledge of Him. The real Creator and Lord of the world is not the principle of the beginning or origin or real essence of all things. If we identify God with this principle, we forget that we have fallen away from God and we repeat and confirm our apostasy by erecting an idol. The real Creator and Lord of the world is the One, and only the One, who befriends us in our very apostasy from Himself, and who in doing so, in confirmation of His creation, has done to us something new and more than creation itself. It is in and by the special act that we recognize the general, and not vice versa. We have to do with a special act of God to us, corresponding to the special nature of our apostasy, and in this special act we have to do with the really immutable." Barth, *Church Dogmatics*, 2:506-507.

[90] Grenz and Olson, *20th Century Theology*, 68.

Hence, for Barth, theology is not in the business of proving things for God. He rejects the idea that theologians' vocation is apologetic, defending the faith with the use of reason.[91] This type of theological approach tends to see God in a manner that is determined by human possibilities. In other words, God is subsumed under the rules and principles of human reason. This is an impossible task, contends Barth. God is mysterious. He does not fit neatly into the rational criteria that human beings have formulated through the use of different sciences. God is transcendent and unapproachable. So, Barth maintains that, if we try to fit God into a pre-programmed human agenda, then we will diminish the uniqueness and specialness of God's self-revelation. McGrath writes in this regard, "If knowledge of God can be achieved independently of God's self-revelation in Christ, then it follows that humanity can dictate the place, time, and means of its knowledge of God."[92] If this is true, then God simply turns into an expression of our own desires and wants. Barth is certainly trying to eschew such an anthropocentric approach that will ultimately veil God's true being and act in the world.

What this contention leads to is Barth's suppression of God's general revelation. For Barth, all God's revelation is "special" because "any revelation which is not 'in Christ' becomes an idol by making competitive claims for the knowledge of God. And any revelation of God which is not redemptive is not a revelation at all."[93] Indeed, if "God's revelation is exclusively 'in Christ,' then there is no theological basis for general revelation."[94] Barth adds, "Jesus Christ, as He is attested to us in Holy Scripture, is the one Word of God, whom we have to hear and whom we have to trust and obey in life and in death," and because of this, "we condemn the false doctrine that the Church can and must recognize as God's revelation, other events and powers, forms and

---

[91] Barth, *Church Dogmatics*, 2/121.

[92] McGrath, *Christian Theology*, 166.

[93] Cited in Gregg Strawbridge, "Karl Barth's Rejection of Natural Theology or an Exegesis of Romans 1:19-20," A paper presented at the 1997 Evangelical Theological Society Meeting in San Francisco.

[94] Ibid.

truths, apart from and alongside this one Word of God."[95] He also declares,

> And if we really do know the true God from his creation without Christ and without the Holy Spirit…how can it be said that the *imago* is materially "entirely lost," that in matters of the proclamation of the Church Scripture is the only norm, and that man can do nothing towards his salvation?[96]

Due to Barth's incessant occupation with the special revelation fulfilled in Christ, there was no room for general revelation in his theological program.

In contrast to Barth's suppression of general revelation and the denial of natural theology, Pannenberg presents a highly polished form of the theology of nature. He claims that God truly reveals himself through nature and history and God's revelation is not "special" or "private" that could be discerned only through pietism; rather, it is "general" and "public" that could even be discerned through the study of natural sciences. For this reason, drawing from Wilhelm Dilthey and Hans-Georg Gadamer, Pannenberg contends that the validity of theological statements must be confirmed within the widest possible context of meaning, which has the potential to include the whole scope of reality, because if we continue to privatize theology, it is going to lose its relevance in the modern world. He writes,

> The price of restricting creation theology to the "repetition" of biblical statements on the subject was that it could no longer be clear to what extent the biblical creation faith applies to this world in which today's humanity lives, and to the world described by the modern natural sciences.[97]

---

[95] Barth, *Church Dogmatics*, 172.

[96] Karl Barth, "No!" in *The Living God: Readings in Christian Theology*, ed. M. J. Erickson (Grand Rapids: Baker Book House, 1973), 132.

[97] Pannenberg, *The Historicity of Nature*, 25.

Essentially Pannenberg is saying that because God is the all-embracing reality, it is reasonable for us to correlate God to all aspects of what goes on in the history of the world.

Is Pannenberg advocating a natural theology like panentheism? This is a tricky question that needs a thorough qualification. Like Barth, Pannenberg rejects natural theology, a belief that we can know God without the aid of God's self-revelation. He declares that "God can be known only if he gives himself to be known."[98] This is the essentially same declaration made by Barth that God reveals himself to us, not that we reveal God on our own.[99] The difference between Pannenberg and Barth becomes apparent when Pannenberg asserts that "the revelation of God must thus attest itself by human experience and natural phenomena as the deity shows itself to be personal in both."[100] What this entails is that the "presentation of Christian teaching cannot begin by presupposing its truth."[101] Rather, "it must face the contesting of the reality and revelation of God in the world."[102] So for Pannenberg, although faith plays a critical role in the expression of theological themes, theological arguments must provide evidence that has the potential to "'prove' the reality of God and the truth of Christian doctrine, showing them to be consistently conceivable, and also confirming them, by the form of presentation."[103]

However, for Barth, the proof of God's revelation is not possible. He writes,

> Thinking we can prove this in some sense, we should really betray the cause, or rather betray the fact that we have confused this cause with some other…We must accept the fact that only

---

[98] Wolfhart Pannenberg, *Systematic Theology* (Grand Rapids: Eerdmans, 1988), 1:189.

[99] Barth, *Church Dogmatics*, 1:10.

[100] Pannenberg, *Systematic Theology*, 1:222.

[101] Ibid., 50.

[102] Ibid.

[103] Ibid., 60.

the Logos of God Himself can provide the proof that we are really talking about Him when we are allegedly doing so.[104]

Is then Pannenberg betraying the doctrine of revelation by asking theologians to show evidence for God's being and act in this world? I believe that Pannenberg is not betraying the doctrine of revelation set forth by Barth. In fact, he is upholding Barth's requirement because he is claiming that we are not proving God, but God who is proving himself as he reveals himself to us. For Pannenberg, God is the all-determining reality, and he is related to and relatable to all aspects of reality since all things owe their existence to God and his continuing sustenance and *creatio continua*. In this respect, God is "proving" and "confirming" his own existence by interacting with his creation as the Creator, and because of God's "general" and "public" engagement, it is possible for us to unveil the divine act and being by examining reality in its widest spectrum possible.

Based on the anthropic evidence, Pannenberg proves his idea of God's universal touch. He contends that "in the history of humanity there has always been in some form of an explicit awareness of God which is linked to the experience of the works of creation."[105] What Pannenberg is saying is that, contra Barth, in his interpretation of Romans, there is an inherent continuity between religious consciousness and our experience of nature as God's creation. Our sense of the infinite God is universal, for all human beings have the "unique freedom" to "move beyond every regulation of his existence"[106] and connect to the "indefinite infinite, of a mystery of being which transcends and upholds human life."[107] Once again, even at this point, Pannenberg emphasizes that such intuition of the infinite is not a matter of faith or innate, but arises from our experience of and critical engagement with the finite

---

[104] Barth, *Church Dogmatics*, 1:161.

[105] Pannenberg, *Systematic Theology*, 1:117.

[106] Wolfhart Pannenberg, *What Is Man? Contemporary Anthropology in Theological Perspective* (Indianapolis: Fortress, 1970), 3.

[107] Pannenberg, *Systematic Theology*, 1:117.

things in the world. [108] For this reason, according to Pannenberg's conception of revelation, natural knowledge of God is a real possibility.

Pannenberg's reformulated natural theology takes us to the next question. If Pannenberg is right to say that all human beings have the ability to know God by studying the things of nature because they are inherently open to God, what is the need for special revelation (e.g., Jesus and his saving act)? Is Pannenberg dismissing salvation-history? Pannenberg does not diminish the value of what he calls "a special history inside the general history of man." [109] He understands the uniqueness of salvation-history. He writes, "It is true, however, that not all events of history are in the same way relevant for the question of salvation, for the question of the wholeness of human life. Here may lie the real point of truth in the position that Salvation-history is characterized by a particular 'line' of events within general history." [110] What he objects is that our attempt to separate salvation-history from general history and treat salvation-history as a radically different history that creates a gap in the entire spectrum of cosmic history. Accusing Oscar Cullmann of making this mistake, Pannenberg asks, "Does God work only in this [salvation-history] 'line' and not also in the other events of [cosmic] history? And is not every act of God, who is love, related in one way or another to the salvation of man?" [111] So, for Pannenberg, it is unthinkable from a theological perspective that salvation-history is disconnected from cosmic history. Here again, we need to ask, does this imply that Pannenberg is committing the fault of reading God from nature?

To reiterate, for Pannenberg, God is known because he has freely decided to reveal himself and act in the world he has created. God's revelation takes priority in Pannenberg's work. We can say for certain

---

[108] Pannenberg, *The Historicity of Nature*, 155. He writes that "even religious awareness can grasp the universe only through intuitions of finite things and states of affairs" and "each intuition is seen as a part of the whole and thus as a revelation of the whole."

[109] Pannenberg, "Salvation-History," translated by Ed. Miller, *The Iliff Review* 37 (1980): 21-25.

[110] Ibid., 24.

[111] Ibid.

that Pannenberg rejects any possibility of a theology based on pure reason.[112] But contra Barth, Pannenberg has decided to do more for theology. In order to eschew the privatization of theology, he has reformulated revealed theology in such a way that theology is now, to borrow McGrath's words, "understood as a demonstration, from the standpoint of faith, of the consonance between that faith and the structures of the world."[113] Pannenberg presupposes the existence of God. Hence, "the search for order in nature is, therefore, not intended to demonstrate that God exists, but to reinforce the plausibility of an already existing belief."[114] However, Pannenberg does not simply want to make theology a mere assertion, but an assertion that is backed up by evidence. So, in Pannenberg's idealization of theology, faith and evidence go hand in hand. He is opting for justified faith, rather than blind faith, which of course, is what fideists ultimately want to defend.

Even when Pannenberg says that there is the possibility of the natural knowledge of God because human beings have the capacity to transcend themselves and able to connect to God intuitively, he is not devaluing the need for special revelation. Our intuitive capacity to know God is vague. It is not explicit. Hence, our natural knowledge in and of itself is always limited, underdetermined, and provisional. It needs to be driven by more explicit expressions found in the Christian systematic presentation of God. Simply put, if we are to draw concentric circles for Pannenberg's conception of revelation, there are three circles that move from natural sciences to human sciences and finally arriving at God's revelation that supervenes and connects all other areas of study. In other words, Pannenberg's theory of God's revelation consists of a series of divinely inspired events, related through a progression from the lower level scientific activities to higher levels of anthropological and theological studies for the sake of unveiling the saving event of the cross and the resurrection of Christ, which is at the center of cosmic history.

---

[112] Pannenberg, *Systematic Theology*, 1:107.

[113] McGrath, *Christian Theology*, 168.

[114] Ibid.

Thus, for Pannenberg, the goal is to move beyond the boundary of each concentric circle. In fact, this push for the threshold crossing accords well with the nature of human beings. According to Pannenberg, humans are made to transcend and be open to the wider world. When we refuse to move beyond the bounds of empiricism that natural sciences tend to focus on, we will never be able to cross over to the study of human sciences upon which we can tackle the metaphysical implications of scientific theories from a hermeneutical and anthropic perspective. So, in light of what Pannenberg has said, such reductionism is going against the grain of becoming a true human. Likewise, when we refuse to move beyond the bounds of anthropocentrism and remain focused on the self and human possibilities, we will be locked in the world of subjectivism and unable to see beyond ourselves, simply grounded in the human nature alone. We must cross the threshold of anthropocentrism and move into the world of divine life.

What we need is a holistic, open-ended approach that is able to pursue something deeper, wider, and higher. We need to keep in mind that God as the all-embracing reality canvasses the entire spectrum of the world; therefore, if we are to be connected to God, we ought to recognize that nature, human, and God are inseparable categories of our study—it is theology's task to correlate them to one another. This is the core of Pannenberg's reformulated revealed theology. He is essentially reformulating Barthian revealed theology and turning it into a theology of nature. He has, in fact, merged special revelation and general revelation into a single unified theology of nature, juxtaposing them as inseparably linked categories of theology. Indeed, we need both as attested by B. B. Warfield.

> Without general revelation, special revelation would lack that basis in the fundamental knowledge of God as the mighty and wise, righteous and good, maker and ruler of all things, apart from which the further revelation of this great God's

interventions in the world for the salvation of sinners could not be intelligible, credible or operative.[115]

In the final analysis, Pannenberg's work has demonstrated that revealed theology does not necessarily isolate itself from the study of nature and man. Rather, the aim of revealed theology is to embrace all of them if we are to stay connected to the all-embracing reality of God. Theology in this respect is a science. Hence, like any other scientists, Pannenberg believes that theologians should not follow the way of theological absolutism, fundamentalism, or fideism, as claimed by Moore. In this light, we are now in position to present a counterargument that will address Moore's concerns for associating theological realism with scientific realism. In the following section, I also add a comment about McMullin's theory of God's atemporality and show that it may be too reductionistic to depict God's transcendence simply in terms of his atemporality.

Countering Moore's Claims

Let's begin with Moore's criticism that theological realism cannot merge with scientific realism because it cannot provide the same context of verification as that of science. My question to Moore is: Why does theology need to provide the same context of verification as that of science? As we have seen from Pannenberg's work, even though theology is cross-fertilized with science, it does not necessarily hold to the scientific requirement of verification. Following Kuhn's idea of normal science, Pannenberg believes that each science, e.g., theological science or natural science, has its own context of verification that may or may not correspond to its counterpart. Indeed, if we were to force theology to follow the verification principle of natural science, then theological science is reduced and restricted to natural science. As Moore has pointed out, theological science is not natural science. Neither is natural science theological science. Thus, the theological

---

[115] B. B. Warfield, *The Inspiration and Authority of the Bible* (Phillipsburg: Presbyterian & Reformed, 1948), 75.

context of verification should be different and unique to that of the scientific context of verification.

Having said this, we still need to show that theology's own verification categories if it is to be correlated to scientific realism. Going back to Pannenberg, we know that, since theology is concerned with God, who is the unified field of reality that covers the vast spectrum of history, the theological context of verification is much wider than natural science. It stretches from nature to God. It consists of the whole history of the cosmos. Hence, theology has to consider the real-life setting as its context of verification, from the experience of day-to-day life, to the investigation of natural events, and finally reaching out to salvation history particularly revealed in and through Jesus Christ. The task of theology is then to show that "Christian teaching must be coherent with all aspects of the reality of the world and all of human life."[116] What this implies is that theological realism is sustained by the dual scientific discipline: that is, the study of nature as it is investigated with the help of natural and human sciences and the study of God as it is investigated with the help of theological science.

What about McMullin's theory of the atemporality of God? Pannenberg has shown that we do not need to speak of God's atemporality in terms of his pure transcendence. God is transcendent and yet immanent. He is the all-determining reality who embraces the whole of creation in the field of relations. This begs the question. Is Pannenberg removing God's eternity at the expense of his emphasis on God's involvement with the world as a unifying reality in the field of relations? Actually, Pannenberg is not marginalizing God's transcendence at the expense of God's immanence, which is the McMullin's main concern. Niels Gregersen confirms this by stating that for Pannenberg,

God is not thought to be an empirical object, as if God existed as one item among others (within the world or beyond the world). Rather God is assumed to be real and effective by being the creative source, but informs, pervades, and surrounds

---

[116] Pannenberg, *The Historicity of Nature*, 7.

everything that exists... The reason is not that God is an absent reality but that God is the encompassing reality, "the one in whom we live and move and have our being" (Acts 17:28).[117]

So, unlike McMullin, although we can emphasize that God is transcendent, we cannot dismiss the fact that God is involved in every aspect of the creaturely process as its Creator and Sustainer. Going back to the concept of the accommodating absolute, we can see that God remains who he is in himself even though he is related to the world of temporality.

Moreover, the idea of eternity, unlike McMullin, cannot simply be equated with the notion of atemporality. The concept of atemporality, even if it really exits, is meaningless because such a thing could only be speculated as non-active, non-being, or non-influential, which has no connection to the temporality of this world. For Pannenberg, it is better to conceive the notion of eternity in terms of God's full embrace of all time: past, present, and future. Because God embraces all reality, he is intimate to all creatures at any moment in history. In this vein, God acts in this world not simply in a deterministic way, but in the manner that befits the one whose time is comprehensive, always guiding the natural process to produce something new. Surely, timeless God is meaningless for us. Rather, it is better theologically to conceive of God who is able to embrace a wide spectrum of time.

The next question we should tackle is: can God be tested? Pannenberg unequivocally states that God cannot be tested, for,

it would be contradictory to his divinity, as the all-determining reality, if he were to make himself available to human beings as a finite reality, reproducible at any time and at will, so that human propositions could be measured against him. God's reality whatever else he might be is not accessible in this way.[118]

---

[117] Niels Henrik Gregersen, Introduction in *Pannenberg's The Historicity of Nature* (West Conshohocken: Templeton, 2008), xvi.

[118] Pannenberg, *The Historicity of Nature*, 16.

As I hinted before, what can be tested is not God, but the implication of God's involvement in this world. More clearly, what we can test in theology is not God himself, but our understanding or statements about God. Since the theological statements about God involve "a systematic presentation of the Christian doctrine of God, of creation, and of human history in terms of a history of salvation,"[119] we must review them in light of theological studies of the Bible, scientific studies of nature, and cultural studies of human life. What brings them together is realistic coherence. So, in this respect, it is safe to say that Pannenberg's realism is a sort of coherentism.

If God is the unified field of reality that encompasses all reality in this world, albeit God does not belong to the world, then there must be a harmonious relationship between these realities, and when we view them in a holistic way, we will be able to unveil the deeper underlying structure of reality that God is involved with; this is precisely the task of theology and metaphysics, which is to generalize the particular views of realism, while combining the works of natural science and human science so that we may have a unified view of reality, which for Pannenberg, without theology, is not possible. Thus, the testing criterion for theology is coherentism. If theology coheres to the realistic vision of other sciences, then theology is fulfilling its duty as a member of the greater scientific society.

Furthermore, given that God is the all-determining reality, theological theories are always underdetermined. In Pannenberg's project, we have seen that all theological theories are underdetermined by data, that is, they can never fully describe God's reality, nor can they be empirically adequate to configure the being as an act of God. God is always bigger than what we can conceive of him. In addition, no theological model can express itself without being accompanied by philosophical and scientific data. Theology is not a stand-alone exercise. It demands interdisciplinary assistance. For this reason, theological programs are always tentative and provisional, waiting to be confirmed and cohere to other sciences. Besides, how can they be able to capture

---

[119] Ibid., 7.

the work of God's creation, which is not a completed affair but something that is on-going? As we have seen in Pannenberg's work, because God is at work in all areas of life, there is variation and spontaneity that can never be captured with a simplistic understanding of reality. God's involvement with reality is too grand, and because of it, our understanding of God's action in this world is always underdetermined.

This is a complete denial of Moore's argument that theological realists cannot talk about underdeterminism of theology. Theological statements can be hypothetical. Pannenberg notes, "Each Christian doctrine remains a hypothetical reconstruction of the universal coherence of the phenomena of God's creation with the theological assumptions concerning the Creator."[120] Because theological statements are hypothetical in nature, they are criticizable based upon the data gleaned from the study of biblical exegesis, human science, and natural science. In this way, we can avoid the error of treating theological statements as absolute or dogmatic. Indeed, theological presentations and examinations of the real-life settings can never be the absolute demonstration of Christian truth. For this reason, theology is a public exercise. Van Huyssteen succinctly summarizes this point.

> The task of a Christian theology is no less than to rethink the Christian tradition in his universal scope. Exactly because God, according to the biblical traditions, has revealed himself in the public realms of history in nature, theology cannot insulate itself behind holy texts and church doctrines, nor hide itself behind havens of piety.[121]

Does this mean that theological realists ought to avoid the absolute category of theology, that is, their faith statements? No. Surely, for Christians, confessional statements are non-negotiable and axiomatic. However, in our discussion of correlating two realisms, what we are focusing on is not the fideistic aspect of theological statements, but the testable statements of theology. Theological statements contain at least

---

[120] Ibid., 8.

[121] Gregersen, "Introduction," xvi.

two hermeneutical implications. One is theoretical and the other fideistic.[122] The theoretical dimension is the one in which we can treat it as a hypothesis, whereas the fideistic dimension as the core belief that sustains the Christian worldview. In Lakatos' language, the theoretical statement is the auxiliary hypothesis that can be tested, and once it is proven to be a successful theory, it can be used to support the hard-core belief system of theology. For example, if we say that Jesus is our God and Savior, we can test the theoretical aspect, that is, the various testimonies of Jesus' miraculous healings that affirm Jesus' messianic ministry, which is the secondary theory of Christian faith. What underwrites both hard core and auxiliary theories is the underlying reality, in this case, Jesus Christ, which unifies and interprets given data.

In the final analysis, what I have attempted to show in this section is that, by drawing upon Pannenberg's work, theological realists do not necessarily follow the way of absolutism as contended by Moore. Moore's understanding of theology is found to be overly reductionistic, treating theology as simply fideistic and ignoring the possibility that theology has another side that is observable, underdetermined, and fallible. In dialogue with Pannenberg, we have found that Moore's understanding of theology is not necessarily the only one. What remains then is the finalization of metascience. Thus, in the final section, combing the works of McMullin and Pannenberg, I outline the contours of metascience and show that theological realism and scientific realism can be correlated by way of metascience. Furthermore, I introduce the usefulness of the metascientific program in the way we cross-fertilize theology and science.

Metascience and Its Implications

What is metascience? Oxford Dictionary defines it as "inquiry into the methodology and philosophical implications of scientific

---

[122] For more details, please see the discussion of the relationship between faith and reason in the following chapter.

investigation."[123] From an interdisciplinary perspective, metascience is an overarching conceptual, methodological bridge that links theology and science without marginalizing the integrity of each discipline. In a nutshell, metascience is an interdisciplinary method undergirded by an integrative realist frame of reference. As stated here, since metascientific interdisciplinarity is undergirded by "integration" and "realism," I investigate each of these categories in detail to highlight its main features and characteristics. First, I start with an integrative feature of metascience.

When we talk about integration, we normally think of the way in which we fuse two competing theories (e.g., one from theology and another from science) and conflate the two so that the weak theory (perhaps, a theological creation theory) is subsumed under the dominant theory (e.g., a scientific evolutionary theory). This is not what metascience is all about. A metascientific integration entails the preservation of differences even while the peculiarities and individualities of each discipline are incorporated into a larger whole in the process of integration. Contra Hegel, it does not seek to generate an abstract form of one-size-fits-all synthesis that could combine the thesis and its antithesis into a unifying *tertium quid*.

Avoiding totalizing tendencies of integration, metascience merges the two standing theories in a complex way. What does it mean to be complex? Useful here is an analogy of changing tires of a bicycle. To change a bicycle tire, we would start by reading a given instruction that we find in the manual that teaches us how to change a tire. If we follow the given instruction to the letter, we expect to solve the problem. With the predetermined set of instructions, we are expected to complete the given task. However, we find that, from the actual results, the instruction from the manual does not produce the "exact" outcome. We are often faced with unexpected results, and in the case of changing a bicycle tire, we may need to spend several hours wrestling to fit the tire

---

[123] Oxford Dictionary, accessed March 12, 2016, https://en.oxforddictionaries.com/definition/metascience.

to the rim with various tools and methods that were not suggested by the instruction.

Of course, there may be an instance in which the instruction may work, and we can produce precisely the same result that is noted in the manual, especially for those who are "good with hands." However, what is more realistic and common is that, even for those savvy experts, there is no guarantee that a combination of expertise, skill, and the detailed interpretation of the instruction would lead to a successful result or a predicted outcome promised by the manual, although it may produce a higher rate of success than the effort of an inexperienced individual. More often than not, this is what actually happens in a scientifically controlled experiment whereby we approach as researchers perform complicated interventions.[124] As many working scientists would admit, scientific experiments do not always produce the results according to the preset formulas, procedures, and expectations. When our model does not work, we assume that something has gone wrong or is lacking, so we go back to the drawing board and search for other possible solutions. The end solution may be simple, but to arrive at a simple solution, scientists must go through a complex process.

Likewise, when we try to patch several non-relatable things together to locate their interrelated meaning, we should not expect a simple outcome. Rather, it would be more natural to see a complex network of ideas intermingling to play its unique role in the unveiling of the true picture of reality out there. In this respect, metascience has a dual heuristic function that involves both the negative and positive operation of science. The negative heuristic produces tensions and frictions that reveal not only the polarity of the two disciplines but also the areas of weaknesses in each discipline's conceptual framework. For instance, a scientific model of evolution reveals nature's own independent ability to generate new species through the mechanism of "natural selection." Such a model is antithetical to the traditional view of the Christian

---

[124] Cf. Joseph A. Maxwell, *A Realist Approach for Qualitative Research* (Los Angeles: Sages, 2012).

creation narrative, which stands on the belief that all creative efforts are attributed to God. The theory of evolution thus plays a negative heuristic for the creation narrative. It not only points out a different view but also discloses the weak spot of the traditional Christian creation narrative, which does not account for the "independent" status of natural processes. Based on the negative heuristic, the scientific model can also function as a positive heuristic. The positive heuristic of the theory of evolution gives theologians a good reason to develop a revised theological concept such as the "evolutionary" creation narrative that speaks of "propensity for increased complexity as built-in and intended by God."[125]

Furthermore, due to the complex nature of the metascientific interface, the transfer of metaphors from science to theology is not only possible but also involves a thorough redescription of scientific metaphors.[126] This is because, as Gregersen has noted, the complicated interface that is built upon the chain of different metaphors gleaned from theology and science involves the transfer from the scientific context to the theological context with a change in the actor-level and the level of the means.[127] For instance, if we claim that God (the actor) has intended for the world to have an evolutionary propensity for increased complexity, then we know that the scientific language of "evolution" has merged with theology except for the fact that the actor has been assigned to "God" rather than to "nature." Likewise, the means by which God acts is an "evolutionary propensity," which was not specified by the traditional Christian doctrines. However, there is a strong caveat to which theology must be attentive in such a conceptual transfer. Gregersen notes, "God possibly could create and transform in other ways than the game of selection (and does so, according to Judeo-Christian doctrines of creation, on both the physical and psychological

---

[125] This is precisely what Peacocke had done for his interdisciplinary program. See Arthur Peacocke, *Theology for a Scientific Age: Being and Becoming—Natural, Divine and Human* (London: SCM, 1993), 152-157.

[126] The term "metaphor" is used generally here to include theories, models, and concepts.

[127] Niels Henrik Gregersen, "A Contextual Coherence Theory," in *Rethinking Theology and Science: Six Models for the Current Dialogue*, eds. Niels Henrik Gregersen and J. Wentzel van Huyssteen (Grand Rapids: Eerdmans, 1998), 214-215.

level)."[128] In other words, the transfer of metaphors from science to theology carries all the "natural" implications of what evolution can do and accomplish, all the while theology refuses to be subsumed under science as the "evolutionary" theory does not exhaustively describe the divine action. Again, the rule of irreversibility applies to prevent natural theology to dominate the theology and science interface. We cannot make deductions "from the nature of selection to the nature of God."[129] For this reason, a thorough redescription is in order, but again, with a caveat.

A redescription from science to theology should never be done univocally or reductively. More clearly, a redescription should not write up a grand theory or a one-size-fits-all paradigm that erases the complexity, differences, and uniqueness of each system, whether it be God, humanity, or nature. Nor should it reduce God, humanity, or nature, to a single rubric of philosophical-naturalist conception such as "evolution" or "physicalism." A redescription from a metascientific point of view needs to preserve not only the uniqueness of each system but also each system's capacity to call forth the order of increased complexity. In this way, a redescription operates with a sufficient room to think of God, humanity, and nature, as co-operating partners producing "increasing complex levels of the emergence of life within the biological domain, each interacting with its environments in various ways."[130]

For this reason, the integrative feature of metascience always operates on the assumption that the world is complex and only a complex methodology may correct the error of riveting science or theology to a single matrix of philosophy. In short, the complex and open structure of metascience, as an interdisciplinary method, drives the correlation between theology and science. What is unique to this method

---

[128] Ibid., 214.

[129] Ibid.

[130] Amos Yong, "*Ruah*, The Primordial Chaos, and the Breath of Life: Emergence Theory and the Creation Narratives in Pneumatological Perspective," in *The Work of the Spirit: Pneumatology and Pentecostalism*, ed. Michael Welker (Grand Rapids: Eerdmans, 2006), 198.

is that scientists are continually encouraged to move beyond one-dimensional thinking, taking into consideration metaphorical extensions that may help even theologians provide a meaningful description of God's action and being in the world vis-à-vis the process of redescription. Hence, the general tenor of metascience is based on the belief that creation is potentially open to higher realities, seeking something that lies beyond its limited context.

Indeed, to be open is to move into a higher and complex level of reality. From an anthropological perspective, man "is always open further, beyond every experience and beyond every given situation" to fulfill an "indefinite obligation."[131] Due to its openness to a higher level of reality, metascientific rationality considers theoretical and metaphysical entities as the possible means to open up theology and science to each other in an attempt to unveil the full scope of reality. It helps both theology and science to acknowledge that reality is multileveled and relatable.

Next, metascience is not only complexly integrative but also underwritten by a realist correlation. To say that there is a realist correlation is to say that first and foremost there exist entities that are mind-independent and distinct from our perception. Real entities, in turn, provide the ontological reference to our conceptual statements. This type of realism is called critical realism. Joseph Maxwell notes in this regard:

> Critical realists thus retain an ontological realism (there is a real world that exists independently of our perceptions, theories, and constructions) while accepting a form of epistemological constructi-vism and relativism (our understanding of this world is inevitably a construction from our own perspectives and standpoint).[132]

But critical realism needs further qualification since, as Elizabeth Frazer and Nicola Lacey contend, "even if one is a realist at the ontological level,

---

[131] Pannenberg, *What Is Man*, 8-9.

[132] Ibid.

146

one could be an epistemological interpretivist...our knowledge of the real world is inevitably interpretive and provisional rather than straightforwardly representational."[133] Surely, there are scholars, who tilt the scale and lean more toward the side of epistemological constructivism such as van Fraassen, denoting that reality as we know it, especially with regard to the unobservable, is a byproduct of our own construction devoid any real ontological value.

Certainly, critical realism has been playing the mediating role for the theology and science interface for many decades, and it was the heartbeat of the theology and science dialogue. However, with its popularity came a wide use by scholars in the field of natural and human sciences. Maxwell provides a list of different versions of critical realism:

> "experiential" realism (Lakoff, 1987), "constructive" (and, later, 'perspectival') realism (Giere, 1999), "subtle" realism (Hammersley, 1992a), "emergent" realism (Henry, Julnes, & Mark, 1998), "natural" realism (Putnam, 1999), "innocent" realism (Haack, 1998, 2003), and "agential" realism (Barad, 2007).[134]

It has been split into so many different versions that we cannot make a difference between which part of it is "critical" and which part of it is "real." In order for us to salvage critical realism for today's use, we must remove anti-realist sentiments that are attached to it. This is precisely what the realist correlation of metascience seeks to accomplish. It takes stock of today's realism and filters out "anti-realist" inclinations so that we can preserve a robust ontological claim of science, as what we have seen in the work of McMullin.

In light of what we have discussed concerning the correlation between scientific realism and theological realism, I list here two key characteristics of the metascientific realist correlation. First, metascientific realism holds that theoretical entities, although not

---

[133] Maxwell, *A Realist Approach*, 5.
[134] Ibid., 4.

directly observable, are part of the real world if they have a real referent. For instance, we can say that a theoretical entity such as gravity and electrons are real because they are referring to a real event in nature. Anthropologically, human social interactions are real since various social systems do exist, and they are responsible for the complexity of historical events such as the dialectics of war and peace. Theologically, the divine action is real because God's creation and redemption are taking place in space and time in and through Jesus Christ and the Holy Spirit. Therefore, theoretical entities are not just conceptual; rather, they are real, although they may not be testable directly like other empirical objects such as trees and rocks. Moreover, contra instrumentalism, theoretical entities are not just useful in the interpretation of what has taken place. Rather, they hold real values in and of themselves because they have the potential to not only refer to actual entities but also unveil the underlying patterns of reality, for they often lead us to explain the complex outworking of natural and social processes.

Second, metascientific realism endorses the concept of "complex realism" in both natural and theological sciences, a concept that replaces modern philosophy of causation such as monism or panentheism. The concept of the complex outworking of reality is an alternative to the regularity theory of causation, which "holds that causality consists simply of regular associations between events or variables, patterns in our data, and denies that we can know anything about supposed 'hidden' mechanisms that produce these regularities."[135] By contrast, from a metascientific realist perspective, the concept of regularity is not necessarily the most fundamental order of the universe, although it is a part of complex particularization. New things can come about and have different causal powers. For instance, the causality in the quantum world is distinct and unique to that of the macro world. In a complex mode, the world process is not just chaotic, nor is it just uniformly patterned. Reality is somewhere in the middle, between chaos and uniformity. In other words, reality is not a closed system that can be restricted to either the theory of chaos or the theory of uniformity.

---

[135] Ibid., 9.

Reality is more uncontrollable and highly complex that may involve both regularity and irregularity to explain its underlying structure. For this reason, as Tony Lawson has argued, demi-regularities better describe the open structure and process of reality. "A demi-regularity… is precisely a partial event regularity which prima facie indicates the occasional, but less than universal, actualization of a mechanism or tendency, over a definite region of space-time."[136] It is not that regular patterns do not exist, nor the regularity is so common that they exist everywhere and universal. Rather, the regularity does happen, but often it is accompanied by unexpected events. From the perspective of metascience, we can learn from both. We learn from the outcomes of our expectations and formulations based on regularity we have become accustomed to; also, we learn from the outcomes that are novel and unconventional.

Metascience in this respect rejects empirical constructivism, which stands on the claim that the term "reality" implies that there is a single way to make a description of this reality as in the case of van Fraassen's empirical adequacy. Although constructivism creates enough room to consider a variegated interpretation of reality within the scope of empirical adequacy, it does not do full justice to multiple realities such as theoretical, social, and theological realities. Metascience fills this gap by exploring the possibility of seeing reality from many different perspectives. In fact, metascience is underwritten by stratified reality.[137]

From a metascientific perspective, reality is stratified because, in the emergent world, there are things which are dependent on one another, as well as there are things which are more fundamental than others. For instance, a social system is depended on the psychology of the individual, and individual psychology is dependent on the biological system underpinning the psychological developments. This is not to say that what belongs to biology is the same as that which belongs to psychology or sociology. Psychology is more "complex" than biology,

---

[136] Jonathan Pratschke, "Realistic Models? Critical Realism and Statistical Models in the Social Sciences," *Philosophica* 71 (2003): 13-38.

[137] For more details on the stratified reality, see Alister E. McGrath, *The Order of Things: Explorations in Scientific Theology* (Malden: Blackwell, 2006).

because the study of cells and subatomic particles does not reveal exhaustively the nature and function of human psychology. To specify human psychology as just a form of actions undertaken by subatomic particles is to deny the complexity and emergent characteristics of reality. Nonetheless, if fundamental things are taken away in the hierarchy of being, then the thing-in-itself ultimately loses its meaning.

As Joseph Maxwell contends, against the anti-realist claims, this type of method does not shift reality "from the empirical world to the realm of imagery and conception…because the empirical world can 'talk back' to our pictures of it or assertions about it—talk back in the sense of challenging and resisting, or not bending to, our images or conceptions of it."[138] In other words, if we are led by the nature of reality, it is more natural to read worldly processes in terms of its complex features (e.g., a stratification of things) rather than in terms of a single matrix such as empirical adequacy that could only side with restrictive paradigms such as naturalism and physicalism. What we need to recognize here is that the relationship between a method and reality must be determined by reality itself. That is, we should locate a method that is determined by the complex nature of reality, rather than force-fitting reality into a predetermined method that may be restricted to a single level of rational activity.

Even if metascience generates a multi-dimensional outlook and opens up one conceptual system to another in order to make a transition to a wider conceptual system, there is a real connection between different conceptual systems.[139] This is due to the fact that, in an emergent ontology, things come together to create a novel phenomenon or meaning from the most basic level of reality. A good example is the variety of ontological status that water carries in the different levels of rational activities. At the elemental level of chemistry, water is depicted with the metaphor of two hydrogen atoms and one oxygen atom that are joined by covalent atomic bonding. At the most basic level of the

---

[138] Maxwell, *A Realist Approach*, 10.

[139] For instance, see Thomas F. Torrance, *Theological Science* (Oxford: Oxford University Press, 1969), 261–62.

macro world, water is simply denoted as the accumulation of water molecules, visible to the naked eye as water droplets. At the hydrologic cycle level, water is seen as a cyclic process that evaporates as steam, condenses as precipitation, and collects precipitation on the ground to be evaporated again. At the organic level, water becomes the agent that sustains life as drinking water for animals and human beings. At the philosophical level, water is the material constituent of all things, at least for an ancient Greek philosopher, Thales. At the theological level, water is metaphorically used to represent Jesus Christ as the "living water" or the "spring of water welling up to eternal life" (Jn. 4:10-15). Despite the fact that in the particular setting water is depicted uniquely that fits the context of that setting via redescription, the reality of water is the common denominator that sustains continuity between different conceptual systems. Hence, all areas of study, even philosophy, and theology, have a realist correlation to lower level scientific activities, and consequently, they have the responsibility to interface with science in order to create a holistic realist paradigm that metascience demands.

In sum, metascience acknowledges that human rationality most effectively advances when it is driven by the study of the underlying structure of reality in a progressive way. It can progress from the past to the future as it recognizes the importance of past achievements, and at the same time, new theories are valued in an attempt to fill the gap left behind by old theories. It is progressive also because the operation of our realist consciousness propels scientific questions of elemental levels into philosophical and eventually theological levels, moving from the study of the particular dimension of reality to a more general and coherent view of reality. This means that metascience always points to something beyond what is empirical and observable. It may not just rely on the answers derived from the empirical method. Rather, it may go beyond the bounds of science to the world of metaphysics and theology. Hence, the theoretical entities that are unobservable play a heuristic role in the development of a congruent realization of different realist visions between theology and science.

Furthermore, because human rationality relies on the belief that "something like the entities and structure postulated by the theories actually exists," metascience is always underdetermined. All theories and models are tentative and provisional. They wait for further discoveries and conjectures that stem from the rigorous attention to reality out there. Therefore, a metascientific framework defies the concept of absolutism. Our statements about reality out there are never settled. They are in the process of being confirmed by new discoveries and observations. In this respect, metascience allows enough room for tensions to spring forth, competing theories to vie for prominence, and rigorous research programs to exist in search of better data and theories that would propel science to a deeper level of understanding. In the final analysis, metascience must frame all human rational activities with its categories of observability, unobservability, underdetermination, and progressive fertility. Before I move to the next chapter, I list five pertinent ways that may assist theology and science to correlate by way of metascience.

1. Metascience provides an interdisciplinary "method" that drives the correlation between theology and science. What is unique to this method is that the correlation starts from scientific realism to theological realism. Scientific realism underwrites theological realism, not vice versa. There are two reasons, one scientific and the other theological. Scientifically, we cannot deny the fact scientific theories have advanced so much that they have unveiled many hidden dimensions of reality. It has been exemplary in the way we ought to correspond and cohere our concepts to actual events and realities in the world. Theologically, the reality of nature has not been studied in a particular way, and theologians have neglected the realist agenda that modern science has proven to be successful. However, what metascience adds to this correlation is that science needs to be stretched beyond one-dimensional thinking and account for its metaphorical extensions as well as metaphysical implications that may even provide a meaningful description of God's action and being in the world. Due to its openness to a higher level of rationality, metascientific rationality considers theoretical and metaphysical entities as the possible means to open up theology and science to continue their efforts to unveil the full scope of reality that is inclusive of the unobservable, without leaving the

empirical ground upon which it stands. It helps both theology and science acknowledge that reality is multileveled and yet relatable.

2. Metascience not only has the potential to underwrite an interdisciplinary method, but also functions as a mediating agent that opens the channel between theology and science. Since theological realism cannot approach scientific data directly, it is required to read scientific theories only at the general level. At the general level, theologians can re-appropriate scientific theories for the theological use and interpret them based upon their potential metaphorical and metaphysical implications. Since we have moved into the world of metascience, theoretical statements are no longer "precise" but sufficiently "vague" as they address philosophical and hermeneutical investigations. The vagueness of general terms, however, does not dismiss the precise meaning of scientific theories, because all meta-scientific terms are referenced to reality, which correlate to the successful theories of science.

3. Metascience can sustain a healthy balance between what is general and what is particular, which is very critical to the theology and science interface. There is a negative role of metascience (e.g., the movement to particularity) and a positive role of metascience (e.g., the movement to generality), and they are complementary. The negative role of metascience tends to prevent a complete reduction of the scientific realist perspective to theological particularities, and vice versa, all the while the positive role opens each scientific metaphorical implication of the particular to a wider community such as theology upon which a new use of the term is emphasized in a general way. The negative role of metascience thus accentuates the non-unitive categories of two realities, such as God and nature, whereas the positive role of metascience stresses the integrative and relatable reality of theology and science.

4. Since metascience brings the scientific realist perspective into the world of theology, a process of "translation" can assist theology to interlace with science. The translation entails a metaphorical extension. This hermeneutical imagination is underwritten by the creative activity of the human mind that complements the productive and reproductive

nature of interpretation. This does not mean that metascientific extensions are antirealistic. It is not necessary for hermeneutical inference to follow constructivism or idealism that limits an imaginative effort as a mere world-making process that has no real component attached to it. Rather, hermeneutical inference propelled by metascience is highly realistic.[140] It is driven by the realist orientations of both science and theology. In science, we let our minds fall under the compulsion of its objective reality, and in theology, our models could only point to the reality that God is involved with, and ultimately reveals the way he stands as the all-embracing reality. Although grounded on this realist commitment, theological realism and scientific realism are still in the process of affirming "something like the entities and structures postulated by the theory actually exist."[141] Hence, it is still in the process of affirming its realist programs. Data, as described and interpreted by theology and science, are provisional versions of reality and that data themselves demand more physical and metaphysical disclosures, which have not yet transpired.

5. Finally, because metascience runs with the engine of analogy, theology and science are likely to compete while theology taking advantage of scientific discoveries and preventing science to be reductionistic. As I have noted previously, the analogical relationship between two opposing poles of theology and science is sustained by the dialectics of similarity-in-difference. This analogical relationship recognizes the threefold conceptual and methodological translation between theological realism and scientific realism: (1) an analogy may say something similar and yet more than the original conceptual device; (2) an analogy may say much less; and (3) an analogy may say something completely different. [142] This analogical consonance and dissonance between theology and science, therefore, reveal what it

---

[140] Torrance writes, "If we are to really understand anything in a true and faithful way we must let our minds fall under the compulsive self-evidence of its objective reality and its intrinsic intelligibility. Only as our minds are seized by the essential nature and truth of things are we able to respond to them in rational conceptual judgments." Thomas F. Torrance, *The Christian Frame of Mind* (Colorado Springs: Helmers & Howard, 1989), 109.

[141] McMullin, "A Case for Scientific Realism," 26.

[142] Pannenberg, *The Historicity of Nature*, 151.

might mean for metascience to demonstrate that, although theology may lay claim of science, the theological use of scientific theories is only analogical and tentative. Even if they are tentative and provisional, theology can certainly, in a progressive way, thanks to scientific advancements, develop a more sophisticated version of the theology of nature that can unveil how God acts in this world.

Concluding Remarks

In this chapter, I demonstrated that theological realism and scientific realism are correlatable by way of metascience. In this way, theological realism is analogically supported by scientific realism all the while it reinforces key methodological criteria of scientific realism such as underdetermination and un/observability that are driven by reality itself. My reliance upon metascience essentially avoids the direct correlation between two realisms. If we were to directly correlate theology and science and their corresponding realist positions, at least one adverse outcome is foreseeable. Theological realism could be confused with scientific realism. If theological realism is confused with scientific realism, the uniqueness of theological explanations will be marginalized, and theistic assumptions will turn into simple naturalistic propositions.[143]

Metascience provides a way out of this dilemma by allowing two realisms to be related indirectly, or more precisely, at the level of *meta-science*. In this way, theology can lay claim of scientific realist justifications such as the argument supported by underdetermination or fallibilism, without either marginalizing theological contents such as God's action in the world or the scientific empirical continuum between the observable and unobservable. Hence, the metascientific approach

---

[143] Teilhard de Chardin and Frank Tipler are two exemplars of a direct correlation. See Pierre Teilhard de Chardin, *The Divine Milieu* (New York: HarperCollins, 1960); and Frank Tipler, *The Physics of Christianity* (New York: Doubleday, 2007). The direct correlation could only confuse the two. In the case of Teilhard, the theory of evolution is conflated with the theology of creation thus leading to panentheism, and in the case of Tipler, the biblical narrative of resurrection turned into a theory of physics. The direct relations between two realisms will destroy the unique realist features of theology and science.

defies Moore's ultimatum that we have only two choices, either to correlate two realisms and fall into the error of turning theology into natural science or accept the non-commensurability of the two and build theological realism solely on faith knowledge.

Through this study, we can see now that theological statements should not necessarily be considered merely axiomatic, absolute, fideistic, non-cognitive, or dogmatic. Rather, we can perceive that theology has a genuine dimension that is underdetermined, fallible, inferential (hermeneutically), realistic, and provisional. In this way, theology may be forced to take seriously theology of nature as a fundamental and ontological criterion for Christian doctrines, crossing my boundaries with science and living amongst the vast array of scientific scholars; indeed, as Pannenberg once quipped, this is what a realist theologian ought to do in the 21st-century. This does not mean that theological realism should be entirely built upon scientific realism. As Moore has pointed out, the God of redemption also plays a key role in identifying the reality of God and his action in this world. We have to recognize at this point that scientific realism is indispensable only in our understanding of the "reality" of nature, upon which a theology of nature can be constructed. To borrow the term from Bernard Lonergan, the correlation between theological realism and scientific realism involves more the intellectual conversion and less religious conversions, though an intellectual conversion is a gateway to religious conversion.

At this juncture, since we are at the midpoint, it is appropriate to add a brief comment concerning what is to be expected in the next two remaining chapters. What I have done thus far is to discuss the problems that are associated with the theology and science interface from the side of natural science. In Chapter One, the discussion of nature provided the starting point of merging God and nature without resorting to naturalistic reductionism or absolutism, and in Chapter Two, scientific realism provided a means for theology to rethink about theological realism that ran afoul to the grains of the old received view of metaphysical realism. Hereafter, especially in the following two chapters, I will shift my focus to two specific theological categories, namely, faith and miracles, to demonstrate that they can function as mediating categories to connect theology and science. Some difficulties associated with this approach are immediately apparent.

Theological categories such as faith and miracles, ironically, have been tabooed in the ethos of scientific society. The warfare model that highlights the conflict between science and theology rests on precisely the propensity of scientists to argue against the theologians' reliance on faith and miracles. As far as faith is concerned, modern scholars such as W. V. Quine see no use for it, because science is not "answerable to any suprascientific tribunal, and not in need of any justification beyond observation and the hypothetical-deductive method." [144] Faith assumptions that are heavily biased are considered stumbling blocks to neutral and value-free science. Similarly, as far as miracles are concerned, modern scholars like Rudolph Bultmann dismiss it as an ancient, outdated, obsolete way to express the world in which we live. According to Bultmann, it has to be treated as "symbols" that can be decoded through existential philosophy. For this reason, the discussion of "faith" and "miracles" do not occupy a large space for the theology and science dialogue. Thus, in an attempt to recover these neglected dimensions of theology, I will bring them to the forefront of the interdisciplinary conversation, and carefully unveil their usefulness and applicability for mending the broken pieces of human rationality.

---

[144] W.V. Quine, *Theories and Things* (Cambridge: Harvard University Press, 1981), 72.

Chapter Three

Faith as Third Rationality

In a large Pentecostal church close to where I live, hundreds of Christian believers gather every Sunday to praise and worship God. Even with a quick glimpse, I often see an exhilarating display of Pentecostal spirituality within the walls of the newly built church sanctuary. There are loud cries of joy. People jump up and down, dancing on the red carpet in front of the altar. The air of excitement is very contagious. Once a few "jumpers" start the engine, the majority of the audience is quickly energized and creates one large deafening noise of shouts and singing. The choir, the band, and the church members all join together in an unrehearsed, spontaneous act of worship.

Streams of tears flow in the midst of the inexplicable moments of ecstasy. They are seized by the pain of sin and express their misery through intense groaning. A few of them drop to the floor claiming that they are healed miraculously by the power of the Holy Spirit and the blood of Jesus Christ. The surrounding fellow worshipers cheer for them with an unceasing chorus of praise and thanksgiving. Soon, a new kind of noise is introduced. People begin to shout in unknown tongues. The Pentecostals are speaking the language of heaven, a gift of the Holy Spirit as denoted in 1 Corinthians 12:10. For them, tongues are clear signs of the encounter with the transcendent God. Without any rational explication, the tongue-speech tells the partakers of the worship that God is present and active in their lives.

Sitting in a pew and watching this free expression of Pentecostal piety, I cannot but wonder how two different contexts can co-exist in today's urban life. On the one hand, we have the majority of common citizens who go about their daily lives without any regard for what goes on inside the church. They are quite comfortable and dismissive of religious spirituality, for all conveniences of life have been provided by the advancement of technology. On the other hand, despite the technological sophistication, spiritual Christians like the Pentecostals have a keen sense of the Holy Spirit. They claim that the encounter with the Spirit often takes place in unanticipated ways, strange and even terrifying perhaps, especially in their most sacred moments.[1] Of course, Pentecostal spirituality does not represent the entirety of Christianity, but it does exemplify one form of Christian life that is starkly different than the ordinary way of secularity in the 21st-century. These two antithetical ways of life bound to clash.

The clash of the two forces of our culture is evident when we are dealing with health issues. For the members of Pentecostal communities of faith, there has always been a tension between receiving healing from spiritual sources and receiving medical treatments from the doctors. Although a recent poll reveals that Pentecostal ministers are interpreting modern medical science as "a God-given blessing," nonetheless, as Amos Yong rightfully notes, "at the present time and at least in some [Pentecostal] circles, there remains the concern that overreliance on medicine will undermine authentic faith in God."[2] This is due to the fact that Pentecostal believers appeal to "faith" healing more so than medical technology. For this reason, during the early years of Pentecostalism, "many sectarian Pentecostal groups, especially in the rural parts of America, rejected medicine and relied solely on the healing power of God, sometimes resulting in the loss of life."[3]

At first glance, a problem of faith can be detected. Faith is seemingly guiding the believers to a wrong path, the path that leads away from scientific knowledge, and as a result, there is the issue of irrationalism. Paul Tillich has warned about a faith-driven irrational behavior and charged Christians to avoid the confusion of subjective overexcitement with a genuine spiritual experience, whatever that genuine spirituality might be.[4] As a matter of fact, the history of Christianity is littered with

---

[1] Frank D. Macchia, "Tongues as a Sign: Towards a Sacramental Understanding of Pentecostal Experience," *Pneuma* 15/1 (1993): 61-76.

[2] Amos Yong, *The Spirit of Creation: Modern Science and Divine Action in the Pentecostal-Charismatic Imagination* (Grand Rapids: Eerdmans, 2011), 6.

[3] Ibid., 5.

[4] Paul Tillich, *Systematic Theology* (Chicago: The University of Chicago Press, 1973), 93.

hostile attitudes toward ecstatic religion that prefers "subjective faith" over "objective reason."[5] Does this mean that faith is purely subjective and untrustworthy? Can "faith" co-operate with reason? Is faith reasonable? Can faith have a similar status of objectivity as reason?

These questions are not new. They have been with us for centuries. However, with respect to scientific rationality, there is a need to revisit the issues related to the interplay of faith and reason. We will need to recast the questions in light of faith's relationship with the modern form of scientific rationality. Can science, including philosophy of science, tell us anything about the nature of faith? If so, how should we define and clarify the nature and function of faith for the contemporary world? Is faith rational? Is it below or above reason? Can faith claim any knowledge? Do we need faith in the scientific world?

In this chapter, I will address these questions, and at the same time, attempt to show that faith is an integrative faculty of the human mind that does not counter or fall under reason but supplements it in such a way that faith and reason provide the basis for a holistic and comprehensive vision of human rationality. I also note that faith is "third rationality" in order to show that faith does not fit neatly into the category of either objectivity (first rationality) or subjectivity (second rationality). Before I flesh out in detail the meaning of faith as third rationality, I investigate the works of Augustine, Descartes, and Kant, respectively, and show why a modern man wants to keep faith and reason separated.

A Historical Survey of the Faith and Reason Relationship

The faith-reason dichotomy follows a long, tumultuous path that stretches from the beginning of ancient philosophy to the modern technological era. For this reason, the faith-reason debate has a history of its own. It is imperative for us to retrace this past, for without it, we would lose our way around in the great maze of this controversial topic.

---

[5] Cf. Stanley M. Burgess, *The Holy Spirit: Ancient Christian Traditions* (Peabody: Hendrickson, 1984).

So we begin with a brief historical survey. As with any other historical survey, I select a few representative figures and their contributions to the debate, namely, Augustine, Descartes, and Kant. Augustine represents the Christian view of faith. He is a good interlocutor for this section because he outlined the premodern idea of faith and its relationship to reason-abled exercises, that is, theology and philosophy. Descartes represents modern philosophy that moved beyond the premodern preoccupation with religious faith and began the systematic dissociation of faith from reason in order to think more about our reason-abled exercises of the mind. And finally, Kant represents the modernist catalyst, who gave the modern world a final push to move into the untested sea of postmodernity with a renewed emphasis on the subject rather than the object, thereby finally creating a clean break between faith and reason. I follow their ways and show the gradual separation of faith and reason.

Augustine: Faith over Reason

The Western Christian theological system has a long history of mingling with Greek philosophy. Such tradition continues to this day.[6] Christian theology in the contemporary world owes its structure and starting point to Greek philosophy, or at least, a modified form of Greek philosophy. Based on the interactive dynamics of working with its handmaid—e.g., Platonic or Aristotelian philosophy—Christian theologians, starting with the patristic period, began to lay the foundation of Christian philosophy. One of the pioneer figures in this area is Augustine. His work is extensively discussed and still finds relevance in today's theological circles because it provides clear and innovative ways to flesh out key theological issues that still haunt Christian believers to this day.

Augustine's work is constitutive of a complex network that interweaves Christian theological topics with Greek philosophical thoughts. It cannot be reduced to a simple strain of the theological or

---

[6] This trend can be traced in the work of panentheists and panpsychists. See Chapter 2.

philosophical system. However, there are distinct philosophical colors that Augustine bears, from which we can begin our discussion. First, he befriended Platonic philosophy with which his theological project was developed.[7] Aristotelianism will come back later in the work of Thomas Aquinas, but in Augustine's days, Platonism was the trend. Augustine's love affair with Platonic philosophy did not begin until his break with Manichean philosophy. In the early years, Augustine was interested in the work of Manichean dualism.[8] Manicheanism is a fourth-century version of Gnosticism. It is more explicitly dualistic than other Greek writings in the sense that Manicheans saw two eternal realms competing with each other. There was the kingdom of light and the kingdom of darkness. The light is good and the darkness evil. The light is the light of reason and the darkness is the confused world of material existence. Manicheans believed that the eternal conflict between good and evil, that is, between light and darkness, took place in such a way that, when the kingdom of light sent the son into the world of darkness, this light was captured and imprisoned in the body. However, when he was persecuted to his death, the body turned out to be a mere phantom. In other words, it was not real. In the end, the victim was raised from the dead, and triumphed over the evil. Therefore, for Manicheans, the body was evil and the way to salvation was found in the light of reason. They had to escape the body in order to find true knowledge.

Augustine may have been attracted to Manichaeism early in his life, but soon, he left the camp because Manichaean dualism had no hope of the victory over evil as the two antithetical kingdoms are locked in everlasting battle. He could not accept the idea of human beings reduced to mere pawns in an everlasting conflict that ultimately had nothing to do with humans from the beginning. One thing that really helped him get beyond Manichaeism was Platonic philosophy.

---

[7] Gerald J. P. O'Daly, *Augustine's Philosophy of Mind* (Berkeley: University of California Press, 1987), 189.

[8] A substantial discussion of Augustine's mingling with Manichaeism is provided by Kam-lun Lee. For more details, see Kam-lun Lee, "Augustine, Manichaeism and the Good" (PhD diss., St. Paul University, 1996).

Augustine details why he followed the ways of Plato in *The City of God*.[9] Here, he finds no reason to promote Manichean corporeal negativism; instead, Augustine sides with Platonic two loves.[10] First, there is the love of the things below, and second, the love of the things above. In the Neoplatonic scheme, there is a desire for the things below which causes the soul to be enslaved by the body. And the escape vis-à-vis an intermediary level on which the intellect resides is possible. It is the intellect that delivers the corrupted desires of the flesh to see the things above. This is the way of Neoplatonic hierarchism.[11] Augustine adopts the story of the two loves but he dismisses the idea that the intellect is the one that saves us from corruption. For Augustine, this is not the source where the hope lies. Our hope is found in Jesus Christ. Therefore, he makes necessary modifications to fit Plato into his Christian faith paradigm.

Augustine attacks the Manichaean doctrine by stating that flesh or body is not the locus of evil. He declares, "We ought not, therefore, to blame our sins and defects on the nature of the flesh, for this is to disparage the Creator. The flesh, in its own kind and order, is good."[12] If our body is not the source of corruption, then why is the flesh so inclined to sin? Augustine gives a short answer. "[B]ecause the will has sinned, the hard necessity of having sin has pursued the sinner."[13] As R. C. Sproul explains, Augustine is arguing that "the freedom that remains in the will always leads to sin. Thus, in the flesh we are free only to sin, a hollow freedom indeed. It is freedom without liberty, a real moral bondage."[14] If free will is enslaved to sin and is in bad shape to seek justice and righteousness, could reason save the day?

---

[9] Augustine, *Concerning the City of God against the Pagans*, trans. Gerald Walsh (New York: The Catholic University of America Press, 2008), Book VIII.

[10] Augustine, *Confessions*, trans. Henry Chadwick (Oxford: Oxford University Press, 2008), Book II.

[11] Stanley J. Grenz, *The Moral Quest: Foundations of Christian Ethics* (Downers Grove: Intervarsity Press, 1997), 135-140.

[12] Augustine, *City of God*, 356.

[13] Augustine, *On Man's Perfection in Righteousness*, 10.

[14] R. C. Sproul, "Augustine and Pelagius," Ligonier Ministries, 1996, accessed November 12, 2016, http://www1.gospelcom.net/HyperNews/get/tt/ttsubrc-06-96.html.

Still, Augustine is not convinced. For him, reason is not exempted from the bondage of a misdirected will, although he speaks highly of human *ratio*.[15] He esteems reason because he bears the burden of the intellectual weight he inherited from the Platonic theistic tradition. Like Plato, Augustine believes that to make sense of any theological statement philosophical contemplation is inevitable. In fact, he argues that Greek philosophy is very close to the Christian truth. Robert Cushman notes in this regard, "Augustine reads Plato as teaching that the 'supreme God visits the mind of the wise with an intelligible and ineffable presence.'"[16] This is why Greek philosophers had knowledge of the existence of God. Their philosophical residence was not too far from that of Christian theologians.

In this respect, according to Augustine, reason is pre-eminent.[17] It defines the image of God, which is the human capacity to be a partaker of the divine nature.[18] Cushman insightfully refers to Augustine's understanding of reason in the following way. "For even in man's fallen condition, his reason is exalted by the divine informing, so that God is the light by which are known whatsoever things are known, temporal or eternal."[19] It is almost as if Augustine is trying to tie together the notion of God's prevenient grace with the universality of reason when he said that we are born with the capacity to think and reason, because, without it, there is no way for us to apprehend not only the power of God but also the beauty and wonder of the universe. Augustine reasons that "I cannot be recollected if absolutely forgotten. If I now find you [God] not in my memory that I am unmindful of you and how shall I find you if I do not remember you?"[20] So, even if we are blinded by sin, such deficiency in us should never erase our capacity to see God and his handiwork, though we see them fuzzily and partially.

---

[15] E.g., Augustine, *Confessions*, 302.

[16] Robert E. Cushman, "Faith and Reason in the Thought of St. Augustine," *Church History* 19/4 (1950): 271-294.

[17] Augustine, *Soliloquies: Augustine's Inner Dialogue*, Book I, 7.

[18] Augustine, *On the Trinity*, Book XIV, 8, 11.

[19] Cushman, "Faith and Reason," 276.

[20] Augustine, *Confessions*, X, 17. Cited in Cushman, "Faith and Reason," 280.

What Augustine wants to say is that there is a general conception of knowledge that is innate to human beings. The capacity to reason is not learned, though learning greatly improves its skills. In this sense, a reason-abled apprehension informs our mind *a priori*. He likens this act of intuition to mathematical experience. "Mathematical propositions are valid because derived *a priori* not *a posteriori*," and "man's memory contains 'the reasons and innumerable laws of numbers and dimensions,' none of which has been imprinted on the memory by any sense of the body."[21] Hence, Augustine sets the stage for Descartes' rationalism to take root in the modern period. Augustine's preference over *a priori* intuition over against sense data is rather a raw form of rationalism that gives hints to Descartes to choose rationalism over empiricism. Perhaps, the correlation between Descartes and Augustine is due to their adaptation to Socratic and Platonic philosophy, since Socrates and Plato are known to follow a deductive reasoning process as opposed to empiricism championed by Aristotle.

However, a question arises. Why do we need faith if we have a divinely given reason which is given to everyone that has the ability to seek out the light of God? For Augustine, reason has its limits.[22] What we need to recognize is that Augustine has some reservations about the world of imperfection. The world of imperfection is what Plato had called the world of appearances, which is an imperfect shadow of the true form, and obviously, there is a gap between the true form and its appearance. Likewise, there is an "infinite qualitative difference" between God and creation, and Augustine could not allow this gap to be closed upon by reason alone. Reason, as it belongs to the human being, is natural. As Cushman notes, reason has "its starting point either in the bodily sense or in the intuition of the mind."[23] It follows then that what is of nature cannot reach out to what is of God without the aid of

---

[21] Cushman, "Faith and Reason," 277. Cf. Augustine, *On Free Choice of the Will*, II, 12, 34.

[22] Cushman, "Faith and Reason," 271.

[23] Ibid., 282.

divine revelation. For Augustine, God is essentially beyond the reaches of human capacity.

Besides, as I have said before, reason has another problem, that is, the problem of the corrupted will misleading it to its demise. According to Augustine, the intellectuals in his own days searched for God, but the God they pursued was not the God of the Bible. Each person seemed to hold his or her own ideas of God, and as a result, there were numerous gods competing for prominence in his day. For Augustine, the rise of polytheism was a clear sign of perversity—human beings are so corrupt that they are not seeking the one true God but a god that fits their likings.[24] The key byproduct of such perversity is the sin of pride. According to Augustine, we are not seeing God, but we are seeing ourselves. We are supplanting God and erecting our own image instead. We are treating ourselves as a divine figure. We have become obsessed with ourselves, and such a coercive inclination comes from man's own will.

It is critical to note that Augustine locates the area of corruption not in our reason-abled faculty of the mind but in the will of man. He explains this by tracing the origin of sin to Adam.[25] Augustine interprets the Genesis Fall narrative in terms of Adam failing to move his will to do the right thing. For Augustine, free will essentially was a gift from God to put to good use. It was free insofar as it had the power of perseverance to know God, and simultaneously, it had the power of the "perverse elevation" that desires self-reliance, which eventually deserts the good, all the while losing the intimate touch with God. The perversion of free will in the end trapped Adam and made him a slave of sin, becoming free from righteousness but enslaved to sin. Consequently, for Augustine, our goal should be to become a slave of righteousness making us free from sin.

The effect of Adam's sin did not end with Adam, as far as Augustine is concerned. Adam's wrong use of his free will has trickled down to his descendants and to all human beings who, thereafter, are bequeathed

---

[24] Augustine, *City of God*, X, 18.

[25] Augustine, *On the Free Choice of the Will*, III, 93.

with the same problem. Our free will is dysfunctional and this problem is universal. It does not function properly, and as a result, we all suffer from the ills of exaggerated desires and appetites that veil the holy and perfect image of God. The final implication of Augustine's analysis is that, although reason is not the problem, it is nonetheless adversely affected by the broken will. Reason is not as clear as it should be. There needs to be a cleansing solution to regain the light of the mind so that we can clearly see the things that we cannot see now. For this purpose, Augustine turns to faith.

Cushman succinctly identifies the salient features of Augustine's understanding of faith. "It is acknowledgment (*agnitio*) of the word of the servant. Preeminently it is love awakened by the lowly form of the historical. It is fundamentally the motion of the heart. It is the conversion of the will through the crumpling of pride."[26] Let me flesh out what this statement means. When Cushman says that Augustine's faith involves acknowledgment, he is actually talking about Augustine's emphasis on the movement of the will. This is differentiated from intellectual activities. The former denotes that the way in which we act and decide based on our desires, and the latter is a conscious mental action that leads to knowledge. So cognition is based on knowledge whereas acknowledgment is based on the consent of the will. In other words, for Augustine, faith is a matter of the heart and reason is a matter of the head. What moves the heart is love, that is, the most powerful faculty of the human mind. So faith is driven by the highest affective power, which is love. Love is the antidote that heals the sickness of selfishness and the sin of pride, which in turn, reorients our *ratio* to function properly.

Going further, for Augustine, love is particular in the sense that it is oriented toward Jesus Christ, and ultimately, to the triune God.[27] Why is he taking us to the God of the Trinity? In Augustine's judgment, reason itself does not lead us to the God of the Trinity. At best, it points to the God of the Greek philosophers. Certainly, the God of the Greek philosophers does not accord to the full version of the Christian story

---

[26] Cushman, "Faith and Reason," 293.

[27] Augustine, *On the Predestination of the Saints*, VIII.

nor is it the religion that leads us to Jesus Christ our Savior. In fact, Augustine insists that the doctrine of the Incarnation is an offense to Greek philosophers.[28] For Greek thinkers, Jesus, a mere man, could not be consubstantial to God the Father. Jesus, if he is God at all, must be a mere appearance of the God of the eternal kingdom of heaven. As the Greek philosophers could not cross the philosophical threshold and pass the theological gate into the kingdom of God due to their high view of reason, Augustine insists that an extra push is necessary, and faith is potentially capable of achieving this goal.

According to Augustine, because there is a great schism between our knowledge of God and what God enlightens us through faith, we need a new light that will inform our mind to see what the knowledge of nature does not see. This light is the Eternal Logos.[29] The divine grace that has come into our own existence has to break the bondage of sin that distorts our will; otherwise, according to Augustine, we can never be able to trust our knowledge. The knowledge of nature in many cases obscures God in such a way that we are unable to distinguish God and ourselves. What Augustine wants us to do is to turn away from our fallen condition that relies on the light of creation, to the light of God that shines brightly against the backdrop of the worldly darkness. The language of turning away reveals the intentional movement of the will that defies Adam's original turning away from God. Our turning away from the world and to God is what faith actuates. In this respect, what we can see is that Augustine correlates faith to the proper movement of the will. Faith signifies the restoration of the will by divine grace.

What about reason? What is the relationship between faith and reason? As I have previously noted, Augustine is not trumping reason for the sake of making faith priority, even though reason has its limitations. However, what he wants to emphasize is the fact that human reason-abled activities should not be completely independent of God's grace. For Augustine, it is imperative that God intervenes and gives extra power to the light of reason that is within us. Faith can help

---

[28] Augustine, *City of God*, X, 28.

[29] Ibid., IX, 16.

us in this regard. Faith empowers us to see God, and only then can we turn to the external world and recognize the handiwork of God. It is Augustine's principle that acknowledgment precedes knowledge, not vice versa. As Cushman notes, "what is not effectively known is precisely what is not adequately loved."[30] We must accept God's offer of grace and allow the love of God to underwrite the knowledge of nature. In this way, Augustine ensures that we see God and the world with clear sight.

Therefore, for Augustine, faith is an indispensable companion to reason. Cushman confirms,

> Reason is operative but at length being cleansed and vigorously lays hold of God, not as an object but in eager and living conversation.... It becomes clear that sin is the cause and occasion of ignorance, and the ground of the aberrations of "natural" reason. Therefore, except a man have faith shall in no wise understand.[31]

In this regard, Paul Helm notes that for Augustine faith is trust in certain propositions.[32] He explains,

> Augustine is not saying that faith is an irrational leap, but that there is an inherent and undesirable incompleteness in matters of faith which impels the believer to gain understanding. Given that the propositions are about an object of love as well as of faith, who would not wish to understand more of the one beloved?[33]

What is certain then is that, in the Augustinian model of faith, faith seeks understanding, and at the same time, cooperating with reason, it deepens the understanding of what our heart acknowledges.

In sum, Augustine seems to place faith above reason as love stands above knowledge, but nonetheless, he never took them apart as

---

[30] Cushman, "Faith and Reason," 274.

[31] Ibid., 294.

[32] Paul Helm, *Faith and Understanding* (Grand Rapids: Eerdmans, 1997), 33.

[33] Ibid.

mutually exclusive categories. However, as we move to Descartes, we will see a more succinct break up between faith and reason, but for now, Augustine's work reveals that faith and reason though distinct are not completely at odds with each other. Neither is the culprit for our errors. The true villain is the movement of the will. It is our wrong desires and wants that distort reason, and faith has to dash onto the scene to pull reason out from the pit of making errors and falling away from the one true God as it heals our will. Consequently, faith has to guide reason. This does not mean that faith does not need reason. Faith still needs reason to explicate and clarify the content of faith.

Before I move to the next topic, allow me to add a brief comment about Adolf von Harnack's claim that "Augustine was never clear about the relation of faith and knowledge."[34] Paul Helm indirectly addresses this question by saying that for Augustine "faith has some cognitive content and so a person needs to have some understanding of this content in order to have faith. Otherwise, how would his faith in God be distinguishable from faith in anyone else?"[35] Contra Harnack, Helm thinks that faith for Augustine is not altogether devoid of the knowledge content. So, who is right?

The question of faith's epistemic status is an important one, as we jump to modernist thinkers such as Descartes and Kant. For them, faith, more specifically, religious faith, does not have any epistemic value, which provided them and their followers the motivation to split up faith and reason as mutually exclusive categories. So, what we need at this point is to see if Augustine found any epistemic value in the outworking of faith. In my opinion, the answer can be both "yes" and "no."

If we put Augustine on the same par with modern thinkers, I would say Augustine's faith has no epistemic value. But is it fair to treat Augustine like a modern philosopher? For sure, Augustine was not a modernist, even if we assumed that he tried to construct his theology in continuation of Greek philosophy. In the modern era, as we shall see in

---

[34] Adolph von Harnack, *History of Dogma*, trans. Neil Buchanan (Oxford: Williams and Norgate, 1898), 5/127.

[35] Helm, *Faith and Understanding*, 27.

the work of Descartes, knowledge is tied to science (e.g., empiricism or rationalism). For modern scholars, know-ledge is not linked to the notion of free will or the love of God; rather, it is linked to either the study of observable data or deductive proofs. For Augustine, faith is neither, for its operation is restricted to the healing of free will and the acknowledgment of God's offer of love.

However, the complexity of Augustine's faith understanding should not stop here. As Helm shows, Augustine knew that faith also is tied to *ratio*, despite his insistence that natural knowledge does not and cannot lead us to the God of the Trinity. Although in Augustine's theological paradigm acknowledgment precedes knowledge, Augustine allowed the human reason-able pursuit to arrive at the knowledge of God. Faith healed reason and reason commandeered by faith produces clear knowledge about God's essence. In this respect, I would agree and say that Augustine's faith has an epistemic value. For Augustine, faith produces knowledge, at least, by way of clarifying what Greek philosophers had missed, the knowledge of our Savior God.

Whether or not Augustine placed a distinct epistemic value on faith, one thing is clear. For Augustine, faith is above reason. He is clear about the fact that reason alone cannot take us to the God of our salvation. For Augustine, concerning the belief in the salvific act of God, there is no need for justification except to recognize, or better yet, to acknowledge the grace that has come to us in and through Jesus Christ. Only after affirming that Jesus Christ is the God-man, which is an absurdity for Greek intellectuals, can we find a deeper understanding of what we have believed. This is the way Augustine set up his theological edifice. Faith, in a strict sense, does not need "understanding" as Greek philosophers do. Faith allows us to see our Savior via the enlightenment of the Holy Spirit. It is faith that guides understanding, not vice versa.[36] Reason is in this sense always at the mercy of faith, since faith is the one that corrects the defect of our will, which in turn, commandeers reason to its right thinking. Only then, faith seeks understanding. However, the

---

[36] For modern scholars, it is reason that guides faith, and thus, the faith statement has a knowledge content only when it is reasonably stated (like Descartes' proof of God).

relationship between faith and knowledge turns sour when we come to Descartes, as they are split apart for the sake of keeping reason as the controlling center of man's cognitive activity.

Descartes' Dualism: The Separation of Faith and Reason

Descartes was born into a world of transition. He lived in a period in which scholars began to search for a new and improved way of thinking about the world we inhabit. In this context, joining a group of maverick scholars who wanted to leave behind the old school and start a new school of thought, Descartes sought a way to put new philosophy in a new wineskin of his time. But how could he begin with a clean slate when there are so many things of the past that need to be cleared away? It was simple for Descartes. He began with skepticism. Skepticism has the potential to reset the current themes of philosophy providing him a new starting point. So, Descartes began his philosophy by treating everything, including our understanding of God, as false. This is clearly the focus of his Meditation.

In *Meditation I*, the first part of his most influential work, he tells us that he does not trust either the philosophical or scientific methods of the past.[37] They are all dubitable. Descartes actually was following the footsteps of Francis Bacon. Bacon also wanted to start anew. He did not like the ways of the past. The error was too grand for him to base his philosophy on past achievements. Metaphorically, he spoke about the four idols of the past to highlight the deficiencies of the old school. They were the idols of the tribe, the idols of the cave, the idols of the marketplace, and the idols of the theater. Bacon was essentially pointing out the error-making practices of past sciences. This is what he said about the idols of the past.

> The illusions [or idols] which have got a hold on men's intellects
> in the past and are now profoundly rooted in them, not only
> block their minds so that it is difficult for truth to gain access,

---

[37] Descartes, *Meditations on First Philosophy*, (Cambridge: Cambridge University Press, 1911), 6-9.

but even when access has been granted and allowed, they will once again, in the very renewal of the sciences, offer resistance and do mischief unless men are forewarned and arm themselves against them as much as possible.[38]

In other words, we are in trouble. We are committing great idolatry by following the wrong ideas and conclusions that we have inherited from the past. What are we to do? We have to go back to the drawing board and lay a new foundation, and this is precisely what Bacon did. He laid the foundation for the scientific inductive method, which ironically is completely antithetical to Descartes' method of deduction.

Although Descartes begins his argument by doubting everything in *Meditation I*, as he gradually unveils his rational program, by the time he reaches *Meditation IV*, he demonstrates that human reason is trustworthy and reliable. Simply put, after clearing away all doubts, Descartes finds *himself* doubting. This is an undeniable rational truth. A simple phrase sums up his finding. "I am, I exist, is necessarily true each time that I pronounce it, or that I mentally conceive it."[39] He takes this uncontestable truth as his epistemic foundation to define all other concepts. What we can see here is Descartes' rationale for taking a deductive approach rather than an empirical method. If we were to follow a Baconian method, we would need to proceed not with a clear and distinct idea in our mind, but by observations that are provisional at best. We would need to amass evidence doing experimentations in a laboratory. Had we built our knowledge upon the empirical foundation, we would only deal with probabilities, not logical certainties. But Descartes is looking for certitude. How can we have certainty when our senses are relative to observational conditions? In search of absolute certainty, Descartes sides with rationalism instead of empiricism.

In Descartes' new program, what comes to the fore is a self-evident truth or intuitive premise, like mathematics. The model for Descartes' rational program is that of a geometric system where we have axioms

---

[38] Francis Bacon, *The New Organon* (Cambridge: Cambridge University Press, 2000), 40.

[39] Descartes, *Meditation II*, 9.

followed by deductive proofs leading to certain conclusions. In his system, what is intuitively true, which is so clear and distinct that it is beyond all doubt, takes precedence over what is empirically testable. The phrase "a clear and distinct idea" is the hallmark of Descartes' writings. For him, a clear and distinct rational system is the only way to diffuse confusion or fuzziness in our mind. A clear and distinct idea in his mind implies that there exists an innate knowledge.

Plato also talked about innate knowledge. However, Plato's philosophy is very different from Descartes. For Plato, innate knowledge comes from our previous existence.[40] It actually came with the pre-existent soul. We are born with our habit of the mind and we have to recollect it, because it came to us as soul-memory. However, for Descartes, the term "innate" denotes that which is native to us, that is, our capacity to sum up ideas here and now.[41] It is not something preexisted. It is not a fictitious knowledge. It is a spontaneous idea that just wells up within the mind. Descartes' view is that our consciousness is immediately aware of the ideas which represent the external reality. So the point here is that there is a cognitive transaction between our mental state and the external realities, and because of it, we cannot really have purely a-subjective knowledge. Thus begins the representational theory of knowledge.

For Descartes, intuition is the only thing that has a direct awareness.[42] In Meditations, he does not say that we have intuitive knowledge of material objects. Nor does he say that we have intuitive knowledge of mathematics. These things have to be proved. They are external to us. We only have intuitive ideas that are immediate to us. We are directly aware of our own ideas, which are clear and distinct. We are taught of those ideas by nature, that is, by the natural light of reason.

---

[40] Plato, "The Sophist as a Species of Imagemaker," in *Plato's Theory of Knowledge: The Theaetetus and the Sophist*, trans. Francis M. Cornford (Mineola: Dover, 2003), 325.

[41] Georges Dicker, *Descartes: An Analytic and Historical Introduction* (Oxford: Oxford University Press, 2013), 198. Cf. Descartes, *The Philosophical Writings of Descartes*, 3 volumes (Cambridge: Cambridge University Press, 1985).

[42] Dicker, *Descartes*, 78-79.

This is an Augustinian metaphor. We need to have the light of reason to understand the content of our faith.

Although Descartes draws from Augustine, [43] he parts with Augustine at this juncture. The difference is that, for Augustine, the light comes from the divine Logos illuminating the object of our knowledge and illuminating the mind for us to understand the God of the Trinity. For Descartes, the light is reason itself; there is no Logos doctrine in Descartes' philosophy. We will come back to this later, but it suffices to say that, for Descartes, the ideas in our mind are only things that are objectively certain and clear. After all, it was Descartes who declared, *"cogito ergo sum"* (I think, therefore I am).

Notice that when he is using the concept of objectivity, he is talking about the quality of an idea, not the form of an idea. In the representational theory of knowledge, it is the idea that is equated to the immediate object of thought, not the thing that it represents. According to Descartes, ideas in our mind make sense of reality, not vice versa. Hence, the external things do not influence the mind *a priori*. Our sense knowledge is always *a posteriori*. This is already affirmed by empiricism. For the empiricist like John Locke, there is no *a priori* knowledge, for the human mind comes with a *tabla rasa* (a clean slate). However, contra empiricism, Descartes argues that the human mind is born with the ability to think about ideas. So the innate ideas exist *a priori*, and by implication, they are clear and distinct unlike the provisional knowledge of empiricism.

Where do these ideas come from, if not preexistent? According to Descartes, they come from God. In *Mediation III*, Descartes claims that our ideas are innate because God has implanted them in us.[44] How does he justify his claim? Descartes begins with the assertion that the idea of an infinite being does not belong to us. How can it be? Our finitude by definition cannot give birth to an infinite being, even if it is just an idea

---

[43] Though a simple claim, this is very controversial. But I follow the analysis put forth by Stephen Menn and see a close connection between Augustine and Descartes, though recognizing there are areas of discontinuity between their works. For more details, see Stephen Menn, *Descartes and Augustine* (Cambridge: Cambridge University Press, 1998).

[44] Descartes, *Meditation III*, 16.

of the infinite. For Descartes, it has to come from God, the source of our transcendence. Descartes' claim makes sense when we think of an idea as objective reality in its own right. It does not make sense when we consider the idea as a mere "concept." Descartes is neither an idealist nor a nominalist in this sense. He is a realist. He considers certain types of ideas in our mind as real and objective. Of course, he is aware of the fact that we can create imaginary things in our mind, but he is not worried about them now. He brings up this issue later. What he wants to emphasize here is that there are certain clear and distinct ideas such as the idea of a thinking thing or the idea of God that has the potential to clear the fuzziness in our mind. So, for Descartes, if and only if our ideas are clear and distinct, they are real. In this respect, our reasonabled capacity is not altogether dimmed. As a matter of fact, it is actually clear and objective.

Furthermore, Descartes argues that if God is perfect in all regards, which he is certainly so, he could not have deceived us, so God has created a faculty in us that are not completely deceptive. Our mind then is enlightened by the light of reason. This argument has a long historical background. For Augustine, enlightenment is the illumination of the Logos that allows the human mind to see the eternal truth of God. In the medieval times, Aquinas picked up this idea of enlightenment but with a slight twist that gave Descartes enough ammunition to develop his own conceptual framework for the innate ideas. According to Aquinas, there is a typical idea of God in our mind.[45] Aquinas does not speak of the Logos enlightening the human mind for this idea to occur; rather, he speaks of the light of reason. He is talking about the light of the natural reason that could shed some ideas of God in our mind. In Aquinas' view, enlightenment is not just about the illumination of the mind of the believer but the illumination of everyone's mind about everything in the world. It is a general knowledge of the universals and such knowledge is possible because of the light of reason that sheds on the human mind. For Aquinas, it is not the Logos shedding the light on the natural reason but the natural reason shining the light on the human mind. This was

---

[45] Leo Elders, *The Philosophical Theology of St. Thomas Aquinas* (New York: Brill, 1990), 59.

implicit in Aquinas, but it was made explicit by Descartes. Augustine's conception of enlightenment has metamorphosed into what he never intended to be, the light of reason instead of the light of the Logos.

So according to Descartes, even in the depths of our doubt, our mind is not lost in darkness. We have a good and functioning rational capacity because the good God would not deceive us by giving us a faulty intellectual faculty. Therefore, Descartes' argument basically pivots on the goodness of God.[46] For Descartes, God is a necessary being. He cannot be a non-existing being. It follows that God's essence is perfect, good, and beautiful. Descartes is actually depending on medieval theology. In medieval theology, God necessarily exists in his perfectness. He is the highest good. He is the God of the absolute. So he is at the top of the hierarchical structure of being and we as contingent beings owe our existence to God. What we can see here is that Descartes' argument is system-dependent. He is arguing within a specifically given paradigm. It is a paradigm he has inherited from his medieval predecessors. The medieval conception of God focused on the essence of God which is related to the discussion of God's existence. God's essence is his existence. He exists in his perfectness because he is not a contingent being.

God's self-existence has another implication. For Descartes, God is his own creator (causa sui).[47] Therefore he is the cause of the idea of himself, God. The introduction of causation in God allows Descartes to explain the existence of God rationally. Insofar as Descartes' divine causality is concerned, the cause of an idea is equivalent to the effect. More clearly, for Descartes, the idea of God has the greatest objective

---

[46] Descartes, *Meditation IV*, 30.

[47] Descartes, *Meditation III*, 15. This idea of divine causation differs from Aquinas. Aquinas demonstrated that God is the cause of the natural order. God is the ultimate cause of things, but he himself is not caused by anything else. Descartes was innovational in this respect since he is introducing a cause in the life of God itself. Also, his divine self-causation implied that there are distinct causative operations in nature. God is the cause of himself and nature has its own causation as well. We see an implicit split between God and nature here. But this was expected as Thomas Hobbes already noted that nature does not need divine causation, for the secondary cause of nature is not dependent on God. For more discussion of Descartes' theory of *causa sui*, see Jean-Luc Marion, *On Descartes' Metaphysical Prism* (Chicago: University of Chicago Press, 1999), 103-118.

degree of reality. It is so clear and distinct that the cause of the idea is its own effect. For this reason, the idea of God's perfectness is the root of our rational clarity. The idea of God is therefore innate. In this line of deductive argument, Descartes insists that God caused the idea of God for us to think of the eternity, for we who are limited by finiteness could never be able to conjure up the infinite.

Descartes' logic continues and tackles another important question. Why could we not say that the idea of God is just a fictional story that our mind made up? In order to address this question, Descartes lays out three kinds of conscious states: conception, imagination, and sensation.[48] First, conception is the thought objects such as the essence of God or the concept of a triangle. They are innate and self-evident. Second, there is an idea of imagination. It gives us a factitious idea about the body. It has the capacity to image things in a creative way like a "flying ring" of our previous illustration. We can also bring up the image of the real thing such as a house. It is voluntary because we deliberately conjure up the image in our mind. There is an external reality involved in the process of imagination. We can imagine a house up on a hill. Therefore, it is essentially a spatial reference. Third, physical sensations are adventitious. If I have a pain in my toe, I know which location or which side of the toe that the pain is located. These sensations are adventitious because they come to you. They are caused by something else other than the self. Thus, the external causes are involuntary. Here, nature becomes our teacher. Nature teaches us by virtue of those sensations.

So, we can see, in Descartes' program, the error of imagination does not come from innate ideas. It comes from the ideas that are factitious or adventitious, the secondary activities of the mind. In order to free the mind from the contamination of the factitious and adventitious ideas, Descartes installs another safety mechanism, the separation of mind and body. For Descartes, they are two different things.[49] They have different essences. They have no essential properties that are in common. They are however by some mysterious or unexplained means conjoined in the

---

[48] Descartes, *Meditation IV*, 26-30.

[49] Ibid., 31.

mind. Certain mental acts cause bodily changes, and by the same token, certain bodily changes produce mental states. Thus, there is a causal interaction. But how does it happen? Why are they related? Descartes comes up with a notion that the interaction takes place in the pineal gland.[50] He pictures the human body containing certain canals through which the animal spirits move about. This is the physiology of the 16th century. The circulation of the blood had not been discovered until the 17th century. For him, the animal spirits somehow influence the gland that in turn affects the brain, and as a result, consciousness changes. So, this is how mind and body supposedly interact. Descartes's treatment of the pineal gland is one of the classical blunders. But he is actually telling us that there is a function of unity between mind and body although the mind and body causal interaction does not explain the essential unity of the self. It would have been better to say that we are a psychosomatic unified being. This language of unity is missing in Descartes's writing.

The issue I have with Descartes at this point is that, as with dualism of mind and body, he goes on and splits up faith and reason as mutually exclusive categories. According to Descartes, faith is an act of the will, not of the intellect. Stephen Menn explains. "Faith must be an act of the will, rather than of the understanding, because faith is a species of judgment, of the mind's assent to something that claims to be true."[51] Again, we can see a similarity in Augustine's writing. Augustine also perceived that faith is tied to an act of the will. As we have seen, for Augustine, free will is where the problem lies. It is malfunctioning due to our sinful nature. It does not pursue God's righteousness; rather, it wants to satisfy the desires of our appetite. Descartes essentially draws on the same idea. Descartes states that "although we do not want to go

---

[50] Daniel Garber lists several sources in which Descartes speaks of this "gland." See Daniel Garber, *Descartes Embodied: Reading Cartesian Philosophy through Cartesian Science* (Cambridge: Cambridge University Press, 2001), 267-268.

[51] Menn, *Descartes and Augustine*, 325.

wrong, nevertheless we go wrong by our own will."[52] The will is the villain that makes our perception dubitable and hazy.

In *Meditation IV*, he explains that the faculty of our judgment comes from the good God, and if God is a good God who does not deceive, he would not have given us a faulty faculty of judgment.[53] This is the same type of argument to that of the clarity of reason. If our judgment has been endowed by God, why is it faulty? According to Descartes, it is faulty because of our imperfection.[54] It is not God's fault. Again, we can hear an Augustinian echo. Augustine had said that the will is dysfunctional due to our sin, the imperfection that we have inherited from Adam, so he vindicated God of all errors. Although Descartes does not go into details of where our imperfection comes from (e.g., Adam's fall), the notion of the existence of our own imperfection was taken for granted.

Descartes expeditiously explains why our freewill is causing all the problems. "They come from the sole fact that since the will is much wider in its range and compass than the understanding, I do not restrain it within the same bounds, but extend it also to things which I do not understand."[55] To state it differently, our free will is attached to those things that are beyond reason. This is due to the fact that understanding often comes after a thorough rational investigation, unlike our judgment that does not subsume under the scrutiny of reason. So, for Descartes, the unrestrained and wide-range activities of freewill are problematic since they are out of the reach of reason. Until reason clarifies that our perceptions are clear and objective, we have to live by what our free will affirms, and in turn, human errors emerge as we rely on the judgment that may or may not be clear and distinct.

Descartes in this respect develops his rational scientific program, a way to avoid human errors. As we have seen, in his philosophical

---

[52] Descartes, "Principles of Philosophy" in *The Philosophical Writings of Descartes*, vol 1, trans. John Cottingham, et al. (Cambridge: Cambridge University Press, 1985), 206.

[53] Descartes, *Meditation IV*, 20.

[54] Ibid.

[55] Ibid., 21.

program, reason is the guiding light, for it controls our free will by pulling on the rein of clear ideas that make us prudent. For Descartes, it is by virtue of mental representations of possible consequences that the mind is able to modify our desires and passions which may lead us in disastrous directions. Descartes thinks that the more clear and distinct idea we have, the greater the mind has the capacity to influence our will to move in a proper direction. What we have then is reason guiding free will and influencing the passion.

So, we now know that, for Descartes, reason is the driving force for his rationalistic program, but we still need to address the issue of clarifying the precise relationship between faith and reason in Descartes' work. There has been a heated debate over Descartes' understanding of faith and reason. However, with the risk of oversimplification, I refer to Descartes' succinct statement that may help clear the air.

> Certain things are believed through faith alone. Such is the mystery of the Incarnation, the Trinity, and the like. Others, however, though they have a certain bearing on faith, can nevertheless be investigated by the natural reason. Among these are generally ranked by the orthodox theologians the existence of God, and the distinction of mind from body. Finally, there are others that belong in no wise to the sphere of faith, but only to the sphere of human reason, e.g., the question of the squaring of the circle or of making gold by the art of alchemy.[56]

Here we can see that Descartes has identified three different ways of looking at faith. The first level is a non-faithful domain. There is no need to include faith in this domain. Faith is completely absent. It is restricted to the level of science. On this level, reason takes the spotlight. When we move to the second level, we meet faith intermingling with reason. The statement of faith, such as our declaration of the existence of a good, perfect, and eternal God, can be justified rationally vis-a-viz the ideas that are clear and distinct in our mind. The catch is that when we arrive at the third level, faith and reason are completely separated from one

---

[56] Descartes, "Notes Directed Against a Certain Programme" in *Descartes: Key Philosophical Writings*, trans. Elizabeth S. Haldane (Hertfordshire: Wordsworth, 1997), 346.

another. Following Augustine, Descartes asserts that the matters of Christian faith such as the mystery of the Incarnation are beyond reason.[57] So, in his new scientific method grounded on his rational program, we find no discussion of the Incarnation or the doctrine of the Trinity. They are taken out of his entire rational scientific program. What happened to Augustine's faith seeking understanding? It seems that this activity is reserved only for the secondary level, which is primarily reserved for church scholars. For this reason, sadly, Descartes' science could not help Augustine, which ended up casting faith into the dungeon of what he calls "mystery."

In short, Descartes unintentionally created a split between faith and reason. Even though he may not have intended as Stephen Menn painstakingly argues, the result speaks volumes. He gradually went after a clear and distinct way, that is, the way of science, and his scientific inclinations have trumped the faith of Christ that reigns supreme in Augustine's theological paradigm. Isolating faith from reason, in the end, created a huge split between theology and science. With this split, the God of the Trinity was seen as an unnecessary component in the scientific program. To save God from completely being dismissed from our rational activities, Kant has stepped in and found a space for faith, not in the area of science of course, but in the realm of morality.

Kant's Second Rationality: Faith and Morality

Kant inherited a problem from his predecessors. It was an epistemological problem. At the time, there were two traditions that proposed their own way of identifying how knowledge is attained. On the one hand, there was the tradition of empiricism. Empiricists such as Francis Bacon, Thomas Hobbs, and John Locke, insisted that knowledge is derived primarily from sense experience. For empiricists, our ideas

---

[57] Descartes' explanation in the preface to the Mediations is helpful here. He writes that "[though] we must believe the Holy Scriptures because they come from God (the reason of this is, that, faith being a gift of God, He who gives the grace to cause us to believe other things can likewise give it to cause us to believe that He exists), we nevertheless could not place this argument before infidels, who might accuse us of reasoning in a circle." Descartes, "Prefatory Note" in *Mediations on First Philosophy*, 1.

come from the perception of external objects. It is the material object that teaches us how to know anything about the world in which we live. On the other hand, there was the tradition of rationalism. Rationalists such as Descartes, Spinoza, and Leibnitz declared that there are axiomatic "first" principles from which everything else can be deduced. These foundational principles are innate and naturally ingrained in the human mind that they emerge spontaneously and self-evidently without any need for justification. Which is true? How do we really attain knowledge? More specifically, how does science attain knowledge?

If we say that science is able to attain knowledge vis-à-vis an empirical method, then physical science takes the spotlight. If we say that science is able to attain knowledge vis-à-vis a rational method, then mathematics becomes the driving force for science. Which one should we choose? Is it physical science that determines the structure of scientific knowledge? Or is it mathematics that determines the structure of scientific knowledge? It is neither, according to Kant. For him, dogmatic metaphysics of empiricism or rationalism is inadequate, because these two metaphysical traditions are one-sided. Kant sought something more holistic and comprehensive than either empiricists or rationalists can provide. In this context, Kant introduced his own philosophy. It is called transcendental philosophy.[58] What follows is a close examination of Kant's philosophy.

In his *Critique of Pure Reason*, Kant invests a substantial amount of space to discuss the nature of transcendental philosophy. What is transcendental philosophy? In brief, it is a philosophical claim that there is an inner structure of the human mind that allows us to make sense of the world in which we live. It emphasizes an *a priori* mental framework that helps us see the world in a certain way. Any-thing about the world we know comes through the grid of *a priori* categories. It is a set of mental preconditions that makes thinking possible; therefore, *a priori*

---

[58] There is a distinction between transcendentalism and transcendence. They are not the same. The former is a philosophical principle that Kant proposes as an alternative to empiricism and rationalism, and the latter is a theo-philosophical concept that depicts otherworldliness. For instance, we can denote that God is transcendent because he is beyond this world, but we cannot say that God is determined by our transcendental way of thinking— God is not the *a priori* category of our mind.

categories are subjective. This is not part of innate ideas, however. Descartes pointed out that we have innate ideas that spontaneously emerge from the mind that is self-evident, clear, and distinct. They in turn function as clear and distinct axiomatic principles upon which the edifice of a rationalistic foundation can be built. Kant is not following this path. Kant's *a priori* framework does not make an axiomatic claim. It does not begin with a set of indubitable self-proclamations such as "I think, therefore I am." It is in itself contentless. It is a formal structure of the mind, which enables us to make judgments.

As an example, Kant speaks of "space" as an *a priori* category that helps us produce sense awareness of the external world. In what aspect is space an *a priori* category? Kant writes,

Space is a necessary representation, *a priori*, which is the ground of all outer intuitions. One can never represent that there is no space, although one can very well think that there are no objects to be encountered in it. It is, therefore, to be regarded as the condition of the possibility of appearances, not as a determination dependent on them, and is an *a priori* representation that necessarily grounds outer appearances.[59]

What we need to see is Kant's differentiation from a phenomenon and the condition of the "possibility of phenomenon." External intuition (e.g., a possibility deduced by a phenomenon) is the way in which we understand the world through our engagement with the external things. Space in this sense is once thought to be an external object. This is what Newton had claimed. For Newton, space is an objective category belonging to the external world.[60] Kant has overturned this idea. For him, "space" is not an external object. Rather, it is an internal structure of the mind upon which we make sense of the spatial relationship possible. It is a grid that is already imbedded in the mind. Without it,

---

[59] Immanuel Kant, *Critique of Pure Reason*, trans. Paul Guyer and Allen W. Wood (Cambridge: Cambridge University Press, 1998), 158.

[60] Robert Disalle, *Understanding Space-Time: The Philosophical Development of Physics from Newton to Einstein* (Cambridge: Cambridge University Press, 2006), 18.

we cannot discern the spatial relationship. As far as Kant is concerned, space is an abstraction of all possible extensions. It is not an object.

For this reason, Kant insists that a specific "form" of space does not belong to the objective world. This is quite different from Aristotle's understanding of "form." [61] Aristotle talked about the relationship between form and external things. According to Aristotle, a form is connected to its physical particular. So for him, the actual substance of a thing is constitutive of form and matter. In this respect, although a form determines the essence of matter, form and matter are not separated. However, Kant overturns the Aristotelian notion of form, and states that a form is not found in or determined by the empirical object. The empirical input does not determine the form of the particular; rather, it is the form, as a mental state, which makes the particular meaningful.

Is Kant following the Platonic notion of form? Kant's way of depicting the *a priori* principle in terms of form is different from Plato. For Plato, unlike Aristotle, an ideal form is otherworldly.[62] It is not to be associated with its particular. If there is a square, insists Plato, there is a square that is perfect in its form in the world of Ideals, and there is a square looking thing (e.g., the appearance of a perfect square) that is in this world of appearances. For Kant, a form of space is not a "perfect" thing that exists beyond this world. Rather, it is a subjective structure in the human mind that makes sense of the spatial extensions of the particular. It is a faculty of the mind. The *a priori* principles themselves do not tell us anything. It just helps us order our thinking in certain ways.

As a result, Kant has changed the way we see things. We no longer see the world from the vantage point of the object. As Kant argues, we cannot be purely objective. Due to the fact that our understanding is filtered through *a priori* categories, it is Kant who made it necessary and universal to say that the human subject contributes to the construction

---

[61] E.g., Aristotle, *Metaphysics*, trans. Hugh Lawson-Tancred (London: Penguin, 1999), 143-147. Also see Gail Fine, *On Ideas: Aristotle's Criticism of Plato's Theory of Forms* (Oxford: Clarendon, 1993).

[62] Michael LaFargue, *Rational Spirituality and Divine Virtue in Plato: A Modern Interpretation and Philosophical Defense of Platonism* (Albany: University of New York Press, 2016), 124.

of meaning. The world we know is the result of our own mental construction. The world of cause-and-effect is the world that we have conceptualized through *a priori* categories of space and time. Whether or not the reality is what we have perceived it to be is another question. The world we have structured in a certain way is different from the world as it is. It is because, for Kant, the world in which it appears to us (*Ding an jich*) cannot be the world the way it is (*Ding ach me*). Thus, the outcome of Kant's transcendental philosophy is the distinction between phenomena and noumena. Such a grand shift in view of the world occasions what we call the Copernican Revolution because object-centeredness has shifted to subject-centeredness. We have a different center of attention after Kant.

Is intellectual reason limited then? For Kant, because we can only know the world in which it appears to us, the rational activity of the human mind is restricted to phenomena. If our epistemic structure is limited, how can we know anything about noumena? Kant says that we will never know vis-à-vis reason.[63] He is agnostic about the knowledge of noumena. Based on intellectual reason, we can never tell whether we can know the thing-in-itself or not. What is certain is that we can have some knowledge of the phenomena. Indeed, it was Kant's intention to limit intellectual reason to the realm of phenomena, as we will see shortly when we discuss another area of reason, that is, practical reason. The limit of reason implies that there is a limit to science. Scientists study not about noumena but about the things that we observe.[64] In this respect, we can label Kant as an empirical realist. Due to this limitation, Kant's proposal is problematic. Immediately, two problems emerge. First, if reason is not utterly objective, is there anything else that can be objective? Second, if reason does not give us the full knowledge of the object, how can we know the reality like God? Anticipating these questions, Kant turns to his *Critique of Practical Reason*.

Because our knowledge extends only to phenomena, Kant is essentially claiming that rational metaphysics is not possible. If we try

---

[63] Kant, *Critique of Pure Reason*, 347.

[64] Ibid., 356.

to prove the existence of God solely based on rational proofs, we will never be successful. This is precisely what Kant has done in his *Critique of Pure Reason*. He systematically discounts ontological, cosmological, and teleological arguments. [65] It follows that the rational proofs themselves do not give us knowledge of God or the thing-in-itself. What does? What other options do we have? Thankfully, we have other faculties of the mind. Kant finds that, besides the faculty of knowing, we have the faculty of free will and the faculty of feeling. For our purpose, we will limit our discussion on Kant's *Critique of Practical Reason*, which deals with primarily the faculty of free will.

We may not have metaphysics of knowledge, but we may have metaphysical beliefs that will give access to the object. At the end of his *Critique of Practical Reason*, Kant concludes that we cannot demonstrate the existence of God rationally, but the knowledge of God is possible on the basis of ethics. Kant, therefore, is a moral realist. In other words, for Kant, there are real moral objects. And based on these real moral objective values, we can prove the existence of God.

Where can we find these moral objects? Kant turns to the inner moral signs that function as the references to the objective qualities in the world.[66] What he is looking for is once again the *a priori* structure of the human mind for the practical reason. There must be a transcendental quality that determines our choice, picking either what is right or what is wrong. What are these principles that determine our moral thinking? Kant states that our inner moral principles are objective qualities of our rationality because they involve some sense of duty. Here he turns to the objectivity of moral laws. While the forms and categories are used in science are purely subjective, for Kant, the categories used in ethics are objective. There are objective corollaries. There are such things as objective moral duties. The difference between right and wrong is surely objective for Kant.

---

[65] Ibid., 551-577. In the section of "Transcendental Dialectic," he counters the traditional proofs of God's existence, that is, the ontological argument, the cosmological argument, and the teleological argument.

[66] Immanuel Kant, *Critique of Practical Reason*, trans. Werner S. Pluhar (Indianapolis: Hackett, 2002), 46-47.

In order to see how Kant justifies this claim, we need to recognize that he brings up the notion of the synthetic *a priori* nature of ethical judgments. [67] Put simply, ethical judgment involves two kinds of influence. On the one hand, there is the empirical input, and on the other hand, there is the *a priori* principle that makes sense of the empirical input. For instance, when we say stealing is wrong, we have a description of what is wrong known as "stealing." This understanding comes from empirical input. We can empirically describe the act of stealing. However, the description of stealing alone does not help us whether it is wrong or not. So, we need an *a priori* concept of wrong, which allows us to see that stealing is wrong. Again, what we have here is an introduction to the *a priori* structure in our moral reflections. By synthesis, our moral awareness is merged with an actual situation. This *a priori* moral principle is not implied from the actual situation, but rather, the inner principle undergirds the explanation of the actual situation. Kant calls *a priori* moral principles categorical imperatives. [68]

This is stated differently in *Groundwork for the Metaphysics of Morals*, but the same idea holds. Here, Kant notes that there is only one thing that is unconditionally good, that is, the good will. [69] We see an echo of Augustine here. Like Augustine, Kant understands that this good will can be corrupted due to the faulty natural inclinations. Hence, in the Kantian program, the moral problem is found in the wrong use of our natural inclinations, which can be twisted or perverted according to our desires. Our desire for happiness is not something that is in itself good and right; thus, it can be misdirected. So, Kant makes a clear distinction between inclinations and a sense of duty that is necessary and universal. Because inclinations move toward the empirical objects, they are impure, and, therefore, we need a stronger sense of duty.

According to Kant, a strong sense of duty gravitates toward *a priori* principles, such as the respect for persons, or our sense of what is right

---

[67] Ibid., 46.

[68] Ibid., 60.

[69] Immanuel Kant, *Groundwork for the Metaphysics of Morals*, trans. Allen W. Wood (New Haven: Yale University Press, 2002), 28.

or wrong. Where does the moral struggle occur? It takes place within the mind trying to choose between our moral obligations and our own desires. What is important for our discussion is that as far as Kant is concerned, moral experience does not involve space and time at all. In other words, the activities of science do not impose on moral thinking. They are two different types of human rational activities. In his discussion of practical reason, Kant turns away from the external world of science, and returns to the inner world of the self. Thus, the turn to the subject is completed. The ultimate reality, or at least our access to it, is via our understanding of right and wrong. Indeed, human subjectivity has taken the center stage.

As a result, Kant has placed another limitation on science. Along with the limits of reason, in which science can investigate what can be observed rather than the thing-in-itself, he has distinguished what is practiced from what is intellectually accessible. Values are discernible through the subjective understanding of what is useful and worthwhile, whereas facts are gleaned through scientific exercises such as mathematics and physics or a combination of the two. Furthermore, since moral values are subjectively judged, they are privately fostered by each individual. This is quite different from scientific activities. Kant has understood that science is largely a public affair. It does not hide its facts from the scrutiny of others, unlike the moral values of an individual. In the end, Kant has successfully split up religion from science. Religion is now a study of ethics, whereas science is the study of nature. This schism implies that religion is not concerned with attaining knowledge. Rather, its goal is to promote moral virtues and the pursuit of the highest good.

In this way, religion is now free from the fetters of rational demand. It does not need to show the rational proof of God to sustain its logical structure. Because religion is not a matter of reason but a matter of attitude and judgment, it does not require evidence or rational argument to justify its belief system. In this respect, he has divorced faith from intellectual reason,[70] on the one hand, and faith from science, on the other. Such dissociation of faith from reason is also emphasized by the role of faith in Kant's transcendental philosophy. According to Kant, the role of faith is regulative as opposed to constitutive. What is the difference between the two? Wayne Pomerleau explains,

> He [Kant] says that ideas can have two possible functions in human thinking. Some (for example, empirical) ideas have a "constitutive" function, in that they can be used to constitute knowledge, while others have only a "regulative" function in that, while they can never constitute knowledge, they do serve the heuristic purpose of regulating our thought and action.[71]

In other words, knowledge is constituted only in the realm of science, and morality is regulated only in the realm of religion. They are mutually exclusive. Religion is regulative and never constitutive of knowledge, while science is constitutive of knowledge, but never regulative of moral duties. In this context, at most, theology is speculative, since according to Kant, the matters of religion do not establish any intellectual knowledge. Kant maintains that if we understand the difference between the regulative and constitutive role of theology and science, respectively, we would not commit the error of anthropomorphism, that is, equating God with our own qualities or the qualities of nature.[72] God is beyond the world of imperfection, and for this reason, Kant is extremely critical of anthropomorphic reading of the Scripture.

At this point, we need to visit Kant's understanding of God. To argue for the existence of God, since he has rebutted all other standing arguments for God's existence, such as ontological, cosmological, and teleological arguments, he opts for the moral argument. In brief, his moral argument runs like this. Everyone is born with a sense of moral

---

[70] Note, I am not saying that Kant has remove reason entirely out of moral discussions. Rather, morality is also rational for Kant. What I am emphasizing here is that he has split faith and reason (e.g., rationalism and empiricism) into mutually exclusive categories.

[71] Wayne P. Pomerleau, "Immanuel Kant: Philosophy of Religion," in *Internet Encyclopedia of Philosophy*, accessed November 16, 2016, http://www.iep.utm.edu/kant-rel.

[72] Kant, *Critique of Practical Reason*, 166, 172.

duty.[73] As such, it needs to be correlated to the highest good. More specifically, there needs to be a perfect correlation of "happiness in exact proportion with the morality of rational being."[74] Since our moral obligations can be achieved, it is not altogether impossible for us to arrive at the highest good. But there is a catch. We are messy. Objectively, the highest good is achievable, but realistically, we fall short of getting there. What we need is a companion to pursue the highest good. Objectively, there is no other person than God, who is perfect in nature and is able to collaborate with us in the achievement of the highest good. In this scenario, morally, God exists necessary and universally. This is Kant's argument for the existence of God. If there is to be a future life, and ultimately, the immortality of the soul, then we have to postulate that there exists the ultimate moral being who would accompany us to our happiness. Thus, Kant's God is a moral God. For him, God is a moral living God who is holy and just.

As the final outcome, in Kant's transcendental philosophy, reason is above faith. Even in his moral realm, it is reason that legislates our moral thinking. Kant was wary of counterfeit religious activities such as ecclesial liturgical practices of his time. He called them pseudo-services.[75] He equated ecclesial worship practices to that of superstition and fanaticism and blamed them for discouraging the believers from seeking moral virtues.[76] The skeptical attitude toward religious rituals that is readily apparent in Kant's writing comes as no surprise, for his predecessors had the same feelings about them. For instance, John Locke writes, "Whereby in effect it [enthusiasm] takes away both reason and revelation, and substitutes in the room of them the ungrounded fancies of a man's own brain, and assumes them for a foundation both of opinion and conduct."[77] The irrationality of religion was so dangerous

---

[73] Cf. Immanuel Kant, *Religion within the Limits of Reason Alone*, trans. Theodore M. Greene and Hoyt H. Hudson (New York: Harper, 1960), Book One.

[74] Kant, *Critique of Pure Reason*, 681.

[75] Kant, *Religion*, 139.

[76] Ibid., 48.

[77] John Locke, "Of Enthusiasm," in *The Philosophical Works of John Locke* (London: George Bell and Sons, 1903), 313.

that Locke asked all parents to "stifle and suppress it [religious feeling] as much as may be."[78] The mood of the time was ripened to put reason above faith. Basil Wiley writes, "Locke's philosophy was the philosophy of an age whose whole effort had been to arrive at truth by exorcizing the phantoms of [religious] imagination."[79] Kant, therefore, followed the trend of modernism. He even dismissed miracles, [80] just like his predecessor Spinoza, and categorized them as superstitions devoid of any moral values. Kant, for this reason, argued that theists should not substitute moral and virtuous conduct for pseudo-services. Morality had to be reasonable, even in the religious realm, and so, Kant asked us to respect "universal human reason as the supremely commanding principle."[81]

Moreover, Kant's attempt to develop "a more authentic way of rationally affirming God's existence"[82] eventually split apart faith and reason, unraveling what Augustine and his medieval followers had done. Not only that, faith and science became mutually exclusive. And as sciences gradually expanded the sphere of influence in the modern culture, faith was set aside as something that opposed reason, or at least, something that was inferior to reason and, therefore, needed reason's guidance. The table has turned. Reason has become the chief faculty of knowing that governs the faculty of the will and affection. The sphere of faith was not only clearly delineated from the sphere of reason, but also lost the spotlight as the primary driving force of human rationality.

The Critical Review of Augustinian, Cartesian, and Kantian Traditions of Faith

---

[78] Richard Kearney, *The Wake of Imagination: Toward a Postmodern Culture* (London: Routledge, 1988), 164.

[79] Basil Wiley, *Seventeenth Century Background: The Thought of the Age in Relation to Religion and Poetry* (New York: Doubleday, 1953), 262-263.

[80] Kant, *Religion*, 51, 54, 57, 74, 77.

[81] Ibid., 152.

[82] Stephen Palmquist, "Kant's Religious Argument for the Existence of God: The Ultimate Dependence of Human Destiny on Divine Assistance," *Faith and philosophy*, 26/1 (2009), 4.

From our historical survey, one thing is clear. The current status of relating faith and reason is dark and gloomy. As Alvin Plantinga opens his paper with a pessimistic tone regarding the relationship between science and religion, the quintessential wisdom of the day is that faith conflicts with reason.[83] Faith and reason turn out to be odd couples. In fact, they are seen as hostile to one another. On the side of science, reason is insulated from the encroachment of faith to eschew the pitfalls of religious subjectivism, and on the side of theology, faith is insulated from reason to eschew the pitfalls of rationalizing faith. The introduction of technological science did not help relieve this tension. The expansion and success of sciences without the aid of faith gave more reasons for modern scholars to keep faith and reason far away from each other.

Essentially, we owe this break-up to misguided thinking that there are only three ways to look at the relationship between faith and reason: (1) faith is above reason; (2) reason is above faith; (3) faith and reason are mutually exclusive because faith is subjective and reason is objective. This is clearly evident in our reading of Augustine, Descartes, and Kant, and as a result, due to their influential works, those who followed their footsteps treated faith and reason the same way as their predecessors. What we need is then to show that these three ways of looking at the faith and reason relationship are inadequate for the postmodern era. Therefore, in this section, I present a critical assessment of these three propositions and expose their shortcomings. In turn, this assessment serves as a guide for our final quest, that is, the formulation of faith as third rationality.

Faith over Reason

After Kant, in the theo-philosophical camps, there had been various attempts to turn the table again and restore faith to its glorious days of

---

[83] Alvin Plantinga, "When Faith and Reason Clash: Evolution and the Bible" *Christian Scholar's Review*, 21/1 (1991): 8-33. He writes, "My question is simple: how shall we Christians deal with apparent conflict between faith and reason, between what we know as Christians and what we know in other ways, between teaching of the Bible and the teachings of science?"

the past. Those who belong to this camp are what I call "Augustinians." They are essentially followers of the Augustinian tradition. One such scholar is Søren Kierkegaard, who argued that true religious knowledge is grounded in faith, not reason.[84] According to Kierkegaard, faith knowledge such as our knowledge of the Incarnation is actually against reason. Like Augustine, Kierkegaard was pessimistic about understanding the concept of the Word made flesh solely on a rational basis. Therefore, in order to understand the counterintuitive event of God becoming man, Kierkegaard demanded nothing less than a leap of faith. In this respect, for Augustinians, theology is reserved for the matters of faith that go beyond the matters of reason. For example, taking the torch from Kierkegaard, Karl Barth set the precedence to systematic theologians of our time by claiming that theology deals with God's self-revelation, not with our reason-abled sciences.[85] Because of Barth's anti-sentiment toward natural theology, the sphere of faith is restricted to three particular loci; Jesus Christ, the Scripture, and the proclamation of the gospel. For Barth, faith is not reliant upon natural knowledge; rather, it is independent of it albeit faith claims are explained in a systematic reasonable fashion. It is due to the fact that there is an infinite qualitative difference between God and his creation. There is no way for us, even if we are equipped with most fancied technology, to move from temporality to eternity. Obviously, Barth's main goal was to overturn the Kantian revolution, attempting to reinstitute the Augustinian approach. For him, faith ought to guide reason, not vice versa. According to the Barthian paradigm, it is faith that guides us to the truth, never reason alone. Consequently, theologians in the Augustinian tradition define faith from a theocentric perspective. From this view, faith unveils the God of the beyond. They follow Augustine, who had no problem of describing God in terms of his otherworldly characteristics. That is, God is eternal, sovereign, and

---

[84] E.g., Søren Kierkegaard, *Provocations: Spiritual Writings of Kierkegaard*, ed. Charles E. Moore (Farmington: Bruderhof, 2002), 72. See a similar analysis from Stephen Evans, *Kierkegaard on Faith and the Self: Collected Essays* (Waco: Baylor University Press, 2006), 298.

[85] Karl Barth, *Church Dogmatics*, ed. G.W. Bromiley and T. F. Torrance (Edinburgh: T&T Clark, 1957), 2:168.

perfect. For them, every aspect of God exceeds and transcends the world he created, and to know this God intimately, faith is necessary.

Not only there are scholars who sided with a pre-modern idea of faith, but also there are scholars like Descartes who insulated faith from reason, treating it as something that deals with what reason cannot access. In the realm of theology, Descartes saw reason as a handmaid to faith in the way we understand God's perfect will and act in this world. The holy temple of God cannot be intruded without the aid of faith. However, for Descartes, this is as far as reason can go. Descartes' rationalistic pessimism could not let intellectual reason to justify why God had to come and take upon human flesh. So, he had no choice but to set aside the hidden secrets of God's salvific work in and through Jesus Christ in the realm of faith which is completely cut off from the realm of science. Consequently, despite the fact that Platonic philosophy came close to identifying the key features of God, such as his goodness, justice, and beauty, nonetheless, reason had no use for religious faith any longer in the Cartesian program.

Going back to those scholars who stand with Augustine, we see that they want to point out that faith is an extraordinary human faculty that allows us to know God who is beyond this world. They believe that reason is this-worldly focused and faith is other-worldly oriented. However, to say that God is beyond this world does not license us to say that faith does not need reason. Assuredly, Augustinian scholars like Kierkegaard and Barth did not reject reason completely even if they deal with the matters of faith. What these scholars rejected was natural theology, not reason *de facto*. As we have seen in the previous chapters, natural theology focuses on the belief that we can come to the knowledge of God without the aid of God's revelation. Put differently, natural theology stands on the conviction that, by examining the natural phenomena and by the power of natural knowledge, we can come to the sufficient knowledge of God—e.g., his being and act in the world. Is such natural theology possible? Augustine rightfully said, "No." However, what we need to understand is that Augustine's rejection of natural theology is not based on the faulty work of reason but based on the faulty work of free will.

Augustine understood that something has gone awry with humanity. He found the problem, not in reason, but in the corrupted part of free will. For Augustine, our volition was so corrupt that it had adversely influenced all areas of human activities, including our use of reason. What is the role of faith then? For Augustine, faith was given as a gift from God to remedy the malfunctioning volition. Once our will is properly healed by faith, we can seek a deeper understanding of God and his act in this world *rationally*. In this respect, even for Augustine, reason is not something that had to be insulated from faith. Rather, reason is the necessary part of working out the details of our faith.

If reason is not all that incompetent, why is it then reason has been put down by fideists? The greatest shift in my judgment occurred during the Reformation. The reason-abled theology that Catholic theologians inherited from Thomas Aquinas and his Aristotelian philosophy did not go well with the Reformers, for Aquinas took a step further than Augustine and noted that reason was not damaged even though our will is fallen. Aquinas had greater confidence in reason than Augustine as he never treated reason as an incompetent human faculty of knowing even though it has its own limits. [86] Reacting against theological rationalists, Martin Luther blatantly pointed out that reason is the Devil's whore.[87] For the Reformers like Luther, the noetic effects of sin that Augustine had spoken about had extended to a wide range of human rational capacity, and as a result, the unredeemed reason was seen as completely distorted and untrustworthy. Faith had all the right values and worth to be on top of the hierarchy of knowledge, and reason was to be treated as a villain that had sided with natural things of this

---

[86] One good example is Aquinas' presentation of analogy of being. In a broad sense, Aquinas' analogy of being points to the fact that the things of this world can function as an "analogy" of God, in which God can be known intellectually and reason-ably. For more detail, see Ralph McInerny, *Aquinas and Analogy* (Washington, D.C.: The Catholic University of America Press, 1996), 51-56.

[87] Martin Luther, "Last Sermon in Wittenberg, Second Sunday in Epiphany, 17 January 1546," in *Dr. Martin Luther's Werke: Kritsche Gesamtsusgabe* (Weimar: Herman Boehlaus Nachfolger, 1941), 51:126. Like Augustine, although Luther preferred the ways of faith, he nonetheless did not dismiss philosophical reasoning altogether. In fact, as Martin E. Marty points out, Luther celebrated "reason as God's gift in his catechisms and through his writings." Martin E. Marty, *Martin Luther: A Life* (New York: Penguin, 2004), 177.

world. As a result, Luther's cry for *sola fide* echoed throughout the churches in the Western world.

Furthermore, modern philosophers and scientists distancing themselves from the matters of faith made things worse. For instance, Spinoza and David Hume found it necessary to say that in the scientific world, there is no need to talk about supernatural elements such as miracles. I will talk more about miracles in the following chapter, but for now, it suffices to say that, for them, biblical miracles are nothing but meaningless claims of superstition. We can even go back to the medieval period, and Aquinas had pointed out that supernatural events belong to the realm of revelation (e.g., biblical narratives) and they do not belong to the realm of nature.[88] Following the Thomist tradition, as we have seen in Descartes' work, by the turn of the 17th century, scholars were slowly assigning a special territory for the sciences in the realm of nature, and human rationality was more and more associated with scientific activities, rather than theological or spiritual exercises that dealt with the supernatural, and with the advancement of sciences, faith was seen as something starkly different than reason.

Going back to the question, is faith above reason? If we say that faith deals with religious matters, does this mean that faith is nonrational? I answer negatively to both questions. Augustine was right to say that even in the case of explaining why God became man, a reason-able justification was necessary. Craig Boyd explains this need succinctly.

> In order to "apprehend" Christ, we must employ our reason. In order to see the distance between God's wisdom and our own human wisdom, we must employ reason. In order to see that a crucified criminal overcomes our sin, we must employ reason. In fact, in order to understand whether reason can or cannot "reconcile" two ideas is to employ reason itself.[89]

---

[88] Rudi te Velde, *Aquinas on God: The "Divine Science" of the Summa Theologiae* (Burlington: Ashgate, 2006), 147.

[89] Craig A. Boyd, "The Synthesis of Reason and Faith Response" in *Faith and Reason: Three Views*, ed. Steve Wilkens (Downers Grove: Intervarsity, 2014), 77-78.

Whether it be for religious or scientific motives, it is wrong to say that faith is above or antithetical to reason. Although reason is faulty in some sense, we cannot say that reason is completely flawed. If we underrate reason, we underrate all theological activities. Are not all theologies reasoned and reasonable activities? Reason allows us to define and shape the cognitive contents of our beliefs. Faith seeks understanding. For this reason, it may not be healthy to say that faith is above reason, even if faith, to a certain extent, structures reason-abled activities. It may be better to say that faith cooperates with reason as partners, because without faith reason is limited, and without reason faith becomes blind. In this respect, it would be absurd to say that two are mutually exclusive. The absurdity of displacing reason for the sake of faith is even more apparent when we discuss the issue of religious absolutism.

Religious absolutism is the major fallout from putting faith over reason. In the name of faith, religious categories such as the Bible, the ecclesial office, or spiritual experiences, are exempted from rational critical investigations. In fact, they are exalted over and above any rational activities, for they are treated as the absolute, infallible categories of faith. They are accepted as true *de facto*. If we treat the Bible as the category of faith standing over and above reason, then it turns into the religious absolute category of biblicism. If we treat the ecclesial office as the category of faith that is indisputably authoritative, then it turns into the religious absolute category of ecclesial imperialism. If we treat spiritual experiences as the category of faith that is unquestionably accepted, then it turns into spiritual absolutism. Let me review each of these categories respectively.

Regarding biblicism, Christian Smith comments, "By 'biblicism' I mean a theory about the Bible that emphasizes the belief in its exclusive authority, infallibility, perspicuity, self-sufficiency, internal consistency, self-evident meaning, and universal applicability." [90] The essence of authority is then unequivocally located in the Bible, which in turn is

---

[90] Christian Smith, *The Bible Made Impossible: Why Biblicism Is Not a Truly Evangelical Reading of Scripture* (Grand Rapids: Brazo, 2011), viii.

treated as the infallible word of God. From a biblicist point of view, no one can raise objections to the authority of Scripture. Cornelius Van Til declares, "No proof for this God and for the truth of his revelation in Scripture can be offered by an appeal to anything in human experience that has not itself received its light from the God whose existence and whose revelation it is supposed to prove."[91] For this reason, Clark Pinnock predicts various theological malaises emerging from biblicism such as "undue hermeneutical anxiety; unfruitful concerns over how perfect the Bible is; preoccupation with the theories of biblical inspiration; anxieties over the extent of the Bible's humanity and historicity; and the threat of criticism."[92] Biblicism, in the end, presents a form of religious absolutism. From such a perspective, significant religious beliefs are reserved only as matters of fact rather than theological categories that may not be precisely pinned down.

But in reality, the Bible is not static, axiomatic, or absolute. Surely, the Bible is the main source for our understanding of God and his act in this world, and it is trustworthy due to the fact that the Spirit-inspired authors of the Bible maintained the integrity of God-given words by staying true to the historicity of biblical events as well as God's self-revelation. However, it nonetheless cannot be considered as "a simple document of propositions easily stated, expounded, and demonstrated."[93] It requires careful reading and interpretation, which demands a rational exercise that supports our beliefs. Hence, theology relies heavily on biblical hermeneutics.

But, will not our interpretation of the Bible introduce errors, for we all are fallible? Due to the inevitability of errors in the way we translate and communicate canonical writings, there had to be another authoritative source that could make sure that the content of the Bible is well-preserved and propagated to the next generation. The task was given to the church. However, it came with its own problem. It

---

[91] Cornelius Van Til, *The Defense of Faith* (Philadelphia: Presbyterian and Reformed, 1955), 126.

[92] Clark H. Pinnock, *Tracking the Maze: Finding Our Way through Modern Theology from an Evangelical Perspective* (Eugene: Wipf and Stock, 1990), 42.

[93] Ibid., 36.

inadvertently gave rise to ecclesial imperialism. One such example is found in Roman Catholicism.

The Catholic Church teaches that the living magisterium (e.g., teaching office of the papacy) is infallible and granted unhindered access to heavenly-sent God's word.[94] Vatican I states that, "we teach and define that it is a divinely revealed dogma that the Roman pontiff, when he speaks ex cathedra, that is, when acting in the office of shepherd and teacher of all Christians, defines, by virtue of his supreme apostolate authority, doctrine concerning faith or morals to be held by the universal church."[95] Once again, the locus of absolutism is identified, but this time, it is located in the office of the church. Indeed, as Pinnock notes,

> there is no escaping from the dimension of church office institution. For how can the church protect itself from living challenges like Gnosticism and modern parallels unless its leaders with the authority to deal decisively with them? The church will need someone to stand in the succession of the apostles and be able to claim the Lord's authority to stand guard of the Scripture and tradition.[96]

However, the infallibility of the church office has given the ecclesial magisterium unbridled power and control over the church, and as a result, the ecclesial office transformed into an imperialistic structure. To remedy this ill, Hans Küng declares that "the Church's being true is not absolutely dependent on quite definite infallible propositions, but on her remaining in the truth throughout all—even erroneous— propositions."[97] In other words, the church's duty is not concerned with the ecclesial teachings that they must be true for all occasions, but that

---

[94] Peter J. Kreeft, *Catholic Christianity: A Complete Catechism of Catholic Beliefs* (San Francisco: Ignatius Press, 1994), 20. For a thorough review of the infallibility of Catholic ecclesial authority, see Hans Küng, *Infallible? An Unresolved Enquiry* (New York: Continuum, 1994).

[95] Vincent McNabb, ed., *The Decrees of the Vatican Council* (New York: Burns & Oates, 1907), 47.

[96] Pinnock, *Tracking the Maze*, 37.

[97] Hans Küng, *Infallible? An Inquiry* (New York: Doubleday, 1971), 182.

they must try to be true, admitting that they are not true all the time. Only with this understanding can we diffuse the criticisms of secularity such as Friedrich Nietzsche, who claimed that the church has impeded the human power to progress due to its misdirected ecclesial teachings.[98] Nietzsche basically pointed out that Christians became powerless to do anything right for themselves, since they were indoctrinated to think that the infallible church will provide answers to all our problems clearly and distinctively. Although Nietzsche's critical evaluation of the church is not entirely true due to his sweeping generalization for not all churches follow the ways of Catholicism, he nonetheless is on target with respect to ecclesial imperialism.

Lastly, concerning spiritual absolutism, there is a problem associated with the turn to the Spirit. The turn to the Spirit in itself is not the problem, however. The issue is with locating the spiritual authority, not in the giver of spiritual gifts (e.g., Holy Spirit), but in the one who has the gift of the Spirit. One good example is the second-century spiritualist movement called the New Prophecy.[99] This is the original prophetic movement credited to Montanus and his two women prophets, Priscilla and Maximilla. Due to the lack and rarity of genuine records, scholars differ greatly as to the tenets and practices of the New Prophecy; however, there is a general consensus concerning the phenomenon of the New Prophecy: ecstatic and aberrant manifestations of the Spirit, authoritative prophetic voices, and ascetic requirements such as prohibition of remarriage and fasting.[100] According to Montanus and women prophets of Phrygia, the Spirit gave them new and authoritative prophecy in a tone of superior revelation compared to ecclesiastical teachings and even Scripture. Montanus taught that the Paraclete was incarnate in the prophetesses Priscilla and Maximilla as

---

[98] Paul Avis, *Faith in the Fires of Criticism: Christianity in Modern Thought* (Eugene: Wipf and Stock, 1995), 55-60. Also see Friedrich Nietzsche, *The Will to Power*, trans. Walter Kaufmann and R. J. Hollingdale (New York: Vintage Books, 1968).

[99] Cecil M. Robeck, *Prophecy in Carthage: Perpetua, Tertullian, and Cyprian* (Cleveland: Pilgrim, 1992), 144.

[100] Ibid., 121. Also refer to the list of oracles of the original Phrygian prophetic trio in Ronald E. Heine, *The Montanist Oracles and Testimonia* (Macon, GA: Mercer University Press, 1989), 3-9.

well as himself. The trio claimed the direct authority of the Spirit. What made the matter worse is that even with the possibility of persecution and severe chastisement from the church, Montanist prophets refused to listen to the ecclesial counsel. Their private experience of the Spirit had no room for the "testing of the Spirit" (e.g., 1 Jn. 4:1).

Anthony Thiselton finds a similar issue with the modern charismatic movement. [101] Although he is not entirely dismissing the spiritual experiences of the Pentecostals, he nonetheless claims that the consequences of identifying prophetic "phenomena" with the Holy Spirit can be disastrous. The possible issues associated with spiritual absolutism are enumerated by Thiselton: (1) The experience of new creation, newness of life, praise, and joy, may degenerate into a loss of the Christian need for waiting, pilgrimage, struggle, and self-discipline; (2) The revelation of a genuinely Trinitarian life in the Holy Spirit may degenerate into a Spirit-centered life, with little focus on Christ; (3) The experience of personal intimacy with God may degenerate into individualism and lack of social concern; (4) Daily renewal and a focus on the promise and new things of the future may degenerate into a disparagement of history, tradition, the past, and continuity; (5) The revelation of prophecies (in the popular sense) may degenerate into an interpretation of all the gifts of the Spirit as a "spontaneous" experience, rather than seeing most of these gifts in terms of settled habits; (6) An appreciation of God's sovereign power to heal may degenerate into an expectancy that God will always do so, as if the end had already arrived; (7) The yielding of one's heart and feelings to God may degenerate into failing to see that the whole person also entails intellect and judgment.[102] Hence, I find Wesley's quadrilateral illuminating. We need to strike a balance between Scripture, tradition, spiritual experience, and reason, and avoid the great travesty of putting one category over the other.

In sum, what we have seen is that the matters of faith, that is, the things of the Bible, of the church, and of spiritual experiences, are not

---

[101] Anthony C. Thiselton, *The Holy Spirit: In Biblical Teaching, through the Centuries, and Today* (Grand Rapids: Eerdmans, 2013), 492.

[102] Ibid.

infallible or absolute. A clear distinction should be made between the absolute and the content of faith that points to the absolute. When the two are confused, the content of faith turns into absolutism. On the one hand, from a Christian perspective, the absolute is none other than the triune God. On the other hand, absolutism is the mix-up of the expressions of faith with the object of faith. The Bible is not God. Neither is the one who holds the church office, nor the one who is filled with the Spirit. No creaturely thing is absolute or infallible. Only God is perfect and infallible. The mix-up of what is perfect and what is not could bring a devastating effect. When we grant a divine status to the Bible, it gives birth to biblicism. When we grant a divine status to the one who holds a church office, it gives birth to ecclesial imperialism. When we confuse the One who gives the gift and the one who receives the gift, we suffer from spiritual absolutism. If we understand that there is a difference between the absolute and absolutism, we would be able to eschew the errors of hardening theological categories into uncriticizable fixed axioms. This is why we must not put faith over reason. When we put faith over reason, we fall into a misguided belief that the matters of faith are absolute, thereby exempting them from the reason-able investigations. Faith cannot be absolute. After reading Wolfhart Pannenberg's work, Clayton makes a similar conclusion:

> Even for the believer, the contents of faith can remain disputable (*strittig*). Religious experience and religious practice may bespeak—and at times create—certainty, but it is possible for religious beliefs to be held hypothetically, in continued dialogue with other religious and nonreligious positions and in conscious openness to criticisms of formulation and content. From the perspective of religious experience, religious beliefs may be viewed as self-authenticating. However, this does not make the search for broader epistemic warrants any less essential if the believer is to achieve an overall coherence of his experience. From other perspectives, namely from those of theoretical reflection, even the truth claim of religious

experience and tradition must be judged as hypothetical and the certainty of faith as a subjective anticipation.[103]

As Clayton argues, our faith expressions should be reasonably criticizable. This does not mean that we should do away with putting our trust in the absolute. Rather, because of our trust in the absolute, our faith claims need to be examined critically and prudently. This is the way of science. If theology is to correlate with science, we need to, at least, move away from the error of absolutism. In this light, Pannenberg writes, "In all the sciences, humility is required: Our affirmations are not by themselves infallible but may be questioned."[104]

Would the critical exercise of faith disrepute the confessional aspect of faith? It does not. On the contrary, the confessional dimension of faith gains traction in the world of many voices due to the fact that it is supported by rationally justifiable theological evidence. For instance, Christians around the world may make the same confession:

Holy, holy, holy! Lord God Almighty!

Early in the morning our song shall rise to Thee;

Holy, holy, holy, merciful and mighty!

God in three Persons, blessed Trinity.[105]

However, despite the universality of this confession, the interpretation of the nature and function of the triune God differs from one denomination to another, and from one culture to another. Because of many voices in the world, our understanding of God can be easily frustrated. Thus, the assistance of a reason-able investigation enlightens our faith claim with justifiable evidence such as the doctrine of

---

[103] Philip Clayton, *Explanation from Physics to Theology: An Essay in Rationality and Religion* (New Haven: Yale University Press, 1989), 144.

[104] Wolfhart Pannenberg, *The Historicity of Nature: Essays on Science and Theology*, ed. Niels Henrik Gregersen (West Conshohocken, Templeton Foundation Press, 2008), 8.

[105] *The Hymnal 1982* (New York: The Church Hymnal Corporation, 1985), 362.

homoousion that may fend off and possibly correct the mis-orientation of the Trinity such as the concept of subordinationism.[106]

Reason over Faith

Unlike those who have stood in line with the Augustinian tradition, the intellectuals of the Enlightenment tradition such as Descartes and Kant turned to the light of reason instead of the authority of faith. The overarching presupposition for them is that reason stands aloof above faith. Reason no longer needs the aid of faith. McGrath writes in this regard, "Enlightenment rationalism may be said to rest upon the belief that unaided human reason can deliver everything that humanity needs to know. There is no need to listen to other voices, having first consulted reason."[107] In fact, faith is seen as an inferior form of human rationality that must be controlled or purified by the power of reason. We can already see the sign of reason acting as the watch dog for faith in Descartes' writings. According to Descartes, the content of faith, especially our understanding of God's essence and existence had to be justified by reason alone. As a result, God was no longer seen as the Unmoved Mover, but a *causa sui*, that is, a self-caused being. In Descartes' program, God had to give a rational explanation of how he exists. It was not enough to say that God just exists without a cause. John Caputo may be right to say that faith was "hauled into court, made to stand before the tribunal of reason."[108]

---

[106] Cf. Kevin Giles, *Eternal Generation of the Son: Maintaining Orthodoxy in Trinitarian Theology* (Downers Grove: Intervarsity Press, 2012); *Jesus and the Father: Modern Evangelicals Reinvent the Doctrine of the Trinity* (Grand Rapids: Zondervan, 2006); *The Trinity and Subordinationism: The Doctrine of God and the Contemporary Gender Debate* (Downers Grove: Intervarsity Press, 2002).

[107] Alister McGrath, *Christian Theology: An Introduction* (Malden: Wiley Blackwell, 2007), 143. He adds, "One of the most graphic portrayal of this enormous confidence in reason is the front piece to the eighteenth-century rationalist philosopher Christian Wolff's ambitiously titled book *Reasonable Thoughts about God, the World, the Human Soul, and just about everything else* (1720)."

[108] John D. Caputo, *Philosophy and Theology* (Nashville: Abingdon, 2006), 23.

While Kant opposed the idea that reason was able to figure out everything in this world, "rationalism"[109] prevailed and reason became not only constitutive of knowledge but also regulative of our beliefs. Although Kant had assigned a unique space for God, rationalists such as Pierre-Simon Laplace removed God from all spheres of knowledge.[110] For this reason, it is now commonly understood that

> God and religion do not have their own island, their own domain or space or playing field. They must build their house of worship on someone else's property. God does not belong to the sphere of knowledge because the domain of knowledge is controlled by the physical sciences. The idea of God as supersensible cause simply does not register in natural science.[111]

Hence, from a rationalist perspective, faith is not to be trusted because it leads to an arcane, mystical path to believe in the things that are probably unreal.

In this context, the faith categories such as prayer and worship, which Kant labeled as pseudo-service, are dismissed as superstitions. In the contemporary setting, D. Z Philips contends that "prayer which, on the surface, appears to be a petition is an essentially irreligious or superstitious attitude, for it attempts to harness the supernatural to the fulfilling of our mundane needs; it is essentially selfish, self-seeking."[112] A root of equating religion with superstition at the expense of reason goes back to Spinoza, who configured various religious categories such as prayer and prophecy in terms of human emotion that has nothing to

---

[109] Here, I differentiate the term "rationalism" from "reason." For me, reason is the basic human faculty of mind. It allows faith to seek understanding. However, as McGrath points out, rationalism is "an exclusive reliance upon human reason alone, and a refusal to allow any weight to be given to divine revelation." McGrath, *Christian Theology*, 144.

[110] Richard Olson, "Physics" in *Science and Religion: A Historical Introduction*, ed. Gary B. Ferngren (Baltimore: John Hopkins University Press, 2002), 303.

[111] Caputo, *Philosophy and Theology*, 30.

[112] Paul Helm, *Faith and Understanding* (Grand Rapids: Eerdmans, 1977), 70. Also see D. Z. Philip, *The Concept of Prayer* (London: Routledge, 1965).

do with reasonableness.[113] In essence, according to Spinoza, when religious faith overpowers reason, religion becomes superstition. Others followed suit and treated religion as nothing more than wishful thinking (Sigmund Freud), a self-projection (Ludwig Feuerbach), or the opium of the people (Karl Marx).

For modern intellectuals, the only remedy for pulling ourselves out of the pit of religious fideism is science. As Kant denoted, there are broadly two types of sciences. One is mathematics and the other physical science. The former is the Cartesian way of justifying beliefs. It begins with clear and distinct ideas that are self-evident and incorrigible. Based on these first principles, we can develop a deductive argument that leads to a definite conclusion. As an example, a deductive argument may contain the following premises. All men are mortal and Socrates is a man. Therefore, the conclusion logically follows that Socrates is mortal. Such a method is clearly visible in the development of Euclidean geometry.

By contrast, physical science does not begin with a self-evident premise. Rather, it depends on sense experience and physical data. The fundamental methodology of physical science is to test all theories against observations of the natural world rather than taking things for granted. No claim is exempt from testing. Evidence is the chief criterion for confirming the validity of an argument. For instance, in order to confirm that Socrates is mortal, the empirical method will not proceed by assuming that all men are mortal and Socrates is a man. Rather, empiricists will look for physical evidence that Socrates indeed was a historical person and that he died at some point in time, which proves empirically that indeed Socrates was a "real" person. Without physical proof, empiricists cannot accept the statement that Socrates was a mortal human being for sure. He could have been an immortal being existing only in the minds of philosophers. Thus, in today's world of science, in order to be certain, deductive and inductive methods are combined to form what is called a hypothetico/deductive method. Science now

---

[113] Baruch Spinoza, *Theological-Political Treatise*, trans. Michael Silverstone, ed. Jonathan Israel (New York: Cambridge University Press, 2007), Chapter 6.

demands both logical coherence and empirical evidence to justify an argument. In his monumental work, *Language, Truth and Logic*, A. J. Ayer famously appealed to "the principle of verification,"[114] which held that for any statement to have meaning it must be either analytically true and/or empirically verifiable. It seems that we have come of age in which the success of science dethroned faith and allowed reason to reign instead. However, this is a misunderstanding. I will demystify this claim and show that it is unscientific to say that reason is above faith.

Reason is not above faith because it is not autonomous. The autonomy of reason is often associated with the superiority of reason. The first error of rationalism is to treat reason as such. Since Descartes, reason is associated with clear and distinct ideas. It is considered as the seat of immediate knowledge. It is free from justification, because it is a source that justifies other things such as faith claims. It forms the foundation of all knowledge. In order to sustain this claim, it was necessary for Descartes and his followers to preserve the purity of reason and began to isolate reason from other error-bound faculty of the human mind such as the movement of will and affection, which had a close association with the movement of faith. I will discuss further the subjective and objective dichotomy in the following section, but it suffices to say here that reason was seen as self-referential and self-sustaining without the need of assistance from other sources of human cognitive activities such as morality and affection.

If we claim that reason is autonomous, we fall into the error of foundationalism. The error that I see is the attempt on the part of foundationalists to ground "the entire edifice of human knowledge on invincible certainty."[115] However, as shown by Clayton, no knowledge is indubitably basic. Instead, knowledge is interdependent. It is supported by different systems of knowledge, such as theology and science, each being connected to its counterpart and ultimately to the whole system of knowledge. According to Grenz and Francke, in this

---

[114] Alfred Jules Ayer, *Language, Truth, and Logic* (Mineola, NY: Dover Publications, 1952), 5-9.

[115] Stanley J. Grenz and John R. Frank, *Beyond Foundationalism: Shaping Theology in a Postmodern Context* (Louisville: Westminster John Knox Press, 2001), 30.

respect, "knowledge is a web of belief (Quine), a nest of beliefs (Kort) or, to cite the more generic designation, a 'conceptual scheme.'"[116] In other words, knowledge is not built upon an indubitable base of first principles, but a collection of partial and conceptual knowledge that taps into all aspects of human life, including religious beliefs.

Does this mean that we have to do away with foundational knowledge completely? No, we do not. We can still base our knowledge on the basic principles, as long as we recognize that those basic principles are not indubitable but criticizable and shareable.[117] It is fair to say that both theology and science, though they may be miles apart with regards to their subject matters, deal with *a priori* concepts such as space and time. A priori concepts are by no means illegitimate because they are intuitively derived. Both Descartes and Kant, in their own way, described the inevitable nature of human cognitive activities that start with the categories that are given or already preprogrammed in our mind to make sense of the world. Reason and faith themselves are such categories. The problem associated with these basic categories is to say that they are utterly incorrigible. If they are treated as incorrigible categories, then they will be automatically exempt from criticisms. If this happens, we circle back to the issue of absolutism. What we need to eschew is myopic rationalism, like naturalism and scientism, that isolate reason from faith.

Regarding naturalism, there is a danger of making nature as the sole determinant of knowledge. As we have discussed in the previous chapter, if naturalism is the only paradigm, there is no other way to explain "otherworldly" phenomena. What if naturalism is unable to explain all events in nature such as the emergence of consciousness? According to naturalists, a gap in the natural explanations is due to the limitation of human cognitive abilities, not due to the existence of other causation such as divine causality. Therefore, from a naturalistic

---

[116] Ibid., 39.

[117] William Alston makes a similar claim. See William Alston, "Two Types of Foundationalism" *Journal of Philosophy* 73/7 (1976): 165-185. He deviates from naïve foundationalism but opts for soft foundationalism—an appeal to justified knowledge rather than following incorrigible epistemic beliefs.

perspective, there is no other option available for theism. Nature is the placeholder for all explanations. In my judgment, this is just a pure display of academic hubris rather than the intellectual outworking of science. We need to understand that science is not naturalism. Science studies nature, but it does not necessarily hold onto the restrictive demands of naturalism. For instance, mathematical realist W.V.O Quine is riveted to the idea that mathematical objects, including highly abstract set theories, are real.[118] In other words, not only physical objects in nature are real, but unobservable abstract objects like mathematical entities are also real. Because of their real property, mathematical objects refer to physical events in the world even though mathematical theories themselves do not refer to any physical events in the world when they are first conceptualized.[119] Although I do not believe that all mathematical objects are real, there are certain sets of mathematical objects, at least, have real semiotic properties that direct us to the real objects "out there." It follows that naturalism is not the only frame of reference on which scientists work. Science depends on other rational categories such as retroduction and intuitionalism as shown by Quine's work.

Regarding scientism, there is a danger of making science the sole measure of truth. Richard Dawkins, for example, rides the crest of scientism, taking the theory of evolution as the primary rubric that measures the viability of both scientific and theological claims. He neither accepts nor counts data as trustworthy if the source of data is

---

[118] Reuben Hersh, *What is Mathematics, Really?* (Oxford: Oxford University Press, 1997), 170-176. For Quine, "It is 'bad faith' to drive a car or switch off an electric light without accepting the reality of the real numbers."

[119] A good example is the power of algebra. Algebraic expressions are normally developed through mathematical manipulations without any regard for natural events. However, Philip Davis notes that "with these representational possibilities at hand, a scientist or mathematician, when confronted with a situation from nature, looks among these possibilities for one that mimics, in a certain sense, the natural situation. Thus, Galileo's formula $s=gt^2$ represents the stone's fall to the Earth, but it can also represent the growth of the area of the circle that arises when a stone is tossed into a pool of still water." We do not know why these mathematical symbolizations can represent nature. So, Philip may be right to say that "we make language, and then language makes us." Philip J. Davis, *Mathematics and Common Sense: A Case of Creative Tension* (Boca Raton: CRC Press, 2006), xl.

outside the sphere of natural sciences.[120] Theological data are thus dismissed even before they are presented to the court of science. No God is permitted in the course of scientism. Atheism in this regard has become a synonym for scientism. Many atheists assume that science is the ultimate source of truth. For instance, Christopher Hitchens states, in his book *God Is Not Great*, "We distrust anything that contradicts science or outrages reason."[121] Atheist Patricia Churchland likewise comments about Charles S. Peirce's pragmatic view of science: "In the idealized long run, the completed science is a true description of reality; there is no other Truth and no other Reality."[122] We can even see Lawrence Krauss' double standard when he contends that it is unreasonable to base theological claims on scientific evidence, while it is reasonable to argue against theological claims based on scientific data.[123] As the philosopher of science, Thomas Kuhn has explained that scientific data and theories are shifting and making modifications constantly, and because of it, scientists have the liberty to explore the world not from a single "proven" perspective but from multiple perspectives that even go against the already "proven" theories. That is how science progresses. So the demand by atheists such as Dawkins, Hitchens, and Krauss, is not the demand of science, but of scientism, since they all think that science already has the truth.

Furthermore, scientism often argues for a purely neutral and value-free science. Hence, scientists often see value-laden and purpose-driven faith having no relationship with science. What makes a statement

---

[120] Cf. Richard Dawkins, *The Selfish Genes* (Oxford: Oxford University Press, 1989); *The God Delusion* (Boston: Houghton Mifflin Co., 2006); *The Magic of Reality: How We Know What's Really True* (New York: Free Press, 2011). Dawkins even introduces a hypothetical biological mechanism called "meme" as the source of our religious mindset. For a thorough counterargument of Dawkins' approach to religion, see Alister E. McGrath, *Dawkins' God: From the Selfish Gene to the God Delusion* (Oxford: John Wiley and Sons, 2015).

[121] Christopher Hitchens, *God Is Not Great: How Religion Poisons Everything* (New York: Twelve, 2007), 5.

[122] Patricia Churchland, *Neurophilosophy: Toward a Unified Science of the Mind-Brain* (Cambridge: MIT Press, 1986), 249.

[123] Cf. Brisbane, Australia, City Bible Forum, Lawrence Krauss and William Lane Craig debate, *Has Science Buried God?* accessed November 16, 2015, https://www.youtube.com/watch?v=U4M4ZUAcyV8.

neutral and value-free? According to Rudolf Carnap, for instance, a statement is neutral and value-free when it meets the criteria of empirical validation.[124] Carnap, for this reason, wanted to severe the metaphysical core from natural sciences, for they are not verifiable empirically. Consequently, Carnap did not hesitate to say that all metaphysical statements are meaningless. However, things have changed since the heyday of logical positivism. As Alan Padgett argues, after the demise of logical positivism, scientists no longer talk about value-free scientific activities. "In the last century, thinkers as various as Heidegger, Polanyi, Kuhn, Gadamer, and Habermas all rejected a 'value-free' or 'neutral' understanding of what counts as good academics (*episteme, scientia,* or *Wissenschaft*)."[125] In fact, Michael Polanyi boldly claims that all sciences operate within a fiduciary system.

Polanyi's main purpose of his book, *Personal Knowledge,* is to demonstrate that no scientific activity is impersonal.[126] Rather, scientific activities are involved with a personal commitment that allows scientists to reach a reliable understanding of the world at large. Colin Weightman correctly assesses Polanyi's work by saying that he follows the postmodern turn and contributes to the overthrowing of scientism in three distinct ways: (1) rational activities are more than logical or explicit, for it demands the tacit dimension of knowing; (2) all knowledge is cast upon a fiduciary framework; and (3) although there is no ground for knowledge, the community of faith plays a critical role as the norm for the determination of truth.[127]

What this means is that all scientists pursue knowledge in the areas of their own discipline, and based on a certain belief system, they hold onto a metaphysical frame of reference such as the concept of order or

---

[124] Rudolf Carnap, "The Elimination of Metaphysics through Logical Analysis of Language" in *Logical empiricism at its peak: Schlick, Carnap, and Neurath,* eds. Maria Neurath and Sahotra Sarkar (New York: Garland, 1996), 10-31.

[125] Alan Padgett, *Science and the Study of God: A Mutuality Model for Theology and Science* (Grand Rapids: Eerdmans, 2003), 114.

[126] Cf. Michael Polanyi, *Personal Knowledge: Towards a Post-Critical Philosophy* (Chicago: University of Chicago Press, 1962).

[127] Colin Weightman, *Theology in a Polanyian Universe: The Theology of Thomas Torrance* (New York: Peter Lang, 1994), 203–220.

contingency that coheres to the norm of the community to which they belong. Hence, scientists, like theologians, hold onto certain values and principles, which they rarely justify by empirical practices. Therefore, all scientific theories are assumption-laden and based on personal commitments. No one is exempt from this personal engagement with the world. Scientists do believe. Even atheist Peter Atkins admits it. "I accept that it is my undemonstrated belief that science can illuminate all the great questions of being, and that I believe in its omnipotence and universal competence."[128] However, he does not stop there but brings up the issue of justification. "These beliefs are of a less demanding kind than the beliefs characteristic of religion, where the justification of the belief will be found on the other side of the grave."[129] I would have to disagree with him on two accounts.

First, the justification of scientific beliefs is not always "more demanding" than religious beliefs. For Atkins, religious beliefs are less demanding than science because religious claims are not supported by empirical evidence. What he is silent on this matter is the fact that scientific statements or theories are not simply justified by empirical facts. There is an ongoing debate in the philosophy of science concerning the question, What constitutes good evidence in science? There is a clear and distinct problem of defining "good evidence" in science. John Norton succinctly summarizes the five major theories vying for prominence in the world of the philosophy of science: uniformity theory, inference to the best explanation, falsification theory, probability theory, and non-uniformity theory. [130] According to Norton, evidence is considered good, if it is tangible, observable, and causally uniform (uniform theory), or if it is a mixture of conjectures and empirical data (inference to the best explanation), or if it is falsifiable rather than verifiable, since verification is impossible (falsification theory), or if it

---

[128] Peter Atkins, "Atheism and Science," in *The Oxford Handbook of Religion and Science*, eds., Philip Clayton and Zachary Simpson (Oxford: Oxford University Press, 2006), 135.

[129] Ibid.

[130] John D. Norton, "A Little Survey of Induction" in *Scientific Evidence: Philosophical Theories and Applications*, ed. Peter Achinstein (Baltimore: The John Hopkins University Press, 2005), 1-5.

increases the probability of the hypothesis (probability theory), or if it is interpreted uniquely within a specific paradigm (non-uniformity theory). The point I want to make here is that there is more than one way to look at evidence, and as such, if we were to follow the Kuhnian paradigm of the non-uniformity theory, then the justification of scientific beliefs cannot be "less demanding" than religious beliefs, since the justification criteria for Atkins' scientism and Christian theology are different and non-conforming.

Second, the justification of religious beliefs is not always found on the other side of the grave. Religious beliefs are sustained by theistic arguments such as metaphysical, psychological, social, hermeneutical, theological, and even scientific evidence. Theistic arguments normally have been accused of relying solely on the internal evidence, such as biblical testimonies, religious experiences, or even inner testimonies of the Holy Spirit, but in the contemporary theological climate, there have been many scholars attempting to justify theistic claims of divine action in the world by interacting with various scientific theories. For instance, exploring territories that are beyond the traditional limits of Christian dogmatics, there are scholars who study God's acts in the realm of chaos,[131] in the quantum world,[132] or in the cosmic history.[133] These scientifically oriented theologians take into consideration data from not only the Bible and church dogmatics, but also the studies of natural and human sciences.

The problem is clear. Atkins' scientism is simply dismissing the evidence provided by theistic apologists *a priori* because "science is the only path to understanding."[134] He states clearly that "there is no other variety of world, and that the 'spiritual' is an illusion generated by a physical brain."[135] In this closed system of the physical world, Atkins

---

[131] Cf. John Polkinghorne, *Belief in God in an Age of Science* (New Haven: Yale University Press, 1998).

[132] Cf. Robert J. Russell, *Cosmology from Alpha to Omega: The Creative Mutual Interaction of Theology and Science* (Minneapolis: Fortress, 2008).

[133] Jürgen Moltmann, *God in Creation* (London: SCM Press, 1985), 206–214.

[134] Atkins, "Atheism and Science," 124.

[135] Ibid.

has decided to disclaim all theistic arguments as superficial and illusory, and, therefore, no evidence is allowed to be submitted in his court of scientism. Once again, Atkins' claim is simply a demand of scientism, not a demand of science. As Norton has shown, evidence in science does not always depend on empirical observations alone. Evidence could be constituted by guess work, metaphorical extensions, coherence to the norm of each paradigm, and even the dismissal of the standing scientific facts in the development of a new theory.

In sum, it is wrong to say that reason is above faith. Science has come a long way since the days of the modern anti-religious sentiment, and in the postmodern context, we even see faith incorporated into all scientific activities. Faith is discovered as the underlying matrix upon which we make sense of the world; hence, it is a co-worker of reason, not a servant to reason. Once we fall into the error of thinking reason as the supreme ruler of faith, we cannot escape from the disillusionment that only reason has the capacity to unveil the truth of things in terms of a this-worldly rubric and neglect the matters of faith that has the capacity to see from the view of otherworldliness.

Faith Is Subjective

Now since we have dealt with the problems of religious absolutism, on the one hand, and scientific absolutism, on the other hand, we are ready to tackle the next issue, that is, the subjectivity of faith. One of the most common ways of describing faith is that it is subjective. Based on this false understanding of faith, faith and reason have been completely separated and have become mutually exclusive—e.g., faith is placed on the subjective pole and reason on its opposite, objective side. We can easily trace this type of distribution in the works of Augustine, Descartes, and Kant, as well as those who followed their footsteps. At least, what we can see from them is that faith has been consistently connected to the subjective aspect of human life. For Augustine, the locus of faith was found in the human free will. Because our will has been marred by sin, it was necessary for God to heal it, and by faith in Jesus Christ, we are made whole once again, and as a result, the entire spectrum of the human faculty of knowing such as reason can be oriented properly to God. Similarly, Descartes followed Augustine and said that faith dealt with the matters of the will, not the matters of reason. Although Descartes understood that faith and reason had to mingle in some instances, it was reason that was objective, and as a result, reason had to play the role of laying out the proper context of justification for faith. When we come to Kant, the separation is all the more distinct and intentional.

Kant's scientific epistemology does not allow us to know the thing-in-itself, and as a result, from the Kantian perspective, only the phenomena of external objects are knowable, which is always a reasonable exercise. In the realm of phenomena, although a variety of different sciences thrived, Kant was not able to find the space for God in this quarter of intellectual reason. Rather, Kant limited God's involvement in the sphere of human activity. Fortunately, Kant did not dismiss faith altogether. He opened two new spaces, which were called "practical reason" and "judgment," in which faith can dwell. The matters of religion thus for Kant were the matters of morality and judgment. Had they mingled with science, they would depreciate the matters of science. Religion was all about our own conduct and subjective movement. It had nothing to do with the objectivity of science. In Kant's program, faith had to be special, because, for him, the idea of God existed completely beyond the boundaries of intellectual reason. Hence, it was easy for him to say that faith is linked to human subjectivity such as the category of imagination, judgment, and morality, rather than the intellectual outworking of science.[136]

Thereafter, with the help of Romanticism and religious pietism, religious faith was thrust into the deeper level of subjectivity, namely, the realm of emotion, rather than the rational exercise of the human

---

[136] We may read all of Kant's works subjectively. Surely, Kant's categorical requirements predominantly lead us to that conclusion. However, Kant does acknowledge that science studies nature realistically (using the empirical method). So, in this sense, Kant is an empirical realist. Cf. Immanuel Kant, *Metaphysical Foundations of Natural Science*, trans. Michael Friedman (Cambridge: Cambridge University Press, 2004).

mind.[137] Romanticism was actually a byproduct of the negative reaction to mechanical philosophy, pushing Kant's program to tilt his subjective inclinations to the extreme. The separation of science and religion in the modern world has led post-Kantian Christian thinkers to associate faith with religious feelings. One fine example would be Friedrich Schleiermacher. Combining both philosophical influences from Kant, Schelling, and Schlegel, and from Christian pietism such as the Moravian Brethren, Schleiermacher postulated that religion is not science, metaphysics, or even a form of knowledge.[138] He thus followed closely to Kant's epistemology. For Schleiermacher, religion was special because it gave rise to an immediate intuition of God. This is where he parted with Kant's theory of religion. For Kant, religion was based on morality, but for Schleiermacher, religion was not really a matter of what we ought to do. Rather, religion was about what we feel.[139]

We need to pay close attention to the term "intuition" in Schleiermacher's writings, since it motivated him to leave behind both intellectual and practical reason. For Schleiermacher, the concept of "intuition" conveyed "some sort of immediate cognitive relation to some sort of object."[140] Thus, there was no need for Schleiermacher to reflect upon the reality of God vis-à-vis rational proofs or moral behaviors. For him, religion was purely an emotional outlet. Regrettably,

---

[137] Luke Maskin's *The Basics of Philosophy* has a good summarized version of Romanticism: "The Romantic view is that reason, objectivity and analysis radically falsify reality by breaking it up into disconnected lifeless entities, and the best way of perceiving reality is through some subjective feeling or intuition, through which we participate in the subject of our knowledge, instead of viewing it from the outside. Nature is an experience, and not an object for manipulation and study, and, once experienced, the individual becomes in tune with his feelings and this is what helps him to create moral values." Luke Maskin, "Romanticism," *The Basics of Philosophy*, 2008, accessed November 17, 2015, http://www.philosophybasics.com/movements_romanticism.html.

[138] Friedrich Schleiermacher, *On Religion*, trans. Richard Crouter (Cambridge: Cambridge University Press, 1996), 22. He writes, "It [religion] does not wish to determine and explain the universe according to its nature as does metaphysics; it does not desire to continue the universe's development and perfect it by the power of freedom and the divine free choice of a human being as does morals. Religion's essence is neither thinking nor acting, but intuition and feeling."

[139] Ibid.

[140] Forster, Michael, "Friedrich Daniel Ernst Schleiermacher," *The Stanford Encyclopedia of Philosophy*, Summer 2015, accessed Oct 12, 2015, http://plato.stanford.edu/arch-ives/sum2015/entries/schleiermacher.

Schleiermacher's extreme subjectivism became a representative model for Christianity in the modern world. Against such a view, there have been attempts by Christian scholars, who endeavored to show that faith is not entirely subjective. One such scholar is Thomas Torrance. His analysis of faith fits well with a holistic conception of rationality that I have envisioned. What follows is a brief review of Torrance's fiduciary program, which later functions as the basis for my conception of faith as a third rationality.

Unquestionably, Torrance has pushed his theological program away from Schleiermacher's camp, for he believes that Schleiermacher had failed to preserve the objective pole of theology by conflating our own religious consciousness with God's self-revelation. According to Torrance, because of the Schleiermacherian turn to subjectivity, religious faith deals with "reflection upon the phenomena of faith rather than with that in which we have faith."[141] Torrance detects the problem of subjectivity in not only the world of religion but also the world of science. Science is suffering from the same malaise. Borrowing the language from Michael Polanyi, he states that the anthropocentric way of structuring our epistemic dimensions allowed the "massive modern absurdity," that is, "the limitation of rational knowledge entirely to what can be tested by reference to observations or logically deduced from them."[142] How could he break the subject and object dualism that is prevalent in our culture? What is the solution? Torrance's solution is simple and direct. If we move away from anthropocentrism, which is the source of obstructive prejudices and reductionism, we can hold fast to objective realism, that is, our epistemic structure which penetrates into the inherent rationality of the object and into what is to be known out of itself, whether it be created existence or God in his revelation to the world.

---

[141] Thomas F. Torrance, *Theological Science* (Oxford: Oxford University Press, 1969), 28.

[142] Thomas F. Torrance, "The Framework of Belief" in *Belief in Science and in Christian Life: The Relevance of Michael Polanyi's Thought for Christian Faith and Life*, ed. Thomas F. Torrance (Eugene: Wipf and Stock, 1980), 7.

Drawing upon Polanyi's fiduciary program, Torrance assumes that there are at least three fiduciary components actively functioning in the way we understand reality "out there." The first component is intelligibility. Torrance's depiction of intelligibility is unique but consistent with his realist program. Unlike Descartes who insisted that our intelligibility is inherent, Torrance suggests that our intelligibility comes from nature as well as from God. Torrance states that "the world, even in its creaturely otherness from God, is held continuously in such an ontological relation to God, the source of all rational order, that there is creatively imparted to it a rationality of its own which is not incongruous with God's rationality."[143] Because of God's orderliness and nature's orderliness, which is contingent upon God's creative act, things are intelligible to us. Torrance takes it to another level and turns this into a "design" argument. "If they [the things in this world] were not orderly in themselves they would not be intelligible to us and would not be open to rational description and explanation."[144] Essentially, Torrance is contending that there is an intimate alignment between the intelligibility of man, the orderliness of nature, and the intelligibility of God, because God has implanted such an order in the creation, although he would not accept the notion that the study of man and nature leads directly to God. What Torrance wants to do is to connect the dots between God, nature, and humanity, at least from a theological realist perspective, and of course, as a believing Christian, his starting point is God. The source of all intelligibility is God. God is the God of order and intelligibility. God brings order out of chaos. Torrance here is following the quintessential testimony of the orthodox Christian tradition. Nature reveals the order imputed by God. We humans are compelled by the intelligibility of both nature and God, and thus, we have our own intelligibility. This is Torrance's first contention.

If our intelligibility is informed by something other than ourselves, then it would be right to say that we are not in control of our knowledge.

---

[143] Thomas F. Torrance, *Divine and Contingent Order* (Edinburgh: T&T Clark, 1998), 35.

[144] Thomas F. Torrance, "The Concept of Order in Theology and Science," *The Princeton Seminary Bulletin* (1984), 130.

If this is the case, what is our role in obtaining specific knowledge about the world? Epistemologically, we can take on the role of either deductive thinker or empirical investigator. For the former, like Descartes' program, we can start with a clear and distinct idea that spontaneously emerges from us, and from it we can make logical connections to come up with a conclusion. For the latter, like John Locke's program, we can start with our observation of empirical objects and find sufficient evidence to prove our hypothesis. However, for Torrance, both Cartesian rationalism and Lockean empiricism are too anthropocentric. That is, knowledge is depended upon human intelligibility, whether it be rational or empirical. The alternative way for Torrance is to the obtainment of knowledge based upon the way we connect to the things out there intuitively.[145] This is Torrance's second contention.

As we have seen, "intuition" is a loaded term. For instance, Descartes' intuition is an *a priori* deductive category and Schleiermacher's intuition is an affective dimension. Torrance takes a slight turn away from Descartes and Schleiermacher by stating that intuition is an objective movement. It is making connections between the intelligibility of nature (or the intelligibility of God) and the intelligibility of the mind as we move out of ourselves to be in touch with the thing-in-itself. So, for Torrance, intuition occurs when we have direct contact with reality, and we are informed by the intelligibility of nature as "we entrust our minds to the orderly and reliable nature of the universe." [146] Understanding the outworking of intelligibility and intuition, we can now talk about faith. Faith is then an integrative force that brings together the subjective and objective pole of our epistemic structure, and this is possible due to the intelligible connection between our mind, God, and nature, which are connected intuitively and implicitly.

Here, we come to Torrance's third point, that is, the tacit dimension of knowing, which again reinforces his idea of "intuition." Torrance draws from Polanyi's notion of personal knowledge again to

---

[145] Torrance, "The Framework of Belief," 9.

[146] Ibid.

substantiate the outworking of tacit knowledge in science and theology. What is a tacit dimension of knowledge? It can be compared to Kant's regulative function of faith. For Kant, faith does not constitute an explicit knowledge, but like a moral compass, it regulates our thought and action. Similarly, Torrance's tacit dimension does not itself produce rational knowledge, because it is not provable or justifiable. It rather regulates our rational activities implicitly in such a way that an explicit form of rational expressions can be identified, articulated, and formed from it.

From a different perspective, Torrance's emphasis on the interplay of the formal and informal interaction can be explained in terms of the binary relationship of the focal and subsidiary awareness. Torrance argues that "in addition to our 'focal awareness' and the explicit knowledge to which it gives rise, we always operate with a 'subsidiary awareness' and an implicit knowledge on which we rely for all our explicit operations."[147] Torrance's argument is understandable since, although we are not always fully conscious of our habits, actions, and surroundings, we are able to think and act because of them. For example, when we solve an algebraic problem for the first time, we painstakingly go through the long steps of solving the problem, but solving the math problem repeatedly for many years, we are able to find the answer immediately and intuitively without the tedious work of outlining each step of mathematical operations. Indeed, it is by this process of being acquainted with the day-day routines in the real world, the tacit dimension of rationality plays a critical role in the formation of explicit statements such as scientific theories and theological doctrines. Living and acting in the world increases the capacity to relate our concepts to the reality around us more directly, and from this direct encounter with the thing-in-itself emerges a possibility of knowledge that is not otherwise possible.[148] Faith thus, according to Torrance, is intelligible, realistic, objective, and implicit.

---

[147] Thomas F. Torrance, "The Place of Michael Polanyi in the Modern Philosophy of Science," *Ethics in Science and Medicine* 7 (1980), 60.

[148] Learning how to swim is a good example. We acquire skills to swim neither by theorizing our bodily motions in water, nor simply observing what takes place when one

If faith is driven by an implicit dimension of knowing, how is it criticizable? The question of criticizability is important, since without criticizability, tacit knowledge once again can be confused with subjective absolutism or naïve foundationalism. Torrance solves this issue by making a difference between working beliefs and ultimate beliefs.[149] Regarding working beliefs, they are given, because they arise "in our minds under the pressure of reality and its inherent intelligibility,"[150] which in turn, function as normative beliefs for a community. However, Torrance notes that,

> all the time the community's normative beliefs are, or ought to be, steadily re-examined in the course of this expansion in understanding, so that they are continuously put to the test and re-appropriated. This can be done, however, only through consistent, responsible commitment to the intelligibility of reality which is the one source of true belief and the ground of its universal authority and validity.[151]

In other words, working beliefs function as an interpretative framework for the critical and constructive work of further inquiry because they are modifiable and criticizable.

Regarding ultimate beliefs, Torrance admits that "they are 'irrefutable as well as unprovable" because "there is no higher or wider system with reference to which they may be demonstrated."[152] For instance, an ultimate belief is a commitment to the notion that there is order in the universe. And this "order is not something that we can ever

---

swims; rather, the actual swimming skills are acquired when we are *in* the water, learning by playing in the water. Only when we are immersed in the pool of water, the theory and observation of swimming come to fruition and become meaningful, for they are applied and embodied through repetition. This means that explicit knowledge becomes meaningful by means of repeated personal indwelling as new and more complex skills emerge from the interaction between explicit and implicit cognitive activities. For a similar explanation, see Jerry H. Gill, *The Tacit Mode: Michael Polanyi's Postmodern Philosophy* (Albany: State University of New York Press, 2000), 47.

[149] Torrance, "The Framework of Belief," 15-24.

[150] Ibid., 15.

[151] Ibid., 21.

[152] Ibid., 19.

prove, for we have to assume order in any attempt at proof or disproof. That is to say, order presupposes an ultimate ground of order, with which we operate at the back of our mind in all rational activity."[153] What Torrance is saying that, without the ultimate belief in the existence of "order," we cannot make sense of what the world is made of, how it behaves, or even the prediction of its final outcomes. In this respect, working beliefs are formulated, tested, and refined because they are contingent upon ultimate beliefs, so ultimate beliefs exercise a regulative control on our on-going scientific and theological inquiry.

The key point for introducing Torrance is that his sophisticated version of faith reveals the fact that faith is not entirely subjective. It has both subjective and objective poles. It is subjective since, in any fiduciary project, we cannot dismiss the role of the affection and passionate conviction in believing what needs to be believed in fidelity to the thing-in-itself. It is objective because faith is associated with the cognitive assent to some aspects of reality, or what Torrance calls "a basic act of recognition in which our minds respond to a pattern or structure inherent in the world around us, which imprint itself upon them."[154] When we marry our fiduciary project with the realistic outlook of the world, we do not have to fall back on the subjectivity of faith, nor do we need to split the two worlds of theology and science as mutually exclusive categories. Rather, if we understand that faith is framed strictly within the context of rational submission to the claims of reality out there, we can eliminate the modern tendency to conflate subjectivity with objectivity, on the one hand, and divide the two without any possibility of a merger, on the other hand.

Faith as Third Rationality

It is time to conclude and state my case for faith as a third rationality. To recap, what I have attempted to do in this chapter is to demonstrate that faith has been misunderstood in many different ways. It is because faith

---

[153] Torrance, "The Concept of Order," 130.

[154] Torrance, "The Framework of Belief," 12.

does not fit neatly into a single category of objectivity or subjectivity; rather, faith is the fundamental structure of the human mind that combines subjectivity and objectivity into a unified whole, and for this reason, it must take the position of third rationality. To unpack the meaning of third rationality, we need to review its precedent categories: objectivity and subjectivity. The former is what I call first rationality. It is commonly noted as "the rational process by which one draws proper deductive inferences from premises or proper inductive inferences from evidence, or properly plausible explanations of observations and phenomena."[155] As I have hinted already, first, rationality does not stand alone. It always remains in tension with second rationality, which is our subjectivity. Subjectivity can be referred to as "how someone's judgment is shaped by personal opinions and feelings instead of outside influences."[156] In other words, subjectivity recognizes that the things in the world are interpreted through the personal, value-laden, and affective dimension of the thinking person.

Faith as third rationality does not fit into either first or second rationality, for it is the "basic act of recognition in which our minds respond to a pattern or structure inherent in the world around us which imprints itself upon them."[157] In a simpler term, we can say that faith is like Kant's conception of an *a priori* category. According to Kant, our experience is meaningful because we see through the lens of an *a priori* category like "space," that is, a basic structure of our mind. Hence, Kant's *a priori* category is regulative in nature. Taking Kant's *a priori* category seriously, I conceive faith as the fundamental structure of our mind that does not constitute an explicit knowledge on its own, but like Kant's *a priori* category, it regulates our thought, action, and feeling to the right direction, that is, to "feel at home with the basic structure of reality." [158] For this reason, faith itself does not generate rational

---

[155] Tom Gilson, "One: The Party of Reason" in *True Reason: Confronting the Irrationality of the New Atheism* (Grand Rapids: Kregel, 2013), 20.

[156] Vocabulary, accessed October 12, 2015, https://www.vocabulary.com/dictionary/subjectivity.

[157] Torrance, "The Framework of Belief," 12.

[158] David A. Pailin, "What Game Is Being Played? The Need for Clarity about the Relationships between Scientific and Theological Understanding," *Zygon* 35/1 (2000), 149.

knowledge explicitly. So, like Torrance, I do not hide the fact that faith is built upon a basic, *a priori* structure of the human mind. However, although it resembles Kant's *a priori* category, it nonetheless differs from Kant's transcendental philosophy because faith not only regulates but also constitutes knowledge, though in an implicit way. As Polanyi and Torrance have shown, faith-as-intuition allows us to penetrate into the intelligibility of nature or God, and as a result, we gain personal knowledge—e.g., tacit knowledge that arises from the personal, real, and intuitive engagement with the world. For this reason, faith knowledge is pre-reflective, non-formal, tacit, inarticulate, and intuitive. Although implicit in nature, faith knowledge becomes the steppingstone for a more nuanced, well-shaped explicit knowledge.

Moreover, because faith functions as a built-in frame of reference upon which we make sense of the world, it combines our objective data with subjective needs, along with intrinsic categories such as working and ultimate beliefs that arise from our implicit transaction with reality. Faith is, therefore, influential in producing workable theories, models, and conceptual systems, upon which we establish our criticizable and expandable expressions. This expression is what I call the secondary statement of faith. In the process of producing a secondary statement of faith, belief categories cohere to the trend and norm of the society, which is to be critically examined by peers to see if they correlate to the objective data from our continual interaction with the reality in question. This is a general description of faith that is operative in all sciences.

From a Christian perspective, faith is not just a secondary movement but also the primary agent that integrates the way we worship, that is, a spontaneous display of our affection toward God, and the way we rationally understand God's being and act vis-à-vis God's self-revelation in and through Jesus Christ. In faith, we correlate what is doctrinal in terms of our existential language to what is fiduciary in terms of our confessional statements. This is what I call the primary statement of faith. In this respect, for Christians, faith is a guide that leads to divine reality, and ultimately, to the Father in and through Jesus Christ by the power of the Holy as it helps us transcend the limits of reason and affection, but nonetheless, merges them with our own existential circumstances for further theological clarifications. Here, in faith, not only subjectivity and objective come together, but also the correlation between God, humanity, and nature is made possible. There is no other rational category that can accomplish such a feat.

Therefore, we must move from faith to faith. We ascend from the secondary dimension of scientific faith to the primary dimension of religious faith, finally arriving at saving faith in Jesus Christ. This means that we all are faith-carriers. By faith, we live, think, and feel our way around the world. Because of faith, we have the passion to pursue what is good, beautiful, and right. Because of faith, we seek the truth. It invokes "confidence in what we hope for and assurance about what we do not see" (Heb. 11:1). Surely, without faith, we cannot sustain the triadic interplay of orthodoxy, orthopraxis, and orthopathos. For faith demands the persistent pursuit of certitude, it constantly searches for the best way to maintain right thinking, right action, and right feeling.

For this reason, I can only place faith in the placeholder called third rationality. There is no other known epistemic rubric to which it can belong. It does not belong to the realm of objectivity, because it does not simply derive from our logical and reason-abled concerns. Neither does it belong to the realm of subjectivity, because it is not determined by our emotions or moods of the day. Rather, faith is the basic structure of the mind underwritten by the deep trust in the reality out there, such as God and nature. It is triggered by implicit awareness of our surrounding which gives rise to explicit statements that could only express partially of what was experienced tacitly. The interplay of the implicit and explicit dimensions of faith will provide the impetus for the fundamental structure of our mind to expand and grow for the sake of keeping a healthy object-subject balance.

Conclusion

In this chapter, based on the critical analysis of Augustinian, Cartesian, and Kantian understanding of faith and drawing from Torrance's work, I have re-appropriated faith as the most basic structure of human rationality that integrates first and second rationality into a nonseparable whole, affirming the idea that faith is related to knowledge, affection, and trust.[159] What I want to accomplish here is to prevent the dichotomization of subject and object, mind and matter, or thought and experience, in order to reinstate the unity of knowing and being under the foundational rubric of faith. This fiduciary framework functions for this book as a catalyst that brings to light the importance of keeping the religious faith intact all the while finding areas of congruence between the faith of science and the faith of Christian religion. This is possible only if we accept not only the continuity but also the discontinuity between the implicit and explicit faith. In this way, we are more capable of recognizing many levels of our cognitive activities that can be correlated in the name of faith so that a gradient of true meaning emerges through the interplay of faith, reason, and affection.

Just to clarify, faith as third rationality is never meant to advocate the Augustinian tradition—e.g., faith is above reason. Although I agree with Augustine's principle that faith seeks understanding, and not vice versa, I have explained this move as a connection between an implicit engagement with reality that always seeks out an explicit explanation. Because the implicit statement requires further support from explicit analyses, these two cognitive activities of faith and reason are complementary rather than hierarchical.

As we move to the final chapter, we are reminded that the integrity of the theology and science cannot be sustained unless we bring to light the ultimate obligation of seeking God and his action in this world, not only from the perspective of naturalism but more importantly from the perspective of supernatural divine causality. For this reason, we turn to the issue of miracles and tackle head-on the inner relation between miracles, divine action, and biblical data.

---

[159] For more details on the definition of faith as "knowledge, assent, and trust" see Francesca Aran Murphy, Balázs M. Mezei, and Kenneth Oakes, *Illuminating Faith: An Invitation to Theology* (New York: Bloomsbury Academics, 2015), Chapter 8. I have nuanced this triad as knowledge, affection, and trust, since "assent" and "trust" are too closely connected and can be bundled up under a common rubric of "acknowledgment."

Chapter Four

Miracles, Divine Action, and the Bible

Thus far, in our assessment of the current status of the bridge that connects theology and science, we have found that there are areas of dangerous pitfalls and cracks such as the naturalistic reductionism and scientific-religious absolutism. More serious was the bridge being torn apart by the separation of theological realism and scientific realism and the dichotomy of faith and reason. We picked up metascientific tools and tried to patch up those areas of weakness, and it seems that our job is nearly complete as we are at the end of the road with one more task remaining. In this chapter, we will be working on the problem of biblical miracles.

Biblical miracles have been controversial for centuries. On the one hand, they have been rejected as fairy tales, legends, or fictional stories made up by ancient novelists. On the other hand, they have been uncritically accepted as divine special interventions, extraordinary events that defy the laws of nature, or God's display of his mighty power to reveal his omnipotence. In our scientific age, miracles clearly separate the camp into two spheres. Either one is a believer or not. There has rarely been any attempt to set a middle course. Does this mean that miracle claims are obstacles to interdisciplinary efforts, for they create dissension? Should we treat miracle claims as the hindrance to the advance of the theology and science interface? Should we remove miracles or any components that are associated with miracles and cast them off the interdisciplinary bridge?

My effort in this chapter is to defend a theological cause and claim that miracles do belong to the bridge. They are not necessarily an obstacle to the advancement of the theology and science interface. Unfortunately, the popular belief seems to side with those who dismiss miracles, or at least, do not find the need to talk about miracles in the scientific age. For this reason, the effort of this chapter is to defend against scholars who say that miracle claims are irrelevant to the scientific age and demonstrate that we can still make some sense out of biblical miracles, despite the scientific gap that exists between the biblical culture and our own settings. I want to show that we who are enjoying the benefits of the state-of-the-art technology should not shy away from speaking about miracles just because they are in the Bible. Miracles should not be the main factor for the cultural and religious schism in contemporary society; rather, they must be well accounted for because they could help us repair the metascientific gap in our culture.

To make my defense, in this chapter, I follow Richard Purtill's suggestion. "The argument for miracles consists of two stages—an argument for the general possibility of miracles, and an argument for the historical actuality (or accuracy) of certain miracles."[1] So the chapter is divided into two main parts. The first part deals with the discussion of the possibility of miracles. The primary dialogue partner in this section is Baruch Spinoza (1632-1677). I engage his rejection of miracles and argue that miracles are possible only if we consider open system metaphysics and divinely guided threshold crossings. The added dimension of this section is the discussion of divine action, which we cannot do without since we are talking about God's extraordinary acts depicted in the Bible. The second part will focus on Rudolf Bultmann's work, and like the preceding section, I will examine Bultmann's dismissal of the historical reliability of miracles and respond critically to his claims in order to sustain the argument that biblical claims are after all historically reliable.

Spinoza and Miracles

Spinoza is often called the philosopher who helped lay the groundwork for a scientific philosophy that was to follow by his successors such as Kant, Schelling, and Hegel.[2] This is so because his theology, ontology,

---

[1] Richard L. Purtill, *Thinking about Religion: A Philosophical Introduction to Religion* (Englewood Cliffs: Prentice-Hall, 1978), 68.

[2] This aspect is highlighted in the work of Steven Nadler and Michael Rocca. Cf. Steven Ladler, *Spinoza's 'Ethics': An Introduction* (New York: Cambridge University Press, 2006); and Michael Della Rocca, *Spinoza* (New York; Routledge, 2008).

and epistemology were constructed from start to finish on a philosophy of naturalism that was truly innovational and unconventional in the cultural climate of his time. Prior to Spinoza, of course, there were thinkers like Francis Bacon and René Descartes, who had attempted to combine science and philosophy in such a way that philosophical science would clarify the nature and work of God in this world. However, although there are areas of continuity between Spinoza and his predecessors, Spinoza's work is unique because it deviates completely away from the orthodox religion, developing a non-traditional view of God and nature.[3] Bacon and Descartes at least tried to stay within the bounds of their inherited theological paradigm, but not Spinoza. In *Theological-Political Treatise* he explicitly states that he wants to do away with the old ways of thinking that plague the minds of his fellow believers, whether they are Christians or Jews, and pave a new trajectory so that justice and harmony could supplant dissension, war, and intolerance of the 18th century Europe.[4]

Moreover, Spinoza is concerned with not only societal dissolution, but also with the dwindling rationality of the citizens, especially those who are churchgoers. He writes,

> They [religious persons] swear that reason is blind and human wisdom fruitless because it cannot show them a sure way of acquiring the empty things they want. On the other hand, they believe that the delirious wanderings of the imagination, dreams and all sorts of childish nonsense are divine replies.[5]

---

[3] Spinoza's three major works are *The Principles of Descartes' Philosophy*, *Theological-Political Treatise*, and *Ethics*. *Theological-Political Treatise* and *Ethics* have been heavily discounted as utterly flawed and useless, anti-Christian, anti-theistic, and anti-social, by his critics like Pierre Bayle. Expecting such criticisms, Spinoza could only publish some of his books anonymously during his life time. He was already in trouble with his Jewish community.

[4] See the preface of Spinoza's *Theological-Political Treatise*. Spinoza, *Theological-Political Treatise*, trans. Michael Silverstone, ed. Jonathan Israel (New York: Cambridge University Press, 2007). Note that there was religious war waging constantly in his day, most violently from 1524 to 1648, following the onset of the Protestant Reformation. The clash between the Catholics, Jews, and Christians was treacherous and fatal, and the reconciliation was nowhere in sight during his time.

[5] Spinoza *Theological-Political Treatise*, 4.

According to Spinoza's assessment, the organized religion of his time had fallen into the error of irrationalism. What caused it? The culprit according to Spinoza is emotion, which makes the church-goers "fluctuate wretchedly between hope and fear."[6] He explains, "When the mind is in a state of doubt, the slightest impulse can easily steer it in any direction, and all the more readily when it is hovering between hope and fear, though it may be confident, pompous and proud enough at other times."[7] Because of the people's inability to make sound, reasonable judgments being swayed by fluctuating emotion, they are, insists Spinoza, "caught up in any superstition."[8]

For Spinoza, calling emotionally driven religion superstition gave him the right to rethink and revise the traditional religious paradigm, especially our understanding of God. The traditional understanding of God trickling down from the medieval period to Descartes is that God and nature are two distinct entities, which are mutually exclusive. Spinoza disagrees with this view. In *Ethics*, he lays out new ground for thinking about God and justifies his proposal by defining the word "substance" as "that which is in itself and is conceived through itself; that is, that which does not need the concept of another thing, from which concept it must be formed."[9] Spinoza is essentially arguing that a substance is something that is self-caused and self-existing. It has its own causality and ontological status. Its existence depends on nothing else. It is a necessary entity.

Going further, based upon his propositions 1 through 10 in *Ethics*, Spinoza argues that a substance cannot be multiple since there can be only one substance.[10] And as proposition 11 states, "God, or substance

---

[6] Ibid., 3.

[7] Ibid.

[8] Ibid.

[9] Spinoza, *Ethics*, trans. Samuel Shirley, ed. Michael L. Morgan (Indianapolis: Hackett, 2002), 217.

[10] Note that for Spinoza the substance is not only a "thing" as we know it today, but also it can mean "causality" or "events," or even "relations" between things. For details on Spinoza's conception of substance, see Beth Lord, *Spinoza's Ethics* (Edinburgh: Edinburgh University Press, 2010), 19-20.

consisting of infinite attributes, each of which expresses eternal and infinite essence, necessarily exists."[11] This implies that there exists only one substance, and this substance is God, and it follows that God exists necessarily. It also means that everything that exists can only exist in God. Moreover, since there can be only one substance in Nature, God and Nature are one and the same. This means that the Spinozian cosmos does not require God to be a creator, since Nature exists necessarily. Surely, this is not the traditional understanding of God. Even his immediate predecessor, Descartes showed that, although a "substance" is a basic immutable independent existing entity with its own corresponding attributes, that is, its permanent properties, there were innumerable substances in the universe because they were created by God. Being a dualist, Descartes even substantiated the mind as an immaterial substance, having a property of its own that is distinct from material objects. In Spinoza's judgment, Descartes had it all wrong. There is only one substance and this one substance is "God or Nature" (*Deus sive Natura*).

How is it then that we have two distinct forms of mind and body? Can monism substantiate the existence of two distinct categories of mind and body? Spinoza has no problem with this distinction. He refers to the attributes and modes of being to make this distinction. [12] According to Spinoza, God has two attributes: thought and extension, which are a dual aspect of single substance, that is, the very essence of God. God has an infinite extension, which is called Nature. It embraces and is made up of every material object in the world. God is also infinite in thought. It embraces and is made up of every kind of thought in the world.

Spinoza also emphasizes that we humans also have these two attributes, namely, mind and body. In fact, these two attributes are evidenced in both infinite and finite modes of being. An infinite mode of thought or extension is, of course, God or Nature. Correspondingly, the finite mode of thought and body are the two aspects of one

---

[11] Spinoza, *Ethics*, 222.

[12] Ibid., 217.

individual human being. We can hear the echo of Platonism here, which notes that the tension between the infinite and finite mode of existence in the world—i.e., a rational intelligible order and a changeable material order. This is what Philip Clayton calls "dual-aspect monism."[13] Dual-aspect monism simply denotes "that the mental and the physical are two different ways to characterize one 'stuff.'"[14] Thus, there is a distinction in the attributes and modes of being, but there is no substance distinction in the world made up of single stuff.

Spinoza's identification of God and nature as one and the same has confused the contemporary scholars, who labeled him as either pantheist or panentheist.[15] In my judgment, if we understand Spinoza's dual-aspect monism, we may say that he has both pantheistic and panentheistic inclinations. God and Nature are identical in substance (pantheism); however, God and nature are distinguishable in attributes and modes of being, albeit God is infinitely greater than the finite modes of nature, whether in thought or body (panentheism). Hence, it is advisable to distinguish "Nature" from "nature," the former denoting a pantheistic all-embracing substance and the latter a panentheistic finite form of nature that is included in the infinite mode of being. To put it in another way, God is, to use Spinoza's term, *Natura Naturans* (Nature naturing) and the world is *Natura Naturata* (nature Natured). The former emphasizes the self-sufficient causality of God as the all-embracing substance of the world, and the latter emphasizes the finite mode of the causal chain of nature that exists in God.

Because of the conflation of God and Nature, Spinoza is now logically privileged to say that everything occurs in Nature is determined by the essence of God.[16] Here, he takes up the medieval notion of God's essence. The medieval notion of God's essence basically

---

[13] Philip Clayton, "Neuroscience, the Human Person, and God" in *Bridging Science and Religion*, ed. Ted Peters and Gaymon Bennett (Minneapolis: Fortress, 2003), 116.

[14] Ibid.

[15] Cf. John W. Cooper, *Panentheism: The Other God of the Philosopher: From Plato to Present* (Grand Rapids: Baker, 2006).

[16] Spinoza writes, "Whatever is, is in God, and nothing can be or be conceived without God." Spinoza, *Ethics*, 224.

says that God is unchanging and immutable.[17] Hence, for Spinoza, Nature is the same way. He notes in *Theological-Political Treatise* that "nothing happens contrary to nature, but nature maintains an eternal, fixed and immutable order."[18] This is easy to prove. Since God is immutable and everything is moved by God or Nature, then the laws of nature are also immutable and unchanging. Based on this explanation, it is wrong to say that the laws of nature are fickle and changeable like the laws and decrees made by human authorities. Such non-standardizable and non-universal form of religious laws does not conform to what nature is supposed to be. So, as far as Spinoza is concerned, they are not "true laws."

What we can see is that Spinoza wants to develop a philosophical primer upon which everything else in the world can be measured and corrected. Of course, this can only be done without the introduction of arbitrariness and relativism. How can we do this? Spinoza turns to science. As a scientist, Spinoza is well aware that "through scientific experiment and rational thinking, human beings have achieved some true knowledge of some of these eternal laws,"[19] just like Baconian and Galilean claims of the universal physical laws that determine how finite bodies are moving and interacting with other bodies. Surely, in Spinoza's opinion, those laws are not human inventions; rather, they are part of God. Merging Spinoza's determinism and monism, we have the rationale for correlating our ways of thinking to the laws of nature, which later provides a pivotal argument against biblical miracles. Beth Lord summarizes the relationship between the physical laws and the laws of inner logic denoted in Spinoza's *Ethic*.

> God, as thinking being, causes there to be infinite intellect: true understanding of everything that exists. Infinite intellect expresses itself as a single continuum of thinking. This continuum is made up of infinite relations of true

---

[17] This is well depicted in Thomistic theism, which draws upon Aristotle concept of pure actuality. For a brief critique on Aristotelian concept of pure actuality, see Michael Welker, *God the Spirit*, trans. John F. Hoffmeyer (Minneapolis: Fortress, 1994), 298-301.

[18] Spinoza *Theological-Political Treatise*, 82.

[19] Lord, *Spinoza's Ethics*, 43.

understanding: the laws of logic. Just as physical laws determine and explain the nature and relations of bodies, logical laws determine and explain the nature of minds and relations of ideas. Human minds are modes of true understanding, and our thinking follows from this logical order. When we have true knowledge, we understand according to the order of logical principles in the infinite intellect. This is one reason why the *Ethics* is composed using the geometrical method. True knowledge is understood logically, and the *Ethics* is a textual representation of true knowledge. The geometrical method best approximates how true ideas are *truly* connected in God.[20]

Essentially, Spinoza is teaching us that our mind functions like the physical things in this world. Because God is everything and everything is in God, it follows that the intelligible mind and the matter in motion are two sides of the one and the same thing. Instead of treating mind and body as separate substances with wholly different properties, contra Descartes, Spinoza sees them as two aspects of the same thing. So our mind supposed to be orderly and reasonable just like the orderliness of nature, thereby not to be swayed by fickle emotions that disturb it. When we depend on our capricious feelings, we would lose this sense of orderliness and fall into the error of thinking God or Nature in terms of superstition.

For this reason, Spinoza makes a distinction between three kinds of knowledge. The first kind of knowledge is referred to as "opinion" or "imagination," which Spinoza labels it as inadequate knowledge.[21] To put it in another way, what is driven by emotion produces only inadequate knowledge. This principle applies to both religion and science. In the case of religion, as we have already seen, inadequate knowledge stems from superstition, which is "variable and unstable as all absurd leaps of the mind and powerful emotions are, and can only

---

[20] Ibid.

[21] For example, see Spinoza, *Ethics*, 267.

be sustained by hope and hatred, anger and deception."[22] According to Spinoza, inadequate knowledge is not only visible in the practice of superstition, but also found in Scripture as well. For instance, he finds that the biblical prophecy is primarily made up of imagination (e.g., a fabrication of the human mind). In this regard, he notes that "prophets were not endowed with more perfect minds than others but only a more vivid power of imagination, as the scriptural narratives also abundantly show."[23] So he concludes that "prophecy by itself cannot provide certainty, because as we have already shown, prophecy depends upon imagination alone."[24] For this reason, Spinoza is pessimistic about biblical prophecies, which cannot be strictly interpretable by the "natural light." For Spinoza, imagination tends to misguide the prophets thinking that there is some entity existing outside of Nature doing things that defy the laws of nature. Since for Spinoza nothing exists outside Nature, this is simply a faulty vision that has no correspondence to reality. In a pantheistic scheme, Spinoza can only perceive nature as having a one-to-one relationship with God. What belongs to this world also belongs to God. Therefore, as far as Spinoza is concerned, the first kind of knowledge, which is inadequate, does not correspond to anything because it is imagined by "the fancies and fantasies of despondent and fearful minds."[25]

In the same vein, Spinoza is skeptical about the surety of empirical studies.[26] Unlike Francis Bacon who was confident that scientific data gleaned from observations and testing reveal the true nature of reality, Spinoza simply asserts that our senses do not give us the complete picture. Spinoza sarcastically writes against Bacon and states that "since the nature of the universe, unlike the nature of the blood, is not limited, but is absolutely infinite, its parts are controlled by the nature of this infinite

---

[22] Spinoza *Theological-Political Treatise*, 5.

[23] Ibid., 27.

[24] Ibid., 28.

[25] Spinoza *Theological-Political Treatise*, 4.

[26] This aspect has been well attested by Eric Schliesser. For more details, see Eric Schliesser, "Spinoza and the Philosophy of Science: Mathematics, Motion, and Being," Philsci Archive, last modified July 10, 2012, accessed January 12, 2016, http://philsci-archive.pitt.edu/id/eprint/9223.

potency in infinite ways and are compelled to undergo infinite variations."[27] Notice his repetition of the word "infinite." He is asserting that the finite mind will never catch up with the infinite. In other words, he is arguing for empirical underdeterminism, which was brought up by Karl Popper much later in the 20th-century. That is to say, empirical knowledge is always merely probable and durable only to a certain extent because nature is too large for us to know everything from our senses. This is not to deny that Spinoza is completely dismissing empirical evidence. According to Spinoza, although empirical evidence cannot give any clear knowledge of reality, especially the essence of things, it can still teach and enlighten us something about nature that will ultimately lead us to the essence of things if we are prudent.

Going further, Spinoza asserts that, like empirical science, mathematical science can never yield adequate knowledge of reality.[28] This is again a counterargument directed to his predecessors like Descartes, Galileo, and Hobbes, who considered mathematics the primary means to access the true knowledge of nature. For Spinoza, the use of measure and number does not reveal to us God's essence and eternity. Simply put, mathematics does not help us see how reality really is but only see how we imagine it to be. He writes,

> Further, inasmuch as we separate the modifications of substance from substance itself, and reduce them to classes, so that we may, as far as is possible, the more readily imagine them, there arises *number*, whereby we limit them. Whence it is clearly to be seen, that measure, time, and number are merely modes of thinking, or, rather, of imagining.[29]

What he is saying here is that science like mathematics is a man-made enterprise, and it will always fall short and never reach God on its own. Again, this does not mean that Spinoza thinks that mathematics is

---

[27] Spinoza, "Letter 32," *Spinoza: The Letters*, trans. Samuel Shirley (Indianapolis: Hackett, 1995), 194.

[28] Spinoza, "Letter 12" in *Spinoza: The Letters*, trans. Samuel Shirley (Indianapolis: Hackett, 1995), 101-107.

[29] Ibid.

fundamentally flawed or unreliable; rather, he simply wants his readers to see that number and measurement do not reveal the ultimate essence of things. So, in the end, Spinoza found himself fighting against empiricists and rationalists of his day, pointing out that neither empirical science nor mathematical science is adequate in itself. For this reason, Eric Schliesser rightfully asserts that Spinoza is not an advocate of the mechanical philosophy of his time, but a fellow traveler of modern science, being ahead of his time.[30]

What then leads us to adequate knowledge? Spinoza proceeds to the next two kinds of knowledge—i.e., reason and intuition, which are categorized as adequate knowledge.[31] In order to understand the particular features of these two kinds of knowledge, we need to know Spinoza's conception of "common notions." He ensures that common notions are steppingstones to adequate knowledge of God or Nature, particularly that God exists necessarily, and is everywhere, and that God's nature is presupposed in all things we conceive. In this monistic ideal, there are three things to note about common notions. First, common notions are fixed and universal because ultimately everything will converge to the one and only substance in the world. Despite the heterogeneous appearance, the things in this world are actually homogenous and systematically connected to each other in a determinative way. Second, just as there are common notions of extension, there must be common notions of thought. In other words, not only things are "common" physically, but so are our thoughts related to each other and to the infinite mode of thought. Third and finally, the source of adequate knowledge is within the nature of the thing itself. To be true means that one acts from one's nature or the essence of things, not from the things themselves like imagination and emotion that are inconsistent and unclear. In short, in Spinoza's philosophical paradigm, common notions guarantee for us clear and distinct ideas that are fixed and universal, which in turn, lead us to adequate knowledge.

---

[30] Schliesser, "Spinoza," 18.

[31] Spinoza, *Ethics*, 267.

Understanding the connection between common notions and adequate knowledge, we can see why Spinoza selects "reason" as the second kind of knowledge. Reason is where thought and extension come together in a unified whole, and functions as a guide to unveil common notions. Unlike false religion or experiential sciences which are underwritten by emotion or imagination, reason allows us to access the essence of things in the form of axiomatic "definitions." [32] These definitions are by no means arbitrary. They are developed through the rigors of inductive and deductive reasoning processes. Once demonstrable definitions are assembled by reason-abled activities and logical thinking, common notions are clarified in terms of axiomatic definitions that no longer need further proof. This is where intuition comes in.

Intuition is the third kind of knowledge that Spinoza mentions. There is a sense of ambiguity as to what Spinoza means when he says that intuition proceeds "from an adequate idea of the formal essence of certain attributes of God to the adequate knowledge of the formal essence of things."[33] There are many different interpretations associated with this statement, such as intuition as inferential knowledge (Schliesser) or intuition as knowledge that extends to eternity (Lord). In my judgment, Spinoza is speaking about intuition as the way to know things "by heart" without the need of going through the rigors of proof. This type of knowledge can be obtained if we know "everything," that is, the essence of things. Since the essence of things is ultimately underwritten by one substance called God or Nature, the essence of things refers to "everything" that there is to be.

Of course, we cannot know everything, and Spinoza is well aware of this fact, but that does not stop us from digging deep into the essence of things by seeing not only in parts but also holistically. Within a broader and holistic perspective, Spinoza ensures that we can intuitively identify axiomatic definitions. In other words, if we move from the idea of God's attributes to the knowledge of the formal essence of things, we

---

[32] For example, see Spinoza, *Ethics*, 217.

[33] Ibid., 267.

may be able to move from inadequate knowledge to adequate knowledge. This can only be done if we have enough critical power to see the whole from the parts. For instance, when we see the finite mode of nature, the existence of the infinite being can be inferred from it as we can think of a large forest just by seeing a few trees. This is not all. According to Spinoza, reason or intuition reveals the fact that the definition of natural things explains how nature behaves, in the same way as physical studies, based upon fixed and universal laws of nature, explaining the matters in motion and at rest, and at the same time, removing any "non-natural" or imaginative ideas from physical science.

Here we can discern Spinoza's way of correlating the bottom-up approach (induction) to the top-down method (deduction). From the first kind of knowledge (imagination) to the second or the third kind of knowledge (reason or intuition), we move from experience to general definitions as scientific philosophy moves from the parts to the whole, and from the second or the third kind of knowledge to the first kind of knowledge, we move from general axiomatic definitions to the observable phenomenon, holistically explaining the behavior of nature via a fixed set of laws. So it is both wrong to say that Spinoza is a simple rationalist who copies Descartes' deductive method, and to say that he is a simple empiricist who follows Baconian inductive science. He employs both inductive and deductive methods all the while understanding the limitation of empirical and mathematical sciences.

Spinoza encourages the same approach to interpreting the Bible. Jonathan Israel explains,

> When studying texts, including Scripture, he [Spinoza] urges us to do the same, seeking out first what is most universal and fundamental in the narrative. What is most universally proclaimed (whether by prophets, scribes, or Christ) in Scripture is "that there is a God, one and omnipotent, who alone is to be adored and cares for all men, loving most those who worship Him and love their neighbor as themselves, etc."[34]

---

[34] Jonathan Israel, "Introduction," in *Benedict de Spinoza: Theological-Political Treatise*, ed. Jonathan Israel (Cambridge: Cambridge University Press, 2007), xvi.

Essentially, Spinoza's biblical interpretative method moves from data to universal meaning, and then descends from the general to the specific, all the while deconstructing "non-natural" or imaginative categories that may veil the true intended meaning of the author.

Like any other sciences, Spinoza realizes that biblical narratives are not true, but historically determined and, therefore, poetic, "inexact, limited, and vague."[35] Despite its vagueness, Spinoza ensures us that, when we apply a scientific method, we can tap into the essence of things and unveil the true meaning based on the truth of things.[36] What is the truth of things? Israel explains, "For Spinoza, the truth of fact is an absolute and purely physical reality grounded on the laws of 'true' philosophy and science, an explanation devoid of all supernatural agents and forces, and all spirits and qualities separate from bodies, being expressed solely in terms of mechanistic cause and effect."[37] This is precisely why Spinoza deems that biblical hermeneutics is historically determined. He writes in this regard,

> The [correct] method of interpreting nature consists above all in constructing a natural history, from which we derive the definitions of natural things, as from certain data. Likewise, to interpret Scripture, we need to assemble a genuine history of it and to deduce the thinking of Scripture's authors by valid inferences from this history, as from certain data and principles.[38]

Therefore, Spinoza asserts that Scripture has two layers of meaning, one imaginative, and the other historical. He equates the former meaning to "revelation" because it "really does transcend human understanding,"[39] and the latter to natural knowledge "for the natural light of reason requires nothing that this light itself does not reach."[40] As

---

[35] Ibid.

[36] Ibid.

[37] Ibid., xii.

[38] Spinoza *Theological-Political Treatise*, 98.

[39] Ibid., 99.

[40] Ibid., 61.

Schliesser notes, "By this [natural light] (then common locution) he means nothing mysterious." [41] According to Spinoza, although the biblical hermeneutics inevitably demands us to give an account of the specific "revelations" and "prophecies," they are not to be trusted as the truth of meaning because they are the byproduct of the prophet's "vivid power of imagination." Thus, we have to go behind them and seek out the truth of meaning by assessing the historical fact that lies beyond the imaginative outworking of biblical narratives. What Spinoza actually wants to say is that the true meaning of a text can be obtained only

> by carefully reconstructing both the historical and linguistic circumstances in which it was written and analyzing the concepts used in terms of a strictly naturalistic interpretation of human nature, that is one that itself makes no appeal to supernatural forces or authority.[42]

Ironically, Spinoza wants to remove theological bias underwritten by imagination, but in lieu of biblical imagination, he has selected the naturalistic philosophical standpoint as the guiding bias for the biblical interpretation. Ultimately, Spinoza does not see the study of Scripture in any way different from the study of nature. In *Theological-Political Treatise*, he affirms this principle by stating that biblical hermeneutics "does not differ from the [correct] method of interpreting nature, but rather is wholly consonant with it."[43] As a result, based on a naturalistic-monistic frame of reference, Spinoza begins to explain away biblical miracles.

Reading Scripture, Spinoza recognizes several key features of biblical miracles. Here are some examples. First, they are depicted as "unusual works of nature" by those who "do not want to know the natural causes of things, partly from devotion and partly from zeal to oppose those who pursue natural philosophy. They desire only to hear about that of which they are most ignorant and consequently about

---

[41] Schliesser, "Spinoza," 11.

[42] Israel, "Introduction," xii.

[43] Spinoza *Theological-Political Treatise*, 98.

which they marvel most."[44] Second, they ascribe to God's governance "ignoring natural causes and evincing wonder at what is outside the normal course of nature, and revere the power of God best when they envisage the power of nature as if it were subdued by God."[45] Third, "the ancients took for a miracle whatever they were unable to explain in the manner the common people normally explained natural things."[46] And lastly, according to Spinoza, those ignorant believers call "'miracles' insofar as the word is used for a phenomenon that conflicts with the order of nature." [47] Essentially, Spinoza is analyzing and defining biblical miracles based on the things of nature. For him, biblical miracles are abnormal because they describe God's work in terms of what is either beyond or opposed to the natural phenomenon. In his opinion, this is surely an erroneous interpretation of Scripture.

According to Spinoza, God's work in nature cannot contravene the laws of nature.[48] As we have seen, in Spinoza's deterministic world, God or Nature is immutable and unchanging. It follows that what goes on in nature as a whole is also governed by a set of fixed and unchanging laws. If God were to change the "laws" that govern nature in any way, he would not be acting according to his perfect essence. He would be no different from the way we humans act. In fact, Spinoza believes that the biblical writers, exaggerating what God has done in the world, faulted on this aspect. Using their own imagination, they anthropomorphized God and confused the infinite mode of being with the finite mode of being. Thus, for Spinoza, God is neither a person nor does he act like

---

[44] Ibid., 81.

[45] Ibid., 82.

[46] Ibid., 84.

[47] Ibid., 85.

[48] Ibid., 91. Spinoza writes in this regard. "Thus, we conclude without reservation that all things that are truly reported to have happened in Scripture necessarily happened according to the laws of nature, as all things do. If anything is found which can be demonstrated conclusively to contradict the laws of nature or which could not possibly to follow from them, we must accept in every case that it was interpolated into the Bible by blasphemous persons. For whatever is contrary to nature, is contrary to reason, and what is contrary to reason, is absurd, and accordingly to be rejected."

one. He is perfectly harmonized with nature. The work of God is the work of nature.

Similarly, God's work in nature cannot go beyond nature. Again, going back to Spinoza's understanding of God or Nature as the all-embracing substance, the one and only substance in which every finite mode of being exists, it would be absurd to speak about God existing outside or beyond this world. So, for Spinoza, the concept of God's intervention is a misrepresentation of what God actually does in this world. God of monism can only work *within* nature, never beyond it. How can all-embracing substance move out of itself to be something else and work against itself? Simply put, if God works beyond nature, he would be acting against the essence of things, and as he has repeatedly demonstrated in his *Ethics,* nothing can act against the essence of things. For example, God is an infinite mode of being according to his essence. If he were to act against his essence, he would be demoted to a finite mode of being, which obviously erases the differentiation between God and man. This is both logically and physically absurd for Spinoza.

Why would the biblical writers or the church goers want to believe that God and nature are basically separate entities? Again, Spinoza turns to the answer that lies in the way we believers want to anthropomorphize God. It is much easier to read into God what we are and what we do than finding out what God actually does via studying rigorously the things of nature. Spinoza reads his society with a particular lens, claiming that religious individuals attribute awe and wonder to those who are domineering, being completely isolated from the rest of the world, sitting atop the most privilege place, controlling and commandeering the world. He feels that people admire God when they think of him as subduing nature. In Spinoza's assessment, God's sovereignty has been misplaced—i.e., God is sovereign because he is far removed from nature, controlling it from a lofty place beyond this world.

As we can see, Spinoza's critical outlook of the traditional religion is essentially tainted by a political agenda, being quite unhappy with the way the society of his day was operating. Human beings were considered unequal because of their race, religion, sex, or class. The same principle applied to the man-nature relationship. Human beings were considered supreme rulers of nature because human essence (such as soul) came from outside of nature, and will return to a place that lies beyond nature. For Spinoza, such misunderstanding brewed nothing but resentment and exploitation that are the ultimate cause of our own destruction. In *Theological-Political Treatise*, Spinoza corrects this misunderstanding by emphatically denoting that a human being is part of nature. No part of humanness is outside of nature. If any part of humanness exists outside of nature, then whatever that part may be, it would not exist at all. Having said this, we can safely conclude that, in Spinoza's philosophical paradigm, divine and human causes correlate to natural causes. Consequently, miracles as divine or human acts must be reinterpreted in light of natural causes.

For instance, Moses' miracles of the ten plagues are tenable insofar as they are natural events—e.g., the locusts came to Egypt by means of a strong east wind and destroyed the land.[49] The splitting up the Red Sea is also explainable naturally. The same kind of a strong east wind blowing over the water all day long dried up the sea. Moreover, Elisha's raising of a supposedly dead boy is a natural event, since Elisha simply warmed up the body by lying on top of the boy for some time. Similarly, Joshua's description of the sun being stopped during the great battle with the five kings is also a natural phenomenon. Behind the fabricated version of the narrative, Spinoza sees that there is a true meaning which is underwritten by the truth of fact. The truth of fact is that the sun did not stop—such an event, of course, would suspend the laws of nature and that would be absurd for Spinoza. Rather, the day seemed longer as a result of "ice which was in the air there at that time" which produced "a greater refraction than normal, or something of that kind." [50] However, the Book of Joshua neither includes nor even hints at such a natural explanation. It is because, insists Spinoza, the author of the text wanted to confirm that the God of Israel was superior to the pagan god

---

[49] Ibid., 90.

[50] Ibid., 34.

246

of the sun.[51] According to Spinoza, the consequence of exaggerated stories is dire. The author of the text, using the language of "miracles," had to say something that is entirely different from what actually occurred.

In this context, Spinoza concludes that biblical miracles are largely imaginary. Although some miracle stories imply a natural explanation that underwrites them, most of the stories do not. It is due to the fact that the writers of the text resorted to "imaginary things and prophetic visions."[52] For Spinoza, many biblical images and visions do not speak for the actual event. They may be used to persuade the readers that God's work is marvelous and awe-inspiring, but in actuality, they do not refer to anything substantial. For instance, when the Old Testament purports that God came down from heaven and Mount Sinai was full of smoke because God descended upon the Israelites, they were speaking of "nothing but apparitions and imaginary things."[53] As we have seen already, for Spinoza, God cannot "come" from outside or descend upon the earth as if his dwelling place is isolated and distinct from the world we live. God is all that there is. All things exist in God. God is not a separate entity from nature. So, for Spinoza, biblical writers were confused and did not know "what really happened with imaginary things and prophetic visions."[54] Thus, according to Spinoza's biblical interpretative method, biblical miracles must be filtered through natural history so that we can unveil hidden natural implications of biblical miracles, on the one hand, and identify faulty, confused, and fabricated stories, on the other hand. In the end, he concludes that, unlike traditional churches, we cannot use biblical miracles as proof of God's existence. It has no historical basis. Even if we prove that biblical miracles are real, they are "limited" occurrences in nature. What is "limited" cannot explain the unlimited mode of being, that is, God.

---

[51] Ibid., 92. He notes in this regard, "Thus partly owing to religion, and partly from preconceived beliefs, they conceived of the thing happening in a totally different way from how it actually occurred, and that is how they reported it."

[52] Ibid., 93.

[53] Ibid.

[54] Ibid.

If the bulk of biblical miracles is faulty, confused, limited, and fabricated, what is the use of this exaggerated and imagined version of biblical miracle narratives? Spinoza does not completely dismiss biblical miracles in particular and Scripture in general. They do have some use for him. The aim of Scripture according to Spinoza is to promote obedience. [55] This implies that the faith narratives, which are predominately fabricated stories, are included in Scripture because they invoke a reverence and awe of God so that believers may keep their simple faith and obey God "in a spirit of sincerity and freedom."[56] In brief, Spinoza sees Scripture as a special kind of book, that is, the book of proper behavior. But since our behavior is properly controlled when we have adequate knowledge, faith needs to be subsumed under reason. What Spinoza has done here is that he has removed the power of faith, the power to see the transcendent, the supernatural works of God, like the miraculous events reported in the Old and New Testament, and replaced the outworking of faith as mere passive "obedience," keeping in line with the order of nature that God has preordained. This sounds very much like a Calvinistic determinism. For this reason, Colin Brown connects Spinoza's work to Calvin's doctrine of predestination. [57] Moreover, faith and reason have been separated. Faith is tied to moral actions, and reason to the natural light that corrects religious imagination, perhaps, giving a new motivation for modern scholars like Kant to bracket morality within the realm of religion.

In the end, Spinoza has reduced biblical miracles as either fabricated stories or events that are underwritten by natural explanations. For Spinoza, it was not possible for God to act supernaturally or transcendentally. It would mean that God would go against his own nature. Although Spinoza was a theist, his monism could only allow him to stay within the bounds of naturalism. So, in actuality, Spinoza was a philosophical naturalist, just like some of the naturalistic atheists of today.

---

[55] Ibid., 172.

[56] Ibid., 10.

[57] Colin Brown, *Miracles and the Critical Mind* (Grand Rapids: Eerdmans, 1984), 32.

Critical Engagement with Spinoza:
Reclaiming Miracles

Spinoza's legacy continues. Modern skeptics like him have emerged left and right after his short-lived academic career. A prime example would be David Hume. He followed suit and dismissed all miracle claims because no laws of nature can be violated by any means.[58] Hume even added that no amount of evidence in this world could ever prove miracle claims.[59] For Hume, miracles neither took place in the past, nor are they taking place today, because they are by definition improbable events. There is simply no analogy in the natural world that fits the miracle narratives. Hume's evidentialist and naturalistic view aligns well with Spinoza, though unlike Spinoza, Hume is an explicit disclaimer of theism. In the wake of the 17th and 18th century skepticism, in Christian circles, scholars are given two choices. They could interpret biblical miracle stories by either dismissing them as meaningless fables or translate them naturalistically so that they make sense to the citizens of the scientific age.

In actuality, these two choices brought up by modern skeptics introduce a false dichotomy. If we choose to work only within the given premise of naturalism, then these two options are logical ways for us to explain away biblical miracles. However, as I have said in the previous chapters, a naturalistic philosophical worldview is not the only option for today's scientific society. We may start not with a single system theory[60] of naturalism, but multiple systems theory, or what I call open system metaphysics. I have already detailed the main features of open system metaphysics in Chapter One so it is sufficient here just to present a quick recap. Open system metaphysics is underpinned by three key features. First, open system thinking recognizes multiple distinct

---

[58] David Hume, "Of Miracles" in *An Enquiry Concerning Human Understanding*, ed. Eric Steinberg (Indianapolis: Hackett, 1993), 87-89.

[59] Ibid., 83.

[60] Note that I am interchangeably using the term "system" and "substance." But since the word "substance" could be narrowly conceived being concerned only with a single entity, I prefer the term "system" because it has the potential to include not only the ontology of substance but also causality and intentionality that are unique to each system.

systems that operate based on their own rules and intentions. For instance, in the case of God, humanity, and nature, these three distinct systems have their own logic and telos that may or may not overlap with one another. Second, open systems are potentially cooperative. Due to the cooperative nature of each system, there is always the possibility to sustain a mutual correlation between different systems. Third, open systems are framed by hierarchical, emergent systems. Although the divine system is not emergent from nature, nonetheless the God of the Trinity, as the highest level of all systems, can exert top-down influence upon nature. The main implication of interpreting reality based upon the open system worldview is the recognition that the natural process is not operating based on the single system that determines all other systems; rather, each system of God, humanity, and nature, brings to the space-time continuum its own causality and ontological elements that may not be explainable solely in terms of natural laws.

Standing on the solid ground of open system metaphysics, we are now in a position to counter Spinoza's arguments and defend the possibility of miracles. I am going to tackle the five major points brought up by Spinoza that are problematic to open system metaphysics. They are as follows: the problem of singular analogy, the dilemma of a deterministic system, the dismissal of imagination, and the miracle as the violation of natural laws.

The Problem of the Single Analogy of Nature

To start with the problem of the single analogy of nature, I would need to revisit Spinoza's interpretation of biblical miracles. According to Spinoza, biblical miracles must be read in terms of how God acts in the world naturally. For Spinoza, there are instances, such as God's use of the strong east wind to split the Red Sea, seem like miracles but they are not. For him, it is simply God working in accordance with the laws of nature. This is true since, in Spinoza's metaphysical paradigm, God does not exist beyond or above nature—i.e., God's causality can never be a supernatural event that is contrary to the fixed order of nature. Thus, for Spinoza, when the biblical narratives refer to God's act in the world as a "supernatural" event, they do not contain any true meaning; rather, they are either fabrication or misunderstanding.

What we can glean from Spinoza's reading of biblical miracles is that he relies on only one analogy, that is, the analogy of nature. For Spinoza, nature is all that there is, and nothing exists beyond or above nature, so the ultimate measuring rod for Spinoza is the natural system. Based upon the single analogy of nature, Spinoza resists against the possibility of the supernatural causation that is associated with biblical miracles. Although Spinoza does not deny the fact that God intervenes in the human and natural affairs, God's work is "limited" to something that is non-supernatural. As a result, biblical miracle narratives have been watered down to either fictional stories or ordinary events made to look extraordinary. In this way, the trustworthiness of the Bible is dramatically reduced. The Bible cannot be wholly trusted. Such skepticism is the result of having a single analogy. However, in the world of multiple systems and multiple analogues, which I believe is a more realistic version of our world, we are not restricted only to natural analogies. We can consider other possibilities, such as our reliance on the transcendental analogy that accounts for the supernatural entity acting in and through nature.

If there is transcendent analogy, which opens up the door to see the things that are greater than the things of nature (e.g., the supernatural work of God), then biblical miracles would not be dismissed as something that is contrary to nature, but a description of things that are above and beyond nature, though occurring within the context of nature. This is precisely what multiple, open systems theory claims. According to the multiple systems theory, the divine system that is uniquely different from what is physical and what is human could bring its own laws and intentions upon the physical or human systems. The divine system that lies above and beyond the world of the physical and the personal means that divine causality may exceed certain ontological and epistemic expectations of the "laws of nature." If divine causality is either equal to or limited by the natural order of things, we cannot but fall into the restrictive matrix of a single system. The multiple systems theory prevents this approach. Hence, in a multiplex world, biblical miracles could be accounted for as the descriptions of divine supernatural causality.

At this point, we need to address Spinoza's concern for supernatural causality. Spinoza accused religious people of looking for supernatural events as a way to confirm God's action in this world. Pursuing God supernaturally became a major impetus for religious people to abandon the idea that God is working in concert with nature, wrongfully viewing that God is the subduing power of nature because he is *super*-natural. For this reason, Spinoza argued that the correlation between miracles and supernatural causality should not be used as proof of God's existence or God's special action in this world.

I agree with Spinoza that we cannot use miracle claims as the proof of God's existence or divine causality, for God is able to work in and through nature in a cooperative manner without violating the laws of nature. Also, extraordinary events could be caused not just by God but also by a physical process or a personal agent.[61] We have seen in the case of a "flying ring" that the extraordinary event of the flying ring was caused by a simple natural event, though it did not fit the "normal expectancy" range of a falling ring. Despite the extraordinary hypothesis of a "flying ring," the cause was never associated with God. Also, even if God is involved with an extraordinary event, as Spinoza has shown, God could use a "natural means" to perform his amazing feat. Nature may have the hidden potential that we may not yet know and act in an extraordinary way. Hence, the miracle in and of itself could not be the gauge for justifying God's extraordinary action in this world, although what lies behind the extraordinary event may be underwritten by supernatural causality. Does this mean that the miracle cannot be discerned supernaturally? My answer is that miracles can be discerned supernaturally only if we recognize that miracle claims are theologically significant.

---

[61] We also need to note the admonition of Matthew 24:24. "False messiahs and false prophets will appear and perform great signs and wonders to deceive, if possible, even the elect."

Looking at biblical miracles such as the parting of the Red Sea, we can see that miracles do occur in the context of the natural order of things. However, what is more obvious here is that the parting of the Red Sea was a demonstration of God working in cooperation with his people and nature for a specific purpose. The miracle of the Red Sea is significant not just because he churned out something that is unusual and extraordinary, which could not have taken place without the special activity of God, but more importantly, because of what was accomplished, that is, the salvation of the people. Miracles in this sense are supernaturally wrought by God not just for a natural purpose (e.g., the demonstration of a marvelous deed) but for a theological purpose, that is, God's deliverance of his people from a dire situation. Of course, a naturalist could say that the parting of the Red Sea is caused by a natural force such as a temporal receding of the sea that the Israelites did not know about. A massive water movement could cause the sea to recede until the entire people of Israel cross the sea on dry ground. However, what is missing in the naturalistic interpretation is the mention of theological implications. For this reason, miracles must include a multi-leveled transcendental analogy, which is framed by a distinct God-talk.

The Problem of a Deterministic System

Next, from reading Spinoza's work, the problem of miracles is associated with the deterministic system. Rather than treating God, humanity, and nature as open systems, Spinoza fixated on a naive determinism to which all things must adhere. His approach vilified the caprice of human behavior both in religious and societal systems. If nature is immutable and fixed, operating on the basis of an unchanging regular pattern of things, then everything that lives and breathes in nature must do the same. Misalignment with nature means misalignment with God, since God is one and the same with Nature.

However, as I have pointed out, in an open system metaphysical framework, determinism is not the only criteria for systematic sustenance. The term "open" signifies the possibility of the world consisting of many indeterministic systems. What is an indeterminate system? We have already seen that indeterminism is demonstrable from the way a human agent acts. However, even without the inclusion of an intentional subject, indeterminism is still explainable. John Polkinghorne's explanation of chaos theory accomplishes this task. A chaotic system denotes the fact that we can never calculate with precise accuracy the exact motion of things even with a supercomputer that has "unlimited computational power, furnished with the details of the states of motion of all the particles in the universe as they are at the present moment."[62] This is because, in any natural system, even one minute change in the initial condition, has the potential to completely change the future outcome of a predictable system.[63] When we know that in this universe there are innumerable particles that are entangled with one another in the massive network of things, any one of countless factors could change the predictable system into a chaotic indeterminate system. Though Polkinghorne's chaos theory may be ultimately determinate in theory, the genuine picture of the chaos system is indeterminate in praxis. So, as Polkinghorne asserts, "there are as many disorderly clouds in the world as there are orderly clocks."[64] Following Polkinghorne, we can say that our world is made up of complex systems of networks as both law-governed and yet ontologically indeterminate.

The implication of indeterminism is clear. In a multiplex world, we are dealing with not only the visible order of things but also open possibilities. In a well-controlled system, we can duplicate a closed system, in which we can identify many variables at work all the while eliminating them to reduce the possibility of chaos. So, in a controlled environment, we may be able to detect predictable patterns at work. However, the real world is not made-up of controllable environments. We could reduce unwanted variables to some extent, but it is practically impossible to identify, let alone eliminate all variables. The matter gets more complicated when an infinite possibility of divine causality is

---

[62] John Polkinghorne, *Exploring Reality: The Intertwining of Science and Religion* (London: SPCK, 2005), 20.

[63] Ibid., 21.

[64] Ibid.

involved. Because God is infinite, his intervention may lead to innumerable possibilities that we may never be able to comprehend. In other words, indeterminism allows enough space for unusual and extraordinary events to take place that defy all known odds. Because of indeterminism, when we do witness an incredible event, we may use only the words that are counterintuitive in nature to describe the event, as in the case of biblical miracles.

But is indeterminism inferior to a deterministic framework like that of Spinoza? Spinoza asserted that the idea of the unknown exacts fear, and in turn, fear leads to unreliable emotions and irrational behaviors. Hence, he saw that indeterminism is an inferior kind of a philosophical system than determinism. Indeed, Spinoza is right in that, if we follow strictly the ways of indeterminism, we would end up with relativism and subjectivism without any means to standardize the God, humanity, and nature relationship.

To tackle this dilemma, we can turn to modern science. In modern science, the problem of relativism and subjectivism has been dealt with in many different ways. But of all different methods, one approach stands tall. It is a process of validating hypotheses and theories based on the testing of evidence whether it be formal or informal. The formal evidence is what Spinoza calls the "truth of things" and the informal evidence is the "truth of meaning" which is evidently based on the truth of things, but with a hint of intelligible interpretations. I will discuss more about the specific role of evidence in determining the reliability of biblical miracles in the next section, but I should say here that evidence requires interpretation. We think that normally science gives more weight to finding the truth of things, but in the postmodern context, this is no longer the trend. As the philosopher of science, Roderick Chisolm, asserts, science is not about getting at the truth of things, but rather, arriving at the truth of meaning, for contemporary scientists now recognize that there is no one single theory that is able to explain the intricate details of all natural phenomena.[65] In this respect, all scientific claims are underdetermined and require sufficient circumstantial

---

[65] Cf. Roderick Chisholm, *Theory of Knowledge* (Englewood Cliffs: Prentice-Hall, 1966).

evidence with clear interpretations to prove not only the reliability of theory but also the usefulness of its explanatory power.

So, in a network of multiple systems, which are comingled with determinate and indeterminate actual occasions, the truth of meaning that Spinoza was looking for can only be achieved based on a critical interpretation of evidence. In other words, the deterrent of an open system is something that is dogmatic, fixed, or absolute, in the way we develop our theories or explanations of natural phenomena, though there may actually be an infallible and absolute reality. At best, due to our epistemic and hermeneutical limitations, all we can do is give our best interpretation of the given evidence and determine whether miracle claims are reliable or not. The implication for interpreting biblical miracles is that they too must be evaluated and interpreted based on evidence. For this reason, the historical-critical method becomes a crucial factor in our understanding of biblical miracles, which will be covered extensively in the following section.

If we accept the possibility of miracles, should we discard the fixed rules of nature? Following Imre Lakatos, I suggest holding onto a dialectical tension between core propositions that function like fixed dogma until proven otherwise by auxiliary hypotheses, which are always indeterminate. Auxiliary hypotheses are always changing since they are constantly revised and changed by new evidence as they are mediated through various models and interpretations that are viable and applicable within a specific context or community. Consequently, all systems have both open and closed ends. They are closed in such a way that they can function based on their own fixed rules and accepted principles, and at the same time, they are open in such a way that they are working progressively toward greater clarity and truth by cooperating with different systems. Based on the open-ended approach, it is not absurd to say that unusual events like biblical miracles may have occurred even though they may defy the set of rules of a closed system of naturalism.

Before we move to the next topic, we need to make one thing clear. We cannot allow one set of fixed laws governing all systems, because, in reality, there is no one set of rules that govern all things. In fact, if we allow one fix system to thrive, it will overwhelm all other systems that have different "rules" and force them to fit into the Procrustean bed of one dominating system, killing off the rest. No one, not even Christianity, is exempt from this type of error. The Spanish Inquisition is a great example in which innocent blood was shed just because of the erroneous belief that one form of Christian religion could be sustained by eradicating other religious communities like the Jews and "heretics." The open system ensures the decentralization of a closed system as well as the preservation of its distinct features by way of refining and renewing its own identity amidst many different views in this world.

The Problem of Imagination

Now we turn to the third issue, that is, the problem of imagination. In association with indeterminate ways of thinking, Spinoza condemned imagination. For Spinoza, imagination is the culprit that creates a make-believe world by fabricating and inventing incredible stories. For this reason, miracles are exemplars of human imagination, that is, the byproduct of human fantasies and fancies. In my judgment, Spinoza's assessment of human imagination is not fair considering the positive input that could be transpired by imagination. Let me mention a few cases in which imagination-as-counterintuition[66] is found to be utterly critical, especially in the world of science.

In science, the chief source of scientific advancement is known to be not only our reasonable alignment with what the natural world reveals, but more significantly, the event of "rupture" or "crisis" that counters the existing paradigms. For instance, according to Alasdair MacIntyre, the basic impulse of scientific advancement is "epistemological crises" stemming from the conflict between the new set of problems and the existing scientific model unable to answer emergent questions. [67]

---

[66] The concept of imagination-as-counterintuition complements well McMullin's imagination-as-retroduction. For more details, see Chapter 2.

[67] Alisdair MacIntyre, "Epistemologial Crises, Dramatic Narrative and the Philosophy of Science," *The Monist* 60/4 (1977): 453-472. Also, for more details on the relationship between scientific crisis and its concomitant philosophical discussions, see Robert Nola and

Similarly, for Thomas Kuhn, science advances as scientists encounter anomalies that existing paradigms fail to explain.[68] Such anomalies become the source of the scientific crisis that ultimately leads to the re-formulation and extension of the existing paradigms. Thus, the contribution of counterintuitive imagination to the development of scientific theories and models optimizes scientific activities as it is the key motif for making a leap of advance in the world of science.

The task of science in this respect is geared toward making discoveries through an imaginative postulation of counterintuitive patterns which explains empirical systems. Such innovative leaps are grounded in and guided by stepping outside common sense and delving deeper into the hidden part of the universe to uncover out-of-the-ordinary elements undergirding observational phenomena.[69] For this reason, the growth of science and mathematics in a certain sense is rooted in counterintuitive logic. Mathematical philosopher Philip Davis explains that "there are mathematical entities, objects, or processes that do not accord with intuition or common sense, and mathematics keeps growing through the creation of new ones" via counterintuitive elements.[70] Although counterintuition defies common sense, without it, scientists cannot explain most natural phenomena rationally and logically, even though counterintuitive elements themselves remain mysterious (e.g., quantum events).[71]

Howard Sankey, *Theories of Scientific Method* (Ithaca: McGill-Queen's University Press, 2007), Chapter 1-4.

[68] Thomas S. Kuhn, *Structure of Scientific Revolution* (Chicago: University of Chicago Press, 1962, c1999), 82.

[69] The search for the "hidden" things of the world continues in the physical science and thinkers in physics currently grapple with the mysterious and logic-defying elements of dark matter and energy. See Ken Freeman and Geoff McNamara, *In Search of Dark Matter* (New York: Springer, 2006).

[70] Philip J. Davis, *Mathematics and Common Sense: A Case of Creative Tension* (Wellesley: A.K. Peters, 2006), 81.

[71] There are innumerable examples in which human ingenuity and counterintuition are displayed in the process of substantiating mathematical postulations. One such case is the creation of geometry. The complex relationship between points, lines, planes, cubes, and even non-Euclidean hyperspace has been unveiled through the culmination of many different creative mathematical manipulations. For more details, see Edward Kasner and James Newman, *Mathematics and the Imagination* (Mineola: Dover, 1967). See also Rudy Rucker,

What this means is that the use of imaginative extensions is not altogether meaningless or erroneous, as purported by Spinoza. In my opinion, imagination-as-counterintuition is an indispensable tool to transcend the limits of the boundary conditions. It is an attempt to see "through" (imaginative) rather than "see as" (representational) so that our vision is directed to the higher and deeper things and causes "out there." It is a way to progress from the limits of our surroundings, making a leap into the world of the unknown. In the case of biblical miracles, these events point to the reality that is higher and greater than what we can comprehend or grasp within the limits of our current systems. It disorients our ways of thinking here and now, creating a crisis event, so that it can reorient us to see the greater things that lie beyond this world. In this sense, ultimately, it is a pointer to God.

Judging from what I have read, Spinoza's angst of using imagination goes deeper in that he blamed the biblical authors for anthropomorphizing God. According to Spinoza, in order for us to see a controlling God like a king of our society, God has been invented as the one who acts, talks, and behaves like us, thereby transforming God into an entity no different from us, a caprice, changeable, emotional, and culturally conditionable being. For him, this is not acceptable. So he concluded that God is not a person; rather he was made a person. Therefore, in Spinoza's final analysis, the truth of the matter is that once we peel off the surface layer and remove the husk of imagination, we can only see God as an immutable and unchangeable *Naturan Naturata*.

It is true that Scripture contains the description of God behaving like a person. For this reason, the Christian traditional doctrine of God does not omit the discussion of God's personhood. However, to speak of God as a person does not necessarily introduce the contingencies and human elements to God.[72] It is beyond the scope of this work to go over the

---

The Fourth Dimension: Toward a Geometry of Higher Reality (Boston: Houghton Mifflin, 1984). Rucker shows that the geometric relationship of the higher dimension reveals the "transient" nature of reality that requires a high level of mathematical imagination to perceive it.

[72] Langdon Gilkey succinctly summarizes this problem. "Both the biblical and orthodox understanding of theological language was univocal. That is, when God was said to have 'acted,' it was believed that he had performed an observable act in space and time so that he functioned as does any secondary cause. And when he was said to have spoken, it was believed that an audible voice was heard by the person addressed. In other words, 'act' and

viability of the personhood of God,[73] but at least, we must distinguish God's personhood from our own personality by stating that God is the absolute person, who is able to accommodate to and assert top-down influence upon different personalities in this world. Even in his absoluteness, due to his accommodation to the things of this world, his action can be described as the way any normal human agent would behave, albeit extraordinarily at times. This does not mean that God's essence can be changed. I have already shown that God is who he is and absolutely so, even when he accommodates to and operates in the finite matrix because he is the power-to-be-himself and the power-to-relate-to-the-other-as-himself.

Despite God's accommodation, as biblical miracle stories show, his action does not always correspond to the rules and laws to which we are accustomed. God is after all infinitely greater than us or any system in this world. Thus, his actions and involvement with the worldly affairs may transcend our common sense as demonstrated by biblical miracle narratives. For this reason, biblical miracles may upset traditional intellectual systems, bringing about an epistemic re-orientation that could lead us to the truth of meaning associated with the things of God. The biblical imagination, therefore, helps us see that God is not just a God who can work in tandem with nature and humans, but also in himself as the infinite mode of being that can bring about extraordinary, counterintuitive events.

Miracles as the Violation of Natural Laws

Moving to the final point, we must now address the problem of seeing miracles as the violation of natural laws. Spinoza could not accept the fact that God performs extraordinary events by overriding the laws of nature. How could God do that when there is only one substance and

---

'speak' were used in the same sense of God as of men. We deny this univocal understanding of theological words. To us, theological verbs such as 'to act,' 'to work,' 'to do,' 'to speak,' 'to reveal,' etc., have no longer the literal meaning of observable actions in space and time or of voices in the air." Langdon Gilkey, "Cosmology, Ontology, and the Travail of Biblical Language," in *God's Activity in the World: The Contemporary Problem*, ed. Owen C. Thomas (Chico: Scholars Press, 1983), 32.

[73] For more detail, please refer to my forthcoming book, *The God of Order*.

one set of laws that govern the universe? In a monistic world where there is no differentiation in essence between God and Nature, God cannot step outside of nature and perform something that is entirely different from the laws of nature. God is, therefore, "refrained" from doing things that are against nature. This is a logically feasible argument if we are assuming that the world is made up of only one substance and God's essence and the things of this world do not really differ in form and content. However, as I have mentioned above, a single system theory does not really esteem the true distinction between God and nature, whereas, in each system, there is a unique set of rules, intentions, and ontological elements that make up the irreducible system.

In an open system, which is undergirded by the multiple, irreducible systems intermingling with each other, the power of God and the power of nature could co-exist as distinct systems. Spinoza rejects this idea, however, because such metaphysical pluralism may lead to the belief that God and nature are two opposing powers in conflict with each other. Such a divisive philosophical worldview could fuel war and confusion that are constantly taking place in our society. Spinoza's concern needs to be taken seriously, and for this reason, the open system must maintain the cooperative effort to actualize its unitive potential to the fullest, although it may be difficult in reality. In fact, this is the true intention of God. As we can discern from the New Testament testimonies, God's true essence is love and peace (e.g., 1 Jn. 4:18; 1 Cor. 14:33). His desire to bring peace and love to the world means that he is asserting top-down influence upon all systems in this world to reconcile them to his divine system in the mode of unity-and-difference. Thus, the goal of the divine system is to lure all systems to create a holistic, cooperative system. In this way, through the cooperative effort guided by the love of God, the conflict and division will be alleviated, and human conditions improve. Indeed, the power of God and the power of nature can create friction; however, contra Spinoza, the incompatibility between the two arises not because the divine system overpowers worldly systems, but because of the power of natural entropy that refuses to cooperate and fall into self-referential reductionism that may defy the loving relationship between God and nature. Consequently, the actual occasions that lead to a conflict should not be thought of as the two powers of God and nature clashing and churning a violent output, one subsuming the other. In actuality, the conflict and war are the result of selfish genes that tend to "steal, kill, and destroy" (Jn 10:10), unwilling to follow the ways of God.

Understanding that God and nature can co-exist as two distinct fields of activity, we are now ready to address the given question. Does God's action in this world contravene the laws of nature? This question becomes difficult on two accounts. First, since we are not considering a single system, but multiple systems that are open to and interact with one another, we need to know how we can distinguish God's action from that of nature and humans. In a single system, we do not need to make this distinction. So, in a single system, the fixed laws of nature explain all events that are taking place in this world. However, in the world of multiple systems, since each system has its own laws and intentions, there is a need to distinguish one from the other. Second, even if we distinguish one system from the other, how could a distinguishable element from one system interact with the other without damaging the integrity of two interacting systems? In Spinoza's monistic paradigm, there is no damage or violation despite the fact that different systems, such as God and nature, interact with each other, because God and nature are ultimately one and the same substance. However, for multiple systems, where there are many different substances and entities that follow different rules, such as God and nature, there must be a disruption if God were to interact with nature because it is inevitable for God to introduce something new into the system. If this happens, would not the integrity of nature fall apart and turn into something that it is not? Let me address these two questions, starting with the last question, for the first question is much more involved.

The first law of thermodynamics has already pointed out that in a closed system energy is neither created nor destroyed. The total amount of energy has to remain the same. This is also called the Principle of the Conservation of Energy. Let me explain this with an illustration. In a closed system, if I burn a piece of paper, the total amount of energy remains the same even though the shape and form of a white rectangular paper changes to a small pile of black ash. The negative energy of the ash and the positive heat energy that the paper gave off during the burning maintain energy equilibrium. This energy equilibrium is natural and binding. The equilibrium would be broken only when some other energy source enters the closed system. For this reason, atheist William Stoeger argues that, when God acts in this world, "energy would be added to a system spontaneously and mysteriously, contravening the conservation of energy."[74] Robert Larmer makes a convincing case against this type of argument.

Larmer insightfully points out that atheists normally divide the Principle of the Conservation of Energy into two parts.[75] The first part states that "energy can neither be created nor destroyed." The second part states that "in an isolated system the total amount of energy remains constant." Larmer asserts that atheists, when they are countering the claims of divine action, refer to the first statement, and deny any possibility of divine intervention. If God were to intervene, then the things that God may add to nature would naturally violate the Principle of the Conservation of Energy. Larmer says that this is not true. The first part actually is a metaphysical statement. A metaphysical statement is not actually a scientific statement, for we have to make a "metaphysical leap" from the second statement to the first. The second statement does not "prove" that the first statement is true. In other words, just because "the total amount of energy remains constant in a closed system," it does not necessarily follow that energy can be neither created nor destroyed. Larmer gives two reasons why this is the case. First, "the theist is able to provide an alternative explanation of the scientific form of truth."[76] From a theistic perspective, God is the only one who is neither created nor destroyed. Since it is a metaphysical assumption, a theistic metaphysical framework could be an alternative

---

[74] William Stoeger, "Describing God's Action in the World in Light of Scientific Knowledge of Reality," in *Chaos and Complexity: Scientific Perspectives on Divine Action*, ed. Robert J. Russell et al. (Vatican City: Vatican Observatory Foundation and the Center for Theology and the Natural Sciences, 1995), 244.

[75] Robert A. Larmer, "The Meanings of Miracle" in *The Cambridge Companion to Miracles*, ed. Graham H. Twelftree (New York: Cambridge University Press, 2011), 40.

[76] Ibid., 41.

to atheists' naturalistic metaphysical assumption. Second, "the metaphysical form is at odds with the Big Bang theory of the origin of the universe."[77] The Big Bang theory claims that the universe had a beginning. If the universe had a beginning, it follows that energy that makes up the universe must have been created at some point, thereby contradicting the statement that energy can neither be created nor destroyed.

What we need to understand at this juncture is that God's involvement with the laws of nature does not necessarily lead to instances of creation or annihilation of energy. It would be easier to refute this claim based on open system metaphysics, since, if the world is ontologically open to a higher level of activities like God and the divine activities can assert top-down influence upon the world, there is no need to follow the strict laws of "a closed system." However, based on the Principle of the Conservation of Energy, we are dealing with a closed system, so God must be able to act in a closed system without altering its laws as well. Is this possible?

Even if we assume that God acts in the closed system of nature, there is no need to alter or change the course of the natural pattern of things. Let me refer to the analogy of the mind-body relationship once again in an attempt to explain the God-nature relationship in a closed system. Recall from our discussion of emergence that our consciousness which has its own rules and systematic developments can assert top-down influence upon the body without changing the shape or form of the body. The body remains what it is even though it is influenced by the mind. Likewise, God who is spirit can interact with nature without changing the integrity of the natural system. A naturalist may say that the mind-body analogy does not fit the bill here since mind and body exist in the common system of one person. Put theistically, the mind-body analogy works if we are promoting substance monism, which defies the traditional understanding of God. I disagree. Even if we say that there are multiple systems, we can still see that the mind can be influenced by another mind through a personal relationship. In a social interaction, the

---

[77] Ibid.

emotional exchange is common, in which one person's mood affects the other, all the while the affected agent may influence the body to react to the emotion like shedding tears.[78] While two personal agents do not belong to the same system (e.g., one person's body), they are nonetheless connected in such a way that a specific psychological-personal interaction could influence one another without damaging the integrity of the physical make-up of both persons. In a similar vein, God as spirit can intervene and influence the world through the development of a personal relationship, without changing the integrity of physical and human systems of this world.[79]

To tackle the second question—i.e., how can we differentiate God's action from that of nature and persons? To address this question, I need to bring up the contemporary divine action project (DAP). A number of different scholars who are engaged with the theology and science interface tested the hypothesis that God could work in a quantum world (Robert Russell),[80] a chaos system (John Polkinghorne),[81] or an emergent process (Philip Clayton)[82] without necessarily violating the laws of nature. This is known as a non-interventionist approach to the DAP. Because of the DAP research, we are now in position to say that there are at least three ways in which God can act in this world: (1) God works in a general way, luring the natural and personal systems to function as cooperative systems; (2) God works in a specific way by responding to

---

[78] As Martin Buber has pointed out, when "I" enter into a special relationship with "Thou," it entails a give-and-take transaction between them, and as a result, both parties of "I-Thou" are influenced by the sharable moments. For more details, see Martin Buber, *I and Thou*, trans. Walter Kaufmann (New York: Touchstone, 1970).

[79] For this reason, I would not accept the ground of being theory proposed by Wesley J. Wildman. Wildman believes that God's relationship to the world is more impersonal than personal. See Wesley J. Wildman, "Ground-of-Being Theologies," in *The Oxford Handbook of Religion and Science*, ed. Philip Clayton (Oxford: Oxford University Press, 2008), 612-632. However, in my judgment, as the Bible shows, God works in a personal way, in a loving fashion, luring the natural processes to his end.

[80] Cf. Robert J. Russell, *Cosmology: From Alpha to Omega: The Creative Mutual Interaction of Theology and Science* (Minneapolis: Fortress, 2008), Chapter 5.

[81] Cf. John Polkinghorne, *Quarks, Chaos, and Christianity: Questions to Science and Religion* (London: SPCK, 2005).

[82] Cf. Philip Clayton, *Mind and Emergence, From Quantum to Consciousness* (New York: Oxford University Press, 2006).

the prayers in an attempt to improve the natural and human conditions; (3) God works in an extraordinary way as a temporary exception to the ordinary course of nature. Most of the scholars have been devoting their time to explore the possibility of the first two ways in which God acts, dismissing the third as primarily a theological task. Let me make comments about the first two approaches before tackling the third position.

Scholars like Russell, Polkinghorne, and Clayton, represent the group of contemporary researchers who adhere to open system metaphysics, albeit in their own unique way. For Russell, the world is open to receive God in the indeterminate system of the quantum world, and similarly, Polkinghorne claims that there is sufficient room for God to act in this world without violating the laws of nature because the world is ontologically open by virtue of the chaotic system. Finally, for Clayton, the world consists of open systems due to the fact that each system is open to higher and complex systems, while higher systems assert top-down influence upon lower systems. Due to this openness, there is no need to worry about God overriding the laws of nature destroying the integrity of natural systems. In this light, God is seen more as a partner who interacts with nature cooperatively and indirectly and less the traditional way of seeing God as a dominant force, intruding and suspending the laws of nature. Although it may be true that God is able to work within quantum, chaos, or emergent systems for that would at least show that nature is ontologically open to God, the weakness of the current DAP research is the lack of fleshing out how it is that God acts supernaturally in the world of quantum, chaos, or emergence. It is all the more difficult to flesh out the precise mechanism of divine action when there are three competing scientifically derived worldviews (e.g., quantum indeterminism, chaos theory, and the theory of emergence). If both God and nature have the potential to create quantum, chaotic, or emergent activities—here, we cannot use the first cause argument since the first cause argument pertains to the divine action that precedes natural events—how can we find out what part of quantum, chaotic, or emergent events qualify as God's action? Why would God choose to act in one way rather than the other? Is not God's action far-reaching and universal?

On a positive note, there seems to be a point of convergence despite their differences in the way theology and science are interfaced. The telos argument seems to be the common denominator for the aforementioned scholars, because it is the best way for them to address the "why" questions. Why is that each system in nature, whether quantum, chaos, or emergent, is ontologically open? Why do multiple systems cooperate with each other? Why do they progress to a higher and more complex level of existence? Why is there life when remaining in an inorganic form seemed much more stable and perpetual? Where is this impetus to be something new, transcending the bounds of its system? From an open system metaphysical viewpoint, these non-interventionists contend that nature is purpose-driven due to the fact that there is an ultimate transcendent system that asserts a top-down influence upon all other systems for a specific end. This is how we discern God's action in nature. Such an approach also provides us with the groundwork to flesh out the real meaning of miracle events.

For my purpose, what I need is a theological assist so that the supernatural causality of the triune God can be incorporated into the divine action project. Here I introduce the entelechy of the Spirit of Christ to tease out the outworking of divine telic processes in nature. I base my understanding of the divinely guided telos on David Coffey's work, so let me briefly review his idea of the entelechy of the Spirit.

As a Jesuit scholar, Coffey is one of the few scholars who has tied the traditional notion of the Holy Spirit (via trinitarian theology) to the whole cosmic process. He believes that the Spirit is behind the whole cosmic evolutionary process. Note that Coffey is not using the term "evolution" is a purely natural sense. He is actually stating that evolution is a Spirit-led activity; thus, evolution consists of both natural and supernatural components.[83] What is the justification for adding a spiritual component to the cosmic evolutionary process?

To justify his claim, Coffey frames his thought upon Pierre Teilhard de Chardin's work. Teilhard has written several books denoting the fact

---

[83] David Coffey, "The Spirit of Christ as Entelechy" *Philosophy and Theology* 13/2 (2001), 372.

that the natural evolutionary process is determined by two types of energy: radial energy and tangential energy. [84] The former is the immaterial force that guides nature to develop complex systems out of a much simpler thing. It is also an inner force in nature that synthesizes different systems in order to unite itself into a greater whole. The latter is the eternal force that cannot be measured by scientific tools. What is important to Teilhard as well as Coffey is that divinely empowered radial energy "fuels the onward march of evolution."[85] According to Teilhard, the guiding light of radial energy may undergo many setbacks and failures while leading the natural system to evolve in the right direction, but nonetheless, it is successful in the end reorienting nature to cross many "critical points."[86]

For Teilhard, the crossing of critical points is a necessary ingredient for the harbinger of the life of the cosmos. Without these crossings, there would not be any progressive breakthrough to a new being that is more complex and sophisticated than the old system. The entire process of complexification is the result of radial energy that provides the impetus for the natural process to synthesize with different systems all the while transcending the limits of its boundary by crossing its own threshold. Teilhard's justification for taking this metaphysical stance is based on his own study of the evolutionary process that starts from the inanimate entities moving up to the animate agents, which in the end, culminates in the hominization of freewill agents.

Despite the usefulness of Teilhard's conception of radial energy, Coffey finds that Teilhard needs a philosophical assist from Karl Rahner.[87] What Coffey wants is a robust transcendental metaphysics that can pull Teilhard's work out of the mire of immanentism. Coffey's move is logical, since Teilhard sees God as the Omega Point to which all

---

[84] E.g., Pierre Teilhard de Chardin, *Christianity and Evolution*, trans. Rene Hague (New York: Harcourt Brace Janovich, 1971); *The Future of Man*, trans. Norman Denny (New York: Harper and Rown, 1964); *The Phenomenon of Man*, trans. Bernard Wall (New York: Harper and Brothers, 1959).

[85] Coffey, "The Spirit of Christ as Entelechy," 372.

[86] Teilhard, *Christianity and Evolution*, 107-108.

[87] Coffey, "The Spirit of Christ as Entelechy," 377.

things will come together, energizing the world from within. In this way, God and nature function as a single system, very similar to that of Spinoza's monism. What went wrong? According to Coffey, Teilhard's error lies in the fact that he dismissed the Christian concept of *creatio ex nihilo*, a doctrine that would ensure the transcendent God who is absolutely different from the natural process. As Coffey has shown, Teilhard, very much like Spinoza, dismissed the idea that God created the world, for he believed that God works only "within" creation, using pre-existent materials to create new things in this world.

Coffey brings Rahner at this point and borrows Rahner's pneumatology to flesh out the meaning of the entelechy of the Spirit. For Rahner, "God 'takes hold,' in Christ's human nature, of the material world at the point at which matter becomes present to itself as spirit."[88] This is a dense statement but what we can see here is that Rahner is basically staking his theology on God's transcendence even though God is intimately involved with the world. For him, God comes to us as a grace offering salvation to all. For this reason, Rahner's conception of the supernatural existential identifies the need to understand that the world is open to God not naturally but supernaturally.

So, what is the entelechy of the Spirit then? Rahner defines the entelechy of the Spirit as God's offer of supernatural revelation in the "whole length and breadth of human history,"[89] which guides and brings to completion of his salvific work in Jesus Christ. Hence, the entelechy of the Spirit is rightfully called the Spirit of Christ. Coffey reads correctly that Rahner's Spirit Christology has a dual movement. On the one hand, the Spirit anticipating God's work of salvation seeks out Christ even before the Christ event, and on the other hand, the Spirit fulfills God's work of salvation after the Easter event.

But it raises the question. How can the Spirit of Christ work prior to the Christ event? Was not the Spirit sent by the Father through Jesus Christ after he was raised from the dead (e.g., John 14:15-27; Acts 2:1-12)? In order to address these questions, Coffey takes us to another

---

[88] Karl Rahner, *Theological Investigations* (New York: The Crossroad, 1991), 5:177.

[89] Ibid., 17/40.

dimension of the Spirit's work, that is, the Spirit's work in creation. He notes that before the Incarnation, the Spirit is seen as the Creator Spirit. Genesis 1:2 hints to this fact as it says that "the Spirit of God was hovering over the waters." Tying the work of the Spirit to the creative process of nature, Coffey in agreement with Teilhard states that the Spirit of Christ is the "force actively guiding and sustaining the activities not only of human beings but also of subhuman beings, rendering them capable of genuine teleological action."[90] The dual aspect of the Spirit of Christ is further advanced by Coffey's return model.

As far as Coffey is concerned, the doctrine of the Trinity has been explained by two different models: the procession model and the return model. The procession model of God shows that the Son proceeds from the Father and sends the Spirit to the world, and the return model shows that the Spirit returns to the Father through the Son. Without marginalizing one model at the expense of the other, Coffey combines the two and notes that we must appreciate both the procession of the Son and the return of the Spirit, from and to the Father, respectively. What Coffey wants to say is that, because of the fact that the Holy Spirit is a mutual bond between the Father and the Son, the procession and the return model are two aspects of the same movement of God. Therefore, it would be wrong to say that the procession is the dominating model over against the return model, or vice versa. Coffey then affirms that there is no discontinuity between the Spirit of Christ working in creation before the Christ event and the Spirit of Christ working in human history after the Easter event. They are two aspects of the same movement of the triune God.

Because we are moving from the Spirit of Christ even before the Incarnation to the Spirit of Christ after the Easter event, there is a spiritual progression. Coffey writes in this regard, "In execution of this process, the Spirit operates in the world, first creating it, then guiding it, by evolution, through the various stages of inanimate matter, through animate matter, to spirit, and thence to Christ and the community

---

[90] Coffey, "The Spirit of Christ as Entelechy," 364.

consciously gathered around him."[91] In this progression, the guiding principle of the Spirit is clear, that is, he is to bring what is divided into a harmonious whole and cross various thresholds in order to achieve the final status of hominization, that is, the final realization of man. Consequently, for Coffey, the final threshold is the critical point of human consciousness, or more specifically, human religious consciousness.

I would have to interject at this junction and point out my disagreement with Coffey's program. I agree with all aspects of his proposal except for his alliance with Rahner's idea of anonymous Christians. Because of the universal outreach of the Spirit of Christ, Coffey drawing upon Rahner believes that the Spirit is working as a guiding principle in non-Christian religions and, hence, non-Christians have the ability to have the salvation faith implicitly, due to the Spirit "drawing to Christ those members who respond, though doing so in a hidden and 'anonymous' way."[92] The mark of the anonymous Christian, such as the "absolute love of neighbor, the acceptance of death, or hope in the future now bespeaks an implicit faith in the absolute bringer of salvation amply fulfills the requirements of the text" of the Gospels.[93] I cannot agree with this idea, especially when we stretch the scope of the Spirit's work into a non-Christian religious arena. Although I agree with Coffey that it is possible for the Spirit of Christ to guide and lure the non-Christian religious people to Christ, an implicit faith would not fulfill the final requirement of crossing the last threshold, that is, the line drawn between many religions and the triune God of Christianity. The only way to be in union with the triune God is to come to Christ in an explicit form of faith. In other words, the saving faith must be expressed unequivocally in Jesus by the power of the Holy Spirit.

Pertaining to the discussion of miracles, what do the entelechy of the Spirit and the crossing of thresholds have to do with miracles? The entelechy of the Spirit has the potential to address the divine causality

---

[91] Ibid., 386.

[92] Ibid., 387.

[93] Ibid., 388.

problem as well as the problem of miracles. First, let me address the divine causality problem. The divine causality problem as I have identified above revolves around the notion that the problem of sorting out divine actions from that of natural and human causality because divine actions are thoroughly intermingled with natural and human processes. The entelechy of the Spirit solves this problem by recognizing the divine action as the one that causes to behave with a specific intention, that is, to cross the threshold, progressing from a lower and simple form of being to a complex and sophisticated system, ultimately marching toward the hominization. The drive for such a progression comes from the will of the triune God, not because God is in the process of becoming, but by his act of grace. I am firmly convinced that the supernatural, divine intervention is a must for the progress toward "hominization." Man is not a byproduct of nature only.

One can counter my claim and say that nature has its own way to break through the critical points and self-transcend, thereby becoming something new and advanced like "man." If we allow the naturally induced self-transcendence to be the primary reason for the crossing of the critical points, we cannot explain the power source that gives nature to fight against entropy. In order to self-transcendent, all natural processes have to counter entropy which is the biggest obstacle for any system to "keep the engine of life running." The second law of thermodynamics states that the total entropy of an isolated system always increases over time, or remains constant in ideal cases where the system is in a completely static state. Let me illustrate by referring to the burning paper. In a closed system, if we burn a piece of paper, it turns into ash. Although the total amount of energy remains the same, the useful amount of energy has changed. Ash is no longer useful. It cannot be burned again and give off heat energy. Thus, what we have is entropy. Entropy is a natural process. Consequently, we see decay, decomposition, and death everywhere. We can speak of the effects of entropy theologically, as the fallen state of affairs in which evil has taken over and turned the natural and human world into estranged systems from God, making these systems isolated and death-bound.

In a real-life setting, despite the various levels of entropic processes, most systems are generating positive output such as cooperation and healthy reconciliation. Where is this positive energy coming from? From the vantage point of Spirit's entelechy, we can see that there is a divine system that counters the entropic processes by sustaining the world with positive influences such as love and forgiveness.[94] God must be opposing the natural tendency to isolate as the entelechy of the Spirit negates the corruption lodged in nature. If we take a naturalist view, the physical process has to counter the entropy on its own, but how? Where does it receive the positive input that can counter decay and death? Why does it want to counter entropy at all? Strictly speaking, from a naturalist point of view, all systems within nature, including human systems, have no reason to fight or counter entropy. [95] It may self-transcend to something new, but the ultimate victor in any closed system will be entropy. Translated into theological language, the fate of a closed system in the natural world is the antithesis of the kingdom of God. The kingdom of God is open to all, and the participants of this kingdom will enjoy an endless flow of God's positive energy that will make entropy meaningless. Thus, from a Christian standpoint, entropy is not the ultimate victor. The guiding force of the Spirit is a transcendent source that counters the entropic processes of nature. The divine system has the potential to counter entropy because it is supernaturally grounded upon divine rules, ontology, and intentions that are not of nature. It follows that the entelechy of the Spirit can introduce positive energy that nature does not have. It provides positive energy in the way it guides the natural and human systems to work together and transcend their limits

---

[94] There is a competing theory, namely, a multiverse theory, that accounts for the origin of "order" in our universe. However, as Rodney Holder has shown, the multiverse theory is not a good alternative here since it does not explain "why is there something rather than nothing?" For more details, see Rodney Holder, *God, the Multiverse, and Everything: Modern Cosmology and the Argument from Design* (Aldershot: Ashgate, 2004).

[95] Atheists like Richard Dawkins erase all traces of telos in nature in their naturalistic framework. For Dawkins, nature is utterly blind and randomly operating without a specific purpose. Cf. Richard Dawkins, *The Blind Watchmaker: Why the Evidence of Evolution Reveals a Universe without Design* (New York: W. W. Norton, 1996). I agree with Dawkins to some extent that nature was supposed to be blind, but in reality, nature does not behave like "a blind" entity. For this reason, scientists are constantly seeking the source of its telic processes.

so that they can break free from the bondage of decay and death, the final inescapable destiny for the isolated, closed systems.

Finally, we come to the problem of miracles. Indeed, based on a closed system of naturalism, miracles are problematic. If the divine source like the entelechy of the Spirit enters into the closed system, miracles, if they can occur in nature at all, have to introduce a new power of causality that overrides the laws of nature. However, the chief problems of miracles disappear if we take into account the supernatural source. In other words, miracles are possible only if we consider the entelechy of the Spirit. From this perspective, miracles are not just natural events, but Spirit-inspired events. If the laws of miracles are spiritual in origin, then they are not something that can be strictly definable within the bounds of the natural world, for by definition, they are more than nature.

What I want to emphasize at this point is that even though miracles are induced by the Spirit, nonetheless, miracles take place in the context of the natural processes. What needs to be remembered from our discussion thus far is that miracles do occur in nature, but they are not merely reducible to natural phenomena. Miracles are unusual and exceptional events because they exceed the manner in which nature produces its orderly patterns. The unusual and exceptional qualities come from the action of the Spirit of Christ, which assists the known course of nature to transcend its bound to something unknown and more complex. In other words, miracles occur when the threshold is crossed, displaying an extraordinary mode of divine activities.

Certainly, we can credit the physical process for crossing certain natural critical points, such as the boiling point of water.[96] When water boils, it crosses the critical point as liquid turns into gas. As identified by Teilhard, this type of threshold-crossing is tangential, that is, the Spirit working with nature in a hidden way, behind the scene, implicitly leading the natural process to its end for the sake of synthesis with the

---

[96] Likewise, a similar thing can happen to the personal system as well. For instance, a person may experience a critical point when she goes through an emotional crisis. The crisis intervention can help her reorient herself to rational behavior, correcting the mistake that led to the emotional crisis.

higher system. However, miracles are not really an implicit threshold-crossing. Rather, it is an explicit form of transcendence that completely changes the ontological make-up of the system. For instance, the resurrection of the dead is a miracle, because the deadness is transformed into something that is living. The healing of the sick is another example. The sick body is transformed into something that is free of disease. Such a systematic and ontological change can only be produced by God alone. It is because, as Thomas Aquinas asserts, a miracle "simply transcends the forces of all created nature, human and angelic."[97]

Although miracles transcend nature, they do not override nature. The aim of the entelechy of the Spirit is to work as a guide, not as a dominating force that exploits or contravenes the natural work. Hence, the invitation of the Spirit is always given in the form of an offer of grace. Once again, referring to Thomas Aquinas, "grace perfects nature." The entelechy of the Spirit or the perfecting work of the Spirit always preserves nature, even though a higher divine causality is involved with nature. What is this perfecting work of the Spirit? The perfecting work of the Spirit is none other than an attempt to prevent each system to close upon itself in an isolated system that ultimately finds its own death due to inevitable entropy. The Spirit guides to Christ, passing through the mundane events of material processes to reach the level of hominization in which God and man can finally be united in Christ by the power of the Spirit sent by the Father. Miracles, therefore, are the result of Christ-seeking moments, changing from implicit dynamics to explicit expressions all the while keeping the laws of nature unscathed. In this respect, miracles are pointers to God, a higher causality that propels lower systems to leave behind self-destructive close systems and break the bounds to be united with Christ, the final return to the infinitely open system, namely, the union with the Father through the mediation of the Son and the Spirit.

---

[97] Quoted from John A. Hardon, "The Concept of Miracle from St. Augustine to Modern Apologetics," Real Presence Association, accessed October 12, 2016, http://www.therealpresence.org/archives/Miracles/Miracles_003.htm.

In the final analysis, we can conclude with a few summarizing statements about miracles. First, miracles can only be denied if we follow the strict naturalist closed system. Scholars like Spinoza, David Hume, and more recently, Antony Flew, were able to rule out miracles because they saw that nature operates as a single system. In this closed system of nature, no causality except that which is underwritten by nature exists. Therefore, miracles as supernaturally driven events create ontological and epistemological dissonance with this restrictive metaphysical system. Second, miracles are only possible if we consider open system metaphysics. Open system metaphysics has enough room for multiple, distinct systems co-operating with one another to transcend the bounds of each system, ascending to higher systems. Such transcendental impetus and thresh-crossing moments are guided and lured by the Spirit. Without divine involvement, we cannot truly explain why each system of nature and humans is transcendent and open to one another and to God. Third, miracles are explicit ways in which the entelechy of the Spirit is revealed. Miracles are explicitly demonstrated extraordinarily and supernaturally by way of threshold crossings that bring about ontological changes. Fourth, miracles attest to the fact that God intrudes nature from outside. His intrusion nevertheless does not compromise the integrity of nature and its laws. Rather, it perfects it by countering various effects of entropy. Fifth, the possibility of miracles can be fleshed out only if we account for the infinitely open system of God and the finitely open-closed system of nature. In this sense, miracles are divine special actions in nature having the capacity to produce new and advanced phenomena via the entelechy of the Spirit. Hence, miracles are the result of a cooperative effort. All three distinct systems, that is, God, humanity, and nature have to work together in tandem to produce unusual and extraordinary events. To add to this statement, God is not an emergent system, which is supervened upon or determined by the natural process. Despite the interaction, all three systems are preserved due to the fact that the top-down influence of higher systems does not suspend the laws of lower systems, nor do the lower systems impose their rules upon higher systems and erase the differences.

Since we have defended the possibility of miracles, we are ready to move to the next section. In the following section, we will focus on more specific problems associated with the historical reliability of biblical miracles. A new set of research questions that we need to deal with is the following. How should we evaluate and determine the reliability of biblical miracle stories? What are the criteria for accepting biblical miracle stories as a historical fact? Why should we accept biblical narratives as the testimony to the actual event that took place in history? Why are biblical miracle narratives reliable at all?

The Historical Reliability of Biblical Miracle Stories: Rethinking Bultmann's Mythical Interpretation of Miracles

In this section, we are going to examine Rudolf Bultmann's work, and on the basis of this analysis, I show that biblical miracles are historically reliable. I have selected Bultmann as my dialogue partner because he is one of the key biblical scholars who tackled the issue of miracles head-on, arriving at his own unique conclusion that all biblical miracle stories are mythical in nature. Although not everyone accepts his claim, the way he investigated biblical texts that involve miracle narratives still stands as the norm for many contemporary New Testament scholars. For this reason, Howard Marshall comments that Bultmann is "probably the most influential New Testament scholar of the 20th century."[98] As a biblical scholar, Bultmann read the Scripture carefully and critically, and he found that biblical miracle narratives have no historical reliability whatsoever because they belong to what he calls "myth." Before we flesh out the meaning of "myth" and Bultmann's dismissive attitude toward biblical miracles, we need to reverse gears and retrace the hermeneutical program that brought him to this conclusion. From my own reading, I observe that Bultmann's hermeneutical method relies upon primarily three related rubrics: *Sitz im Leben*, oral transmission,

---

[98] I. Howard Marshall, *I Believe in the Historical Jesus* (Grand Rapids: Eerdmans, 1977), 12.

and fictional writings. So I start with a close examination of each of these rubrics.

Sitz im Leben

In his book, *The History of the Synoptic Tradition*, Bultmann makes clear that "the [biblical] literature, in which the life of a given community, even the primitive Christian community, has taken shape, springs out of quite definite conditions and wants of life."[99] This life situation is what he calls *"Sitz im Leben."* For Bultmann, the examination of life settings takes precedence over critically studying the text of the Scripture, because biblical authors imposed the understanding of his own contemporary world upon the entire make-up of biblical narratives. Bultmann insists that no literary work can eschew not only cultural colorings but more importantly the intrusion of the author's needs and wants.[100] He is essentially saying that the author's presupposition determines and shapes the form of a literary work. Therefore, he is more concerned with the *Sitz im Leben* of the early church and less the *Sitz im Leben* of the text. We can see this tendency in the methodology revealed in *The History of the Synoptic Tradition*, which shows that Bultmann's interpretative process moves from the believing community's *Sitz im Leben* to the text, not vice versa. This particular biblical move reverses the normal way that the historical-critical method works, which starts from the text and then moves to the context to unveil the ancient meaning of the text.

Bultmann's odd way of looking at New Testament's *Sitz im Leben* turns the focus away from the actual meaning of the biblical text to the identification of the presupposition of the early church. Consequently, Bultmann pays attention to how the early church influenced the creation of biblical narratives and explains the way the early church modified

---

[99] Rudolph Bultmann, *The History of the Synoptic Tradition*, trans. John Marsh (New York: Harper and Row, 1963), 4.

[100] For more detail, see Rudolf Bultmann, "Is Exegesis without Presuppositions Possible?" in *New Testament and Mythology and Other Basic Writings*, ed. Schubert M. Ogden (Philadelphia: Fortress, 1984), 145-154.

and remodified the original sayings about Jesus to fit the needs and wants of the church. For example, concerning the messiahship of Jesus, Bultmann argues that, in the original version of Jesus' teachings and sayings, there was no mention of Jesus' messiahship—Jesus was not even conscious of his messiahship.[101] Why was Jesus depicted as the Messiah in the New Testament? Bultmann writes, "It is an Easter-story projected backward into Jesus' life-time, just like the story of the Transfiguration."[102] Consequently, Bultmann dismisses the sayings and deeds of Jesus if similar ideas and concepts are found in early Christian sources. He is essentially following the criterion of dissimilarity.[103] In other words, he rejects all ideas that lead to the exaltation of Jesus and blames the early church for contaminating the true picture of biblical sayings by overly elevating Jesus even to the status of God.

Bultmann further supports his idea that Scripture has been severely modified by the early church by supposing that many miracles stories were borrowed from the Hellenic culture in which the early church flourished. Bultmann succinctly explains, "Synoptic miracle stories have grown up in the same atmosphere as the Jewish and Hellenistic miracle stories."[104] He goes on and lists many similar miracle stories that were common in the early church settings—e.g., exorcisms of demons, healings, raisings from the dead, and nature miracles. Bultmann asserts that these "[Hellenic] folk stories of miracles and miracle motifs have come into the oral tradition, a process which is quite plain in Mk. 5:1-21."[105] Bultmann is essentially saying that the original sayings have been tempered by the early church leaders as they reinterpreted those sayings reflective of Hellenic cultural settings. In the end, the investigation of the *Sitz im Leben* of the church unveiled for Bultmann the early church's

---

[101] Rudolf Bultmann, *Theology of the New Testament*, v.1 (New York: Charles Scribner's Sons, 1951), 26.

[102] Ibid.

[103] The criterion of dissimilarity and its cognate principles are succinctly explained by I. Howard Marshall. See Marshall, *I Believe in the Historical Jesus*, 201-207.

[104] Bultmann, *The History of the Synoptic Tradition*, 231.

[105] Ibid.

tempering with the original communication about Jesus' sayings and deeds.

Oral Transmission

Bultmann has no doubt that the earliest form of the biblical tradition is orally constructed and transmitted.[106] He also notes that, in some cases, there may have been short pieces of writings that supplemented the oral narratives, but due to the lack of solid evidence, he does not want to say that we can really verify whether or not there were written documents supporting the earliest form of oral traditions; thus, as far as Bultmann is concerned, biblical stories must have been circulated by word of mouth from one person to another without relying on the written text.

As demonstrated well by Bultmann in *The History of the Synoptic Tradition*, orally developed traditions cause some problems. They are essentially unreliable. Bultmann supports this claim in two ways. First, oral transmission is so fluid that it can be easily altered and modified by the hearers. He argues that, when "folk stories of miracles and miracle motifs have come into the oral tradition," the original meaning is lost and, after layers of adding on the modified form of sayings, for the words normally change when the stories are passed from one person to another, the final form we have is entirely different from the original.[107] In fact, Bultmann assumes that we can never go back to the actual historical event and uncover what precisely took place just by reading biblical narratives. All we can do with the given text is to peel away as much as we can the added layers and salvage pieces of the original sayings of the Bible.

---

[106] Rudolf Bultmann, "The Study of the Synoptic Gospels" in *Form Criticism: A New Method of New Testament Research* (Chicago: Willett, Clark and Company, 1934), 25-26. He writes, "It may be seen quite clearly that the original tradition was made up almost entirely of brief single units (sayings or short narratives), and that almost all references to time and place which serve to connect up the single sections into a larger context are the editorial work of the evangelists."

[107] Bultmann, *The History of the Synoptic Tradition*, 231.

Second, oral transmission never intended to maintain well-organized and coherent narratives. According to Bultmann, because they have circulated orally, the original form of dominical sayings had no real textual continuity from one piece of narratives to another. What most likely had happened in the ancient times was that short, pithy sayings that could be easily remembered were passed down from one person to another, and because of the time and geographical gap, there must have been many snippets of stories concerning Jesus' deeds and words floating around in the Palestinian and Hellenic community. Because of the inevitable time and geographical gap, as shown by Bultmann in his exegesis of miracle stories, biblical narratives contradicted each other.[108] Such disconnected pithy sayings do not present for the early church a coherent picture of Jesus' sayings and deeds, and thus, it was up the early church to fix this problem and create a coherent picture by the use of literary accretions.[109] Consequently, as Randall Hardman notes, "Bultmann's model presumes much more variety, freedom, and creativity than we actually find within the synoptic Gospels."[110] Indeed, Bultmann's assumption does not account for the fact that the oral tradition, especially in religious settings, can maintain a high degree of stability that is comparable to the written text.

Mythical Writings

In the end, Bultmann considers biblical miracle narratives as mythical stories that were invented by the early church to promote the welfare of the ecclesial community. For Bultmann, myth, according to the current standard of science, is fictional. However, in ancient times, mythical stories may have understood to carry some truth value; thus, unlike other liberal biblical scholars like David Strauss before him, he does not

---

[108] For instance, Bultmann takes issue with the narrative of a man being healed on the Sabbath. There are three different accounts with the same form, revealing three variants of a single saying. For more details, see Bultmann, *The History of the Synoptic Tradition*, 12-16.

[109] A variety of literary accretions is shown in Bultmann, *The History of the Synoptic Tradition*, 241-244.

[110] Randall Hardman, "Historical Evidence of the Gospels" in *True Reason: Confronting the Irrationality of the New Atheism*, ed. Tom Gilson (Grand Rapids: Kregel, 2013), 239.

want to remove the mythical elements in the Bible but translate them by filtering out all mythical elements and find the true meaning that lies behind the fictional writings. Why were biblical miracle stories told in mythical terms? Bultmann assigns several factors in the early church that allowed biblical authors to include mythical elements in the Bible.

The first factor he mentions is the mythical worldview upon which all biblical writers depended. Biblical writers lived in a time when myth played a critical role in the way people understood the things in this world. So, according to Bultmann, the ancient community had a mythical view of the world, seeing the world as a three-tiered structure. On the highest tier is God ruling over the world. On the lowest tier is the earth where humans and animals dwell. In the middle lie spiritual beings such as angels and demons. However, Bultmann asserts that, from a scientific perspective, there is no such thing as angels and demons.[111] The world we know operates based on the natural process. We just have a single system of nature. Thus, from the standpoint of modern man, the three-tiered universe is a primitive view of the world that is obsolete and irrelevant in the contemporary scientific society.

In the context of mythical worldview, insists Bultmann, Jewish and Hellenic miracle stories were uncritically accepted and synthesized into the original oral traditions. Based on Bultmann's belief that all interpretations and literary works are filtered through the interpreter's cultural setting and particular worldview, we can only say that the final product of biblical miracle narratives is shaped by the Jewish and Hellenic mythical stories. They became the template upon which the edited pieces of biblical literature were produced. As we can only talk about the movement of a solar system based on contemporary theories of science, biblical writers could only speak about the events that they heard through the grapevine on the basis of the most common form of communication, that is, the mythical story-telling.

---

[111] Rudolf Bultmann, "New Testament and Mythology?" in *New Testament and Mythology and Other Basic Writings*, ed. Schubert M. Ogden (Philadelphia: Fortress, 1984), 4. He writes, "For us the stars are physical bodies whose motion is regulated by cosmic law; they are not demonic beings who can enslave men and women to serve them."

The second factor he presents is the biblical authors' use of literary accretions and theological embellishments. Bultmann believes that the writers of the early church had unrestrained freedom to add literary devices, modify the original story, and even embellish what they heard to suit the need of the church. For this reason, Bultmann asserts that the Gospel authors had no intention of working as historiographers; rather, their job was to function as a "novelist"[112] writing short narratives that may attract readers by adding marvelous deeds and sayings of Jesus. To support this claim, Bultmann presents both literary and theological examples.

Literally, based on his own critical reading of the New Testament, he argues that the addition of geographical locations, personal names, and conjunctions such as the ancient literary device called "καί" may have portrayed biblical narratives as coherent, real events.[113] What is even more interesting for Bultmann is narrative discrepancies and variants found in the Gospels. As an example, looking at Mark 3:1-6, Bultmann finds in this pericope the description of Jesus' "Sabbath healing of the man with the withered hand."[114] Even though Markan narratives are the earliest form of written text, Bultmann notes that there are editorial insertions such as "πάλιν to link it with the context."[115] Also, he asserts that verse 6 includes biographical information, which is not relevant to the pericope, so he identifies it as another sign of an editorial accretion. Compared to other healing narratives in the Gospels, Bultmann treats Mark 3:1-6 with more respect since he believes that it is "an organically complete apothegm."[116]

That is not all. He finds a parallel pithy saying in Luke 14:1-6 and Luke 13:10-17. Here, Bultmann points out that the editorial work is more explicit and dramatic, since Luke 14:1-6 adds an introduction to Mark 3:1-6 and changes the wording to specify "the Sabbath healing of the

---

[112] Bultmann, *The History of the Synoptic Tradition*, 241.

[113] Ibid., 242.

[114] Ibid., 12.

[115] Ibid.

[116] Ibid.

man with the dropsy"[117] rather than the original version of healing "the man with the withered hand." Worse yet, for Bultmann, Luke 13:10-17 reveals that this narrative differs significantly from not only Mark 3:1-6 but also Luke 14:1-6, for the story is now changed to "the Sabbath healing of the crippled woman."[118] For Bultmann, such invention is the telltale sign of mythical elements in the Bible. Also, according to Bultmann, the conclusion of Luke 13:10-17 is another editorial addition since it ends with an editorial comment, "the miracle has to be followed by the report of the shame and confusion of the critics."[119] Moreover, he finds a new layer in verse 17, namely, the second part of verse 17, which for him is an editorial work for "the rejoicing of the multitude is a theme which originally would be placed at the end of the miracle story proper." [120] In short, because Bultmann sees a common pattern of a literary form that runs through Mark 3:1-6, Luke 14:1-6, and Luke 13:10-17, he accepts them as a single story, but the variants in the story that are traceable in the threefold narrative is, insofar as Bultmann is concerned, a clear sign that the original narrative has been changed into three different stories by the editor.

Moreover, theologically, insists Bultmann, there have been many cases in which the deeds of Jesus have been amplified and changed by the Gospel authors. Due to the limitation of this paper, I introduce one such case of what Bultmann calls, "the Baptismal legend."[121] Bultmann contends that the baptism narrative of Mark 1:9-11 is a legend. He writes, "The miraculous moment is essential to it and its edifying purpose is clear."[122] So, although it reads like a "historical" narrative, it takes the form of Persian and Egyptian legend as a "representation of the divine power, which fills kings in the form of a bird."[123] According to Bultmann, this is due to the fact that the early church writers preferred to exalt Jesus

---

[117] Ibid.

[118] Ibid.

[119] Ibid., 13.

[120] Ibid.

[121] Ibid., 249.

[122] Ibid.

[123] Ibid. 250.

to the status of a deity. He, therefore, contends that, in the original setting, Jesus was merely baptized by John like any other man, but this act of consecration could not qualify Jesus as the one who overcomes death. Bultmann insists that due to the resurrection of Jesus—which is another biblical myth—the church had to make Jesus a divine person. Hence, to embellish Jesus' baptismal narrative, the early church writers introduced the Holy Spirit, the sign of the divine power coming from on high, to solidify Jesus' divine Messiahship.[124] Thus, Bultmann concludes that the mythical story of the divine origin of Jesus that may have been circulating in the early church was read into the baptismal narrative, and what we ended up is a mythical story of Jesus being filled with the Holy Spirit.

In the final analysis, Bultmann points to the fact that the Bible is full of fictional writings, and as a result, he would not treat the Bible as a reliable historical document. For him, the truth of the story cannot be discerned because biblical narratives had been doctored by the Gospel authors, who had no concern for the historicity of Jesus and his deeds. For Bultmann, the Gospel writers were essentially novelists who wrote history-like mythical stories to idealize and exalt Jesus. Thus, there is no biographical information of Jesus in the Bible; rather, the Gospel narratives concerning Jesus are fictional with little historical value.

Does this mean that Bultmann found no use for the New Testament? Fortunately, he did. Like his predecessors Martin Kähler and Martin Debelius, he could not talk about the faith of Christianity in terms of the historicity of the Gospels, but he was able to talk about faith in terms of "kerygma." What is kerygma? In the words of Bultmann, it is "the message of God's decisive act in Christ."[125] We would need to cross a few more ideas before we can fully unpack what he means by "the message of God's decisive act in Christ," but here it suffices to say that he is looking for the original meaning of the Bible that is hidden behind

---

[124] Ibid. Bultmann believes that the baptismal myth is a derivative of Hellenic legend. He writes, "But since this conviction [that Jesus is the Messiah] could naturally not be derived from John's baptism, but could only, in my view, grow up in a Christian, through first in an Hellenistic environment, it follows that the Baptismal legend is firstly Hellenic origin."

[125] Bultmann, "New Testament and Mythology," 12.

mythical narratives so that he can translate it into today's language by cross-examining it with scientific naturalism and existential philosophy. This process takes a special label coined by Bultmann—i.e., "demythologization."

As an illustration, let us look at Bultmann's demythologization of Jesus' resurrection in his book, *New Testament and Mythology*. He considers Jesus' resurrection a myth because it does not fit the scientific view of the day. He writes, "A dead person being brought back to physical life is unimaginable."[126] No modern man is able to accept this story as a matter of fact. How can it be intelligible when "God's action is evidently tied up with natural occurrences in some completely unintelligible way"?[127] According to Bultmann, to speak of resurrection literally is to sacrifice our intelligence (*sacrificium intellectus*). Therefore, Bultmann warns that we should not be so ignorant and naïve and say that men and women of today who are more familiar with electric lights and radios than ancient mythologies base their faith in the wonder world of the New Testament. Bultmann declares sternly that we are living in the scientific world, in which events in the world are explained by natural processes.[128] There is no need to include the supernatural. The world of the supernatural is the world of myth. And "the mythical world picture is a thing of the past"[129] that is completely obsolete and irrelevant to today's worldview. So, based on scientific naturalism, Bultmann suggests that we ought to revise the resurrection narrative by the "facts that impress one as real."[130] How do we accomplish this when there is nothing historical about the biblical resurrection narrative?

According to Bultmann, the "facts that impress one as real" come to us by way of not only scientific naturalism but also existential philosophy, which in Bultmann's judgment, are two aspects of the same thing. He notes in this regard, "The world picture formed by modern

---

[126] Ibid., 7.

[127] Ibid.

[128] Ibid., 8.

[129] Ibid., 3.

[130] Ibid.

natural science and, in the second place, our own self-understanding, according to which we each understand our self to be a closed inner unity that is not open to the interference of supernatural power."[131] We can hear the echo of Spinoza here. Spinoza also said that our mode of intelligence and the laws of nature are two aspects of the same thing, the former leads to the truth of meaning and the latter to the truth of facts. What Bultmann wants to say is that via the merger of natural science and existentialism, theology is justified by "the decision for a consistent biological world view, that is the common basis on which the question of decision can arise."[132] In essence, like Spinoza, Bultmann highlights nature as the only acceptable criterion for theological interpretations, while rejecting the supernatural system. For this reason, according to Bultmann, the literal view of Jesus' resurrection is not just an unexplainable event, but more importantly, it says nothing to us. It would be a meaningless event if we were to take the resurrection narrative at face value. Since the biblical miracle has no authenticating power, Jesus' resurrection can only be an object of faith.[133] So he leaves history behind and looks to faith knowledge. To find the faith-meaning of resurrection, Bultmann asks his audience to turn to the existential interpretation of Jesus' cross-event.[134]

Since, for Bultmann, Jesus' resurrection has no historical value, it can only be understood in terms another event, that is, the cross of Jesus. The death on the cross, although it is a historical event, has an existential meaning behind the colorful and dramatic sacrificial myth. In the words of Bultmann, "Jesus' death on the cross is not to be seen as a human death but rather as God's liberating judgment of the world, the judgment that as such robs death of its power." [135] In translation, Bultmann is suggesting that we should free ourselves from the bondage

---

[131] Ibid., 6.

[132] Ibid.

[133] Ibid., 40.

[134] For an in-depth analysis of the relationship between Bultmann's existential theology and Heidegger's existential philosophy, please see John MacQuarrie, *An Existential Theology: A Comparison of Heidegger and Bultmann* (London: SCM Press, 1955).

[135] Ibid., 36.

of this world, the world full of fear and anxiety that defies the authentic existence. When we exercise our free will (e.g., making our own decisions) and correlate ourselves with "God's decisive act in Christ," "we are freed from anxiety, from frantically clinging to what is available and disposable."[136] What happens when we exercise our freedom to be authentic? We will "open ourselves freely to the future."[137] This is the appropriate movement from being inauthentic to becoming authentic. Bultmann also speaks of this change in terms of eschatology when he says, "To exist, however, means to exist eschatologically, to be 'a new creation.'"[138]

For Bultmann, becoming a new creation is the true meaning of Jesus' resurrection. Here, Bultmann once again sees Jesus' cross and resurrection as two aspects of one "cosmic occurrence." They are connected since both speak about the pursuit of becoming authentic existence, the former denotes the turning away from the world for the sake of reorienting ourselves to the authentic existence, and the latter finally finding the possibility of becoming authentic by losing the old baggage we carry. In this way, the true meaning of resurrection is unveiled. Resurrection is none other than the pursuit of the authentic human existence that we must lay hold of by resolve. The authentic human existence, in turn, gives us true freedom. Thus, according to Bultmann, accepting Jesus' resurrection as the object of our faith, we should no longer live in the past. We should no longer be satisfied with fear and anxiety. Instead, we must make our decision now and lead a new life that is "appropriate to creation."[139] What is appropriate to creation? Bultmann notes that what is of nature is appropriate to creation.[140] Consequently, we circle back to the original declaration— being authentic is being free from the supernatural, that is, being free from myth.

---

[136] Ibid., 20.

[137] Ibid., 18.

[138] Ibid., 19.

[139] Ibid., 25.

[140] Ibid.

This is the result of Bultmann's demythologization. Consequently, Jesus' resurrection has no miraculous component. The deconstructed meaning of resurrection takes the form of an existential ideal that strips away the antiquated worldview expressed in what Bultmann calls "objectifying" language. For Bultmann, myth objectifies God as if we can know something about God in a supernatural way. Bultmann insists that this is a mistake. Thus, like Spinoza, Bultmann rejects supernaturalism and disconnects all supernatural elements from the Bible in the name of demythologization. Due to the utter rejection of supernaturalism, Bultmann could only translate biblical miracles, like resurrection, in light of the liberating power-to-be, not as the actual event of a dead person returning to life. Bultmann tells us that he had to change miracle narratives in this way, because the Bible is full of invented, fictional stories. Unless he changes biblical stories, he is afraid that, in the 20th century, no one in the right mind will accept them as a matter of fact and take the Bible seriously. So, for Bultmann, the one and only way to save the Bible from utter dismissal is demythologization, translating it into existential language, which aligns well with the scientific naturalist worldview.

A Theological Response to Bultmann's Anti-Miracle Hermeneutics

At this junction, we need to ask, is Bultmann's way of reading the Bible the only way to interpret biblical miracle stories? Craig Blomberg thinks otherwise. Blomberg, based upon the work of a well-known New Testament scholar, N. T. Wright, lists three distinct trajectories of current biblical historical research:

(1) Some scholars—the smallest percentage—find it is appropriate to apply the standard criteria of historical investigation to the Gospels but believe that the results prove largely negative: not much turns out to be historically probable. (2) More commonly, others believe that it is methodologically inappropriate to apply historical criteria to documents that were first of all intended to be theological. (3) A final group,

perhaps a plurality among fully credentialed New Testament scholars today, agrees with the first in the use of the criteria but argues that the results actually make the historicity of the main contours of the canonical Gospels more probable than not.[141]

Accordingly, Bultmann's work likely falls under the first or second group.

If the majority of the New Testament scholars apply the standard criteria of historical investigation to the Gospels like Bultmann, how do they come up with such a drastically different conclusion than that of Bultmann's hermeneutical paradigm? Why does the third group on the list believe that the Gospels are historically reliable when others do not? To answer these questions, I review the work of a selected group of New Testament scholars that belong to the third group, such as Howard Marshall, F. F. Bruce, and Gary Habermas, who claim that not only the Gospels are historically grounded but also the early church came into being on the basis of Jesus' actual sayings and deeds. I am not going to review Bultmann's philosophical and scientific categories, since I have already covered extensively in the preceding section and demonstrated that a single system of naturalism can only explain away the supernatural elements of the Bible and falls short of explaining the miracle phenomenon. Evidently, Bultmann has also taken the same philosophical and scientific stance as that of Spinoza, so I am not going to repeat the work of countering the single system theory. What I will focus on in the following section is how the third group, as identified by Blomberg, justifies the historicity of the Gospels. And, based on their work, I reject Bultmann's hermeneutical paradigm all the while claiming the historical reliability of biblical miracles. I begin with the results of Howard Marshall.

Marshall contends that, contra Bultmann, the writers of the Gospels were not "blind as bats." If the writers had no historical data, Bultmann may be right to say that the Gospel authors had to invent stories to fill in the gaps and organize the disconnected pieces of information they

---

[141] Craig L. Blomberg, *The Historical Reliability of the Gospels* (Downers Grove: Intervarsity Press, 2007), 17.

received from their predecessors. However, based upon recent New Testament scholarship, Marshall finds that the true *Sitz im Leben* of the church is that they were working with well-organized "'tradition history' — i.e., the development of the tradition from its earliest forms to the point at which it was put into writing and found its way into the Gospels."[142] According to Marshall, scholars like Heinz Schurmann saw a plausible tradition history developing even before the post-Easter *Sitz im Leben*. Although Schurmann was more interested in the sociological make-up of the pre-Easter *Sitz im Leben*, he nonetheless discovered that there existed a pre-Easter *Sitz im Leben* such as the life setting of Jesus' disciples during the ministry of Jesus. Thus, Marshall contends that "if they regarded him as teacher or prophet, or something more than this, they must have had some relationship to what he said, for a teacher or prophet is nothing without his teaching or prophecy."[143]

Pushing the envelope even further, Marshall mentions several scholars who have identified Jesus' *Sitz im Leben*. One such scholar is Harald Riesenfeld who had suggested that there was a rabbinic tradition handed down from Jesus to the fixed circle of his disciples.[144] If there was a rabbinic tradition undergirding the early church movement, Jesus' teachings and deeds must have carried significant weight. Even if Jesus' teachings and deeds were transmitted orally, they must have been done with great care and fidelity — i.e., "each pupil learning accurately by heart what they heard from his teacher, and then passing it on."[145] Although there are skeptics who do not accept the theory proposed by Riesenfeld and his followers like Birger Gerhardsoon, as insisted by W. D. Davies, one of those skeptics, we can safely say that,

> they have forcibly compelled the recognition of the structural parallelism between much in Primitive Christianity and Pharisaic Judaism. This means, in our judgment, that they have made it far more historically probable and reasonably credible,

---

[142] I. Howard Marshall, *I Believe in the Historical Jesus* (Grand Rapids: Eerdmans, 1977), 200.

[143] Ibid., 197.

[144] Ibid., 195.

[145] Ibid.

over against the skepticism of much form criticism, that in the
Gospels we are within hearing of the authentic voice and within
sight of the authentic activity of Jesus of Nazareth, however
much muffled and obscured these may be by the process of
transmission.[146]

Thus, unlike Bultmann who has focused primarily on the church's *Sitz
im Leben* that was allegedly read into the stories about Jesus, Marshall's
examination of the earlier tradition reveals that there was a pre-ecclesial
Sitz im Leben that Bultmann may have missed. We can see this also in
Bultmann's discussion of Jesus' messiahship.

One of the strong arguments put forth by Bultmann is that the early
church read the messiahship of Jesus into the earlier oral traditions,
which had no interest in Jesus' messiahship, so that Jesus can be deified
and gain a superhuman status like all other gods in the Hellenic era, but
scholars like Michael Bird have found that this is not the case. Bird
contends that Jesus' messiahship belonged to the history tradition of
Jesus. According to Bird, the error comes from the scholars like Rudolf
Bultmann, Ferdinand Hahn, Petr Pokorny, and Maurice Casey, all of
whom assert that the early church invented the idea of Jesus as the
Messiah to some extent to venerate Jesus as their Savior and King. He
argues, in his book, *Jesus is the Christs,* that "the messianic identity of
Jesus is the earliest and most basic claim of early Christology."[147] His
contention is clear. Jesus' messiahship was not a late category conjured
up by the early church; rather, it was an indispensable component of
Jesus' self-awareness and his ministry from which the self-
understanding of the church arose. What is his rationale for taking this
stance?

He shows that, although not all Jews in the first century anticipated
eagerly for a messiah, among those Jewish groups who did wait
anxiously for the Messiah, there was a common set of beliefs that went
around the Jewish community concerning the coming Messiah. Bird

---

[146] Ibid., 196.

[147] Michael F. Bird, *Jesus is the Christ: The Messianic Testimony of the Gospels*
(Downers Grove: Intervarsity, 2012), 4.

writes, "The shared thread of Jewish messianism in the various tapestries that hung around from time to time was a future hope for a royal eschatological deliverer to liberate Israel and establish a renewed Jewish kingdom."[148] In this light, Bird insists that the Jewish community had, to some degree, the knowledge of the coming Messiah, and Jesus in this particular milieu came to fulfill these anticipated messianic expectations. In fact, Bird claims that Jesus was aware of his messianic title and duty during his ministry and started the messianic tradition for the early church. He enumerates six key evidence: (1) Jesus' self-understanding was based on Isaiah 61, which exhibits an explicit appeal to a Spirit-anointed ministry; (2) Jesus' central message had to do with the kingdom of God; (3) Jesus alluded to his royal functions tracing back to David and Solomon; (4) "I have come" sayings align well with Jewish messianic literature; (5) Jesus' performed messianic duties during the final week of his ministry—e.g., triumphal entry, prophecy about the rebuilding the temple, the passion scene depicting the messianic shepherd, and so on; (6) Jesus was crucified having the title of "king of the Jews." [149] For this reason, Bird is convinced that the messianic movement arose from Jesus' own teachings and ministry.

Therefore, insists Bird, the knowledge of the coming Messiah could not have originated in the early church. So, for him, Bultmann was wrong to say that the idea of resurrection is a derivative of the early church's exaltation of Jesus as the Messiah. According to Bird, there is no precedence for deducing messiahship from his resurrection. He writes, "How does 'resurrected' equal 'Messiah'?"[150] He goes on to show that the New Testament mentions the resurrection of the dead in other places such as Mark 6 and Revelation 11, but they are not associated with the messianic claim. Therefore, according to Bird, Jesus' resurrection was not the only cause of Jesus's exaltation, venerating him as the divine Messiah. Rather,

---

[148] Ibid., 5.

[149] Ibid., 8-9.

[150] Ibid., 6.

it was remembrance of Jesus as an anointed prophet, testimony to his royal and eschatological role in a future kingdom, impressions he made upon his disciples by his teaching, fresh memories of his death on a messianic charge, knowledge of his Davidic family origins, belief in his resurrection, the experience of the Spirit[151]

that led the early church to reflect on Jesus' messiahship. Accordingly, Bird concludes that, "more likely, the Gospels were written between AD 70-100 when belief in Jesus as Israel's Messiah had been in currency for forty years or more. The Gospels were composed as conscious attempts to promote the gospel of Jesus, serve as an introduction to Israel's Messiah, and offer an explanation for the emergence of a messianic community."[152]

Not only that the existence of an earlier tradition of Jesus' messiahship supports the idea that biblical authors were piecing together historical data but so is the idea that biblical authors had relied on the eyewitness accounts. There are a number of different biblical scholars who make this claim, most notably by F. F. Bruce, Richard Bauckham, Howard Marshall, and Gary Habermas, renowned New Testament scholars who provide us with a crux of the argument. So, I introduce their arguments here.

To start with Bruce, he contends that "the first three Gospels were written at a time when many were alive who could remember the things that Jesus said and did, and some at least would still be alive when the fourth Gospel was written."[153] This means that, as it is noted in Luke 1:1-4, the Gospel writers verified their writings by checking their accuracy based upon eyewitness accounts.[154] In this regard, Bruce confirms that

---

[151] Ibid., 11.

[152] Ibid., 30.

[153] F. F. Bruce, *The New Testament Documents: Are They Reliable?* (Grand Rapids: Eerdmans, 1982), 13. He adds, "When, some fifty days after the crucifixion, the disciples began their public proclamation of the gospel; they put forward as the chief argument for their claims about Jesus the fact of His rising from the dead. 'We saw him alive.'"

[154] This argument has been contested most strongly by Bart D. Ehrman. He succinctly summarizes his points in his blog (https://ehrmanblog.org/question-about-eyewitnesses-and-the-gospels). I mention three points here. First, the contents of the New Testament are written

the phrase "we are witnesses of these things" (Acts: 5:32) was the constant and confident assertion of biblical writers.

Similarly, Marshall asserts that biblical narratives are not the byproduct of modification but a recording of what actually took place. According to Marshall, the visible patterns in the Gospels, for example, the stories of healings,

> fall into fairly regular patterns: there is a description of the situation requiring a cure, an account of what the healer does, and a description of the effects of the healer's action both in terms of the actual cure and in terms of the reaction produced in any observers.[155]

However, just because of this regularity, insists Marshall, we cannot assume that they are made up stories, the variants of a common ancient myth. Rather, the commonality of these patterns may imply that the stories must have been constructed and transmitted according to the common story-telling patterns of the day as noted in the Gospels. Thus, Bultmann's account of Luke 14:1-6 and Luke 13:10-17 as the variants of Mark 3:1-6 could be three distinct eyewitness accounts that were told in a similar pattern. It is highly probable that the regular patterns in the

---

many years after Jesus' death, so most eyewitnesses probably already passed away. Second, even if eyewitnesses were alive at the time of drafting the Gospels, there is no proof that the authors checked their data against the eyewitness reports. Third, eyewitness accounts were transmitted orally, and orally transmitted data always change. It is due to the fact that human memory is not reliable. Because of these reasons (and more), Ehrman dismisses eyewitness accounts as a non-viable option for deciding the historicity of the Bible. For more details, see Bart D. Ehrman, *Forgery and Counterforgery: The Use of Literary Deceit in Early Christian Polemics* (New York: Oxford University Press, 2013). For a counterargument against Ehrman's view, read Timothy Paul Jones, *Misquoting Truth: A Guide to the Fallacies of Bart Ehrman's "Misquoting Jesus"* (Downers Grove: Intervarsity Press, 2007); and Craig Blomberg's *Can We Still Believe the Bible? An Evangelical Engagement with Contemporary Questions* (Grand Rapids: Brazo, 2014). To add my opinion, I do not think Ehrman's arguments are persuasive on two accounts. First, as Bruce notes, the Gospels themselves make it clear that their writings were based on eyewitness accounts. The mistrust comes not from the reading the Bible carefully and critically but from his own view of the Bible as "forgery." Second, human memory surely is fallible, but we cannot discount wholly the value of memory. Ehrman in his book, *Forgery*, recalls his own journey from being an evangelical writer to becoming an agnostic scholar. Isn't this narrative based on his memory? We need to at least give some credit to memory for recalling the truth of the past events.

[155] Marshall, *I Believe in the Historical Jesus*, 173-174.

Gospels could be the sign of people memorizing the actual event based on common linguistic makers.[156]

Such a historical recording and memorizing activity is further supported by notetaking activities. Bruce refers to the first-century Christian writer, Papias, who affirmed that Matthew complied the "Logia" in the Hebrew speech.[157] We do not have a clear idea of what this "Logia" entailed, but it is safe to say that Matthew may have taken notes of Jesus' teachings during the heyday of Jesus' ministry. He writes in this regard, "The evidence indicates that the written sources of our Synoptic Gospels are not later than AD 60; some of them have even been traced back to notes taken of our Lord's teaching while His words were actually being uttered."[158] Likewise, Marshall, drawing upon the work of C. H. Dodd, confirms that "the early preaching of the church probably contained a rough outline of the ministry of Jesus."[159] What this means is that the early church had access to Jesus' sayings and deeds all based on eyewitness accounts that were verified by checking with the living eyewitnesses and disciples of Jesus.

Thus, Bultmann's assumption that biblical data related to chronological markers, such as names of persons and geographical identifications, are signs of the work of a novelist might be missing the fact that they are actual markers of historical narratives. It is quite normal to read eyewitness accounts including chronological markers, names of persons, and geographical identifications, for these components preserve the integrity of the stories.[160] In other words, these

---

[156] Bruce, *The New Testament Documents*, 39. Bruce says that there is a sign of memorization markers in the Bible, especially the Lord's sayings. He writes, "Another interesting fact which comes to light when we try to reconstruct the original Aramaic in which our Lord's sayings in all the Gospels were spoken is that many of these sayings exhibit poetical features." Poetical features that Bruce mentions here are memorization markers (e.g., linguistic repetitions), rather than imaginary word-pictures as what poetry may invoke in our days.

[157] Ibid., 36.

[158] Ibid., 45.

[159] Marshall, *I Believe in the Historical Jesus*, 165.

[160] Richard Bauckham, *Jesus and the Eyewitnesses: The Gospels as Eyewitness Testimony* (Grand Rapids: Eerdmans, 2006), 39-92.

markers do not necessarily support a myth-theory. That would be a shallow assumption. Rather, as Richard Bauckham asserts, if we read the Gospels carefully and critically, we can see that the authors of the Gospels were guided by historical events and treated chronological markers, names of persons, and geographical identifications as the markers of real-life events, not the markers of invented stories.

Of course, Bultmann is right to say that the biblical authors were adding things such as conjunctions and parenthetical remarks, but those additions do not alter the crux of historical data. In other words, they function as secondary linguistic devices supporting and clarifying the primary historical data of Jesus' sayings and deeds. Miracle narratives such as Jesus' resurrection, therefore, are historically based stories, which were transmitted to the early church from the earlier sources of historical data. This point is well made by Gary Habermas in his explanation of Jesus' resurrection.

Like Bultmann, Habermas relies heavily on Paul's account to show that "after his death, Jesus appeared alive to his followers,"[161] although he finds the corroborative work between Pauline and non-Pauline materials in the New Testament. Habermas employs a unique method of what he calls, "the minimal fact approach."[162] Michael Licona explains, "Habermas has compiled a list of more than 2,200 sources...in which experts have written on the resurrection from 1975 to the present. He has identified minimal facts that are strongly evidenced and which are regarded as historical by a large majority of scholars, including skeptics."[163] He cites scholars like Reginald Fuller who asserts that "within a few weeks after the crucifixion Jesus' disciples came to believe this is one of the indisputable facts of history."[164] But more likely, the

---

[161] Gary R. Habermas, "The Resurrection Appearances of Jesus," in *In Defense of Miracles: A Comprehensive Case for God's Action in History*, ed. R. Douglas Geivett and Gary R. Habermas (Downers Grove: Intervarsity, 1997), 262.

[162] Also see Gary R. Habermas, *The Case for the Resurrection of Jesus* (Grand Rapids: Kregel, 2004), 43-51.

[163] This is quoted in Lee Strobel, *The Case for the Real Jesus* (Grand Rapids: Zondervan, 2007), 112.

[164] Habermas, "The Resurrection," 262.

earliest resurrection account along with the recognition of Jesus as a divine figure was put into a creedal form a few years after the resurrection, as contended by James Dunn.[165] Nonetheless, Habermas makes a compelling point here that the early creedal formula that describes the resurrection quickly formed after Jesus' death and resurrection.

He gives primarily four major facts gleaned from Paul's testimonies: Paul's reception of the creedal account of Jesus' resurrection, Jesus' appearance to Paul himself, Paul's testimony that his message was given the stamp of approval by other apostles, and Paul's own confirmation of their appearance reports.[166] Habermas reasons that there is rarely any contention amongst the New Testament scholars and skeptics that Paul was a real figure who had enough education and intelligence to write accurately as he can about the events that took place during his lifetime. According to Habermas, Paul, therefore, is one of the favorite New Testament figures upon which we can verify the records of the Gospels. For instance, 1 Corinthians 15:3-8 shows that Paul had received an early form of eyewitness accounts drafted in a creedal form that testifies to Jesus' burial and resurrection "on the third day according to the Scriptures" (1 Cor. 15:4).[167] Paul then lists the eyewitnesses who had checked the data for him, including James and the apostles (1 Cor. 15:7). He ends the testimony stating the fact that "he appeared to me also" (1 Cor. 15:8). Habermas confidently claims that 1 Corinthians 15:3-8 is historically reliable, for according to Hans von Campenhausen, "[t]his account meets all the demands of historical reliability that could possibly be made of such a text."[168] He also notes that in Galatians 2:6 Paul writes, "they added nothing to my message."[169] "They" denotes the apostles he met in Jerusalem, namely, Peter, James, and John (Gal. 2:8-9). This shows that Paul's data and apostle's memory matched. They

---

[165] James Dunn, *The Evidence for Jesus* (Louisville: The Westminster Press, 1985), 61.

[166] Habermas, "The Resurrection," 270.

[167] Ibid., 264-267.

[168] Ibid., 264.

[169] Ibid, 267.

were preaching about the same Jesus who was resurrected three days after his death, revealing himself to his followers.

Going further, Habermas shows that non-Pauline materials also attest to the actual appearance of Jesus. I list seven items: (1) the empty tomb, (2) disciples own accounts of Jesus' physical appearances after his death, (3) the ontological and spiritual transformation of Jesus' disciples (4), the resurrection narrative being central to disciples' preaching, (5) the rapid expansion of the church (6) the Jewish believers making Sunday their primary day of worship (7), the so-called family skeptic, James, being converted to the faith after the resurrection.[170] In other places, he has given more reasons to believe in the historical facts about Jesus' resurrection but the items I present here give sufficient evidence that the resurrection account is based on the historical fact.[171]

Contra Bultmann, who argued that the resurrection is a biblical myth that has no historical foundation, Habermas demonstrates with sufficient evidence that "it is almost impossible to dispute that at the historical roots of Christianity lie some visionary experiences of the first Christians, who understood them as appearances of Jesus, raised by God from the dead."[172]

Although we have demonstrated the historical claim of Jesus' resurrection, we need to address one additional comment from Bultmann. Bultmann showed that there are signs of theological adornment in the Gospels. For instance, Jesus' resurrection changed the identity of Jesus as man to Jesus as a divine figure. Even if we say that Jesus' resurrection is historically grounded, we need to know when and how the Christology of the early church developed and influenced the writings of the Gospel miracles. This issue is taken up by F. F. Bruce.

---

[170] He talks about these points in detail in his book, *The Case for the Resurrection of Jesus*.

[171] He also notes that, drawing upon C. H. Dodd's work, the resurrection appearance narrative found in Matthew 28:8-10, John 20:19-21, and Luke 24:36-49 are based on early creedal materials. Habermas, "The Resurrection," 268.

[172] James Dunn's words quoted in Habermas, "The Resurrection," 263.

Bruce writes, "But, while Christ's resurrection was proclaimed by the early Christians as a historical event, it had more than a merely historical significance for them." [173] For Bruce, the theological significance of Jesus' resurrection is "the grand demonstration of the Messiahship of Jesus."[174] However parting with Bultmann here, he adds that this theological adornment "did not make Him Messiah, but it proved that He was Messiah," as Paul notes, "He was declared to be the Son of God with power...by the resurrection of the dead."[175] So the theological meaning of the resurrection points to the fact that, "in Christ, the power and grace of God entered into human history to bring about the world's redemption."[176] Basically, Bruce is telling us that the miracle of Jesus' resurrection is a theological pointer to God's redemptive act in this world. For this reason, Bruce refers to the miracles of the fourth Gospel denoting as "signs and wonders." He writes in this regard, "'signs and wonders' is a frequent phrase, as if to teach us that the miracles are not related merely for their capacity of begetting wonder in the hearers and readers, but also because of what they signified...They were signs of the messianic age, such as had been foretold by the prophets of old."[177] Bruce argues that the messianic age, in turn, denotes that "the power of God has entered into human life."[178] The implication of the power coming from above is clear. There will be an ontological transformation.

We may be under the dominion of the entropic power of nature, struggling with ailments and death. However, the power of Christ heals the sick and resurrects the dead. According to Bruce, the same power of healing and resurrection operates on the same level as the power to forgive sins.[179] Because we have forgiveness and reconciliation in and through Jesus Christ, we are now under the dominion of God, living in a messianic age. So, Bruce affirms that the miracle narratives are clear

---

[173] Bruce, *The New Testament Documents*, 66.

[174] Ibid.

[175] Ibid., 66-67.

[176] Ibid., 67.

[177] Ibid., 69.

[178] Ibid., 70.

[179] Ibid.

signs of the intermingling of God, humanity, and nature. These three systems are cooperating in an extraordinary way to bring about an ontological transformation that may help us transcend entropy and ascend to the messianic age in which all three systems of God, humanity, and nature, are opened to one another. If we follow Bultmann's program, there would be no ontological change associated with divine special actions; rather, there would only be an existential realization of who we are in a reductionistic, naturalistic way.

What needs to be clarified at this point is that Bruce is not talking about the theology of the messianic age giving the biblical authors impetus to invent the miracle stories. Bruce actually contends that all biblical miracles, including resurrection and nature miracles, are historically grounded.[180] From history emerged the church's theology, not vice versa. Such compelling theology of the early church could not have stood up to the test had it not based on the true event. If no one received healing from Jesus, from what authority could Jesus and the church say that "your sins are forgiven?" The only way to sustain the authority of the church's theology is the historical data and the apostolic tradition that verified the miracle testimonies.

Bultmann may have read too much of the early church's theology into history and end up losing history altogether. Of course, as Bultmann has said, we cannot deny the fact that the early church's theological interpretation has seeped into Gospel narratives. However, it is highly probable that the bulk of the early church's theological renderings, as shown by a number of different New Testament scholars mentioned in this section, must have been a late addition to the primary historical data that gave the theological impetus to call Jesus "Lord and Savior."

Conclusion

We may now conclude that biblical miracle narratives are theological pointers to God's special act and his supernatural causality. However, we have seen that in both Spinoza's and Bultmann's work the inclusion

---

[180] Ibid., 74.

of the supernatural was problematic. Spinoza handled this problem by way of either dismissing the supernatural element as a non-viable option for his naturalism or interpreting them as recently realized natural phenomena. For Bultmann, miracle narratives in the Bible were nothing less than the invention of the early church writers who promoted their own ideas of Jesus being utterly influenced by the Hellenic culture that freely accepted supernatural entities intermingling with nature to produce extraordinary events such as healing the sick and raising the dead. Bultmann contended that these primitive ideas belong to the first-century church; they do not belong to the 20th-century scientific world in which natural sciences have proved that our universe is the world underwritten by natural processes, not the world undergirded by spiritual beings or supernatural causes.

The issue, therefore, is clear. Miracles cannot be explained unless we show that the world is not a single system. Unless we account for many different systems in this world, including God, which may not be explainable strictly in terms of natural processes, miracles will continue to be misinterpreted. To solve this problem, I propose to consider open system metaphysics. Open system metaphysics take into consideration that the world is a complex network of many different systems, some natural, and some supernatural. In this way, open system metaphysics ensures God's involvement with the world with the possibility of his special miraculous interventions. With the possibility of God's miraculous intervention in nature, the divine action is not explained away by the naturalistic rationalization that operates on the assumption that all God's actions fall under the laws of nature. I agree that miracles do not violate the laws of nature, but I cannot say that God's action is just that, the process of nature. Miracles break the chain of this reductionism.

We need to mention one additional component, the divinely guided threshold crossing. In other words, miracles are special manifestations of God's extraordinary works that lead to threshold crossings. What I mean here is that miracles occur when the higher divine system (God) intersects with the lower system (man and nature), bringing about a transcendental occurrence that goes beyond the possibility of lower systematic activities. For instance, the lower system of nature or humanity cannot reverse the process of entropy such as death. The intrusion of the higher divine system to the lower system—without damaging the integrity of the lower system like the mind and body relationship—brings about an extraordinary event like the resurrection that may not be rationalized simply in terms of lower system logic. Simply put, miracles transcend the natural logic even though they occur in the context of nature, and thus, they demand an explanation not only from natural and human existential circumstances but, more importantly, from metaphysical and theological viewpoints. This is my way of declaring that the consideration of miracles does not have to leave the scientific mindset as we deal with open system metaphysics, nor does it reduce to secular rationalization, as miracles demand us to go beyond secular reason and into the territory of theology.

This theory of miracles is predicated upon a cooperative effort between God, humanity, and nature, and only when these systems work together, and at the same time, transcend creaturely limit conditions with the help of divine interventions, miracles can take place. To reiterate, in this divinely inspired transcending event, miracles have to do with something more than what is natural. Miracles are theological pointers that direct us to the messianic age of the future that has penetrated the kingdom on earth here and now through the Spirit of Christ. Indeed, they are signs and wonders for the messianic age, to borrow the words from F. F. Bruce. If we accept Jesus as the Messiah and live in the power of the Holy Spirit in this messianic age, we will be able to see the things of God at a higher level of divine activity that transforms and "perfects" nature. Otherwise, we will be restricted to the activities of the lower system, unable to discern the higher level of theological causality. Paul speaks in this regard, "The person without the Spirit does not accept the things that come from the Spirit of God but considers them foolishness, and cannot understand them because they are discerned only through the Spirit" (1. Cor. 2:14). This openness to the "Spirit" means that the final transition moves from restrictive naturalism to an unbounded infinite system of God's inner life.[181]

For this reason, as Bruce has shown, when we read the Gospels, although we should pay attention to historical data first, we must not forget that biblical miracles have theological referents that direct us to God himself. If we rely solely on the naturalistic historical-critical method, we will run into the problem of robbing the biblical narratives of all their theological significance. Conversely, if we remove the significance of history from miracles, as Bultmann had done, we would lose sight of all historical data that are associated with miracle narratives. What we have to realize is that biblical miracle stories did take place — i.e., "something of a very wonderful and impressive nature happened, in which the disciples saw the glory of God revealed in their Master."[182]

Before I end, one important thing to note is that, although we ascertain the possibility and historicity of biblical miracles, we cannot say that we know precisely how each miracle played out to the extent that we can draft a formula that may invoke the same miracles today. In order to duplicate biblical miracles, we would need to construct a laboratory of a controlled environment, which is absurd. We cannot "control" the divine action, nor can we control all aspects of the natural environment in which miracles have taken place. Simply put, miracles are not "controlled" events. They are the spontaneous and free acts of God integrated into the natural and human processes. They should not be treated as something that can be domesticated for our own use here and now. They occur within God's special salvific purpose, as shown in the time of Jesus' ministry. This does not mean that miracles belong only to the past. If miracles are signs and wonders of the messianic age, which

---

[181] To note, I am not arguing for "supernaturalism." Supernaturalism tends to focus on the supernatural act of God as a way for us to escape from unpleasant realities and find relief in the wish-fulfilling God. Bruce makes an important comment about miracles in this regard. "Our Lord did not esteem very highly the kind of belief that arose simply from witnessing miracles. His desire was that men should realize what these things signified." In other words, miracles are not the ends but means to an end, that is, our final redemption and the fulfillment of God's kingdom. For this reason, miracles function only as pointers to God's salvific act. Bruce, *The New Testament Documents*, 69.

[182] Ibid.

has come here and now, they are legitimate events even in today's scientific environment.[183] As a matter of fact, their significance is not reduced at all because of the advancement of science. Rather, they are all the more needed to counter scientific reductionism and reveal the ultimate telos for this world—i.e., the confirmation that the messianic age has come to deliver this world from the entropic-bound self-centeredness.

---

[183] Like Craig Keener, I also believe that the miracles take place in our current contemporary settings. Keene details the biblical miraculous events that are occurring around the world today. Read Craig Keener, *Miracles: The Credibility of the New Testament Accounts*, 2 vols. (Grand Rapids: Baker, 2011).

Epilogue

I conclude with a personal reflection regarding the task of a theologian working in the 21st-century scientific age. Although doing theology scientifically is not always welcomed, it is safe to say that the bridge that connects theology and science has become a permanent fixture in the contemporary academic world.[1] In fact, the bridge we have now will be ever expanding, for the passion and zeal for the interdisciplinary studies have not died down yet. With the attention drawn to the bridge and the increased traffic on the bridge, it is more urgent that theologians and scientists keep looking for ways to clear away potentially dangerous objects that may stifle the free movement on the bridge. This was one of the main tasks for this book.

Surely, there are still many stumbling blocks on the bridge that I have not dealt with in this book, primarily due to its limited space and scope. One such obstacle is the evolutionism-creationism debate. There are many subcategories that are attached to this debate such as the issue of the origins or the role of ecclesial and public education, which makes the debate even more complex and controversial. The problem I have is not with the way we hold to different views; rather, I am more concerned with the way in which this debate is making our society fragmentary. Proponents of creationism do not want to be reconciled with evolutionists. Neither do evolutionists want to find a middle way and shake hands with creationists. Biblical creation narratives and the theory of evolution are seen as antithetical, and no one wants to listen to the voice from the other camp. In this respect, the job of theo-scientific scholars is to work continuously and find a way to handle these types of impediments so that the public is aware that theology and science, though they may hold to different views, could enrich each other by keeping the conversation open to one another.

---

[1] I am grateful for Robert J. Russell for introducing the bridge metaphor to describe the theology and science relationship. For his illustration, see Robert J. Russell, "Foreword," in *Bridging Theology and Science*, ed. Ted Peters and Gaymon Bennett (Minneapolis: Fortress, 2003), ix-x.

It is good that we focus on the clearing way of obstacles on the bridge, but if our attention is drawn solely to the bridge itself, we tend to suffer from a tunnel vision and lose sight of the original aim, that is, the preservation and betterment of the two forces of our culture: religion and science. We have two main components that sustain the integrity of the bridge, that is, God and nature. Because I am coming from a theological camp, my primary concern is God, but because the study of God extends to the study of nature, I see the need to lay a theological path in the outdoor of nature as well. However, due to our myopic visions, there seems to be a trend that is adversely affecting the theology and science interface.

As I tried to show in this book, theologians can play the game of interfacing theology and science by borrowing new scientific findings and their theoretical and metaphysical implications. However, when theologians borrow the playing field from science, they need to remember that it is wrong to read the playing rules of science into God and alter God's essence to fit the scientific agenda. Surely, theology of nature can be modified and sustained upon borrowed scientific concepts for we have come a long way since the Thomistic adoption of Aristotelian science, but the very essence of God should not be amended simply because we have a new vision of the natural world. If we consistently make this mistake, theologians would rely more and more on reductionistic metaphysics such as naturalism than a holistic paradigm such as open system metaphysics that accounts for the dynamic interplay of God, humanity, and nature. I sense this trajectory as I examine the current status of theology. Theologians today unapologetically accept the naturalistic presuppositions, and as a result, they have little regard for the supernatural. There seems to be a large crowd of theo-scientists who are riding on the bandwagon of naturalism, leaving behind the traditional Christian understanding of God. We must stop committing the sin of modifying the doctrine of God simply based on the metaphysical framework we learned from naturalism.

In order to prevent this type of error, I suggest that theologians evaluate cautiously various naturalistic worldviews out there. The peril of naturalistic worldview is present and clear, namely, the employment of naturalistic metaphysics by which all ideas of God and his created beings are interpreted. As a theologian engaged in the theology and science dialogue, I must warn that we cannot simply point to what is in nature and argue that the same thing is in God. The "this-is-that" approach should be carefully weighted when there is a possibility of the "this-is-not-that" connection between God and the world. This does not mean that we should completely avoid various naturalistic metaphysical proposals handed to us from the modern period to the contemporary era. That would be throwing the baby out with the bathwater. What I urge is to find a mediating position upon which we can build a more open approach to the cross-fertilization of theology and science without having to fight for one single, dominant metaphysics.

In his book, I introduced many metaphysical paradigms such as panentheism, religious naturalism, process metaphysics, and the theory of emergence. After the demise of logical positivism, metaphysics has gained a new driving force, and for this reason, many different metaphysical views have been introduced. The buffet of metaphysics has left this generation with a dilemma, however. Which one should we choose to see the world realistically and truthfully? What metaphysical worldview is right for today's scientific world? To solve this problem of multiplicity, theo-scientific scholars have been looking for a single metaphysical matrix under which all other metaphysics can be subsumed. In my judgment, this is a wrong approach. I agree that for any interdisciplinary project it is critical to ascertain a dominant metaphysical lens through which we can see the line of continuity in the midst of many different strands of thought crisscrossing the landscape. However, we must take this approach with caution. There is a danger of reducing all metaphysics into a single dominant matrix. This is certainly not the spirit of interdisciplinary studies. The proper way to interface different disciplines is to recognize the distinct contribution of each system all the while finding specific areas of consonance. In this postmodern context, looking for a universal matrix is a dead-end approach. We need to be more sensitive to the multiplicity of voices out there. So, I opt for an open system metaphysical approach. It allows us to take advantage of the metaphysical development from many different fields of study, such as physics, biology, and theology, and underwrite a holistic metaphysical stance that comes out of the theology and science dialogue in particular, and the interplay of God, humanity, and nature, in general. Hence, open system metaphysics is always provisional, growing, and networked, adapting to the changing environment of this world.

The main implication of putting theology and science under the holistic metaphysics of open systems is the recognition that there are at least three analogical relationships between theology and science—i.e., realist analogy, personal analogy, and transcendental analogy. I have discussed these components in detail elsewhere [2] so let me briefly explain what they are. First, realist analogy ensures that both theology and science adapt to the worldview of critical realism. As we have seen, critical realism is a way we see reality existing independent of the mind, and at the same time, we recognize that mind-independent reality requires our interpretation via the use of models and signs. In this light, Arthur Peacocke writes that both theology and science "aim to depict reality; both use metaphorical languages and models that are revisable in the light of experiments and of experiences. The aim of both is to tell as true a story as possible."[3] This means that the work of theology falls within the scientific requirement of taking realist components seriously. Our concepts and ideas about the world derive from the actuality of what goes on in the world, not according to what we want to see the "world as." So, theological science underwritten by realist analogy penetrates to the inner dynamics of "being" and "existence" all the while giving accounts to the relationship between the concept and its referent.

Second, personal analogy prevents realist analogy to fall under a rubric of sterile physicalism or materialism. It does not pivot theology or science to the belief that the world is operated based on brute, senseless, purposeless, and entropic "stuff" that is bound to be destroyed by the degrading forces of nature. Rather, the world is

---

[2] Cf. Aaron Yom, *Number, Word, and Spirit: Rethinking T. F. Torrance's Theological Science from a Pneumatological Perspective* (New York: Peter Lang, 2018).

[3] Arthur Peacocke, "'The End of All Our Exploring' in Science and Theology," *Zygon* 39/2 (2004), 416.

purposeful, hopeful, and cooperative, due to the fact that there is positive energy imputed by a divine system that guides and lures the entire cosmic event to its fulfillment, that is, to be in relation with personal agents in the kingdom of God. With this personal analogy, we do not stop describing reality as they are merely in themselves, but take into consideration the interplay of the known and the knower. This does not mean that we, as intentional and conscious agents, impose our own ideas upon the things in this world, and turn the world into a subjective matrix. Rather, personal analogy helps us correlate reality to our concept by way of maintaining the principle of double agency, that is, the cooperative interplay of concepts and reality in the way we understand the world.

Third, transcendental analogy takes a step further and allows theology and science to move beyond their limits and come into the world of metascience, ultimately arriving at a divine matrix. Although scientists may not be interested in God-talk, nonetheless, the transcendental analogy will assist them, at least, to take advantage of metascientific and metaphysical implications of theology. They could acknowledge that there is a kind of objectivity that does not rest simply on empirical adequacy, for our knowledge of the transcendent emerges from the contact with divine reality which requires an act of discernment beyond common natural observations. In other words, via metascience, they could move from investigating what is physical to what is metaphysical and theological.

From a theological perspective, transcendental analogy also has to do with God's act in space and time, for the ultimate driving force of transcendental analogy is the divine system. Consequently, as theologians, we have to see history being laden with divine actions and lures that transpire the natural process to transcend its limits and cross the thresholds. That is to say, transcendental analogy ultimately leads us to a theological reflection, opening ourselves to the infinite causality of God. This does not mean that we are leading science to some supra-historical event that has nothing to do with actual events in history; rather, transcendental analogy emerges from a realistic-historical study all the while exploring nature without reducing God's action to merely natural phenomenon.

In the final analysis, we need to inject these three analogies to the theology and science dialogue so that we can sustain the growth and progress of both theology and science in the 21st-century and beyond. The neglect of any one of these categories could result in the shoddy practice of favoring one metaphysical paradigm over the many. By cutting off one worldview in favor of another, we may defy the purpose of our interdisciplinary efforts to maintain a fruitful dialogue between God, humanity, and nature. We must keep multiple lenses and through them, we may be able to see a glimpse of continuity between our differences. I end with a final caveat from Thomas F. Torrance.

> As I see it, this is the great story of modern thought, whether it be in theology, science, or philosophy: the struggle for fidelity, for appropriate methods and apposite modes of speech, and therefore for the proper adaptation of the human subject to the object of his knowledge, whether it be God or the world of nature or man; but it is also the story of the struggles of man with himself, for somehow the more he comes to know, the more masterful he tries to be and the more he imposes himself upon reality, the more he gets in the way of his own progress. It is here that positive theology should have so much to offer, for it is concerned with right relations between man and God, with the healing and repairing of the human subject through humility before God, with the control of his convictions by what is ultimately given and real, with emancipation from arbitrary individualism, and thus with genuine objectivity in which man learns to love God and his neighbor, not for his own sake, but for their sakes.[4]

---

[4] Thomas F. Torrance, *Theological Science* (Oxford: Oxford University Press, 1969), xiii.

Bibliography

Allais, Lucy. *Manifest Reality: Kant's Idealism and His Realism.* Oxford: Oxford University Press, 2015.

Allen, Paul L. *Ernan McMullin and Critical Realism in the Science-Theology Dialogue.* London: Routledge, 2006.

Aristotle. *Metaphysics*, translated by Hugh Lawson-Tancred. London: Penguin, 1999.

Armstrong, D. M. *A World of States of Affairs.* Cambridge: Cambridge University Press, 1997.

Augustine. *Concerning the City of God against the Pagans*, translated by Gerald Walsh. Washington, DC: The Catholic University of America Press, 2008.

Augustine. *Confessions*, translated by Henry Chadwick. Oxford: Oxford University Press, 2008.

Austin, Brian D. "Randomness, Omniscience, and Divine Action." In *Facets of Faith and Science*, edited by Jitse Van Der Meer. New York: University Press of America, 1997.

Avis, Paul. *Faith in the Fires of Criticism: Christianity in Modern Thought.* Eugene: Wipf and Stock, 1995.

Ayer, Alfred Jules. *Language, Truth, and Logic.* Mineola, NY: Dover Publications, 1952.

Bacon, Francis. *The New Organon.* Cambridge: Cambridge University Press, 2000.

Barbour, Ian G. *Religion in an Age of Science: Gifford Lectures Series.* New York: Harper Collins, 1990.

_____. *Religion and Science: Historical and Contemporary Issues.* New York: Harper One, 1990.

Barth, Karl. *Church Dogmatics*, edited by G.W. Bromiley and T. F. Torrance. Edinburgh: T&T Clark, 1957.

_____. *The Epistle to the Romans*, translated by Edwyn Hoskyns. Oxford: Oxford University Press, 1933.

Bauckham, Richard. *Jesus and the Eyewitnesses: The Gospels as Eyewitness Testimony*. Grand Rapids: Eerdmans, 2006.

Bennett, Jane. *Vibrant Matter: A Political Ecology of Things*. Durham: Duke University Press, 2010.

Berger, Peter. *The Sacred Canopy. Elements of a Sociological Theory of Religion*. Garden City: Doubleday, 1967.

Bird, Michael F. *Jesus is the Christ: The Messianic Testimony of the Gospels*. Downers Grove: Intervarsity, 2012.

Blomberg, Craig L. *The Historical Reliability of the Gospels*. Downers Grove: Intervarsity Press, 2007.

_____. *Can We Still Believe the Bible? An Evangelical Engagement with Contemporary Questions*. Grand Rapids: Brazo, 2014.

Boa, Kenneth and Robert M. Bowman. *Faith Has Its Reasons: Integrative Approaches to Defending the Christian Faith*. Downers Grove: Intervarsity Press, 2005.

Bonhoeffer, Dietrich. *The Cost of Discipleship*. New York: Touchstone, 1995.

Bowman, Gary. *Essential Quantum Mechanics*. New York: Oxford University Press, 2008.

Boyd, Craig A. "The Synthesis of Reason and Faith Response." In *Faith and Reason: Three Views*, edited by Steve Wilkens. Downers Grove: Intervarsity, 2014.

Bracken, Joseph A. *Christianity and Process Thought: Spirituality for a Changing World*. West Conshohocken: Templeton Foundation Press, 2006.

_____. *The One in the Many: A Contemporary Reconstruction of the God-World Relationship*. Grand Rapids: Eerdmans, 2001.

_____. *The World in the Trinity: Open-Ended Systems in Science and Religion*. Minneapolis: Fortress, 2014.

Bradie, Michael. "Models, Metaphors and Scientific Realism," *Nature and System* 2 (1980): 3-20.

Brown, Colin. *Miracles and the Critical Mind*. Grand Rapids: Eerdmans, 1984.

Bruce, F. F. *The New Testament Documents: Are They Reliable?* Grand Rapids: Eerdmans, 1982.

Buber, Martin. *I and Thou*, translated by Walter Kaufmann. New York: Touchstone, 1970.

Bultmann, Rudolf. *Existence and Faith*, translated by Schubert M. Ogden. London: Hodder and Stroughton, 1961.

_____. "Is Exegesis without Presuppositions Possible?" In *New Testament and Mythology and Other Basic Writings*, edited by Schubert M. Ogden. Philadelphia: Fortress, 1984.

_____. "New Testament and Mythology?" In *New Testament and Mythology and Other Basic Writings*, edited by Schubert M. Ogden. Philadelphia: Fortress, 1984.

_____. "The Study of the Synoptic Gospels." In *Form Criticism: A New Method of New Testament Research*. Chicago: Willett, Clark and Company, 1934.

_____. *Theology of the New Testament*, v.1. New York: Charles Scribner's Sons, 1951.

_____. *The History of the Synoptic Tradition*, translated by John Marsh. New York: Harper and Row, 1963.

Burgess, Stanley M. *The Holy Spirit: Ancient Christian Traditions*. Peabody: Hendrickson, 1984.

Caputo, John D. *Philosophy and Theology*. Nashville: Abingdon, 2006.

Carrier, Richard. *Sense and Goodness without God: A Defense of Metaphysical Naturalism.* Bloomington: Authorhouse, 2005.

Chalker, William H. *Science and Faith: Understanding Meaning, Method, and Truth*. Louisville: Westminster John Knox Press, 2006.

Chiovene, Michael L. *The One God: A Critically Developed Evangelical Doctrine of Trinitarian Unity*. Eugene: Pickwick, 2009.

Chisholm, Roderick. *Theory of Knowledge*. Englewood Cliffs: Prentice-Hall, 1966.

Churchland, Patricia. *Neurophilosophy: Toward a Unified Science of the Mind-Brain*. Cambridge: MIT Press, 1986.

Churchland, Paul M. *Matter and Consciousness*. Cambridge: MIT Press, 1984.

Clark, Thomas W. *Encountering Naturalism: A Worldview and Its Uses*. Somerville: Center for Naturalism, 2007.

Clarke, David S. *Panpsychism and the Religious Attitude*. New York: State University of New York, 2003.

Clayton, Philip. *Adventures in the Spirit: God, World, Divine Action*. Minneapolis: Fortress, 2008.

_____. *Explanation from Physics to Theology: An Essay in Rationality and Religion*. New Haven: Yale University Press, 1989.

_____. *Mind and Emergence, From Quantum to Consciousness*. New York: Oxford University Press, 2006.

Cobb, John B. *God and the World*. Eugene: Wipf and Stock, 1998.

_____. *Christ in a Pluralistic Age*. Eugene: Wipf and Stock, 1998.

Compton, Arthur. "Foreword." In Werner Heisenberg's *The Physical Principles of the Quantum Theory*. Chicago: University of Chicago, 1930.

Cooper, John. *Panentheism, the Other God of the Philosophers: From Plato to the Present*. Grand Rapids: Baker, 2008.

Coulson, Charles. *Science and Christian Belief*. London: Fontana, 1957.

Crick, Francis. *Of Molecules and Men*. New York: Prometheus, 2004.

Cullmann, Oscar. *Salvation in History*. New York: Harper & Row, 1967.

Cupitt, Don. *Taking Leave of God*. London: SCM Press, 1980.

Danto, Arthur C. "Naturalism." In *The Encyclopedia of Philosophy*, edited by Paul Edwards. New York: Macmillan, 1967.

Davis, Philip J. and Reuben Hersh. *The Mathematical Experience*. New York: Houghton Mifflin Company, 1998.

Davis, Philip J. *Mathematics and Common Sense: A Case of Creative Tension*. Boca Raton: CRC Press, 2006.

Dawkins, Richard. *The Blind Watchmaker: Why the Evidence of Evolution Reveals a Universe without Design*. New York: W. W. Norton, 1996.

_____. *The Selfish Gene*. Oxford; Oxford University Press, 1989.

Dembski, William A. *The Design of Life: Discovering Signs of Intelligence in Biological Systems*. Dallas: The Foundation for Thought and Ethics, 2008.

Dennett, Daniel. *Freedom Evolves*. New York: Penguin, 2003.

Descartes. "Notes Directed Against a Certain Programme." In *Descartes: Key Philosophical Writings*, translated by Elizabeth S. Haldane. Hertfordshire: Wordsworth, 1997.

_____. "Principles of Philosophy." In *The Philosophical Writings of Descartes*, vol 1., translated by John Cottingham. Cambridge: Cambridge University Press, 1985.

_____. *Meditations on First Philosophy*. Cambridge: Cambridge University Press, 1911.

_____. *The Philosophical Writings of Descartes*. Cambridge: Cambridge University Press, 1985.

Dewey, John. *The Later Works, 1925-1953*, edited by Jo Ann Boydston. Carbondale: Southern Illinois University Press.

Dicker, Georges. *Berkeley's Idealism: A Critical Examination.* New York: Oxford University Press, 2011.

_____. *Descartes: An Analytic and Historical Introduction.* Oxford: Oxford University Press, 2013.

Disalle, Robert. *Understanding Space-Time: The Philosophical Development of Physics from Newton to Einstein.* Cambridge: Cambridge University Press, 2006.

Dodds, Michael J. *Unlocking Divine Action: Contemporary Science and Thomas Aquinas.* Washington, D.C.: The Catholic University Press of America, 2012.

Drees, Willem B. "Should Religious Naturalists Promote a Naturalistic Religion?" *Zygon* 33/4 (1998), 619.

_____. *Religion, Science and Naturalism.* New York: Cambridge University Press, 1996.

Drescher, Gary L. *Good and Real: Demystifying Paradoxes from Physics to Ethics.* Cambridge: The MIT Press, 2006.

Dunn, James. *The Evidence for Jesus* (Louisville: The Westminster Press, 1985.

Edwards, Denis. *Breath of Life: A Theology of the Creator Spirit.* Maryknoll: Orbis, 2004.

_____. *How God Acts: Creation, Redemption, and Special Divine Action.* Minneapolis: Fortress, 2012.

Ehrman, Bart D. *Forgery and Counterforgery: The Use of Literary Deceit in Early Christian Polemics.* New York: Oxford University Press, 2013.

Elders, Leo. *The Philosophical Theology of St. Thomas Aquinas*. New York: Brill, 1990.

Emerson, Ralph Waldo. *Nature*. Boston: James Munroe and Company, 1849.

Evans, Stephan. *Faith beyond Reason: A Kierkegaardian Account*. Grand Rapids: Eerdmans, 1998.

_____. *Kierkegaard on Faith and the Self: Collected Essays*. Waco: Baylor University Press, 2006.

Farley, Wendy. *Tragic Vision and Divine Compassion: A Contemporary Theodicy*. Louisville: Westminster John Knox, 1990.

Farnham, Surrey. *Science and Faith within Reason: Reality, Creation, Life and Design*. Burlington: Ashgate, 2011.

Fine, Arthur. *The Shaky Game: The Shaky Game: Einstein Realism and the Quantum Theory*. Chicago: The University of Chicago Press, 1996.

Fine, Gail. *On Ideas: Aristotle's Criticism of Plato's Theory of Forms*. Oxford: Clarendon, 1993.

Flanagan, Owen. *The Geography of Morals: Varieties of Moral Possibility*. Oxford: Oxford University Press, 2017.

Fodor, Jerry A. "Making Mind Matter More." In *A Theory of Content and Other Essays.* Cambridge: MIT Press, 1990.

Fraassen, Bas C. van. "To Save the Phenomena." In *Scientific Realism*, edited by Jarrett Leplin. Berkeley: University of California, 1984.

_____. *The Scientific Image*. Oxford: Clarendon, 1980.

Frank, Philipp. *Philosophy of Science: The Link between Science and Philosophy*. Mineola: Dover, 2004.

Freeman, Ken and Geoff McNamara. *In Search of Dark Matter*. New York: Springer, 2006.

Friedman, Michael. *Reconsidering Logical Positivism*. New York: Cambridge University Press, 1999.

Garber, Daniel. *Descartes Embodied: Reading Cartesian Philosophy through Cartesian Science*. Cambridge: Cambridge University Press, 2001.

Giberson, Karl. *The Language of Science and Faith: Straight Answers to Genuine Questions*. Downers Grove: Intervarsity Press, 2011.

Giles, Kevin. *Eternal Generation of the Son: Maintaining Orthodoxy in Trinitarian Theology*. Downers Grove: Intervarsity Press, 2012.

_____. *Jesus and the Father: Modern Evangelicals Reinvent the Doctrine of the Trinity*. Grand Rapids: Zondervan, 2006.

_____. *The Trinity and Subordinationism: The Doctrine of God and the Contemporary Gender Debate*. Downers Grove: Intervarsity Press, 2002.

_____. *The Tacit Mode: Michael Polanyi's Postmodern Philosophy*. Albany: State University of New York Press, 2000.

Goodenough, Ursula. *The Sacred Depths of Nature*. New York: Oxford University Press, 1998.

Grant, Edward. "Aristotle and Aristotelianism." In *Science and Religion: A Historical Introduction*, edited by Gary B. Ferngren. Baltimore: The John Hopkins University Press, 2002.

Greene, Joshua. *Moral Tribes: Emotion, Reason, and the Gap between Us and Them*. New York: Penguin, 2014.

Gregersen, Niels Henrik. "Emergence and Complexity." In *The Oxford Handbook of Religion and Science,* edited by Philip Clayton. Oxford: Oxford University Press, 2008.

_____. Introduction in *Pannenberg's The Historicity of Nature*. West Conshohocken: Templeton, 2008.

Grenz, Stanley J. *Reason for Hope: The Systematic Theology of Wolfhart Pannenberg*. Grand Rapids: Eerdmans, 2005.

_____. *Renewing the Center: Evangelical Theology in a Post-Theological Era*. Grand Rapids: Baker Academics, 2006.

_____. *The Moral Quest: Foundations of Christian Ethics*. Downers Grove: Intervarsity Press, 1997.

Grenz, Stanley J. and John R. Frank. Beyond Foundationalism: Shaping Theology in a Postmodern Context. Louisville: Westminster John Knox Press, 2001.

Grenz, Stanley J. and Roger E. Olson. 20th Century Theology: God and the World in a Transitional Age. Downers Grove: Intervarsity Press,1992.

Griffin, David R. *Panentheism and Scientific Naturalism: Rethinking Evil, Morality, Religious Experience, Religious Pluralism, and the Academic Study of Religion*. Claremont: Process Century Press, 2014.

Habermas, Gary R. *The Case for the Resurrection of Jesus*. Grand Rapids: Kregel, 2004.

Hahn, Roger. *Pierre Simon Laplace, 1749-1827: A Determined Scientist*. Cambridge: Harvard University Press, 2005.

Hardman, Randall. "Historical Evidence of the Gospels." In *True Reason: Confronting the Irrationality of the New Atheism*, edited by Tom Gilson. Grand Rapids: Kregel, 2013.

Harnack, Adolph. *History of Dogma*, trans. Neil BuchananOxford: Williams and Norgate, 1898), 5/127.

Haught, John F. *Christianity and Science: Toward a Theology of Nature*. Maryknoll: Orbis, 2007.

_____. *Science and Faith: A New Introduction*. New York: Paulist, 2012.

Hebblethwaite, Brian. *The Philosophical Theology of Austin Farrer*. Leuven: Peeters, 2007.

Hegel. *The Phenomenology of Mind*. New York: Harper and Row, 1967.

Heine, Ronald E. *The Montanist Oracles and Testimonia*. Macon, GA: Mercer University Press, 1989.

Helm, Paul. *Faith and Understanding*. Grand Rapids: Eerdmans, 1997.

_____. *Faith with Reason*. Oxford: Oxford University Press, 2000.

Hench, L. L. *Science, Faith, and Ethics*. London: Imperial College Press, 2001.

Hersh, Reuben. *What is Mathematics, Really?*. Oxford: Oxford University Press, 1997.

Hickman, Louise. *Chance or Providence: Religious Perspectives on Divine Action*. Newcastle: Cambridge Scholars Publishing, 2014.

Hitchens, Christopher. *God Is Not Great: How Religion Poisons Everything*. New York: Twelve, 2009.

Holder, Rodney. *God, the Multiverse, and Everything: Modern Cosmology and the Argument from Design*. Aldershot: Ashgate, 2004.

Holder, Rodney. *The Heavens Declare: Natural Theology and the Legacy of Karl Barth*. West Conshohocken: Templeton Foundation Press, 2012.

Hume, David. "Of Miracles." In *An Enquiry Concerning Human Understanding*, edited by Eric Steinberg. Indianapolis: Hackett, 1993.

Huyssteen, Wentzel Van. *Theology and the Justification of Faith: Constructing Theories in Systematic Theology*. Grand Rapids: Eerdmans, 1988.

Israel, Jonathan. "Introduction," in *Benedict de Spinoza: Theological-Political Treatise*, edited by Jonathan Israel. Cambridge: Cambridge University Press, 2007.

Jaeger, Werner. *Paideia: The Ideals of Greek Culture*, vol. 1, trans. Gilbert Highet. New York: Oxford University Press, 1965.

John B. Cobb, Jr., and David R. Griffin. *Process Theology: An Introductory Exposition*. Westminster John Knox Press, 1976.

Jones, Timothy Paul. *Misquoting Truth: A Guide to the Fallacies of Bart Ehrman's "Misquoting Jesus."* Downers Grove: Intervarsity Press, 2007.

Kant, Immanuel. *Critique of Pure Reason*, translated by Paul Guyer and Allen W. Wood. Cambridge: Cambridge University Press, 1998.

_____. *Religion within the Limits of Reason Alone*, translated by Theodore M. Greene and Hoyt H. Hudson. New York: Harper, 1960.

Kasner, Edward and James Newman. *Mathematics and the Imagination.* Mineola: Dover, 1967.

Kauffman, Stuart. "Cosmic Mind?" *Theology and Science* 14/1 (2016): 36-47.

_____. *Reinventing the Sacred: The New Science, Reason, and Religion*. New York: Basic Books, 2008.

Kaufman, Gordon D. *God the Problem*. Cambridge: Harvard University Press, 1972.

Kearney, Richard. *The Wake of Imagination: Toward a Postmodern Culture*. London: Routledge, 1988.

Keener, Craig. *Miracles: The Credibility of the New Testament Accounts*, 2 vols. Grand Rapids: Baker, 2011.

Keller, Catherine. *On the Mystery: Discerning Divinity in Process*. Minneapolis: Fortress, 2008.

Kierkegaard, Søren. *Provocations: Spiritual Writings of Kierkegaard*, edited by Charles E. Moore. Farmington: Bruderhof, 2002.

Kim, Jaegwon. *Physicalism, or Something Near Enough*. Princeton: Princeton University Press, 2005.

_____. *Mind in a Physical World: An Essay on the Mind-Body Problem and Mental Causation*. Cambridge: MIT Press, 1998.

Kirk, Andrew J. *The Future of Reason, Science and Faith Following Modernity and Post-modernity*. Burlington: Ashgate, 2007.

Kline, Morris. *Mathematics and the Search for Knowledge*. Oxford: Oxford University Press, 1985.

Koch, Christof. *The Quest for Consciousness: A Neurobiological Approach*. Englewood: Roberts and Company, 2004.

Krauss, Lawrence M. *A Universe from Nothing: Why There is Something Rather than Nothing*. New York: Free Press, 2012.

Kreeft, Peter J. *Catholic Christianity: A Complete Catechism of Catholic Beliefs*. San Francisco: Ignatius Press, 1994.

Kuhn, Thomas S. *Structure of Scientific Revolution*. Chicago: University of Chicago Press, 1962, c1999.

Küng, Hans. *Infallible? An Unresolved Enquiry*. New York: Continuum, 1994.

Ladler, Steven. *Spinoza's 'Ethics': An Introduction*. New York: Cambridge University Press, 2006.

Larmer, Robert A. "The Meanings of Miracle" in *The Cambridge Companion to Miracles*, edited by Graham H. Twelftree. New York: Cambridge University Press, 2011.

Laudan, Larry. *Science and Relativism: Some Key Controversies in the Philosophy of Science.* Chicago: University of Chicago Press, 1990.

Lee, Kam-lun. "Augustine, Manichaeism and the Good." PhD diss., St. Paul University, 1996.

Locke, John. "Of Enthusiasm," In *The Philosophical Works of John Locke*. London: George Bell and Sons, 1903.

Lockwood, Michael. *Mind, Brain, and the Quantum: The Compound "I".* Malden: Blackwell, 1991.

Lonergan, Bernard. *Insight: A Study of Human Understanding.* Toronto: University of Toronto Press, 1992.

Lonergan, Bernard. *Method in Theology.* London: Darton, Longman, and Todd, 1972.

Lord, Beth. *Spinoza's Ethics.* Edinburgh: Edinburgh University Press, 2010.

Luther, Martin. "Last Sermon in Wittenberg, Second Sunday in Epiphany, 17 January 1546," in *Dr. Martin Luther's Werke: Kritsche Gesamtsusgabe* (Weimar: Herman Boehlaus Nachfolger, 1941), 51:126.

Macchia, Frank D. "Tongues as a Sign: Towards a Sacramental Understanding of Pentecostal Experience," *Pneuma* 15/1 (1993): 61-76.

MacIntyre, Alisdair. "Epistemologial Crises, Dramatic Narrative and the Philosophy of Science," *The Monist* 60/4 (1977): 453-472.

MacQuarrie, John. *An Existential Theology: A Comparison of Heidegger and Bultmann.* London: SCM Press, 1955.

Marion, Jean-Luc. *On Descartes' Metaphysical Prism*. Chicago: University of Chicago Press, 1999.

Marshall, Howard. *I Believe in the Historical Jesus*. Grand Rapids: Eerdmans, 1977.

Marty, Martin E. *Martin Luther: A Life*. New York: Penguin, 2004.

Maxwell, Joseph A. *A Realist Approach for Qualitative Research*. Los Angeles: Sages, 2012.

McDowell, John. *Mind and World*. Cambridge: Harvard University Press, 1994.

McFague, Sallie. *The Body of God: An Ecological Theology*. Minneapolis: Augsburg Fortress, 1993.

McGrath, Alister E. *Dawkins' God: From the Selfish Gene to the God Delusion*. Oxford: John Wiley and Sons, 2015.

_____. *The Foundations of Dialogue in Science and Religion*. Malden: Blackwell, 1998.

_____. *The Open Secret: A New Vision for Natural Theology*. Oxford: Blackwell, 2008.

_____. *The Order of Things: Explorations in Scientific Theology*. Malden: Blackwell, 2006.

_____. *The Science of God*. Grand Rapids: Eerdmans, 2004.

_____. *Christian Theology: An Introduction*. Malden: Wiley Blackwell, 2007.

McInerny, Ralph. *Aquinas and Analogy*. Washington, D.C.: The Catholic University of America Press, 1996.

McLaughlin, Brian P. "The Rise and Fall of British Emergentism." In *Emergence or Reduction? Essays on the Prospect of a Nonreductive Physicalism*. Edited by Ansgar Beckerman, et al. Berlin: Walter de Gruyter, 1992.

McLeish, Tom. *Faith and Wisdom in Science*. Oxford: Oxford University Press, 2014.

McMullin, Ernan. "A Case for Scientific Realism," in *Scientific Realism*, edited by Jarrett Leplin. Berkeley: University of California, 1984.

_____. "Religion and Cosmology." In Norris Hetherington, ed. *Cosmology: Historical, Literary, Philosophical, Religious and Scientific Perspectives*. New York: Garland, 1993.

Meillassoux, Quentin. *After Finitude: An Essay on the Necessity of Contingency*, translated by Ray Brassier. New York: Continuum, 2008.

Meland, Bernard E. *The Secularization of Modern Cultures*. New York: Oxford University Press, 1966.

Melnyk, Andrew. *A Physicalist Manifesto: Thoroughly Modern Materialism*. Cambridge University Press, 2003.

Menn, Stephen. *Descartes and Augustine*. Cambridge, UK; Cambridge University Press, 2020.

Mesle, Robert C. *Process Theology: A Basic Introduction*. St. Louis: Chalice, 1993.

Milbank, John. "Faith, Reason, and Imagination: The Study of Theology and Philosophy in the 21st Century," *Transversalités* 101/1 (2007): 69-86.

Molnar, George. *Powers: A Study in Metaphysics*. Oxford: Oxford University Press, 2003.

Moltmann, Jurgen. *God in Creation: A New Theology of Creation and the Spirit of God*. Minneapolis: Fortress, 1993.

Moore, Andrew. "Theological Realism and the Observability of God," *International Journal of Systematic Theology*, 2/1 (2000): 79-99.

Moreland, J. P. *Consciousness and the Existence of God: A Theistic Argument*. New York: Routledge, 2008.

_____. *The Recalcitrant Imago Dei: Human Persons and the Failure of Naturalism*. London: SCM, 2009.

Moreland, J. P. *The Soul: How We Know It's Real and Why It Matters?* Chicago: Moody, 2014.

Muir, John. *Steep Trails*. Boston: Houghton Mifflin Company, 1918.

Murphy, Francesca Aran, Balázs M. Mezei, and Kenneth Oakes. *Illuminating Faith: An Invitation to Theology*. New York: Bloomsbury Academics, 2015.

Murphy, Nancey. *Bodies and Souls, or Spirited Bodies?* Cambridge: Cambridge University Press, 2006.

_____. *Theology in the Age of Scientific Reasoning*. Ithaca: Cornell University Press, 1990.

Niebuhr, Richard H. *The Meaning of Revelation*. New York: MacMillan.

Nietzsche, Friedrich. *The Will to Power*, translated by Walter Kaufmann and R. J. Hollingdale. New York: Vintage Books, 1968.

Nola, Robert and Howard Sankey. *Theories of Scientific Method*. Ithaca: McGill-Queen's University Press, 2007.

O'Daly, Gerald J. P. *Augustine's Philosophy of Mind*. Berkeley: University of California Press, 1987.

Olson, Richard. "Physics" in *Science and Religion: A Historical Introduction*, edited by Gary B. Ferngren. Baltimore: John Hopkins University Press, 2002.

Pannenberg, Wolfhart. "God as Spirit—and Natural Science," *Zygon* 36/4 (2001): 783-825.

_____. *Systematic Theology*. Grand Rapids: Eerdmans, 1988.

_____. *The Historicity of Nature: Essays on Science and Theology*, edited by Niels Henrik Gregersen. West Conshohocken: Templeton Foundation Press, 2008.

_____. *What Is Man? Contemporary Anthropology in Theological Perspective*. Indianapolis: Fortress, 1970.

Peacocke, Arthur. "The End of All Our Exploring' in Science and Theology," *Zygon* 39/2 (2004), 413-29.

_____. *Creation and the World of Science: The Re-shaping of Belief*. Oxford: Oxford University Press, 2004.

_____. *Intimations of Reality: Critical Realism in Science and Religion*. Notre Dame: University of Notre Dame Press, 1984.

_____. *Theology for a Scientific Age: Being and Becoming—Natural, Divine and Human*. London: SCM, 1993.

_____. *Theology for the Scientific Age*. London: SCM Press, 1993.

Peters, Ted. "The Cosmic Mind: Entanglement over Physics, Panpsychism, and the Trinity," *Theology and Science* 14/1 (2016).

_____. *God—The Word's Future: Systematic Theology for a Postmodern Era*. Minneapolis: Fortress, 1992.

_____. *Playing God: Genetic Determinism and Human Freedom*. London: Routledge, 1997.

Philip, D. Z. *The Concept of Prayer*. London: Routledge, 1965.

Pinnock, Clark H. *Tracking the Maze: Finding Our Way through Modern Theology from an Evangelical Perspective*. Eugene: Wipf and Stock, 1990.

Plantinga, Alvin. *Faith and Rationality: Reason and Belief in God*. Notre Dame: Notre Dame University Press, 1991.

_____. *Where the Conflict Really Lies: Science, Religion, and Naturalism*. Oxford: Oxford University Press, 2011.

Plato. "The Sophist as a Species of Imagemaker." In *Plato's Theory of Knowledge: The Theaetetus and the Sophist*, translated by Francis M. Cornford. Mineola: Dover, 2003.

Poland, Jeffrey. *Physicalism: The Philosophical Foundations.* Oxford University Press, 1994.

Polanyi, Michael. *Personal Knowledge: Towards a Post-Critical Philosophy.* Chicago: The University of Chicago Press, 1962.

_____. *Science, Faith and Society.* Chicago: University of Chicago Press, 1964.

Polkinghorne, John. "Chaos Theory and Divine Action," In *Religion and Science: History, Method and Dialogue*, edited by W. M. Richardson and W. J. Wildman. London: Routledge, 1996.

_____. *Belief in God in an Age of Science.* New Haven: Yale University Press, 1998.

_____. *Exploring Reality: The Intertwining of Science and Religion.* London: SPCK, 2005.

_____. *Quarks, Chaos, and Christianity: Questions to Science and Religion.* London: SPCK, 2005.

_____. *Reason and Reality: The Relationship between Science and Theology.* London: Trinity Press International, 1991.

_____. *Science and Providence.* London: SPCK, 1989.

_____. *Science and Theology: An Introduction.* Minneapolis: Fortress, 1998.

_____. *The Faith of a Physicist.* Princeton: Princeton University Press, 1994.

Pratschke, Jonathan. "Realistic Models? Critical Realism and Statistical Models in the Social Sciences," *Philosophica* 71 (2003): 13-38.

Purtill, Richard L. *Thinking about Religion: A Philosophical Introduction to Religion.* Englewood Cliffs: Prentice-Hall, 1978.

Putnam, Hilary. *Reason, Truth and History*. Cambridge: Cambridge University Press, 1981.

Quine, W.V. *Theories and Things*. Cambridge: Harvard University Press, 1981.

Rahner, Karl. *Theological Investigations*. New York: The Crossroad, 1991.

Ramm, Bernard L. *The God Who Makes a Difference: A Christian Appeal to Reason*. Waco: Word Books, 1972.

Robeck, Cecil M. *Prophecy in Carthage: Perpetua, Tertullian, and Cyprian*. Cleveland: Pilgrim, 1992.

Rocca, Michael Della. *Spinoza*. New York; Routledge, 2008.

Rucker, Rudy. *The Fourth Dimension: Toward a Geometry of Higher Reality.* Boston: Houghton Mifflin, 1984.

Russell, Robert J. *Bridging Theology and Science*, edited by Ted Peters and Gaymon Bennett. Minneapolis: Fortress, 2003.

_____. *Cosmology from Alpha to Omega: The Creative Mutual Interaction of Theology and Science*. Minneapolis: Fortress, 2008.

Sanders, Fred. "The Strange Legacy of Theologian Wolfhart Pannenberg," September 2014 *Christianity Today*.

Saunders, Nicholas. *Divine Action and Modern Science*. New York: Cambridge University Press, 2002.

Schalow, Frank. *Heidegger and the Quest for the Sacred: From Thought to the Sanctuary of Faith*. London: Springer, 2001.

Schleiermacher, Friedrich. *On Religion*, translated by Richard Crouter. Cambridge: Cambridge University Press, 1996.

Schleiermacher, Friedrich. *The Christian Faith*. New York: T&T Clark, 1999.

Schloss, Jeffrey P. "Evolutionary Theory and Religious Belief." In *The Oxford Handbook of Religion and Science,* edited by Philip Clayton. Oxford: Oxford University Press, 2008.

Scott, Peter. *A Political Theology of Nature.* Cambridge: Cambridge University Press, 2003.

Searle, John R. *Seeing Things as They Are; A Theory of Perception.* Oxford: Oxford University Press, 2015.

_____. *The Rediscovery of the Mind.* Cambridge: The MIT Press, 1992.

Sellars, Roy W. *Religion Coming of Age.* New York: McMillan, 1928.

Sellars, Wilfred. *Science, Perception, and Reality.* London: Routledge, 1963.

Shaviro, Steven. The Universe of Things: On Speculative Realism. Minneapolis: University of Minnesota Press, 2014.

Smith, Christian. *The Bible Made Impossible: Why Biblicism Is Not a Truly Evangelical Reading of Scripture.* Grand Rapids: Brazo, 2011.

Smith, Wilfred. Cantwell *Faith and Belief.* Princeton: Princeton University Press, 1979.

Soler, Lena. *Rethinking Scientific Change and Theory Comparison: Stability, Ruptures, Incommensurabilities?* Dordrecht, Springer, 2008.

Soskice, Janet. *Metaphor and Religious Language.* Oxford: Clarendon, 1987.

Southgate, Christopher and Michael Poole. "Introduction." In *God, Humanity, and Cosmos,* edited by Christopher Southgate. New York: T&T Clark, 2011.

Spinoza, Baruch. *Ethics,* translated by Samuel Shirley, edited by Michael L. Morgan. Indianapolis: Hackett, 2002.

_____. *Theological-Political Treatise*. Spinoza, *Theological-Political Treatise*, translated by Michael Silverstone, edited by Jonathan Israel. New York: Cambridge University Press, 2007.

_____. "Letter 12" in *Spinoza: The Letters*, translated by Samuel Shirley. Indianapolis: Hackett, 1995.

_____. *Ethics*, trans. Samuel Shirley, edited by Michael L. Morgan. Indianapolis: Hackett, 2002.

Stone, Jerome A. *Religious Naturalism Today: The Rebirth of a Forgotten Alternative*. Albany: State University of New York Press, 2008.

Strawson, Galen. *Selves: An Essay in Revisionary Metaphysics*. Oxford: Oxford University Press, 2009.

Strobel, Lee. *The Case for the Real Jesus.* Grand Rapids: Zondervan, 2007.

Stroud, Barry. "The Charm of Naturalism." In *Proceedings and Addresses of the American Philosophical Association*.

Thacker, Eugene. *In the Dust of This Planet: Horror of Philosophy.* Alresford: Zero, 2011.

Thiselton, Anthony C. *The Holy Spirit: In Biblical Teaching, through the Centuries, and Today*. Grand Rapids: Eerdmans, 2013.

Tillich, Paul. *Courage to Be*. New Haven: Yale University Press, 1952.

_____. *Systematic Theology*. Chicago: The University of Chicago Press, 1973.

Tipler, Frank. *The Physics of Christianity*. New York: Doubleday, 2007.

Torrance, Thomas F. "The Concept of Order in Theology and Science," *The Princeton Seminary Bulletin* (1984).

_____. *Christian Theology and Scientific Culture*. New York: Oxford University Press, 1981.

_____. *The Christian Doctrine of God, One Being Three Persons*. Edinburgh: T&T Clark, 1996.

_____. *The Christian Frame of Mind*. Colorado Springs: Helmers & Howard, 1989.

_____. *Theological Science*. Oxford: Oxford University Press, 1969.

_____. *Theology in Reconstruction*. London: SCM Press, 1965.

Tracy, Thomas F. "Scientific Perspectives on Divine Action? Mapping the Options," *Theology and Science* 2/2 (2004): 196-201.

Trigg, Roger. *Rationality and Religion: Does Faith Need Reason?* Malden: Wiley-Blackwell, 1998.

Ward, Keith. *Divine Action: Examining God's Role in an Open and Emergent Universe*. West Conshohocken: Templeton Press, 2007.

Warfield, B. B. *The Inspiration and Authority of the Bible*. Phillipsburg: Presbyterian & Reformed, 1948.

Wegter-McNelly, Kirk. *The Entangled God: Divine Relationality and Quantum Physics*. New York: Routledge, 2011.

Weightman, Colin. *Theology in a Polanyian Universe: The Theology of Thomas Torrance*. New York: Peter Lang, 1994.

Welker, Michael. *Creation and Reality*. Minneapolis: Fortress, 1999.

_____. *God the Spirit*, translated by John F. Hoffmeyer. Minneapolis: Fortress, 1994.

Wheeler, John. *Quantum Theory and Measurement*. Princeton: Princeton University Press, 1983.

White, Lynn T. "The Historical Roots of Our Ecologic Crisis." In *Ecology and Religion in History*, edited by David Spring and Eileen Spring. New York: Harper and Row, 1974.

_____. *Medieval Technology and Social Change*. Oxford University Press, 1962.

Whitehead, Alfred North. *Modes of Thought*. New York: The Free Press, 1968.

Wigner, Eugene. *Symmetries and Reflections: Scientific Essays of Eugene P. Wigner*. Woodbridge: Ox Bow Press, 1979.

Wildman, Wesley J. "Ground-of-Being Theologies." In *The Oxford Handbook of Religion and Science*, edited by Philip Clayton. Oxford: Oxford University Press, 2008.

_____. *Science and Religious Anthropology: A Spiritually Evocative Naturalist Interpretation of Human Life*. New York: Routledge, 2016.

Wiley, Basil. *Seventeenth Century Background: The Thought of the Age in Relation to Religion and Poetry*. New York: Doubleday, 1953.

Yom, Aaron. *Number, Word, and Spirit: Rethinking T. F. Torrance's Theological Science from a Pneumatological Perspective*. New York: Peter Lang, 2018.

Yong, Amos. *The Spirit of Creation: Modern Science and Divine Action in the Pentecostal-Charismatic Imagination*. Grand Rapids: Eerdmans, 2011.

Index

coherentism, 16, 139

Compton, Arthur, 96

constructive empiricist, 12

constructivism, 94, 147, 149, 154

continental realism, 45

Cooper, John, 50, 52, 63, 64, 125, 126, 234

correlationism, 45, 46, 50, 51, 52, 73

counterintuition, 257, 258, 259

creatio ex nihilo, 77, 269

critical realism, 8, 12, 110, 149

Danto, 60

Davis, Philip, 18, 210, 258

demythologization, 286, 289

Descartes, René, 36, 46, 48, 95, 108, 160, 161, 165, 170, 171, 172, 173, 174, 175, 176, 177, 178, 179, 180, 181, 182, 183, 184, 193, 195, 197, 205, 208, 209, 215, 216, 219, 220, 231, 232, 233, 236, 238, 241

determinism, 20, 22, 25, 235, 248, 253, 255

Dewey, John, 10, 95

eco-theology, 5

eliminationism, 47-48

Elisha, 246

emergence, 20, 25, 34, 42, 43, 50, 54, 55, 60, 66, 145, 209, 264, 266, 294, 309

ethics, 3, 4, 14, 33, 163, 221, 230, 231, 232, 233, 234, 235, 236, 239, 240, 245

exclusivism, 91

faith and reason, 26, 27, 141, 160, 161, 168, 170, 179, 181, 182, 190, 192, 193, 215, 216, 227, 229, 248

faith rationality, 2, 19

Farrer, Austin, 22-23

Feuerbach, Ludwig, 207

Fichte, J. G., 74, 75

Flew, Anthony, 276

foundationalism, 15, 16, 208, 209, 222

Frank, Jackson, 43

free will, 85, 163, 166, 167, 171, 179, 180, 181, 187, 195, 196, 215

Gadamer, George, 130, 212

Gerhardsoon, Birger, 291

Gregersen, Niels, 1, 4, 9, 38, 137, 138, 140, 144, 204

Grenz, Stanley, 16, 62, 119, 120, 127, 128, 163, 208

Habermas, Gary, 212, 290, 294, 297, 298, 299

Hegel, G. W. F., 36, 50, 64, 74, 75, 142, 230

Heidegger, Martin, 87, 212, 287

Hitchens, Christopher, 38, 211

Hobbs, Thomas, 182

Holy Spirit, 18, 57, 71, 73, 75, 79, 84, 90, 91, 108, 116, 120, 123, 130, 148, 158, 159, 160, 171, 201, 202, 214, 267, 270, 271, 285, 303

Hume, David, 6, 21, 197, 249, 276

hypothetical-deductive method, 100, 157

Incarnation, 77, 88, 127, 168, 181, 182, 194, 270

interdisciplinary scholars, 20, 24

intuition, 17, 132, 133, 165, 174, 184, 217, 220, 225, 239, 240, 241, 258

Kauffman, Stuart, 4, 52

Kierkegaard, 72, 127, 194, 195

Kim, Jaewon, 3, 41

Laplace, Pierre-Simon, 20, 95, 206

Locke, John, 175, 182, 191, 192, 220

Lonergan, Bernard, 18, 72, 73, 156

Lord, Beth, 232, 235

monism, 33, 51, 80, 148, 233, 234, 235, 245, 248, 264, 269

Montanus, 201

Muir, John, 29

non-interventionism, 2, 21

non-uniformity theory, 213-214

panpsychism, 4, 44, 45, 47, 49, 50, 51, 52, 53, 56, 69, 77, 80, 86

Pinnock, Clark, 2, 199-200

Polkinghorne, John, 7, 8, 20, 21, 23, 24, 25, 96, 113, 117, 124, 214, 254, 265, 266

pure actuality, 67, 74, 235

Rahner, Karl, 67, 74, 235

Shaviro, Steven, 4, 46, 48, 49

Sitz im Leben, 277, 278, 279, 291, 292

Spinoza, Baruch, 33, 36, 50, 183, 192, 197, 206, 207, 230, 231, 232, 233, 234, 235, 236, 237, 238, 239, 240, 241, 242, 243, 244, 245, 246, 247, 248, 249, 250, 251, 252, 253, 255, 256, 257, 259, 260, 261, 262, 269, 276, 287, 289, 290, 301, 302

speculative realism, 4, 46

Stone, Jerome, 3, 58, 61, 87

Strawson, Galen, 4, 10, 49, 50

substance dualism, 53, 56, 69, 77

thermodynamics, 21, 262, 272

Van Huyssteen, J. Wentzel, 1, 140

Weightman, Colin, 16-17, 212

Whiteheadian metaphysics, 48, 78

Wigner, Eugene, 97-98